Toward a Global Psychology:
Theory, Research, Intervention, and Pedagogy

International Psychology Series

Sponsored by the Division of International Psychology (52) of the American Psychological Association

This new series highlights the ways in which newly evolving practices and paradigms are affecting our understanding of how to conceptualize human beings and their problems, how to study and help them, and how to educate and train psychologists.

Candidates for the series are books that synthesize current bodies of knowledge about important psychological questions from international, cross-cultural, cultural, or multidisciplinary perspectives. Prospective authors or volume editors are invited to place psychological findings and issues in their sociocultural contexts and to construct theoretical frameworks within which readers can understand human lives as shaped by both global and more local sociocultural forces. The series includes volumes concerned with the understanding and resolution of urgent problems that have no borders, such as intergroup conflict, health, the natural environment, and the plight of disempowered groups. Other volumes will be focused on the discovery of genuine universals in human functioning through the study of psychological phenomena in different contexts, sometimes using alternative methods.

Inquiries about publishing in the series may be directed to the series editors.

International Psychology Series books published by Lawrence Erlbaum Associates

Stevens/Gielen • *Toward a Global Psychology: Theory, Research, Intervention, and Pedagogy* (2007).

Toward a Global Psychology: Theory, Research, Intervention, and Pedagogy

Edited by

Michael J. Stevens
Illinois State University

Uwe P. Gielen
Saint Francis College

Psychology Press
Taylor & Francis Group

New York   London

First Published by Lawrence Erlbaum Associates, Inc., Publishers
10 Industrial Avenue
Mahwah, New Jersey 07430

Reprinted 2010 by Psychology Press

Lawrence Erlbaum Associates, Inc., Publishers
10 Industrial Avenue
Mahwah, New Jersey 07430
www.erlbaum.com

Cover design by Tomai Maridou

Library of Congress Cataloging-in-Publication Data

Toward a global psychology : theory, research, intervention, and peda-
    gogy / Michael J. Stevens and Uwe P. Gielen, editors.
        p. cm. — (Global and cross-cultural psychology)
    Includes bibliographical references and index.
ISBN 978-0-8058-5375-9 — 0-8058-5375-8 (cloth)
ISBN 978-0-8058-5376-6 — 0-8058-5376-6 (pbk.)
ISBN 978-1-4106-1399-8 — 1-4106-1399-2 (e book)
1. Psychology. 2. Ethnopsychology. I. Stevens, Michael J., 1954–
    II. Gielen, Uwe P. (Uwe Peter), 1940– III. Series.
BF121.T665 2006
150.9—dc22
                                                    2006003208
                                                        CIP

For Rachel, my daughter, a rare young woman who, though just beginning her own life's journey, has already made the world a better place.

MJS

To the memory of Lawrence Kohlberg, who strove for a more universal conception of justice.

UPG

Contents

Foreword

Kurt Pawlik
University of Hamburg

It gave me pleasure to accept the Editors' invitation to contribute a Foreword to *Toward a Global Psychology: Theory, Research, Intervention, and Pedagogy*, which highlights the significance of and perspectives on the globalizing psychology. This is not to say that psychological science has not been open for worldwide cooperation and exchange in the past, ever since its beginnings as a distinct discipline. Indeed a first international congress in psychology took place as early as 1889 in Paris, France (under the name, International Congress of Physiological Psychology), and its most recent successor, the 28th International Congress of Psychology, which convened in 2004 in Beijing, China, attracted more than 6,000 participants from around the world. Also, the international exchange of graduate students in psychology since the early 1880s is already documented, as recorded, for example, by Edwin G. Boring for the German universities of Göttingen and Leipzig. And, over the years the volume and scope of cross-national research cooperation in psychology has seen a steep and impressive rise, most notably since the 1960s and 1970s.

Then, what is so new in recent developments up to the present-day movement toward a global psychology? I would like to stress four points, which run like thematic guidelines through the chapters of *Toward a Global Psychology*.

First, like many other sciences, psychology too has succeeded in setting up powerful and efficient cross-national structures of organization for the promotion of scientific and professional forms of exchange, ranging from regional to global in scale. As President of the International Union of Psychological Science (IUPsyS), the "U.N. of psychology" as some like to call it, I had ample opportunity to appreciate the IUPsyS as a miraculous platform for convening in psychology new projects of international cooperation and capacity-building in research and applied practice. Furthermore, the IUPsyS has become *the* operative arm for psychology to engage in international scientific collaboration with other disciplines and with global governmental structures under the aegis of the U.N. To a large extent, this globalizing of psychology has been fostered through its founding and ongoing membership in the International Social Science Council and its complementary membership since 1982 in the International Council for Science. *Toward a Global Psychology* is a resource-rich road map into the dynamics and merits of globalizing psychology.

Collaborative efforts of this type reveal a second *ordre du jour* for global psychology: to prepare for a two-fold extension of its heuristic dimension, namely the enlargement of units of study and the establishment of multidisciplinarity. Not only action tasks in applied professional work, but also topics in basic research often reach beyond the single individual as the unit of study and/or transcend the conceptual framework and methodological toolbox of psychology. Social psychology, organizational psychology, cognitive neuropsychology, psycholinguistics, and clinical-counseling psychology each holds a stockpile of well-documented examples. Research and applied work in the fields of human migration, environment-friendly behavior, or interethnic conflict becomes virtually impossible if we restrict the unit of study to the individual level and fail to cooperate, in open partnership, with other social and natural sciences. And, all too often, social issues that call for psychological expertise and action extend across borders of nations and even regions. The context in which these issues are situated make for a tough laboratory when it comes to preparing the necessary conceptual, methodological, and practical extensions in and of psychology. The examples presented in *Toward a Global Psychology* highlight the pressing need for global strategies to guide research and applied work vis-à-vis such issues in psychology.

A third function of the movement toward a global psychology touches upon the conceptual and methodological universality of psychology, or at least of certain fields within psychological science. Although there is unequivocal experimental evidence that the structure and process characteristics of human cognition, human behavioral learning, and human motivation and emotion are genuinely universal, this does not necessarily hold for their content and for culture-bound determinants of their mental and behavioral outcomes. It is well documented, for example, how languages and cultures may differ in the way they conceptualize intra-familial relationships and kinship connections and how this will affect social roles and rules. Social psychology has revealed striking differences between typically Western and typically Chinese rules of conduct for properly initiating and structuring verbal communication. Still more fundamental, psychological concepts are often referred to by terms borrowed from everyday language, like *intelligence*, *mind*, or *emotion*. To the extent that they differ between language communities in their connotation, theories employing these concepts and research devised to elaborate on them need an underpinning grounded in normative expertise if a common intellectual base is ever to be established. *Toward a Global Psychology* is rich in examples and recommendations with respect to the challenge of establishing universality in psychology.

My fourth and last point relates to the role of psychology as an agent and actor in international affairs at large. As of today, so much is empirically known and theoretically understood about human behavior—about human actions producing or mitigating interpersonal conflict or about individual and cultural differences—yet so little of it is brought to bear in terms of world governance and diplomacy. Other social and, even more so, natural sciences are far ahead of psychology in this, as an analysis of international procedures and structures (e.g., at the U.N.) easily verifies. Here, a truly novel field of professional psychology and a new specialization in psychological science is opening up, for which we must lay the foundations now in curriculum development and graduate training. And, foremost and above all, we must become creative in "giving psychology away," as George Miller requested, also in the arena of global governance and scientific advisory bodies, as other disciplines have done already, including economics, law, and political science. Research-based knowledge and theory-guided analytical capacity already enable psychology to serve as expert agent, as success stories of psychology's advisement to governments and policy-makers have shown at subnational and national levels (e.g., in crime prevention or in labor-management relationships).

I would like to close this Foreword by expressing the hope that *Toward a Global Psychology: Theory, Research, Intervention, and Pedagogy* will capture the attention of psychologists and help to shape the development of a global psychology, and, for the reasons just enumerated, it surely deserves our strong support as we face the demands of the 21st century.

Preface

Michael J. Stevens
Illinois State University

Uwe P. Gielen
Saint Francis College

In recent years, the number of psychologists and psychology students around the world has grown considerably, with increases being especially visible outside the United States. At the same time, the process of globalization has exerted a major impact on psychology everywhere. However, whereas the globalizing of psychology has accelerated in recent years, no book is currently available that delineates global psychology with a coherent view to theory, research, intervention, and pedagogy.

Furthermore, it is widely recognized that paradigms of human behavior developed by Western psychologists are not entirely compatible with the global phenomena to which they are applied. A psychology based too often on U.S. college undergraduates has fallen short of providing a satisfactory approach when transferred from the laboratory to problems and issues that are constituted in culture, economics, history, politics, and religion. As global psychology becomes a "buzz word" in academic and professional circles, the time is ripe for a volume that meets the needs of scientists and practitioners of such a psychology.

Toward a Global Psychology: Theory, Research, Intervention, and Pedagogy aims to define a mostly new field while bridging the divide between scholarship and application. Global psychology seeks to enhance communication and collaboration among psychologists worldwide through scholarship, advocacy, education, and networking. Global psychology also seeks to discover genuine universals through the study of psychological phenomena-in-context. Finally, global psychology encompasses the application of psychological science to pressing global concerns, such as overpopulation, global warming, HIV/AIDS, and human trafficking. These concerns, like others that confront the world, are complex and multi-determined. As such, global psychology recognizes that alternative and multidisciplinary theories, research methods, interventions, and pedagogies are needed to understand more fully and respond more effectively to concerns that transcend country and region.

Unlike the few existing volumes on psychology as defined and practiced around the world, our book will give its readers a richer appreciation of how to approach a global psychology as researchers, practitioners, and trainers. We build upon the extant literature on global psychology by offering readers the detailed information they need to participate meaningfully in the field. The distinctiveness of our book, then, is its systematic and utilitarian presentation of conceptual, methodological, and strategic knowledge for constructive engagement in the science and practice of psychology in an increasingly globalized world.

Part I of *Toward a Global Psychology*, Welcome to Global Psychology, introduces the specialty of global psychology and orients readers to the following three sections of the book.

The four chapters of part II, The Emergence of Psychology Around the World, provide a more detailed introduction to global psychology. They address global perspectives on the history of psychology, current trends in psychology worldwide, problems and issues confronting psychologists in the non-Western and developing regions of the world, and the indigenization movement in psychology.

The six chapters of part III, Theory, Research, Practice, and Training in Global Psychology, give a systematic overview of existing and new approaches to the work of international psychologists: conceptual perspectives, research methods, interventions both psychotherapeutic and macrosocial, professional psychology and licensure, and education and training for a global psychology. These chapters reflect the widespread and rapid advance of a more contextually sensitive psychology, yet preserve useful applications of mainstream paradigms. As noted previously, the distinctive contribution of part III, and of our book in general, is its articulation of how psychologists can apply theoretical formulations, investigative methodologies, intervention techniques, and training procedures to explain, study, change, and prepare professionals to respond to global problems and issues that have significant psychological dimensions.

The lone chapter of part IV, Challenges and Prospects for a Global Psychology, offers practical guidelines for psychologists and psychology students who wish to become involved in psychology around the world.

In the Epilogue we provide evidence to support the globalizing of psychology, a grand synthesis of the themes common to various chapters, and predictions about the future of global psychology. These questions must be addressed if its models, research strategies, practical applications, and training are to mature further.

Thus, *Toward a Global Psychology* is a timely contribution to the maturing speciality of global psychology that offers a systematic orientation and utilitarian content intended to meet the needs of scientists and practitioners alike. It also prepares readers for how the discipline of psychology might be transformed from the way in which it is currently constituted. No volume currently available covers a similar range of topics on such a grand scale.

There are three audiences for *Toward a Global Psychology*: American psychologists, psychology students from virtually all scientific and applied specialities within the discipline (e.g., cultural, social, developmental, I/O, and clinical), and those from abroad with interests in global psychology. We seek to inform U.S. readers about theory, research, intervention, and pedagogy in psychology around the world in order to reduce the isolation and parochialism of U.S. psychology. U.S. psychology has tended to disregard the contributions of non-Western and recent advances in European psychologies along with the professional experiences of foreign psychologists, trained in the United States, who have returned to their countries of origin. As American psychology faces the challenges of the 21st century (e.g., migration, terrorism), it must raise awareness and understanding of the contextually embedded nature of the discipline and profession, and provide a foundation for meaningful transnational dialogue and collaboration To this end, we hope to contribute to American psychology's recent commitment to globalize its conceptual, investigative, practical, and training base and to narrow the gaps that separate these elements.

Psychologists and psychology students overseas have limited access to the global literature on psychology. Moreover, many foreign psychologists and psychology students, including those who are connected to the Internet and World Wide Web, continue to be exposed mainly to Western psychology with the complaint that it is de-contextualized and of limited applicability. *Toward a Global Psychology* seeks to offset the consequences of such bias through its adoption of a global, multidisciplinary perspective on psychology and encouragement of transnational communication and collaboration on matters of contemporary significance. Our book will inform readers from around the world about global problems and issues that confront psychology by synthesizing culturally informed scholarship with culturally sensitive application to achieve a meaningful praxis.

Whether for domestic or international consumption, *Toward a Global Psychology* has relevance for scholars and professionals and for graduate and advanced undergraduate students interested in international and cross-cultural psychology. Our book will also prove valuable as required reading in courses on global psychology or as adjunct literature in courses on the history of psychology; clinical, counseling, and school psychology; and social and industrial-organizational psychology. To this end, we developed a sample syllabus for a course on global psychology (see Appendix A), in which we identify specific chapters of the book as required readings for weekly topics. Outside of psychology, our book will find a voice in courses in anthropology and sociology, history and political science, and curriculum and instruction. Given the growing importance of globalizing psychology in the United States and elsewhere, we believe that *Toward a Global Psychology* will assume a central place in this movement.

In order to assure sufficient breadth and scope, and to attract an eminent team of international contributors, we formed an editorial advisory board, chaired by Dr. Juris G. Draguns. Members of the board included renowned psychologists from Africa (Dr. A. Bame Nsamenang), Asia (Dr. T. S. Saraswathi), Europe (Dr. Kurt Pawlik), Latin America (Dr. Rubén Ardila), the Middle East (Dr. Ramadan A. Ahmed), and the Pacific Rim (Dr. Cristina Jayme Montiel). The duties of our editorial advisors included identifying and recruiting potential chapter authors, who in their judgment were among the most expert or influential in a particular domain of global psychology; they also assisted in enlisting international colleagues with whom primary authors of chapters collaborated. The final set of chapter authors included psychologists of unparalleled stature in their respective fields who brought a genuinely international focus and expertise to the book. Our editorial advisors and outside experts reviewed drafts of chapters as they became available; the additions and modifications that they recommended contributed immeasurably to the quality of those chapters and to our book as a whole. For example, in order to minimize the risk of ethnocentric bias and to advance global psychology generally, we asked our editorial advisors to comment on the appropriate infusion of psychological literature published in languages other than English so as to ensure representation of the well developed, yet relatively unknown French, German, Japanese, Russian, and Spanish perspectives.

We also developed a fine-grained Author's Guide that we believed would facilitate the preparation of holistic chapters on various dimensions of global psychology. As a result, the chapters of *Toward a Global Psychology* balance theory, research, and practice and underscore meaningful ties among them. To attain additional coherence and enhance lucidity, the book's chapters integrate case examples that highlight key concerns and challenges in the international application of theory, research, intervention, and pedagogy, as well as articulate ways of overcoming them. In this way, readers will come away with a better appreciation of the assets and liabilities of the transnational application of conceptual models, investigative methodologies, strategies for intervention, and approaches to professional training. For example, chapter 1 synthesizes existing descriptions of global psychology into a succinct and useful definition, compares and contrasts global psychology to related fields (e.g., cross-cultural psychology, ethnic studies, economic psychology, and political psychology) in order to give readers a canonical map within which to place this specialty, and articulates the scope of global psychology, with particular attention paid to phenomena of contemporary significance (e.g., intergroup conflict, threats to the natural environment, risks to physical and mental health, especially for women, children and adolescents, and migrants and refugees). Each chapter also includes a short list of influential readings.

Finally, in addition to integrating theory, research, and practice through case illustrations and infusing the non-English language literature in psychology, *Toward a Global Psychology* features a consistent format and style. Brief introductions to each part of the book include summaries of each chapter contained therein that highlight the connections between chapters organized within the same part.

Acknowledgements

Toward a Global Psychology: Theory, Research, Intervention, and Pedagogy could not have succeeded without the untiring efforts of many to whom we owe a debt of gratitude. We thank the Board of the Division of International Psychology of the American Psychological Association for their support of a book series on *Global and Cross-Cultural Psychology*, edited by Dr. Uwe P. Gielen and Dr. Harold Takooshian under the imprimatur of Lawrence Erlbaum Associates, Inc., of which this volume is the first.

We were exceedingly gratified to assemble a distinguished editorial advisory board, led by Dr. Juris G. Draguns and which included Dr. Ramadan A. Ahmed, Dr. Rubén Ardila, Dr. Cristina Jayme Montiel, Dr. A. Bame Nsamenang, Dr. Kurt Pawlik (who also kindly agreed to write the Foreword to *Toward a Global Psychology*), and Dr. T.S. Saraswathi; all served skillfully, graciously providing advice and input whenever called upon.

Of course, we deeply appreciate the authors for their expertise and devotion in preparing chapters, especially our primary authors Dr. Michael J. Stevens, Dr. John D. Hogan, Dr. Elizabeth Nair, Dr. Juan José Sánchez-Sosa, Dr. Uichol Kim, Dr. Fathali M. Moghaddam, Dr. Graham B. Stead, Dr. Juris G. Draguns, Dr. Michael G. Wessells, Dr. Jean L. Pettifor, Dr. Anthony J. Marsella, and Dr. Harold Takooshian.

We are indebted to the experts from around the world whom we invited to review chapter drafts; their comments were invariably thoughtful and constructive.

We also express our appreciation to the University Seminars at Columbia University for assistance in preparing the manuscript for publication. Material drawn from this work was presented to the University Seminar on Ethics, Moral Education, and Society.

We also thank our editors at Lawrence Erlbaum Associates, most notably Dr. Susan Milmoe, now retired, and Ms. Debra Riegert, for their guidance and support at every stage in the preparation of this book, particularly in making the many details related to its publication so manageable.

Finally, we appreciate the patience of our respective loved ones, who tolerated the many evenings and weekends we sacrificed to edit *Toward a Global Psychology*.

I

WELCOME TO A GLOBAL PSYCHOLOGY

Part I of *Toward a Global Psychology: Theory, Research, Intervention, and Pedagogy* contains a single chapter written by the book's senior editor, Michael J. Stevens. As the title of the chapter indicates, "Orientation to a Global Psychology" offers a definition of this specialty and a general framework for the three parts of the book that follow. Ironically, in considering the historical contributions to the discipline and profession of psychology, it soon becomes evident that psychology has long been global. Yet, the global dimension of psychology has been explicitly recognized and established as a specialty only recently, particularly by psychologists in Western nations. It seems that economic, political, social, and technological forces are exerting a profound influence on the globalizing of psychology, breaking down parochial and, at times, ethnocentric theories, investigative methods, applications, and models of training.

Chapter 1 describes the mission of global psychology as that of promoting communication and collaboration among psychologists worldwide. Communication and collaboration are becoming hallmarks of the efforts of globally oriented psychologists to understand and respond to urgent transnational concerns, such as intergroup conflict, threats to the natural environment, and risks to physical and mental health, especially among women, children and adolescents, and migrants and refugees. To give a more diverse and complete overview of the global concerns mentioned above, Stevens infuses this chapter with publications authored by experts in non-Western countries and draws upon the relatively unknown non-English-language literature.

As attested to by the chapters in Part II: The Emergence of Psychology Around the World, the transnational concerns just mentioned are among the central foci of a growing number of globally oriented psychologists in both industrial and less-developed countries. To address these global concerns more effectively, psychologists have come to recognize that alternative and emerging perspectives, which emphasize the situated and relational nature of human action and experience (e.g., indigenous psychologies), must complement the mainstream, reductionistic paradigm. The value and promise of these "new" conceptual, empirical, practical, and training approaches are echoed in the chapters that comprise Part III: Theory, Research, Practice, and Training in Global Psychology. Likewise, "Orientation to a Global Psychology" underscores the necessity for contemporary psychologists to acquire and utilize a multidisciplinary, multilevel, and contextually sensitive foundation of knowledge and skill as they approach their science and practice; this call is also sounded throughout the book.

Stevens closes with an invitation to psychologists and psychology students to engage their counterparts worldwide in "horizontal" dialogue, to exploit familiar means and to fashion new means of advancing psychological science and practice to a genuinely global footing, one that imbues psychology with greater unity and purpose. These aims are detailed further in Part IV: Challenges and Prospects for a Global Psychology.

1

Orientation to a Global Psychology

Michael J. Stevens
Illinois State University

INTRODUCTION

The global proliferation of psychology is evident not only in the rising
numbers of psychologists and psychology students, but also in the growth
of scientific and applied specialization and the psychological organizations, journals, and training programs that represent these specialties
(Stevens & Wedding, 2004a). Furthermore, psychology is experiencing
rejuvenation throughout the world. Witness the restoration and development of psychology in East European countries that have transitioned
from communism to alternative economic and political systems (e.g.,
Poland) as well as the surge in psychological science and practice in
South American nations with healthy economies and political institutions (e.g., Brazil; Jing, 2000; Stevens & Wedding, 2004b). In part II,
chapters 2 and 3 trace the diverse roots of these trends and enlarge on their
current status. The connection between stable economic and political conditions and the growth of psychology is revealed by the expectations of governments, business and industry, and the public that psychology address
national challenges and promote personal well being in response to modernization (Jing, 2000; Stevens & Wedding, 2004a). This is certainly the
case in developing countries (e.g., China; Jing, 2000; Stevens &
Wedding, 2004b), which create jobs for psychologists, allocate resources

for psychological research, practice, and training, and pass legislation that legitimizes and safeguards psychology (Stevens & Wedding, 2004b). There is more to say on psychology in the developing world in part II, chapter 4.

Although there are approximately 277,000 employed psychologists in the United States (U.S. Census Bureau, 2003), the proportion of American psychologists relative to the number of psychologists worldwide will likely shrink due to the vigorous expansion of psychology elsewhere (Jing, 2000; Tikkanen, 2005). The trends I noted previously have also launched a swing away from reductionistic psychology (i.e., an approach to understanding, derived from Cartesian philosophy, in which complex psychological phenomena are dismantled into their constituent parts and whose interactions are explained in objective and linear terms) to alternative psychologies, many of which, owing to their normative focus, capture the diverse worldviews of other countries and regions whose history and culture are non-Western. In part II, chapter 5 analyzes one manifestation of this shift: the movement toward indigenization. Today, reductionistic psychology is seldom applied uncritically to phenomena situated in the non-Western world due to the belief, often grounded in experience, that its compartmentalized descriptions and causal explanations tend to have limited scientific and practical relevance (Gergen, 2001; Stevens & Wedding, 2004a). Although such outcomes often disappoint novice international consumers of reductionistic psychology, they are not surprising. Reductionistic psychology is relatively decontextualized, tends to dismantle the unity that gives psychological phenomena their rich meaning, and is perceived as hegemonic and oppressive in its claim of objectivity and universality (Horowitz, 2004).

The perception that reductionistic psychology is of limited global usefulness has triggered paradigmatic adjustments in various parts of the world, including the United States (Horowitz, 2004; Nsamenang, 2004). Some of these have become more fully differentiated and recognized perspectives, such as multiculturalism and indigenization. Others have emerged recently or are evolving slowly, and reflect a normative realignment of psychology across regions that share a language or religion (e.g., Islamic psychology across the Muslim world; Stevens & Wedding, 2004b). These developments illustrate how psychology is evolving beyond mainstream reductionism and strengthen the call for Western psychologists to dialogue with their international colleagues (Gergen; 2001; Stevens & Wedding, 2004a). Such dialogue holds the promise of broadening the conceptual, methodological, and practical knowledge and skills of Western psychologists as they face the multidetermined, multilayered, and contextually embedded psychological phenomena of the 21st century. For example, African psychologists have identified the many overlapping factors that underlie the unequal exchange between Western and African cultures and argue that greater representation of the African experience in psychology would add richness and relevance to the discipline (Nsamenang, 2004). One sign of widening dialogue is the growing contribution by authors from outside the United States to the psychological literature, as indexed by databases such as PsycLIT. However, the coverage of research from less developed nations is lean, and abstracts in languages other than English have declined since the 1980s (Adair, Coelho, & Luna, 2002), creating a parallel trend toward homogeneity and uniformity. German psychologists have also expressed a need to internationalize their research and practice, with some German journals seeking to publish more globally representative studies (Borkenhagen, Schumacher, & Braehler, 2002). Chapters 6 through 9 in part III sample a number of alternative psychological theories, research methods, and interventions both small and large that are more responsive to the nuanced worlds in which people live; if integrated with reductionistic psychology, they offer the possibility for discovering genuine universals in human functioning.

Global psychology is relatively new as a specialty within psychology and as an unfolding process within the discipline and profession. I begin this orientation with a review of extant descriptions of global psychology and then attempt to synthesize these into a clear and complete definition of its mission and scope. I then compare and contrast the domain of global psychology to that of related fields, such as cross-cultural psychology and ethnic studies, in order to articulate the canonical map within which to place this specialty. I also present two relatively new and unfamiliar fields that are of increasing importance to a global psychology: economic psychology and political psychology. Rather than review international scholarship in traditional areas of psychology or emerging alternative psychologies, I next survey the range of convenience of global psychology and highlight its scientific and applied relevance to foci of worldwide concern. Of the many pressing issues which the world now faces, three have profound implications: intergroup conflict, threats to the natural environment, and risks to physical and mental health, particularly among women, children, and adolescents, and migrants and refugees. I approach these topics with two overarching goals: (a) to impart a coherent, albeit abbreviated, conceptual, empirical, and practical perspective on the work of globally oriented psychologists (see the five chapters of part III) and (b) to sample literature published by authors from less developed countries as well as the relatively unknown non-English-language literature (i.e., French, German, Japanese, and Spanish) in order to provide a rich contemporary and global view of each topic (see the four chapters of part II).

DEFINITIONS AND DISTINCTIONS

Before defining the mission and scope of global psychology, and examining it in relation to cross-cultural psychology and ethnic studies, it is important to clarify the terms: *global* and *international*. Although used somewhat interchangeably, they have subtle differences in meaning. *The Oxford English Dictionary* gives the following definition for global:

> ... pertaining to or involving the world, worldwide. (1993, p. 1101)

and defines international as:

> Existing, occurring, or carried on between nations ... Agreed on by many nations; used by, or able to be used by (the people of) many nations. (1993, p. 1397)

Both terms speak to demographic, economic, political, and technological macro-processes that contribute to international, interregional, and worldwide networks. Both reflect activity that occurs and has relevance beyond state boundaries. With respect to psychology, the use of either term connotes that its history, current trends, theories, research methods, interventions, practice regulations, and curricula transcend local and national limitations. Both terms imply a diversity of scientific and applied foci, both circumscribed and far-reaching, that involves communication and collaboration among scholars, practitioners, and educators worldwide. However, because the globalizing of psychology is nascent and evolving, it would be more accurate to refer to areas of psychological science and practice that have not yet attained a truly global footing as *international*. Similarly, the term *global* implies paradigmatic universality, which has been questioned by critics of reductionistic psychology and by those who reject attempts to meld alternative and reductionistic psychologies (Gergen, 2001; Horowitz, 2004; Stevens & Wedding, 2004a). Here, too, the term *international* is preferred given its greater sensitivity to the degree of fit between a psychology and the context to which it is applied. In short, although the terms *global* and *international* are synonymous in some instances, they are not identical, with *international* articulating a special case of global. Owing to these subtleties of definition, both terms are used judiciously throughout this book.

Global Psychology

Although the *Encyclopedia of Psychology* does not have an entry for *global psychology*, it offers a definition of its closely related counterpart, *international psychology*:

> ... scientific or professional activities (organizations, exchanges, and research enterprises) of a psychological nature involving groups of psychologists in two or more nations. Such activities are generally aimed at advancing psychological science or improving the practice of psychology through organizational efforts in one or more nations ... Occasionally the term *international psychology* is also used to designate the social psychology of international relations. (Holtzman, 2000, p. 343)

Global psychology has a distinct mission and scope of scientific knowledge and professional practice that differentiate it from other disciplinary specialties (Stevens & Wedding, 2004a). Global psychology operates to increase the frequency, broaden the scope, and enhance the meaningfulness of communication and collaboration among psychologists and psychology students with shared interests from diverse countries and cultures.

Efforts to globalize psychology have four foci, all of which serve to heighten global consciousness: scholarship, advocacy, the curriculum, and networking (Velayo, 2004). In terms of scholarship global psychology seeks to provide greater access to needed resources, such as psychological literature in multiple languages (Stevens & Wedding, 2004a, 2004b), to strengthen the methodological capacities of psychologists (e.g., the International Union of Psychological Sciences's Advanced Research Training Seminars), to facilitate collaborative research (e.g., Social Science Research Council), and to sensitize investigators to the hazards of implicit ethnocentric bias as well as encourage the further development of contextually sensitive, normative paradigms. Global psychology advocates committed involvement with psychological associations that represent the worldwide interests of psychologists and psychology students (e.g., International Association of Applied Psychology, International Psychology Student Organization) as well as scientific and policy-making entities in which psychology has an official presence (e.g., International Council of Science, U.N.). In part III, chapter 10 describes how professional psychologists and psychological organizations facilitate scholarship and encourage participation globally. With respect to creating a curriculum to meet the needs of the global community (e.g., University of Hawaii, United States), global psychology encourages the expansion of distance-learning (e.g., National University of Singapore), appreciation of diversity through creative pedagogies (e.g., Utkal University, India), completion of internships at foreign institutions (e.g., Universidade de São Paolo, Brazil), and mentoring of students who show enthusiasm for global psychology. In part III, chapter 11 elaborates on approaches for preparing a new generation of competent, globally oriented psychologists. As important as scholarship, advocacy, and the curriculum are to global psychology's mission of worldwide communication and collaboration, networking is, perhaps, the most important. The global psychology of the 21st century demands a readiness to exploit existing and emerging technologies (e.g., translation software), funding to support travel abroad (e.g., International Research and Exchanges Board), programming at national, regional, and international conferences that maximizes the diversity of participants, and expanding venues, especially regional ones, to accelerate the exchange of ideas, data, and practices (e.g., Middle East and North Africa Regional Conference of Psychology). In part IV, chapter 12 enumerates the many ways psychologists and psychology students can become globally engaged. The epilogue offers a glimpse of the agenda and challenges to global psychology in the context of its history and current status.

As implied by the above definition, there is more to global psychology than its mission to promote communication and collaboration. Global psychology also encompasses the application of psychological science and practice to a range of issues encompassing the world (Jing, 2000; Stevens & Wedding, 2004a). Among the most pressing of these are global terrorism, global warming, overpopulation, the worldwide spread of HIV/AIDS, and trafficking in human beings. These problems, like others that confront the world, are multidetermined, multilayered, and constituted in economics, history, politics, psychology, religion, and culture. As such, globally oriented psychologists recognize that alternative, multidisciplinary theories, research strategies, and interventions are required to understand more fully and respond more effectively to these concerns. Three particularly urgent global issues are examined later in this chapter, including intergroup conflict, threats to the natural environment, and risks to physical and mental health. Many of these topics are also addressed either directly or through case examples in the chapters that follow.

Cross-Cultural Psychology

Unlike global psychology, cross-cultural psychology addresses behavior and experience as they occur in different cultures and is often viewed as subsuming both contemporary cross-cultural psychology and cultural psychology (Jing, 2000; Triandis, 2000a). Contemporary cross-cultural psychologists measure psychological phenomena equivalently across cultures to determine the generality of such phenomena. Hence, contemporary cross-cultural psychology reflects a universalist or *etic* model of human functioning. Cultural psychology acknowledges the bi-directional relationship between culture and psychological phenomena and articulates how language, myth and tradition, and social discourse construct psychological phenomena (Triandis, 2000a). Because cultural psychology entails the investigation of a single culture, rather than cultural comparison, cultural psychologists adhere to a relativistic or *emic* perspective of human functioning. Contemporary cross-cultural psychology and cultural psychology are elements of global psychology. For example, globally oriented psychologists compare various response patterns exhibited by members of distinct groups who share assumptions and experiences (Jing, 2000). Likewise, these psychologists appreciate that the theories, methods, and techniques that guide their activities are situated in the same multidisciplinary crucible out of which culture is formed.

Ethnic Studies

Ethnic studies is another field that overlaps with, but does not duplicate global psychology. Ethnic studies, like cultural psychology, construes a person's identity in terms of a particular subgroup within a surrounding social context that claims a common cultural, racial, religious, linguistic, and/or geographic ancestry (Phinney, 2000). It focuses on the affective, cognitive, and evaluative elements that comprise ethnic identity, changes in ethnic identity over time and circumstances, prejudice, the relationship between ethnic minority and dominant majority groups within a society, and the acculturation of migrants, refugees, and indigenous peoples. Ethnic studies is integral to global psychology. For example, globally oriented psychologists are attuned to intergroup relations and advocate a multidisciplinary approach to understanding and improving such relations.

Unlike cross-cultural psychology and ethnic studies, the mission of global psychology is to increase the breadth and depth of communication and collaboration among the world's psychologists, which gives it a distinct process focus. Global psychology's application of psychological science and practice to concerns that traverse national borders also gives it a wider range of convenience than cross-cultural psychology or ethnic studies.

Economic and Political Psychology

Economic psychology and political psychology are two psychological fields that are relatively unfamiliar to psychologists in the U.S., but which have relevance for psychology as it begins to address topics of global significance. Globalization is such a topic. Since the 1990s, the pace and scope of worldwide integration have accelerated dramatically through the movement of goods and capital, expansion of human rights and democratic institutions, dissemination of information, and mass migration of peoples. As a result, globalization has created a compressed and contentious world, one to which economic and political psychology can offer much (Hermans & Kempen, 1998).

Though well established in Europe, economic psychology is an emerging field that melds economics and psychology. Economic psychologists investigate how economic systems explain specific individual behavior (e.g., consumer choice, saving money), the influence of social capital on macro-economic growth (e.g., the correlation of interpersonal trust with national wealth), and the cocreated natures of economic systems and normative social interaction through which members of any society master the tasks of daily living (Guerin, 2003; Rodriguez Kauth, 2002). To address such a diversity of topics authoritatively, economic psychology has become an integrative field that will likely assume a more prominent role in social analysis and policy formulation.

Political psychology centers on the relationship between political and psychological processes. It encompasses the study of political belief systems, attitudes, and behavior, the influence of mass media, and leadership as well as, more recently, information processing and the relationship of affect to political cognition and decision making. Another area of interest stresses a holistic view of politics, analyzing the capacity of macro-social structures to transform intra- and interpersonal processes as well as the mechanisms whereby normative interactional patterns resist or modulate imposed macro-social structures (McDermott, 2004). Political psychology has also become a voice for greater social relevance and social action. As a disciplinary gadfly, political psychologists cajole mainstream psychology to consider alternative perspectives and methods, grounded in anthropology, economics, history, and sociology, that better account for the contemporary realities of human affairs (e.g., conflict resolution, international relations, terrorism; Dorna, 2002; McDermott, 2004).

THREE CONCERNS OF GLOBAL SIGNIFICANCE

It is time now to survey the recent English and non-English language literature on three intersecting areas of worldwide concern on which scientific and applied psychology can be brought to bear: intergroup conflict, threats to the natural environment, and risks to the physical and mental health of women, children and adolescents, and migrants and refugees. As will become apparent, each of these concerns has multidisciplinary, multilayered, and global dimensions. In addition, although these concerns are presented separately, each is interwoven with every other concern. For example, intergroup violence (e.g., civil war) can have devastating effects on the natural environment and on physical and mental health. Environmental conditions (e.g., overcrowding) can impact intergroup relations and health (see Rainham & McDowell, 2005, for an analysis of data from 152 countries showing an inverse relationship between environmental sustainability and population health). And the health problems of women, children and adolescents, and migrants and refugees (e.g., HIV/AIDS) can heighten intergroup tensions.

Intergroup Conflict

During the 1990s intergroup conflict either intensified or erupted in various parts of the world, reaching genocidal levels in Bosnia and Rwanda. The prospect for peace in the 21st century has not improved as evidenced by ongoing violence in the Middle East and Central Africa. Globally oriented psychologists face the daunting task of understanding intergroup conflict and working for peace. They appreciate the importance of addressing the structural conditions and cultural norms that interact to produce systemic violence. They also recognize the importance of drawing on local strengths and resources when negotiating an end to intergroup violence, in facilitating a resolution of the entrenched and interlaced issues that engender such violence, and in implementing positive-sum solutions that nurture and sustain individual and collective well-being (Stevens, & Wedding, 2004a; Wessells, 2000).

Collective worldviews facilitate or inhibit intergroup conflict. These worldviews are shared, stable explanations for past, present, and anticipated events and mediate the emotions and actions of groups. The myriad of collective worldviews reflects the possible ways in which different groups sample information from their environments (Triandis, 2000b). Some groups tend to sample internal processes (e.g., attitudes) versus external processes (e.g., social roles). Others weigh ascribed attributes (e.g., ethnicity) more heavily than attained attributes (e.g., achievement). Once formed, collective worldviews are considered axiomatic by a significant proportion of the group and provide a way for members to identify with and become socialized into the group. Collective worldviews may contain distortions, such as the selective recall of a group's history and embellished historical narratives. These distortions are seldom examined carefully; when they are questioned, the group may sanction, marginalize, or evict the doubting member. Thus, collective worldviews have the potential to inflame intergroup conflict when they preclude impartial evaluation within a group and block the correction of miscommunication between groups (Stevens & Wedding, 2004a; Triandis, 2000b).

Eidelson and Eidelson (2003) described four overlapping collective worldviews that encourage intergroup conflict: superiority, injustice, vulnerability, and distrust. Reminiscent of social identity theory, shared beliefs about in-group superiority may propel a group to adopt violence when its social advantage is threatened or when it seeks to reclaim its appropriated status (e.g., Hitler's pursuit of *Lebensraum*). The collective worldview of injustice fortifies a group's conviction that its grievances against another group are righteous. Whether real or imagined, collective perceptions of injustice bolster group loyalty, blame an external entity for its suffering, and fuel violence (e.g., political and economic asymmetry in Sri Lanka has nourished ethnic grievances and violent competition for resources tied to power; Korf, 2005). The collective worldview of vulnerability reflects the shared expectation of impending threat to a group's values and traditions, and to its existence, which intensifies cohesion and can lead to pre-emptive violence against a threatening target (e.g., the genocidal policies of Hutus against Tutsis). The collective worldview of distrust assumes predatory intent by another group. It often brings forth generalized suspiciousness and negative stereotypes of an alleged persecutory group that are immune to contradiction (e.g., the fragile relations and, hence, fragile peace talks between Israelis and Palestinians), and which can justify violence. Plainly, these collective worldviews, either individual or in combination, impede the cessation of intergroup violence, the resolution of its causes, and the creation of a lasting peace.

Researchers are studying these collective worldviews, increasingly employing qualitative methods that place fewer restrictions on the expression of worldviews than do quantitative methods. Durrheim and Dixon (2004) used a discursive approach to show how racial attitudes are woven into the daily lives of white South Africans. The researchers were coparticipants in the investigation, underscoring the view that psychological phenomena exist not only as cognitive representations, but also as social constructions. Discourse analysis was used to discover how the meaning of prejudice is constructed and defended during a conversation within a specific setting. The analysis revealed features of racial prejudice not easily operationalized or quantified, but which are relevant to understanding attitude formation and change (e.g., expressions of racial attitudes and stereotypes are often equivocal and implied).

Stopping intergroup violence, resolving the issues that interact to produce such violence, and building cultures of tolerance entail the identification of variables that soften collective worldviews (Eidelson & Eidelson, 2003; Wessells, 2000), and occasionally facilitate natural outbreaks of peace (e.g., the peaceful separation of the former Czechoslovakia into two republics). Social identity theory is a perspective from which strategies for peace have been derived. Social identity theory holds that individuals prefer to belong to groups that are categorized as respected because membership in such groups provides positive self-definition (Hewstone & Greenland, 2000). To reduce intergroup conflict, psychologists are modifying the structure of group categorizations via recategorization and crossed categorization, such that members of adversarial groups come to see themselves as having comparable status and more shared attributes, respectively (Hewstone & Greenland, 2000). Social identity theory also suggests that increased contact between hostile groups can foster tolerance. The integrated education movement in Northern Ireland was inaugurated by the government to soften ethnopolitical attitudes and nurture reconciliation through a common curriculum that encourages multiple avenues for increased contact between Catholic and Protestant school children. Integrated education has positively affected in-group identity, out-group attitudes, and forgiveness and holds promise for building social cohesion where intractable intergroup conflict has existed (McGlynn, Niens, Cairns, & Hewstone, 2004).

Cultivating peaceful societies also involves increasing social capital, namely norms of reciprocity, civic virtues, and interpersonal trust

(Wessells, 2000). The International Association for the Evaluation of Educational Achievement evaluated the success of educational programs in building civic attitudes, knowledge, and participation among students in emerging democracies. Schools whose curricula included information about and demonstrations of democratic practices were most effective in promoting civic knowledge and participation (Torney-Purta, Lehmann, Oswald, & Schulz, 2001). These findings also support structural efforts to match training materials and group activities with the social norms and political culture of specific countries so as to deepen responsible citizenship among youngsters, thereby preventing intergroup violence.

The United Nations General Assembly (1998) defined a culture of peace as a set of attitudes, behaviors, and values that reject violence, seek to prevent intergroup conflict by addressing its origins, and aim to resolve conflict through dialogue and negotiation. Although the U.N. was advancing global norms for a peaceful world, the third element of its definition presents a hurdle for those engaged in any peace process. Dialogue occurs in a cultural context, one in which disputing parties may have markedly different strategic goals and styles that can determine the success or failure of negotiations. For example, the Western approach to negotiation is characterized by integrative goals (i.e., individualistic values) as well as a confrontational (i.e., high power) and transactional (i.e., context-free information) style, whereas non-Western cultures prefer distributive goals (i.e., collectivistic values) and an egalitarian (i.e., low power) and situated (i.e., context-rich information) approach to dispute resolution (Brett, 2000). In Asia, a significant amount of intergroup violence is structural, with governments oppressing their citizens and/or conditions that sustain economic and power inequality between ethnic groups. Thus, strategies for peace in Asia should include the promotion of beliefs and values that are consistent with economic and political democratization (Montiel, 2003). Psychologists working for peace in Asia must also be attuned to the importance of establishing a personal and particularistic form of trust with leaders of groups in conflict (Montiel, 2003). They must also recognize that successful efforts at establishing peace may require the involvement of figureheads and spiritual representatives, given their cultural authority and, hence, wherewithal to influence the conduct of belligerents.

Threats to the Natural Environment

Human beings have exploited the natural environment for ages, but industrialization and overpopulation over the last two centuries have transformed the environment on a global scale. Delhi offers a prime example of how a rapidly growing population and unfettered industrial output can produce an environmental crisis (Nagdeve, 2004). The burning of fossil fuels, over-working of farmland and fish stocks, and disposal of synthetic products have despoiled the environment to the degree that terms such as *dead zone* and *global warming* are now part of the global lexicon. Environment degradation is a significant global concern. First, many adverse effects of environmental exploitation are co-occurring and impact multiple, interrelated environmental systems at once (e.g., the atmosphere, oceans, ecosystems). Second, relatively circumscribed changes to the environment have accrued and have increasingly far-reaching consequences (e.g., acid rain, deforestation). Environmental trends that present a genuine global threat include the depletion of ozone, melting of polar ice caps, and changes in climate.

Degradation of the environment may be construed in economic and political terms as well as psychologically. Some have noted that environmental exploitation is inherent to free market democracies given their individualistic orientation and valuing of efficiency and growth (Vlek, 2000). Like free market democracies, reductionistic psychology finds itself pitted against the environment. Reductionism in psychology obtains from a worldview in which the person is separate from nature and possesses unlimited capacities that are ideally fulfilled through plumbing the depths of the world's natural resources. In fairness, communist countries have been notorious for environmental exploitation given Marxism's instrumental stance toward nature. Its limitations notwithstanding, reductionistic psychology is germane to a comprehensive understanding of and solution to global environmental problems because these problems are fundamentally behavioral (Vlek, 2000; Winter, 2000).

Psychologists worldwide have launched research programs grounded in applied behavior analysis, information processing, and social psychology to identify the prerequisites of sustainable development, targeting risk perception, cognitive and affective environmental awareness, choice behavior, and lifestyle values (Winter, 2000). Montada and Kals (2000) found that awareness of global environmental risks, perceived injustices in the distribution of benefits and costs resulting from environmental exploitation, and the belief that individual and corporate actors have the responsibility and means to protect the environment predicted commitment to preserve the global commons.

Psychologists are also laboring to slow and reverse the effects of environmental exploitation by devising models of, and strategies for, environmental problem solving at the individual, communal, and institutional level. Among the latter are pedagogies to promote moderation in consumer behavior, partnerships with business and industry to invest in conservation, and consultation with governmental agencies on policies and legislation that would enforce environmentally responsible action (Stevens & Wedding, 2004a; Winter, 2000). An especially persistent challenge has been to reduce cultural barriers to the adoption of contraceptive practices that curb population growth. Together with physicians, psychologists are adjusting contraceptive techniques and service–delivery systems to the preferences of local cultures in order to meet the needs of diverse peoples who seek to control their fertility in a satisfying, yet dignified manner (David & Russo, 2003).

Efforts to identify factors that contribute to pro-environmental behavior are truly worldwide. In Germany, psychologists are investigating how behavioral costs and social norms determine environmentally friendly attitudes and conservation behavior in different social contexts (Steinheider et al., 1999). Japanese psychologists have found that conservation behavior among city dwellers is tied more to personal benefits than to potentially positive consequences for the environment per se (Hayashi & Kubo, 1997). Psychologists in Spain are refining a dynamic-situational model for such pro-environmental behavior as recycling, buying ecological products, and energy and water conservation that delineates the interaction between attitudinal and contextual variables (Berenguer, Corraliza, Martin, & Oceja, 2001). Of special interest are multidisciplinary and international approaches to environmental issues within geographic regions and the role of natural and social scientists in advising governments of the imperative of sound environmental policies. Lidskog and Sundqvist (2004) describe the formation of a consensual environmental science, involving networks of experts in the natural and social sciences from various countries. Their collaborative work on sustainable growth has led to the codification of multilateral policies, including the Convention on Long-Range Transboundary Air Pollution. Similar multidisciplinary, scientific–political, and regional cooperation has contributed to the Alpine Agreement, which established environmental safeguards via regulation of the transportation infrastructure of countries situated along the Southern Alps. Psychologists are also studying the process of building consensus among adversarial parties (e.g., environmental activists vs. leaders of industry, countries with conflicting interests) and identifying variables that empower science to inform regulatory authorities and shape public opinion (e.g., credibility) (Lidskog & Sundqvist, 2004; Vlek, 2000).

Given the difficulties in managing environmental problems, experts in the natural and social sciences will need to continue forming international networks dedicated to the development of multilayered responses to the global environmental crisis (Stevens & Wedding, 2004a). The commons dilemma is a popular, multidisciplinary framework that has stimulated conceptual, empirical, and applied research worldwide (Vlek, 2000). The commons dilemma describes a fundamental conflict between the near-term individual, economic, and social benefits of unfettered human activity and the risks and costs to the collective environment that amass over time. Because there is no definitive solution to the commons dilemma, governments must seek a sustainable balance between the benefits and risks or costs of decisions that affect the environment. The psychological component of managing collective risks and costs revolves around awareness of collective risk, weighing collective risk against personal gain, and strengthening behavioral restraint. Clearly, psychological science and practice alone cannot succeed in generating the national, regional, and global compromises needed for sustainable growth. Progress will hinge upon the further integration of psychological concepts and techniques with those of anthropology (e.g., cultural values), economics (e.g., decision making), engineering (e.g., energy use), political science (e.g., policy formation), and sociology (e.g., structural change).

Risks to Physical and Mental Health

In this section, I examine the risks to physical and mental health posed by a growing number of converging factors that adversely impact the lives of many of the world's people, particularly women, children and adolescents, and migrants and refugees.

Physical Health

The emergence of health psychology in the 1970s reflected a shift in the patterns of illness and death in the industrialized world (Stevens & Wedding, 2004a). Cancer, heart disease, stroke, and accidents supplanted infectious diseases as leading causes of death, with lifestyle choices (e.g., poor diet, under-exercising, smoking) predicting a substantial proportion of these changes. However, in the underdeveloped world, millions have no choice about living in poverty and/or under political oppression. As a result, these peoples are more prone to suffer child mortality, infectious disease, malnutrition, dreadful living and work conditions, inadequate education and health care, and trauma and social isolation. In the less developed world, there are signs of the growing adverse outcomes of globalization on physical and mental health. Witness the rising incidence of eating disorders among adolescent females in Hong Kong, suggesting that exposure to the individualistic consumer culture of the West is eroding traditional communal values that heretofore insulated young women from dysfunctional eating (Lin, Tseng, & Yeh, 1994). Physical and mental health are influenced by an intricate constellation of cultural, economic, environmental, political, social, and psychological variables that must be identified and understood through multidisciplinary and international research. Hence, any systematic attempt to reduce illness and disability or to promote health must include education, law, medicine, public health, and psychology.

A large and growing proportion of the world's population lives in poverty (e.g., 2.8 billion live on less than $2 per day), with the gap between rich and poor within and between countries expanding (United Nations Population Fund, 2004). Notwithstanding the strong relationship between poverty and various indices of physical health (e.g., malnutrition, disease, mortality), few psychologists in the industrialized world have displayed interest in the psychosocial causes and effects of poverty (see Carr & Sloan, 2003). Some have examined attributions of poverty in order to account for the disturbing reality in which affluent individuals, including psychologists, neglect and marginalize the poor. Hine and Montiel (1999) discovered that Canadian respondents attributed poverty to natural causes, including low intelligence and various forms of social unrest, whereas Filipinos attributed poverty to incompetent and corrupt governments and to the poor themselves. Consistent with research on domestic poverty, attributions about global poverty mediated the relationship between political ideology and antipoverty activism, with activism predicted most strongly by attributions of exploitation that were made less often by social conservatives. Practically speaking, antipoverty activism might be increased through attributional retraining, whereby misconceptions are dispelled about the characterological basis of poverty, and information is provided on the contribution of exploitation to poverty.

Other psychologists argue that redressing unequal access to life-sustaining resources requires that poverty be construed as a human rights violation and the eradication of poverty as a moral obligation (Mbonda, 2004). Poverty, then, can be understood as suffering caused by unjust deprivation of the resources needed to live in freedom and dignity. That the world is becoming a global community suggests a collective duty to root-out poverty. Because the moral construction of poverty is embedded in society and culture, such efforts need not be uniform in their particulars, but rather adhere to universal principles of justice. Accordingly, psychologists are developing strategies to enhance good governance by increasing political stability and crafting policies that nurture economic and social development (Boucher, 2003). Psychologists recommend community empowerment as key to any systemic approach to reduce poverty and the overcrowding, malnutrition, and disease that obtain from it. They collaborate with community leaders to reconfigure political and institutional resources, capitalize on local self-help networks, and mobilize community members to social action.

Given the inordinate burden of poverty on women (United Nations Population Fund, 2004), the importance of empowering women cannot be overstated. Poverty, together with entrenched norms of gender inequality, contributes to multiple reproductive health problems, particularly for women in the less developed world (Murphy, 2003; United Nations Population Fund, 2004). Women's greater malnutrition puts them at risk for maternal mortality and chronic pelvic inflammatory disease. The Program of Action put forth by the 1994 International Conference on Population Development supports rights-based, integrative services that target women's reproductive health needs, and it has been adopted by the World Bank, World Health Organization, and International Planned Parenthood Association (Murphy, 2003). In addition to these reforms, psychologists are empowering women through didactic and experiential strategies designed to cultivate self-awareness, social consciousness, and an independent, proactive identity; of course, such approaches must be supported by community, national, and international programs that safeguard the empowerment process.

Recent studies have also illuminated the role of ethnic economies in the adaptation and integration of migrants and refugees (Light, 2004). Ethnic economies that are tolerated by the wider community insulate migrants and refugees from poverty by affording them employment and housing. Given the certitude of continued migration throughout the world due to rapid population growth in less developed countries and relaxed barriers to migration (Richmond, 2002), psychologists have informed officials at various levels of government of the wisdom in adopting policies that are favorable toward ethnic economies. In fact, the Commission on Global Governance (1995) recommended that governments coordinate international migration in a systematic fashion to ensure a multilateral commitment to human rights, including freedom from poverty.

HIV/AIDS is having widespread and ruinous effects at the personal and familial as well as national and regional levels, with over 38 million cases worldwide (United Nations Population Fund, 2004). Intersecting economic, political, social, and cultural factors contribute to the spread of HIV/AIDS, reflecting the multi-determined nature of the disease and multidisciplinary responses needed to arrest it. HIV/AIDS in sub-Saharan Africa is a case in point. The prevalence of HIV/AIDS in women and men between 15 and 49 years of age is 26% and 33%, respectively (United Nations Population Fund, 2004). Aside from the impact on health of intergroup conflict, poverty, and migration, indigenous values and customs may heighten rates of infection and the challenges of managing the disease (Kalichman & Simbayi, 2004). Many African cultures promote high-risk cultural practices, including rites of sexual initiation and proof of fertility before marriage. Spiritually, many Africans attribute illness to a supernatural force transmitted by a malevolent person or group. Given this reality, effective treatment must include a cosmological account of the symptoms of the disease, often by a local healer. Furthermore, some Africans do not distinguish sharply between life and death. Because death brings people in contact with cherished ancestral spirits, the past and present are blurred, one consequence of which is a relatively low concern about contracting a potentially fatal disease. If psychologists hope for a meaningful role in combating the global HIV/AIDS pandemic, they must begin to dialogue, not only with political leaders and the health care system, but also with nontraditional local healers in order to meld indigenous worldviews with modern health practices. Such an approach has reduced the incidence of HIV/AIDS in Uganda through popular multimedia campaigns to increase knowledge and use of condoms and reduce the number of sex partners (Parkhurst & Lush, 2004).

Women.   Women, especially teenage girls, are 2 to 4 times as vulnerable to HIV/AIDS as men (Murphy, 2003; United Nations Population Fund, 2004). Moreover, their greater poverty and economic dependence lead many women toward promiscuous sex and prostitution for survival. In countries with traditionally demarcated gender roles, many women feel obliged to have unprotected sex even when they suspect infidelity, preferring to risk infection over criticism, abuse, and/or abandonment. These psychological and cultural realities dovetail with studies that underscore the universal role of interpersonal and social variables in mediating couples' intention to practice safe sex (e.g., Lanfranchi & Touzard, 2000). With the help of psychologists, the Office of Population and Reproductive Health of the U.S. Agency for International Development has developed holistic and contextually sensitive programs for women's reproductive health that integrate HIV/AIDS prevention with family planning, maternal health, and gender issues.

Children and Adolescents. Many of the world's children and adolescents live in poverty and have few opportunities for a more promising future (e.g., in the Arab world, 26% of boys and 48% of girls over 14 years old are illiterate; Saraswathi & Larson, 2002; United Nations Population Fund, 2004). There is much need for social policies and action that rescue children and adolescents from lives geared toward survival, and harness their potential. In addition, globalization has created many disturbing contrasts for today's youth that make forming a stable identity more daunting than ever (Gielen & Chumachenko, 2004). Although many children and adolescents successfully adapt to the vicissitudes of globalization (e.g., a bicultural identity formed around local and global cultures), other accommodations are problematic and feature alienation, marginalization, and acculturative stress (Gielen & Chumachenko, 2004). Coupled with a future foreclosed by poverty and lack of opportunity, children and adolescents with incomplete or maladapted identities may be drawn toward unhealthy lifestyles that are likely to include unsafe sex with more sex partners, starting at a younger age and extending over a longer period of time (Gielen & Chumachenko, 2004; Saraswathi & Larson, 2002). Among the objectives outlined by the U.N. General Assembly (1996) to ensure the self-sufficiency and participation in society of adolescents is improvement in education for reproductive health and for the prevention of HIV/AIDS. Psychologists are integral to the multidisciplinary, multilayered, and global approach required to meet this objective. To help adolescents operationalize such concepts as safe sex, of which they have a rudimentary understanding from conventional sex education, psychologists have developed interactive DVDs in which adolescents can intervene at critical choice points while viewing a couple who encounter various sexual situations. This interactive tool not only has closed adolescents' knowledge gap, but also yielded greater abstinence and fewer sexually transmitted infections than standard sex education (Downs et al., 2004).

Migrants and Refugees.   Each year an estimated four million people travel illegally across national borders (Gushulak & MacPherson, 2000). In today's rapidly globalizing world, ever more people will relocate in search of opportunities to improve their lives or to escape intergroup conflict, environmental disasters, and economic and political oppression. The trend toward greater control over national borders has paradoxically increased the illegal movement of people. Such movement entails health risks to migrants and refugees. Although the health risks to migrants and refugees have not been studied systematically, descriptive accounts suggest that they are significant for this population as well as the population in the country of destination (Gushulak & MacPherson, 2000). These health risks range from minor to life threatening (e.g., HIV/AIDS) and are being examined within and across discrete stages of the migratory process: predeparture, the journey, and destination. Multidisciplinary experts have hypothesized a number of factors that may contribute to the health of migrants and refugees in these stages: Health conditions in the country of origin and social equity (e.g., poverty) bear upon the predeparture stage; type of transportation, environmental conditions, and psychosocial factors (e.g., violence) impact the journey; and barriers to social programs, acquired health problems, and noncommunicable diseases (e.g., sexual abuse) have relevance upon arrival. Several international foundations, such as TAMPEP, are mapping the demography and distribution of migrants and refugees in the sex industry in hopes of containing the international transmission of HIV/AIDS (Wallman, 2001). A global response to the health hazards of migration mandates a multidisciplinary and international effort at various levels (e.g., government agencies, scientific and professional organizations, individual experts) to recognize, define, measure, and address the biopsychosocial factors that impact the health of migrants and refugees. Among the most important challenges for psychologists is the assessment of the health of migrants and refugees, design of holistic interventions to arrest and prevent illness at different stages of migration, and evaluation of programs that provide care for sick migrants and refugees (Gushulak & MacPherson, 2000). Specific to HIV/AIDS among migrant and refugee sex workers, psychologists are developing streetwise and culturally appropriate information and approaches to education, networking with physicians and social service agencies, mediating between migrants and refugees and local authorities, and empowering migrant and refugee communities in order to prevent infection and promote sexual health (Wallman, 2001).

Mental Health

Although symptoms of psychopathology vary markedly worldwide (Draguns & Tanaka-Matsumi, 2003), thorny conceptual, definitional, and psychometric issues threaten the integrity of cross-cultural research on psychopathology. Likewise, it has proved difficult to identify the core and presumably universal dimensions of different forms of psycho-pathology. Epidemiological studies have found comparable incidence rates and symptom constellations for certain disorders across countries and cultures, especially for major depression and schizophrenia (Draguns & Tanaka-Matsumi, 2003). Depressed persons generally exhibit sadness, anhedonia, limited attention and concentration, low energy, poor self-esteem, and suicidal ideation, with guilt showing the greatest intercul-tural variation. Schizophrenia also has fairly similar incidence rates internationally and cross-culturally, and is manifested by confusion, lack of insight, blunted affect, delusions, hallucinations, ideas of reference, and the experience of control, with its onset and course varying according to a country's level of industrialization.

In addition to epidemiological research, psychologists are investigating whether cultural expressions of psychopathology become more or less vari-able as symptom severity increases, if elements of certain cultures induce psychopathology (e.g., eating disorders in Western nations), and how mas-sive changes introduced by globalization impact the form and level of psy-chopathology worldwide (Draguns & Tanaka-Matsumi, 2003). Draguns and Tanaka-Matsumi (2003) pursue a research agenda that articulates a potential connection between psychopathological symptoms and cultural characteristics, derived from Hofstede's (2001) five cultural dimensions (i.e., individualism–collectivism, power distance, masculinity–femininity, uncertainty avoidance, and dynamism orientation), although these dichoto-mies have been questioned in view of the increased cultural complexity and heterogeneity engendered by globalization (Hermans & Kempen, 1998).

Approaches to the remediation and prevention of psychological suffer-ing around the globe increasingly entail interventions that do not originate in reductionistic psychology (Gielen, Fish, & Draguns, 2004; Stevens & Wedding, 2004a). Psychologists have discovered that imported psychotherapeutic models and methods are not equally applicable within different cultural, economic, historical, political, religious, and social con-texts and must, therefore, be substantially modified (e.g., the use of action research to identify local factors that contribute to resilience and can form the basis for culturally meaningful and beneficial mental health services). These transformations often assume a relationship between mental health, human rights, and the struggle against injustice. Many Latin American psychologists, for example, construe mental illness as a reasonable accommodation to oppressive forces, such as discrimination, poverty, and trauma, rather than as caused by organic and intrapsychic disregulation (Comas-Díaz, Lykes, & Alarcón, 1998). Consequently, these practitioners eschew medication management and corrective therapies (e.g., behavior modification) in favor of approaches that target social injustice and involve activism and advocacy.

Psychologists worldwide are devising procedures that match the lives of people they seek to help, such as bearing witness and attitudinal healing. These approaches are used to raise individual and collective awareness of how oppression impacts mental health and to transform alienation and despair into affirmation, solidarity, and empowerment; it is assumed that contexts producing suffering may also contribute to recovery, and that those who have been victimized may become agents of contextual change (Wessells, 2000). Ethnopolitical psychotherapy is an eclectic approach whose goals are to enhance people's capacity to analyze the causes and consequences of their position within society and undertake transformative action individually and collectively (Comas-Díaz et al., 1998). Ethnopolitical psychotherapy has been utilized in indigenous communities in Guatemala that report distrust, weakened traditional values, and fear of violence after decades of civil unrest (Martin Beristain, Gonzalez, & Paez, 1999). Bearing witness to survivors' testimony of trauma and loss facilitates individual and collective recovery and supports community mobilization for accurate institutional memory and justice. The Association St. Camille de Lellis, a Catholic charity for the mentally ill, operates a community program built upon the economic, sociopolitical, and cultural realities in the Côte d'Ivoire (Morin, Attoungbre, & Dallaire, 2002). The program empowers people through narrative procedures to assume greater responsibility for themselves and also strengthens local resources and networks that support interdependence. Other community-oriented interventions that offer support and cultivate interpersonal bonds are employed in collectivistic nations, such as Japan, to prevent depression in workers (Katauke & Shoji, 2000).

Before examining the mental health concerns of women, children and adolescents, and migrants and refugees, it is important to note the growing synthesis of traditional healing and modern therapies in industrialized and less developed parts of the world. This synthesis comes from a growing recognition of the salience of indigenous representations of mental illness and health—as opposed to Western approaches—and explains their limited success when introduced in different cultural contexts. For example, folk and modern psychological treatment have been success-fully integrated in the mental health services offered to ethnic Turks residing in Germany (Assion, Dana, & Heinemann, 1999).

Women.   Researchers have consistently found that the incidence of depression among women is twice that of men, with the ratio between men and women for major depression at approximately 1:4 (Draguns & Tanaka-Matsumi, 2003). Aside from their greater willingness to acknowl-edge symptoms and seek treatment, psychologists have attributed the gender difference in depression to the fact that women are socialized into less powerful and lower status roles and, hence, have harsher economic and social lives and fewer opportunities to improve their lot. Of particu-lar interest is the proposed link between violence against women and their report of depression. It is not uncommon to learn via the media of the global traffic in women and cases of female genital mutilation and honor killing in conservative, male-dominated countries. Entire commu-nities of women have been raped and traumatized in the course of ethnic conflict, as occurred in Bosnia-Herzegovina, Rwanda, and Sudan. Globally, one third of women have been beaten, raped, and/or abused psychologi-cally within intimate relationships (Murphy, 2003). Added to the physi-cal harm and injury, domestic violence increases women's risk for depression, substance abuse, and suicide. International and cross-cultural variability notwithstanding, domestic violence appears tied to the inter-action of cognitive (e.g., asymmetrical gender roles, implicit theories that accept interpersonal violence) and ecological (e.g., conservative religious values, weak political and civil institutions) factors (Malley-Morrison, 2004). In Russia, the incidence of domestic violence covaries with indi-cators of national economic and political stability. The rates of domestic violence and teenage prostitution in Israel tend to increase during eco-nomic downturns and political violence. Buoyed by the recommenda-tions of the International Conference on Population and Development for integrative interventions to combat all violence against women every-where (Malley-Morrison, 2004; Murphy, 2003), psychologists serve on multidisciplinary teams that design ecological programs to heal and empower battered women, improve batterers' emotional regulation and verbal communication, and re-socialize families whose implicit theories favor violence (Haesevoets, 2003).

Children and Adolescents.   Tragically, upwards of 300,000 children
and adolescents in over 80 countries have been recruited or forced to
engage in violent conflicts (Parson, 2000). Some volunteer, seeking
revenge upon their enemies, martyrdom, or economic viability. Others
are coerced and/or manipulated to serve and remain in militias and other
armed groups. While serving as cooks, laborers, prostitutes, spies, guards,
and fighters, these youth experience and witness extreme violence,
including the murder of family members and friends, and the destruction
of their homes and communities. Children and adolescents, who reside in
places that experience intractable conflict like the Middle East, are
exposed daily to such violence. The psychological sequelae of exposure to
violent conflict include acute and posttraumatic stress disorders, mood disorders, externalizing and disruptive behaviors, and somatic complaints as
well as changed developmental trajectories (Aptekar, 2004; Parson, 2000).
Research is underway to identify variables that exacerbate or insulate the
psychological effects of exposure to violent conflict, including the level and
duration of exposure, gender, personal resources, and family and community factors. For example, the degree to which Palestinian children participate in the Intifada is positively correlated with deficits in attention,
memory, and self-esteem; however, some of these children appear to be
buffered from exposure to violence by psychological flexibility (Qouta, El-
Sarraj, & Punamaeki, 2001). These findings, coupled with cross-cultural
research on how youngsters cope and develop (Aptekar, 2004; Frydenberg
et al., 2003), can lead to more effective and efficient remedial and preventive interventions for at-risk children and adolescents.

Globally oriented psychologists have become part of the multidisciplinary and multi-layered process of post-conflict reconstruction (Wessells
& Monteiro, 2004). In addition to healing psychological wounds, psychologists assist children and adolescents associated with violent conflict
in becoming reintegrated within mainstream society. Often, those who
participate in violent conflict, regardless of whether their involvement
was involuntary or peripheral, experience discrimination and marginalization. These youngsters may be barred from returning to school and,
consequently, may join groups of other ostracized peers whose hopelessness and resentment fuel antisocial violence. Psychologists have part-
nered with governments, relief agencies, and local leaders to forge
programs that meld psychological with cultural, political, and spiritual
elements in order to salvage shattered lives. Specific interventions that
must be tailored to impoverished and unsafe conditions include reconsti-
tuting families, education and vocational training, supporting adults and

caregivers, and strengthening the capacity of communities to build a better future (Wessells & Monteiro, 2004).

Migrants and Refugees. Finally, there is a burgeoning literature on the acculturative stress of migrants and refugees especially in Europe, owing to the fall of communism and emergence of the European Union, and in Canada, whose social policies invite relocation there. Psychological and somatic indicators of the acculturative stress of migrants and refugees appear inversely related to psychological hardiness, positive attitudes toward acculturation, social support within the family and emigrant community, language proficiency, level of participation in the host society, and the absence of discrimination (Miller & Rasco, 2004). Other studies have reported that self-esteem buffers migrants and refugees from the adverse psychosocial impact of discrimination, with parental support and traditional values contributing to self-esteem (e.g., Jasinskaja-Lahti & Liebkind, 2001). Psychologists have also proposed theoretical frameworks to explain the acculturative adjustment of migrants and refugees (Schmitz, 2003). The Interactive Acculturation model predicts cooperative or conflictual relations between migrants and refugees and members of their host community based on the interaction of complementary or opposing acculturative orientations held by these groups (Bourhis, Moiese, Perreault, & Senecal, 1997). Lastly, given evidence that discrimination stigmatizes migrants and refugees and intensifies their perception of and anger at being structurally disadvantaged, European psychologists are formulating a pluralistic, rather than an integrative model for social cohesion in which different ethnic constituencies are ensured equal access to political participation and encouraged to preserve their distinct cultural identity (Bilbeny, 2003).

CONCLUSION

This orientation began with a definition of global psychology, and a cautionary note that the term *global* is more inclusive than *international* and that both terms should be used judiciously given their nuances. The mission of global psychology is to promote communication and collaboration among psychologists worldwide via scholarship, advocacy, the curriculum, and networking. Global psychology can be distinguished from the cross-cultural psychology and ethnic studies, and has links to two specialties that are relatively unfamiliar to psychologists in the United States: economic psychology and political psychology. The orientation also surveyed the recent English and non-English language literature on three intersecting global concerns that are relevant to scientific and applied psychology in the industrialized and less developed worlds: intergroup conflict, threats to the natural environment, and risks to physical and mental health, particularly among women, children and adolescents, and migrants and refugees. Throughout this survey, I underscored the need for and value of approaching these concerns from reductionistic as well as through alternative perspectives (see part II, chapters 2–5) and from a multidisciplinary, multi-layered, and contextually sensitive foundation of knowledge and skill (see part III, chapters 6 through 11).

As its editors, we hope that *Toward a Global Psychology: Theory, Research, Intervention, and Pedagogy* will equip readers to engage their counterparts worldwide as researchers, practitioners, and trainers (see part IV, chapter 12). We further hope that readers will become more involved globally, joining or establishing collegial networks to address in innovative ways the urgent global concerns described earlier. Increased involvement and openness to dialogue will reflect an expanding vista that invites all psychologists to pursue a psychology that is more unified, meaningful, and socially responsible.

RECOMMENDED READINGS

Bond, M. H. (1997). *Working at the interface of cultures: Eighteen lives in social science.* London, UK: Routledge.

Carr, S. C., & Schumaker, J. F. (Eds.). (1996). *Psychology and the developing world.* Westport, CT: Praeger.

David, H. P., & Buchanan, J. (2003). International psychology. In D. K. Freedheim (Ed.), *Handbook of psychology: History of psychology* (Vol. 1, pp. 509–533). New York: Wiley.

Eysenck, M. W. (2004). *Psychology: An international perspective.* Hove, UK: Psychology Press.

Gielen, U. P. (Ed.). (in press). *Conversations with international psychologists.* Greenwich, CT: Information Age Pubishing.

Hofstede, G. J., Pedersen, P., & Hofstede, G. (2002). *Exploring culture: Exercises, stories and synthetic cultures.* Yarmouth, ME: Intercultural Press.

Matsumoto, D., & Juang, L. (2004). *Culture and psychology* (3rd ed.). Belmont, CA: Wadsworth.

Pawlik, K., & Rosenzweig, M. R. (Eds.). (2000). *International handbook of psychology.* Thousand Oaks, CA: Sage.

Prilleltensky, I., & Fox, D. (Eds.). (1997). *Critical psychology: An introduction.* London: Sage.

Stevens, M. J., & Wedding, D. (Eds.). (2004). *Handbook of international psychology.* New York: Brunner-Routledge.

Stevens, M. J., & Wedding, D. (Eds.). (2006). *Psychology: IUPsyS global resource* [CD-ROM] (7th ed.). Hove, UK: Psychology Press.

REFERENCES

Adair, J. G., Coelho, A. E. L., & Luna, J. R. (2002). How international is psychology? *International Journal of Psychology, 37*, 160–170.

Aptekar, L. (2004). The changing developmental dynamics of children in particularly difficult circumstances: Examples of street and war-traumatized children. In U. P. Gielen & J. Roopnarine (Eds.), *Children and adolescence: Cross-cultural perspectives and applications* (pp. 377–410). Westport, CT: Praeger.

Assion, H.-J., Dana, I., & Heinemann, F. (1999). Volksmediziniche Praktiken bei psychiatrischen Patienten tuerkischer Herkunft in Deutschland [Indigenous medicine for psychiatric patients of Turkish origin living in Germany] [Abstract]. *Fortschritte der Neurologie, Psychiatrie, 67*, 12–20.

Berenguer, J., Corraliza, J. A., Martin, R., & Oceja, L. V. (2001). Preocupacion ecologica y acciones ambienales. Un proceso interactivo [Ecological concern and pro-environmental actions: An interactive process]. *Estudios de Psicología, 22*, 37–52.

Bilbeny, N. (2003). Por una Europa de la inclusion social [For a socially inclusive Europe]. *Anuario de Psicología, 33*, 597–608.

Borkenhagen, A., Schumacher, J., & Braehler, E. (2002). Die Forderung nach Internationalisierung der deutschen Psychologie am Beispiel der *Zeitschrift für Pädagogische Psychologie* [The demand for internationalization of German psychology demonstrated by the *Zeitschrift für Pädagogische Psychologie*] [Abstract]. *Zeitschrift für Pädagogische Psychologie, 16*, 233–241.

Boucher, M. (2003). Turbulences, controle et regulation sociales: Modèles securitaires et democratiques dans des quartiers populaires [Turbulence, control and social regulation: Security oriented and democratic models in working-class neighborhoods] [Abstract]. *Deviance et Société, 27*, 161–182.

Bourhis, R. Y., Moise, L. C., Perreault, S., & Senecal, S. (1997). Towards an interactive acculturation model: A social psychological approach. *International Journal of Psychology, 32*, 369–386.

Brett, J. M. (2000). Culture and negotiation. *International Journal of Psychology, 35*, 97–104.

Carr, S., & Sloan, T. (Eds.). (2003). *Poverty: International perspectives.* New York: Plenum.

Comas-Díaz, L., Lykes, M. B., & Alarcón, R. D. (1998). Ethnic conflict and the psychology of liberation in Guatemala, Peru, and Puerto Rico. *American Psychologist, 53*, 778–792.

Commission on Global Governance. (1995). *Our global neighborhood.* New York: Oxford University Press.

David, H. P., & Russo, N. F. (2003). Psychology, population, and reproductive behavior. *American Psychologist, 58*, 193–196.

Dorna, A. (2002). La psicología política. Ausencia de proyectos pol ticos y la crisis de las ciencias sociales [Political psychology: Absence of political projects and the crisis of the social science]. *Psicología Política, 24*, 31–44.

Downs, J. S., Murray, P. J., Bruin, W. B., Penrose, L., Palmgren, C., & Fischhoff, B. (2004). Interactive video behavioral intervention to reduce adolescent females' STD risk: A randomized controlled trial. *Social Science and Medicine, 38*, 65–67.

Draguns, J. G., & Tanaka-Matsumi, J. (2003). Assessment of psychopathology across and within cultures: Issues and findings. *Behavior Research and Therapy, 41*, 755–776.

Durrheim, K., & Dixon, J. (2004). Attitudes in the fiber of everyday life: The discourse of racial evaluation and the lived experience of desegregation. *American Psychologist, 59*, 626–636.

Eidelson, R. J., & Eidelson. J. I. (2003). Dangerous ideas: Five beliefs that propel groups toward conflict. *American Psychologist, 58*, 182–192.

Frydenberg, E., Lewis, R., Kennedy, G., Ardíla, R., Frindte, W., & Hannoun, R. (2003). Coping with concerns: An exploratory comparison of Australian, Colombian, German, and Palestinian adolescents. *Journal of Youth and Adolescence, 32*, 59–66.

Gergen, K. J. (2001). Psychological science in a postmodern context. *American Psychologist, 56*, 803–813.

Gielen, U. P., & Chumachenko, O. (2004). All the world's children: The impact of global demographic trends and economic disparities. In U. P. Gielen & J. Roopnarine (Eds.), *Childhood and adolescence: Cross-cultural perspectives and applications* (pp. 81–109). Westport, CT: Praeger.

Gielen, U. P., Fish, M. J., & Draguns, J. G. (Eds.). (2004). *Handbook of culture, therapy, and healing.* Mahwah, NJ: Lawrance Erlbaum Associates.

Guerin, B. (2003). Putting a radical socialness into consumer behavior analysis. *Journal of Economic Psychology, 24*, 697–718.

Gushulak, B. D., & MacPherson, D. W. (2000). Health issues associated with the smuggling and trafficking of migrants. *Journal of Immigrant Health, 2*, 67–78.

Haesevoets, Y.-H. (2003). La souffrance des families maltraitantes à l'épreuve de l'intervention: Vers une éthique de l'intervention medico-psycho-sociales [Suffering experienced by abusive families confronted with intervention by social services: Toward the ethics of medico-psycho-social intervention] [Abstract]. *Evolution Psychiatrique, 68*, 509–529.

Hayashi, O., & Kubo, N. (1997). The reasons and conditions for sustained global environment conservation behavior. *Japanese Journal of Social Psychology, 13*, 33–42.

Hermans, H. J. M., & Kempen, H. J. G. (1998). Moving cultures: The perilous problems of cultural dichotomies in a globalizing society. *American Psychologist, 53*, 1111–1120.

Hewstone, M., & Greenland, K. (2000). Intergroup conflict. *International Journal of Psychology, 35*, 136–144.

Hine, D. W., & Montiel, C. J. (1999). Poverty in developing nations: A cross-cultural attributional analysis. *European Journal of Social Psychology, 29*, 943–959.

Hofstede, G. (2001). *Culture's consequences: Comparing values, institutions and organizations across nations* (2nd ed.). Thousand Oaks, CA: Sage.

Holtzman, W. (2000). International psychology. In A. E. Kazdin (Ed.), *Encyclopedia of psychology* (Vol. 4, pp. 343–345). Washington, DC: American Psychological Association.

Horowitz, I. L. (2004). Two cultures of science: The limits of positivism. *International Social Science Journal, 56*, 429–437.

Jasinskaja-Lahti, I., & Liebkind, K. (2001). Perceived discrimination and psychological adjustment among Russian-speaking immigrant adolescents in Finland. *International Journal of Psychology, 36*, 174–185.

Jing, Q. (2000). International psychology. In K. Pawlik & M. R. Rosenzweig (Eds.), *The international handbook of psychology* (pp. 570–584). Thousand Oaks, CA: Sage.

Kalichman, S. C., & Simbayi, L. (2004). Traditional beliefs about the cause of AIDS and AIDS-related stigma in South Africa. *AIDS Care*, *16*, 572–580.

Katauke, Y., & Shoji, I. (2000). The influence of reciprocity of social support on mental health among workers. *Japanese Journal of Counseling Science*, *33*, 249–255.

Korf, B. (2005). Rethinking the greed-grievance nexus: Property rights and the political economy of war in Sri Lanka. *Journal of Peace Research*, *42*, 201–217.

Lanfranchi, J.-B., & Touzard, H. (2000). Étude d'un modèle de la motivation à se protéger contre le SIDA [Testing a model of motivation for protection against AIDS] [Abstract]. *Cahiers Internationaux de Psychologie Sociale*, *47–48*, 110–130.

Lidskog, R., & Sundqvist, G. (2004). From consensus to credibility. *Innovation: European Journal of Social Sciences*, *17*, 205–226.

Light, I. (2004). Immigration and ethnic economies in giant cities. *International Social Science Journal*, *56*, 385–398.

Lin, T.-Y., Tseng, W.-S., & Yeh, E.-K. (Eds.). (1994). *Chinese societies and mental health*. Hong Kong: Oxford University Press.

Malley-Morrrison, K. (Ed.). (2004). *International perspectives on family violence and abuse: A cognitive ecological approach*. Mahwah, NJ: Lawrence Erlbaum Associates.

Martin Beristain, C. M., Gonzalez, J. L., & Paez, D. (1999). Memoria colectiva y genocidio político en Guatemala. Antecedentes y efectos de los procesos de la memoria colectiva [Collective memory of political genocide in Guatemala: Antecedents and effects of collective memory processes]. *Psicología Política*, *18*, 77–99.

Mbonda, E.-M. (2004). Poverty as a violation of human rights: Towards a right to non-poverty. *International Social Science Journal*, *56*, 277–288.

McDermott, R. (2004). *Political psychology in international relations*. Ann Arbor, MI: University of Michigan Press.

McGlynn, C., Niens, U., Cairns, E., & Hewstone, M. (2004). Moving out of conflict: The contribution of integrated schools in Northern Ireland to identity, attitudes, forgiveness, and reconciliation. *Journal of Peace Education*, *1*, 147–163.

Miller, K., & Rasco, L. (Eds.). (2004). *The mental health of refugees: Ecological approaches to healing and adaptation*. Mahwah, NJ: Lawrence Erlbaum Associates.

Montada, L., & Kals, E. (2000). Political implications of psychological research on ecological justice and proenvironmental behavior. *International Journal of Psychology*, *35*, 168–176.

Montiel, C. J. (2003). Peace psychology in Asia. *Peace and Conflict: Journal of Peace Psychology*, *9*, 195–218.

Morin, P., Attoungbre, C., & Dallaire, B. (2002). L'association St. Camille de Lellis en Côte d'Ivoire: Innovations, potentiel et limites d'une pratique issue des damnés de la terre [The Association St. Camille de Lellis in Côte d'Ivoire: Innovations, potential, and limits of a practice coming from the "wretched of the earth"]. *Canadian Journal of Community Mental Health*, *21*, 139–149.

Murphy, E. M. (2003). Being born female is dangerous for your health. *American Psychologist*, *58*, 205–210.

Nagdeve, D. A. (2004). Environmental pollution and control: A case study of Delhi mega city. *Population and Environment*, *25*, 461–473.

Nsamenang, A. B. (2004). *Cultures of human development and education: Challenges to growing up African*. Hauppauge, NY: Nova Science Publishers.

Oxford University Press. (1993). *The new shorter Oxford English dictionary*. New York: Author.

Parkhurst, J. O., & Lush, L. (2004). The political environment of HIV: Lessons from a comparison of Uganda and South Africa. *Social Science and Medicine, 59*, 1913–1924.

Parson, E. R. (2000). Understanding children with war-zone traumatic stress exposed to the world's violent environments. *Journal of Contemporary Psychotherapy, 30*, 325–340.

Phinney, J. S. (2000). Ethnic identity. In A. E. Kazdin (Ed.), *Encyclopedia of psychology* (Vol. 3, pp. 254–259). Washington, DC: American Psychological Association.

Qouta, S., El-Sarraj, E., & Punamaeki, R.-L. (2001). Mental flexibility as resiliency factor among children exposed to political violence. *International Journal of Psychology, 36*, 1–7.

Rainham, D., & McDowell, I. (2005). The sustainability of population health. *Population and Environment, 26*, 303–324.

Richmond, A. H. (2002). Globalization: Implications for immigrants and refugees. *Ethnic and Racial Studies, 25*, 707–727.

Rodriguez Kauth, A. (2002). Algunas relaciones entre la psicología y la economía [Some relations between psychology and economy]. *Psicología Política, 25*, 37–48.

Saraswathi, T. S., & Larson, R. W. (2002). Adolescence in global perspective: An agenda for social policy. In B. B. Brown, R. W. Larson, & T. S. Saraswathi (Eds.), *The world's youth: Adolescence in eight regions of the globe* (pp. 344–362). New York: Cambridge University Press.

Schmitz, P. G. (2003). Psychosocial factors of immigration and emigration: An introduction. In L. L. Adler & U. P. Gielen (Eds.), *Migration: Immigration and emigration in international perspective* (pp. 23–50). Westport, CT: Praeger.

Steinheider, B., Fay, D., Hilburger, T., Hust, I., Prinz, L., Vogelgesang, F., & Hormuth, S. E. (1999). Soziale Normen als Prädiktoren von umweltbezogenem Verhalten [Social norms as predictors of environmental behavior] [Abstract]. *Zeitschrift für Sozialpsychologie, 30*, 40–56.

Stevens, M. J., & Wedding, D. (2004a). International psychology: An overview. In M. J. Stevens & D. Wedding (Eds.), *Handbook of international psychology* (pp. 1–23). New York: Brunner-Routledge.

Stevens, M. J., & Wedding, D. (2004b). International psychology: A synthesis. In M. J. Stevens & D. Wedding (Eds.), *Handbook of international psychology* (pp. 481–500). New York: Brunner-Routledge.

Tikkanen, T. (2005). *The present status and future prospects of the profession of psychologists in Europe*. Paper presented to the European Congress of Psychology, Grenada, Spain. Retrieved August 25, 2005, from http://www.efpa.be/news.php?ID=12

Torney-Purta, J., Lehmann, R., Oswald, H., & Schulz, W. (2001). *Citizenship and education in twenty-eight countries: Civic knowledge and engagement at age fourteen*. Amsterdam: International Association for the Evaluation of Educational Achievement.

Triandis, H. C. (2000a). Cross-cultural psychology. In A. E. Kazdin (Ed.), *Encyclopedia of psychology* (Vol. 2, pp. 361–364). Washington, DC: American Psychological Association.

Triandis, H. C. (2000b). Culture and conflict. *International Journal of Psychology, 35,* 145–152.

United Nations General Assembly. (1996). *World program for youth to the year 2000 and beyond* [GA resolution 50/81].

United Nations General Assembly. (1998). *Culture of peace* [GA resolution 52/13].

United Nations Population Fund. (2004). *State of world population 2004. The Cairo consensus at ten: Population, reproductive health and the global effort to end poverty.* New York: Author.

U.S. Census Bureau. (2003). *Statistical abstract of the United States: 2003. Section 12: Labor force, employment, and earnings* (pp. 381–432). Retrieved September 9, 2005, from http://www.census.gov/prod/2004pubs/03statap/labor.pdf

Velayo, R. S. (2004). Extending our research: Focal points that help internationalize psychology. *International Psychology Reporter, 8,* 1–4.

Vlek, C. (2000). Essential psychology for environmental policy making. *International Journal of Psychology, 35,* 153–167.

Wallman, S. (2001). Global threats, local options, personal risk: Dimensions of migrant sex work in Europe. *Health, Risk and Society, 3,* 75–87.

Wessells, M. G. (2000). Contributions of psychology of peace and nonviolent conflict resolution. In K. Pawlik & M. R. Rosenzweig (Eds.), *The international handbook of psychology* (pp. 526–533). Thousand Oaks, CA: Sage.

Wessells, M., & Monteiro, C. (2004). Healing the wounds following protracted conflict in Angola: A community-based approach to assisting war-affected children. In U. P. Gielen, M. J. Fish, & J. G. Draguns (Eds.), *Handbook of culture, therapy, and healing* (pp. 321–341). Mahwah, NJ: Lawrence Erlbaum Associates.

Winter, D. D. N. (2000). Some big ideas for some big problems. *American Psychologist, 55,* 516–522.

II

THE EMERGENCE OF PSYCHOLOGY AROUND THE WORLD

Part II of *Toward a Global Psychology: Theory, Research, Intervention, and Pedagogy* contains: chapter 2, International Perspectives on the History of Psychology by John Hogan and Thomas Vaccaro; chapter 3, Current Trends in Global Psychology by Elizabeth Nair, Rubén Ardila, and Michael J. Stevens; chapter 4, Theory, Research, and Practice in Psychology in the Developing (Majority) World by Juan José Sánchez-Sosa and Angélica Riveros; and chapter 5, Development of Indigenous Psychologies: Understanding People in a Global Context by Uichol Kim and Young-Shin Park. Each of these chapters speaks to the origins and development of a more global psychology; collectively, they offer a global view of the evolution and contemporary standing of the field, emphasizing important events and processes in the less familiar non-Western world.

Hogan and Vaccaro in chapter 2 date modern psychology to its first appearance in the latter part of the 19th century in western Europe and the United States. Although psychology is often said to have begun with the founding of Wilhelm Wundt's laboratory in Germany, it actually arose in several countries at approximately the same time. As a result of these multiple beginnings, psychology was an international enterprise virtually from its inception. Hogan and Vaccaro trace and explain the historical shifts in the center of psychology from Europe to the United States, and note that, as the United States came to dominate the discipline, its psychology became increasingly insular and less responsive to the refinements and innovations taking place elsewhere in the world.

This refrain is heard repeatedly throughout part II of the book and the volume as a whole. As a result of the parochialism of U.S. psychology, there have been ongoing efforts in many countries to develop a psychology of greater relevance to local cultures and needs, a call that is also reflected in virtually every chapter, but particularly in chapter 3, which covers current trends in global psychology, and chapters 4 and 5, which examine psychology in the developing world and the indigenization movement in psychology, and in chapters 6 and 10 of part III, which examine possible alternative psychologies that emphasize normative systems and trends toward the globalized practice of professional psychology. Thankfully, these efforts to fashion a global psychology have taken root and are contributing to a redefinition of psychology in North America, western Europe, and the world generally. The strength of chapter 2, then, lies in its integration of a scattered literature, which offers an informative, if not comprehensive, summary of the development of psychology in different parts of the world.

Building upon the origins and evolution of international psychology associations presented in chapter 2 and anticipating the more detailed description of such organizations in chapter 12, Nair, Ardila, and Stevens survey a variety of international and regional psychology organizations with an eye toward their global mission, goals, activities, and accomplishments. The better known of these organizations include the International Union of Psychological Science and International Association of Applied Psychology. Other smaller, but formidable international psychology organizations include the International Association for Cross-Cultural Psychology and the International Society for the Study of Behavioral Development. Regional associations of rising influence are the European Federation of Psychologists' Associations and the Interamerican Society of Psychology. More and more, these international and regional psychology organizations are expanding their membership to embrace psychologists in Africa, Asia, eastern Europe, and Latin America and forging ties with governmental and other policy-making entities, such as the U.N. and the World Health Organization, in order to inform policy through psychological science. International and regional associations also seek to achieve consensus on training standards for psychologists and ethical guidelines for the practice of psychology. Nair, Ardila, and Stevens also survey contemporary trends in scientific and professional psychology worldwide (e.g., the growth and feminization of psychology) as well as selected regional developments in such key geographical areas as eastern Asia, Europe, and Latin America. The authors conclude with a call for greater regional and global cooperation and collaboration in order to address pressing contemporary concerns that have psychological dimensions.

According to Sánchez-Sosa and Riveros, the science and practice of psychology in the developing (majority) world shares the philosophical, theoretical, and methodological antecedents of psychology found elsewhere, consistent with the international history of psychology given in chapter 2. The authors trace how most seminal schools of thought in psychology spread from Europe and then the United States to developing countries, where psychology was typically born in universities, especially in countries with strong traditions of higher education. Since national or regional culture quickly pervaded the academic development of psychology, perhaps the most salient feature of psychology in the developing world is its diversity, as is documented by the regional trends reviewed in chapter 3 and indigenous models for understanding people-in-context described in chapter 5. However, intermediate levels of economic and social development often impose comparable generalized circumstances for the progress of psychology in these countries, such as the scarcity of resources. After defining what is meant by a "developing country," Sánchez-Sosa and Riveros trace how scientific and professional psychology are affected by a country's level of development and offer recommendations for facilitating psychology in the developing world; some of these recommendations foreshadow the credentialing for transnational mobility and training for social activism emphasized in chapters 10 and 11, respectively. Sánchez-Sosa and Riveros also provide a data set that serves as an informal index of the research activities of psychologists in many developing countries. This last contribution is an especially important, if not unique, addition to what we know about the recent work of a majority of the world's psychologists.

In chapter 5, Kim and Park offer an analysis of indigenous psychology within a global context. In the first part of their chapter, the authors distinguish unilateral globalization from enlightened globalization. Echoing the criticisms leveled in chapters 2 and 4 of part II, Kim and Park proceed to articulate the limitations of general psychology. They continue by defining indigenous psychology and by presenting a transactional model of science that captures the underlying tenets of indigenous psychology: human beings are construed as agents of their own action and are motivated to understand, manage, and control their environment. Their presentation foreshadows chapters 6 and 7 of part III in which alternative psychologies and qualitative research are seen as providing the conceptual foundation and investigative methodology necessary for a global psychology. Kim and Park then define culture and outline several key dimensions on which cultures differ. Next, the authors offer an indigenous and cultural analysis of achievement in eastern Asia by reviewing empirical studies on academic achievement and organizational climate, both of which account for the extraordinary scientific and economic success in that region of the world. The authors' comprehensive description and explanation of how culture co-creates educational and organizational success in eastern Asia provide a unique example of a phenomenon-in-context.

2

International Perspectives on the History of Psychology

John D. Hogan and Thomas P. Vaccaro
St. John's University

When one understands psychological science to be a byproduct of the Western tradition, fashioned by particular cultural and historical considerations, the door is opened to a fresh consideration of the practice of psychology in the global context. —Gergen, Gulerce, Lock, & Misra (1996, p. 496)

In this chapter, we explore the history of psychology from an international perspective. We argue that the discipline is best understood and appreciated by adopting such a perspective. Moreover, we believe that an appreciation of the history of international psychology will open a window for understanding the future of psychology (see chapter 3, this volume).

INTRODUCTION

International psychology, in a limited form, has been a part of psychology virtually from its beginning as a scientific discipline. Soon after the formal founding of psychology in the latter part of the 19th century, students began traveling to distant universities to study the new science, and scholars from different nations actively began trading information. An international conference on psychology was organized in 1889 only 10 years after Wilhelm Wundt (1832–1920) founded the first experimental laboratory in psychology. However, the interest in viewing psychology from an international perspective has not always been uniform or consistent.

39

The lack of interest in a global psychology was directly related to the growing dominance of the United States in the field. Beginning after World War I, and increasingly throughout the 1930s, the United States became the most important force in world psychology, and it retained that leadership for decades. In the period after World War II, the growth of psychology in the United States was so great compared to the rest of the world that U.S. students were told psychology was an American discipline and that there was little to learn from anyone else (Fowler, 1998a). Only now, more than a century after the modern founding of the discipline, has psychology in the United States begun to appreciate how limited its view has been.

The recent growth of interest in international psychology was inevitable, given current world conditions. Travel among countries has never been easier or cheaper, with many opportunities for scientific exchange. Modes of communication have accelerated at such a pace that it is almost impossible for an active scholar to remain isolated from psychology in other countries. Political changes, such as the emergence of the European Union (EU), have forced nations to join together in common goals. Moreover, the longstanding dominance of U.S. psychology is diminishing. The result of all of these changes has been to create a more decentralized discipline, making it necessary for scholars to adopt a greater world perspective. Simultaneously, some scholars from outside of the United States have questioned the applicability of U.S.-based psychology to their own cultures. The result has been the emergence of so-called indigenous psychologies, a trend that may have important implications for the future of psychology (see chapter 5).

The benefits of adopting an international approach are readily apparent. When viewed cross-nationally, psychology as a whole can be understood more fully and more deeply. The differences in psychology among nations illustrate the extent to which the field is embedded in the cultures from which it grew. By taking a global perspective, lines of communication are open for the exploration of new approaches. The simple juxtaposition of Eastern and Western philosophies, for example, can create an enormous source for new ideas. Conceptual and methodological variety throughout the world highlight the different ways in which questions are asked and explored. Various sociopolitical perspectives suggest other possible avenues of growth and direction. In short, adopting a global approach to psychology holds the potential for understanding the discipline in a way that is available from no other source.

IN THE BEGINNING

Psychology, in its most general sense, has been present since the dawn of humankind and knows no national boundaries. Our ancestors were making observations of psychological phenomena and drawing conclusions about them long before any psychological terminology had been introduced. Many of these observations, which derived from both oral and written traditions, were codified and became parts of their respective cultures.

Most Westerners are likely to recognize the names of early Greek philosophers, such as Plato (circa 427–347 B.C.E.) or Aristotle (384–322 B.C.E.), even if they cannot identify their specific contributions to psychology. They would probably be less successful in identifying the contributions of non-Western philosophers, such as Confucius (551–479 B.C.E.), the renowned Chinese teacher, or Avicenna (980–1037), the Persian philosopher and physician, even using their Western names. Virtually every culture has produced individuals who addressed some of the same questions that modern-day psychologists address. But, there is a fundamental difference. Most of these early contributors would be considered "pre-psychologists" in the sense that they did not make use of the scientific methods that would later become available.

The appearance of a modern, scientific psychology is usually linked to a very specific time and place. Many historians use the founding date of the psychology laboratory at the University of Leipzig in 1879 as the starting point for experimental psychology. Wundt, the laboratory's founder, has been identified as the first person who was unquestionably a psychologist in the modern mold (Boring, 1929). But in England, Francis Galton (1822–1911) was also making systematic observations of human beings by the early 1880s, using an approach that was entirely different from Wundt's. William James (1842–1910), in the United States., was teaching psychology at Harvard University, with a demonstration laboratory, as early as 1875. By bending the rules only a little, we would be able to include several additional pioneers as well. (See David & Buchanan, 2003, for a chronology of important milestones in international psychology.)

It is clear that modern psychology had multiple beginnings. Its emergence took place largely in the Western world, particularly in Europe and the U.S. Although psychology appeared in a variety of forms, most involved a systematic attempt to satisfy the requirements of science, a relatively new undertaking at that time. Two implicit questions emerged almost immediately: What should this new science study, and how should such studies be conducted? The approaches and subject matters were different enough among the pioneers to raise questions about the future direction of the discipline. By the early 1880s, there was already a proposal to organize a meeting to share information about the emerging science. The convening of an international meeting for those interested in the new discipline was the first concrete example of what would later be called "international psychology."

International Congresses of Psychology

The First International Congress of Psychology met in Paris in 1889 under the leadership of Jean-Martin Charcot (1825–1893), honorary president, and Th odule Ribot (1839–1916), president. Charcot was the noted neurologist from La Salpêtrière, and Ribot was renowned as the first teacher of experimental psychology in France. In all, the conference hosted 203 attendees from 20 countries, giving early evidence of the cross-national character of the discipline.

Among those present were experts in various fields, including philosophy and neurology; psychology had not yet been firmly established as a discipline. But among the attendees were some of the most important contributors to psychology in its pioneer years, including Wilhelm Wundt, Francis Galton, Alfred Binet, William James, and Pierre Janet. Many of the topics at the conference reflected the applied direction that psychology was already taking, and also included discussions of hypnotism and parapsychology. In his inaugural address, Ribot spoke of the hopes and goals that he and the congress had for the new discipline. For Ribot, psychology was a pure science, whose primary methods were observation and experimentation (Misiak & Sexton, 1966).

While preparations were underway for the first congress, a committee was formed to ensure that there would be future congresses. And, indeed, they continued on a relatively regular basis: London (1892), Munich (1896), Paris (1900), Rome (1905), Geneva (1909)—at which point they were interrupted by World War I. After they resumed—Oxford (1923), Groningen (1926), New Haven (1929), Copenhagen (1932), Paris (1937)—they were interrupted again, this time by World War II. Finally, at the meeting of the 12th Congress in Edinburgh (1948), the committee for the congress was abolished and a new structure was established. At the next congress in Stockholm (1951), the new structure was implemented and the International Union of Scientific Psychology (IUSP) was born. In 1965, the IUSP was renamed the International

Union of Psychological Science (IUPsyS), and the IUPsyS continues today as one of the premier organizations in international psychology.

The 9th International Congress, held at Yale University in New Haven in 1929, was a particularly important one for United States interests. In addition to being the first congress to be held in the United States, the American Psychological Association (APA) gave up its annual meeting in deference to the international one. The total attendance at the conference was 826, the highest number of attendees since international conferences began, and a record that would not be exceeded for several decades. Seven hundred and twenty-two members of the APA attended, almost three quarters of the entire APA membership (Hilgard, 1987).

There were also 104 international visitors from 21 countries present at that congress. Among the luminaries attending from Europe were Ivan Pavlov, Charles Spearman, Jean Piaget, Wolfgang Köhler, and Henri Pieron (Hilgard, 1987). In addition to visitors from Europe, the conference hosted representatives from China, Egypt, India, Japan, New Zealand, and Australia. If the world needed a reminder that the United States was emerging as an important center for psychology, this conference offered strong evidence. But the conference also pointed to the growing importance of psychology around the world, particularly outside of Europe and the United States.

BEYOND THE PIONEER PERIOD

In the decades immediately following the founding of experimental psychology in Leipzig, the center for psychology remained in Europe. Germany was the most active country, and the United Kingdom and France followed behind, but not too closely. The United States was also active and important, but it was a relative neophyte in educational areas and it still looked to Europe for direction. (See Britt, 1942, for an examination of European influences on American psychology from 1600–1900.) It was important for early U.S. students hoping to be recognized as scholars to have either a European degree or, at the very least, some European education. For students interested in psychology, the most important educational destination was Wundt's laboratory in Leipzig.

After founding the laboratory, Wundt continued to solidify his position as the father of experimental psychology, primarily through his publications and his students. Although other scientists were exploring the new psychology, Wundt became the most important one. Students traveled from all over the world to learn about this new science under his tutelage. Leipzig became the most important center of learning for psychology in the world; the number of doctoral students graduated during Wundt's tenure was unequaled by any other institution. Many of Wundt's students returned home to become leaders of psychology in their own countries. Some even established laboratories designed specifically to resemble his laboratory at Leipzig, for example, in Japan (Blumenthal, 1985).

Not surprisingly, many of Wundt's students were German and they included several who became prominent in the discipline: Oswald Külpe, Hugo Münsterberg, Ernst Meumann, Karl Marbe, and Emil Kraepelin. Among the notable Americans who studied with Wundt were James McKeen Cattell, Lightner Witmer, Charles Judd, Walter D. Scott, and Edward A. Pace. Other international students included: Vladimir Bekhterev, Georgy Chelpanov, and Nikolay Lange (Russia); Joseph Fröbes and Friedrich Kiesow (Italy); Alfred Lehman (Denmark); Ernst Dürr and G. F. Lipps (Switzerland); Matataro Matsumoto (Japan); Benjamin Bourdon and Victor Henri (France); W. G. Smith and Charles Spearman (Great Britain); Th. Voreas (Greece); Cai Yuanpei (China); and A. Mahrburg and W. Witwicki (Poland; Jing, 2000; Jing & Fu, 2001; Misiak & Sexton, 1966). Virtually all of these students became leaders of psychology in their respective countries. Wundt's success in introducing the world to psychology through his students is without parallel.

Despite this success, however, Wundt's brand of psychology did not travel well. When students left his laboratory, they were apt to modify what they learned in ways that the master would not approve. Psychology had already shown itself to be particularly responsive to its national context, as with the French focus on psychopathology and British focus on individual differences and statistics. Now, those forces became even more pronounced, and psychology in various countries began to develop in ways that were often peculiar to their culture and climate. This would become particularly evident in some Asian countries where Western scientific psychology would be merged with more ancient philosophical beliefs (Misiak & Sexton, 1966).

In the United States, psychology began to divorce itself not only from Wundt's brand of psychology, but to some degree from European psychology as well. In terms of subject matter and focus, it owed more to Darwin and Galton than it did to Wundt. Rather than exploring common features of humankind, it focused on the role of individual differences and adaptation. As U.S. psychology grew in size and importance, it placed more emphasis on practical, objective, and quantitative issues than its European counterparts, with less emphasis on the philosophical issues and underpinnings more common to European psychology (Sexton & Misiak, 1984). These differences would increase with time.

GROWTH OF PSYCHOLOGY

No country provided such a fertile ground for the new psychology as the United States. In 1892, it became the first to establish a national psychology association, the APA. By 1900, there were 41 psychology laboratories at various colleges and universities in the United States, more than in the rest of the world combined (Pawlik & Rosenzweig, 2000). Although the number of psychologists was initially small—in its first year the APA had 31 members—the rate of growth was impressive. For a long period of time, the APA doubled its membership in each succeeding decade (Hogan, 1995). By 2004, the APA had more than 100,000 members excluding students, the largest psychology association in the world by far. Its annual convention typically attracts 12,000 to 20,000 people from the United States and around the world (Fowler & Newman, 2004).

France and the United Kingdom, pioneering countries in psychology, had early psychology associations, both begun in 1901. Germany established its first national psychology association in 1904. Surprisingly, between 1879 and the end of Word War II, only 13 countries had established national psychology associations (Jing, 2000). Other nations were still developing such organizations well into the 1970s and 1980s, strong evidence that they were in the early stages of a national commitment to psychology. In general, industrialized nations with an early exposure to Wundt or American psychology were the first to organize such associations; less developed countries, including Arab countries and those in South America and Africa, were among the last. (See Jing, 2000, p. 574 for an extensive list of national associations and their founding dates.)

The strong growth that characterized U.S. psychology for so long has now leveled off. No longer are there dramatic increases in the number of psychologists each year. In fact, the number of new doctorates has remained at approximately the same level for more than a decade. However, other countries have experienced a tremendous upsurge in the number of psychologists. Recently, Stevens and Wedding (2004) reported substantial increases in the number of psychologists, in some cases up to

100%, in Israel, Brazil, South Africa, and Spain in just the last decade. The potential for growth among developing nations is even greater. The most populous nations in the world have surprisingly few psychologists relative to their population. For instance, China, with a population approaching 1.3 billion, is estimated to have approximately 10,000 psychologists. By contrast, the U.S., with a population less than one-fourth that of China, has at least 25 times more psychologists.

Whereas American psychologists were once thought to constitute more than half of all the psychologists in the world, their relative portion of the world's psychologists has been substantially reduced in the last 20 years. A decade ago, one estimate put the figure at slightly less than 40% (Hogan, 1995); a few years later, another estimate suggested the figure was as low as 20% to 25% (Rosenzweig, 1999). It is important to note that in these surveys local definitions are used to define "psychologist" and they can be highly variable. In the United States, Canada, and parts of Europe, a psychologist frequently holds a Ph.D. or an equivalent degree. The modal degree for psychologists around the world is more likely to be the Master's degree or its equivalent.

In some respects, the United States has dominated the world of psychology through the sheer size and power of its resources. The APA has an annual budget of more than 80 million dollars and a publication program equal to that of many major publishing houses. Recently, it has published more than 50 books annually. APA's database, *PsycINFO*, contains abstracts of books, book chapters, dissertations, and articles from more than 1,800 journals published around the world (Fowler & Newman, 2004). The number of academic psychologists in the United States is greater than that of any other nation, perhaps greater than all of them combined. Not surprisingly, the United States. remains the research center for psychology around the world.

Despite all of those strengths, it would be wrong to think that the United States is the only important contributor to psychology internationally. Several nations have more psychologists per unit of population: Norway, Israel, Spain, and Argentina. Clearly, those countries have strong interests in psychology. Still, they do not have the same resources. The result of this imbalance is frequently a critical one. Many countries are forced to use U.S. textbooks in their classrooms because it would be uneconomical to do otherwise. Because of their audience and circulation, U.S. journals are greatly prized as avenues for publication. The result is to promote a brand of psychology in many countries that is more U.S.-based than it should be.

U.S. PSYCHOLOGY VERSUS OTHER PSYCHOLOGIES

As a result of the imbalance of resources among nations, other countries have often tried to imitate psychology in the United States. It used to be rather common, for example, to hear reports of developing nations adopting United States psychological tests for their own use, but not bothering to re-standardize or re-norm them. Other countries have reported that university professors will choose research topics of little relevance to their own nation and culture, but which they believe are more appealing because of their resemblance to U.S. research. Gergen et al. (1996) describe the situation in India where, for many years, only Western psychology was taught in universities and a concerted effort was made to ignore Indian culture and thought. Fortunately, there has been a reversal of this trend, coupled with ongoing attempts to develop an indigenous Indian psychology.

Recent decades have seen a substantial effort to form a more cooperative kind of psychology among European nations. Beginning in the late 1970s, representatives from a dozen national associations came together to draft a constitution and bylaws for a new organization (Lunt, 1996). By 1981, their efforts resulted in the founding of the European Federation of Psychologists' Associations (EFPA). Among other issues, the EFPA provides a vehicle for developing common standards for training and ethical practice among European countries (Lunt & Poortinga, 1996; see chapter 10 on the globalizing of professional psychology, including training standards and ethics codes). By 2005, the association represented more than 200,000 psychologists in 31 countries, a little more than half of all the psychologists in the member countries.

The Bologna Accord, approved by the European Ministers of Education in 1999, provides for a single model of higher education throughout Europe, from baccalaureate to doctoral degrees. The plan is to implement the model within the next few years. Following the Bologna Accord, a directive was issued in 2002 concerning the recognition of professional qualifications so that, for instance, psychology would be regulated at the European level instead of country by country. Consistent with that directive, the EFPA is developing a European Diploma in Psychology (EuroPsy) that would result in the automatic recognition of professional qualifications for psychologists throughout the EU. This would provide mobility for those with the degree, as well as ensure a certain level of quality of professional services (Tikkanen, 2004). Arriving at mutually agreeable standards for professional psychology has not been a simple task, given the enormous historical differences in training, even among these culturally related nations.

Consistent with the North American Free Trade Agreement (NAFTA), there have been attempts in North America to develop common standards in training and licensing for psychology across countries. Beginning in 1995, a group called the Trilateral Forum has been meeting to encourage communication among Canada, Mexico, and the United States. Since that initial meeting, there have been significant changes in training and accreditation in Mexico's educational system, and the implementation of a new agreement in Canada that permits psychologists licensed in one province to practice in another (Bailey, 2004). Their quest for common standards continues.

FACTORS AFFECTING THE GROWTH AND DEVELOPMENT OF PSYCHOLOGY

There are many factors that determine the extent to which psychology can grow in a particular country. History, culture, ideology, politics, and the economy have been among the most important. Some nations have had strong philosophical foundations in psychology, but failed to make the transition to modern scientific psychology until recent decades. This has been true for the bulk of Arab countries, for example. Many undeveloped nations still cannot afford the "luxury" of psychology, as can be seen in some African nations. But, the impact of political ideology and war has been among the most important determinants in the development of psychology, and the effect has not always been predictable.

In the United States, World War I was instrumental in introducing psychological testing to a large segment of the population and, ultimately, it laid the groundwork for the acceptance of psychological tests. Following World War II, the return of soldiers in need of mental health services set the stage for the emergence of clinical psychology in the United States. In Europe, World War I dramatically hindered the development of psychology in several countries, particularly Germany. As a result of the war, publications in psychology in the United States began to outnumber German ones, and Germany would never achieve that dominance again (Pawlik & Rosenzweig, 2000).

Psychology in Germany was also profoundly affected by the seizure of power by the Nazis in 1933. One of the immediate effects was the enormous flight of German and Austrian intellectuals to other countries, particularly to the United States by Jews and anti-fascists. Seven scientists holding psychology chairs at German universities were among those who emigrated. Those leaving Germany and Austria included: the leading Gestalt psychologists, Max Wertheimer, Kurt Koffka, and Wolfgang Köhler; psychoanalysts such as Alfred Adler, Erik Erikson, Sigmund and Anna Freud, Erich Fromm, and Karen Horney; and other notable contributors such as William Stern, Charlotte and Karl Bühler, Fritz Heider, Kurt Goldstein, Paul Lazarsfeld, Otto Selz, and David Katz (Groebel, 1992). Despite this tremendous loss, however, university training for professional psychologists continued during this period, albeit with a politicized curriculum. Professional psychology actually grew in Germany during the Nazi era, particularly because of the central role of German psychologists in the selection of personnel for the *Wehrmacht* (Geuter, 1987; Graumann, 1997). Although political sycophants with lesser scientific qualifications tended to be appointed for university chairs, several new chairs were established, thus furthering the institutionalization of psychology in Germany.

The arrival of communism in the Soviet Union had a dramatic impact on the growth of the discipline there. Although Wundt's form of psychology was introduced into Russia before the turn of the 20th century, it had only a few decades to develop. With the revolution of 1917 and the dominance of communism, Wundtian forms of psychology were eventually discarded. They were replaced by a form of psychology based on the philosophy of dialectical materialism. This philosophy, developed by Marx and Engels, and later modified and promoted by Lenin, would become the foundation for Russian psychology for decades to come. The central unit of study in this system is not the individual, but society, a startling departure for many so-called traditional approaches. After World War II, this brand of psychology would become the state policy for almost all communist countries (Jing, 2000). Nonetheless, the Pavlovian school remained influential, as did the work of Nebylitsin and Luria on individual differences and neuropsychology, respectively.

War and political ideology have had an important impact on the development of psychology, as does the economic development of a country. When resources are limited, those resources will be directed to areas of greatest need. Psychology has not always been seen as an essential element in all societies; for many, it has been a privilege associated with a high standard of living. As much as developing nations may want to make use of modern psychology—and they typically prefer it in its applied form—they cannot afford the research that usually goes with it (see chapter 4 for more on psychology in the majority world).

Jing (2000) quantified the relationship between two indicators of national development and psychology. The correlation between a country's gross national product (GNP) and the number of psychologists was sufficiently high (.44) to suggest that GNP could be used as a rough predictor of the relative number of psychologists in a country. The Human Development Index (HDI) was also investigated. The HDI is a U.N. derived measure that reflects several quality-of-life issues including life expectancy and adult literacy. The HDI and number of psychologists in a country were also significantly correlated (.51). In addition, countries that had a high HDI were much more likely to belong to the IUPsyS. Conversely, countries with a low HDI were unlikely to belong to the IUPsyS.

DISSATISFACTION WITH U.S. DOMINANCE IN PSYCHOLOGY

Many in the United States psychologists have been dissatisfied with the provincialism of their psychology and have been openly critical of it. One prominent American historian of psychology called American psychology "xenophobic" (Sexton, 1983). Despite the impact of its psychology, it has been pointed out that the United States has never made important theoretical contributions to psychology on the order of Sigmund Freud, Jean Piaget, Lev Vygotsky, and others. Moreover, many of the greatest contributions to psychology, from intelligence testing to the correlation coefficient, psychoanalysis, Gestalt psychology, and even the Rorschach, came to psychology from non-U.S. sources (Sexton & Misiak, 1984).

Moghaddam (1987) argues that there are really "three worlds" of psychological research and practice, all different from one another. The first is found in the United States, the second in other industrialized nations, and the last in developing countries. The United States has a very strong influence on the latter two, and this relationship tends to be largely unidirectional. U.S. psychologists pay little attention to psychology in other countries. They tend not to read foreign journals and appear to have little interest in exploring non-U.S. theories, methods, or practices (Gielen & Pagan, 1993). This attitude is likely to put U.S. psychologists at a disadvantage in tomorrow's world.

It is worth noting that the U.S. was late in recognizing the value of the work of some important international contributors to psychology, such as Swiss-born Piaget and Russian-born Vygotsky. Eventually, both Piaget and Vygotsky generated a great deal of research in the United States, but this occurred long after they were well known in Europe and other parts of the world. Perhaps, if the United States had been more open to international contributors, these benefits to developmental psychology could have come much sooner. It is difficult to know how many other important figures may have gone unrecognized in the United States, particularly from the Eastern world.

Although the United States is the single greatest contributor to scientific articles in psychology, there is evidence that some changes are taking place. Bauserman (1997) examined abstracts in PsychLIT, a CD-ROM version of *Psychological Abstracts*, produced by the APA. At the time of his inquiry, PsychLIT indexed approximately 1,330 psychology and psychology-related journals from around the world (the number of journals that PsychLIT indexes has grown substantially since then). Bauserman found that between 1975 and 1994, there was a drop of 15.6% in the percent of total articles originating from the United States. No other country experienced such a loss. Most other countries experienced small gains, with the United Kingdom the largest at 3.1%. A few east European countries showed small losses, probably as a result of economic and political turmoil in those countries. Not surprisingly, for most developing nations the overall contribution was small. The author concluded that the relative contribution of various countries to the psychological literature was consistent with the population density of psychologists in those countries. Adair, Coêlho, and Luna (2002), in their more recent review of PsychLIT, found that only 55% of the articles originated from the United States, a figure they judged to be surprisingly small.

DISSATISFACTION WITH WESTERN PSYCHOLOGY

Some writers have noted the irrelevance of traditional Western psychology within certain cultures. For instance, Gergen et al. (1996) describe clinical psychology as practiced among the Maori of New Zealand. Commentators there often view psychology as a political act and a means of social control, with no more relevance to the lives of the Maori than reading a horoscope. In trying to understand the issue, Gergen et al. wrote, "The map of the self is different in each culture, and each culture could be said to require its own separate psychological science" (p. 499). With the increase in multicultural and multiethnic concerns around the world, an understanding of the psychology of different nations and cultures may become critical (see chapter 6 for related material on the emergence of alternative psychologies).

These comments are not meant to be unfriendly toward U.S. psychology, which has served as an important caretaker for psychology for many decades. Rather, they are made to point out the limited reach of any psychology that proceeds from a single culture or national origin. As Ardila (1982a) argued, "... as long as the discipline is so much influenced by one culture (and it does not matter which culture), there cannot be a truly international psychology" (p. 328). For many years, U.S. academic psychology has been dominated by the experimental approach and, for several decades, the behaviorist position was the only acceptable position at leading universities. But, as Kim and Berry (1993) note, Wundt himself considered the experimental approach to have many limitations, with other leading central European psychologists resisting the embrace of behaviorism and instead emphasizing conscious experience and private mental processes as key elements of their psychology.

Wundt (1916) spent the last two decades of his life writing a 10-volume work that he titled *Völkerpsychologie* (often translated as folk or cultural psychology) in which he argued that many so-called psychological phenomena were significantly affected by the language and culture in which they appeared. He believed that his "socio-cultural" form of psychology would eventually eclipse the more limited experimental form (Danziger, 1983). In effect, he argued that different cultures give birth to different psychologies, precisely the argument of the current-day indigenous psychologies. The dominance of one model, in this case the U.S. one, has muted the impact and appearance of other models and potential models.

THE LANGUAGE DEBATE

One of the reasons that U.S. psychologists do not read the research and writing of other countries is that they cannot; they are typically monolingual. This was not true in the early years of the discipline when some of the U.S. pioneers, like William James, could read and write in four or five languages. Until the 1960s, it was common for U.S. universities to require knowledge of one or two foreign languages before the doctoral degree was granted. This is no longer true. Language requirements have been all but eliminated from contemporary U.S. doctoral training. Despite the relatively recent appearance of cheap, fast, and efficient methods of international communication, including the Internet and e-mail, the interaction among countries remains largely unidirectional (i.e., in the export of U.S. psychology) and English-oriented.

The use of English as the principal language of communication in psychology has stimulated considerable discussion in the past. There was an intense debate in Germany several decades ago about the appropriate language for psychological publications, with the pro-English exponents (e.g., Lienert, 1977) as adamant as the pro-German supporters (e.g., Traxel, 1979). Ardila (1982a, 1993), a noted expert in Latin-American psychology, later commented on the argument from a different geographical and cultural perspective. More recently, Draguns (2001) has revived discussion of the issue. Draguns argued that, "... a truly international psychology is obstructed at this point by the massive disregard of contributions that are published in languages other than English" (p. 1019). Although Draguns endorses the use of English as the principal language of communication in psychology, he criticizes its use as the only language of psychology.

The language debate among all the major participants appears to involve a few basic issues. They include the following specific arguments. There are benefits to be obtained from publishing in English, including a visibility that can be achieved in no other language. In addition, international conferences conducted only in English, a trend for several decades now, are convenient for many English-speaking participants. But, important research and writing is being conducted outside of English-speaking countries, and it is not true that the best work will be automatically translated into English. In fact, such translations are the exception. Moreover, language is responsible for the development of psychological concepts themselves. A psychology conceived of and implemented in only one language will be limited by that language. Such limitations work against the development of a truly international psychology.

EMERGING COUNTRIES IN PSYCHOLOGY

The Arab World

For historical, cultural, and political reasons, some countries and regions have begun to develop a modern scientific psychology only in recent decades. The Arab world is a case in point. Despite a rich tradition of philosophical writers, such as Abou-Baker al-Razy (864–925) and Ibn Sina (980–1037), who made important observations directly related to psychology, the transition to modern psychology took place very slowly and generated little interest. When experimental psychology was introduced at the turn of the 20th century, it floundered, and there were no important developments until the 1940s and 1950s when psychology first made its appearance as a separate academic discipline (Soueif & Ahmed, 2001). Finally, in the mid-1970s, independent departments of psychology appeared and psychology began to take on some of the modern trappings found in many other countries. Even now, there are several Arab countries where psychology remains largely undeveloped (Ahmed & Gielen, 1998). Most Arab universities have psychology departments, but these are often underfunded, and few have psychology programs at the doctoral level.

Egypt has served as the gateway for psychology in the Arab world. The dominance of Egyptian psychology is, in part, due to the efforts of several pioneering Egyptian psychologists trained abroad, who introduced the discipline relatively early. But Egypt's dominance should also be seen in the context of Egyptian sociopolitical movements toward modernity and secular enlightenment that originated in the 19th century. It is estimated that about 70% of all Arab psychologists are Egyptian, and psychology publications in Egypt outnumber those in the rest of the Arab countries combined (Ahmed & Gielen, 1998).

Traditional research in experimental psychology is very limited, as are publications in these areas. Furthermore, because most publications are written in Arabic, the work of Arab psychologists is often not recognized by the non-Arab world. Most departments of psychology are affiliated with faculties of arts or faculties of education. Hence, many Arab psychologists are not perceived as genuine scientists. The public image of psychologists in the Arab world is not strong, although psychologists are generally recognized for their contributions to special education and human services (Soueif & Ahmed, 2001).

Despite the distance that Arab psychology has come in its short existence, it remains in its early stages with much to be done. Nonetheless, it has great potential for further growth (Ahmed, 1998). Future challenges for Arab psychology include facilitating greater regional cooperation and coordination of research efforts. Furthermore, it has been argued that Arab psychology should rely less on the indiscriminate and haphazard importation of U.S. psychology and make the discipline more relevant to the culture and social realities of the Arab world (Ahmed & Gielen, 1998).

Emerging Psychology in Asia

Many countries in Asia showed sharply renewed interest in psychology in the period immediately following World War II. Most of them, with the notable exception of China, were strongly influenced by Western psychology. However, the overall development of psychology in Asia has remained at a rudimentary level. Only Japan can be considered to be in a somewhat advanced stage.

Japan was influenced by Western psychology not long after the founding of the laboratory at Leipzig. Its two pioneers were Yujiro Motora (1858–1912) and Matataro Matsumoto (1865–1943), both of whom received some of their education in the U.S. Motora received his Ph.D. under G. Stanley Hall at Johns Hopkins University in 1888. He subsequently was appointed the first Japanese professor of psychology at the University of Tokyo and became a revered figure in that nation's psychology. Matsumoto completed his research at Yale University under E. W. Scripture. He later visited laboratories in Europe and was strongly influenced by his work with Wundt. He established the nation's first psychology laboratory at the University of Tokyo (1903). Later, when he moved to Kyoto University, he established a laboratory there as well. When Motora died, Matsumoto succeeded him at the University of Tokyo (Misiak & Sexton, 1966).

At first, the development of scientific psychology moved slowly in Japan, but by 1911 a psychology journal had been established and new textbooks were being written. By 1914, behaviorism was introduced into Japan and, in 1920, Gestalt psychology. Following World War II, the United States became an increasingly important influence on Japanese psychology, which continued to grow rapidly, expanding its expertise in testing, and moving into more applied areas, including child and industrial/organizational psychology (Misiak & Sexton, 1966).

Psychology in Japan has developed to an advanced stage comparable to the state of psychology in many Western countries. The discipline has sound academic foundations, and is diversely applied and represented by several large psychological associations. Furthermore, Japanese psychologists have begun the process of indigenization and have adapted many Western tools and constructs to the Japanese language and culture. According to recent estimates, Japan has only about 20,000 psychologists, of whom considerably fewer are in practice, providing services for a population of more than 127 million (Tanaka-Matsumi & Otsui, 2004). However, recent educational reforms and several newly established graduate programs will ensure further growth. Future challenges for Japanese psychology include providing services for Japan's aging population and developing legislation to regulate licensing on a national level.

Modern psychology was introduced into China by Cai Yuanpei, a prominent educational reformer who had studied under Wundt in Leipzig, and by other pioneering Chinese psychologists trained in America and Germany (Jing & Fu, 2001). The first psychological laboratory in China was established in 1917 under Yuanpei's presidency at Peking University. Besides the United States, Japan was probably the most important influence on early Chinese psychology. In the late 19th century, China initiated broad educational reforms based on the Japanese model, and began an extensive academic exchange with Japan (Blowers, 2000). A consequence of this exchange was that Japanese ideas on psychology and education were implemented in Chinese teachers' training, and psychology's role in education remained significant even as Western psychology was rejected.

Chinese psychology had a promising beginning, but its development stalled with the onset of the Sino-Japanese War and World War II. Following the 1949 revolution, China rejected Western psychology in favor of the Soviet model of dialectical materialism (Jing & Fu, 2001), and, during the Cultural Revolution, psychology was rejected almost entirely. Chinese psychology was not reinstated until the late 1970s, but it has shown strong movement toward professionalization and diversification of research efforts due to the patronage of the Chinese Academy of Sciences and, more recently, the economic and political impact of globablization on China.

Psychology in India has had a particularly mixed heritage. Its long-standing philosophical traditions promoted certain practices of mental health (e.g., Yoga Nidra). However, many of its early psychologists were educated in the British tradition that emphasized statistics and individual differences. These two emphases did not sit well together. The first psychology laboratory was established at Calcutta University in 1906 under the direction of N. N. Sengupta, who had studied with Hugo Münsterberg at Harvard University (Misiak & Sexton, 1966). Still, most psychology was taught as a form of philosophy by philosophers.

Clinical psychology and intelligence testing have been central to Indian psychology since its inception. Psychoanalysis was long an influential orientation in Indian psychology, but behavioral and cognitive approaches have increasingly come to dominate the field. Although India has more than 100 universities with graduate programs in psychology, access to psychological services is limited, particularly in rural areas. A future challenge for India is to develop legislation governing the licensing and functions of Indian psychologists. At this time, Indian psychologists have developed their own standards through professional organizations, and many have adopted the APA's ethical guidelines. However, India has a large number of unqualified "pseudo-professionals" offering psychological services to the detriment of consumers and the profession at large (Barnes, 2004, p. 233).

Psychology in the remaining Asian countries, with the exception of Singapore and the Philippines, remains at a very low level. One clear index of its lack of relevance is the ratio between the population and the number of psychologists in each country. With the exception of Japan, most Asian countries have very few psychologists relative to their population.

Psychology in Sub-Saharan Africa

It is difficult to generalize regarding the state of psychology across countries in a region with such diverse cultures, people, and political conditions as sub-Saharan Africa. Furthermore, there is a paucity of published research on psychology in this continent (Holdstock, 2000). However, certain commonalities may be noted, many of which are shared by developing countries on other continents.

In most sub-Saharan countries, psychology was established as a science and a profession during or after the 1960s, which is relatively late compared to Western countries. The discipline was introduced mainly by African psychologists trained abroad or by Western educators and missionaries. As a result, psychology is still largely regarded as a Western science. For the most part, psychologists in sub-Saharan countries lack the capacity to produce knowledge. This is due to a number of factors: psychology is a relatively new discipline in those countries; there is political instability in certain areas of this region; and there is scarce funding for many educational institutions. Hence, psychologists in sub-Saharan Africa are primarily importers of psychological knowledge. Historically, the transfer of psychology from Western countries to Africa has been problematic because Western psychology has not been adequately adapted to the culture and social realities of sub-Saharan countries (Mpofu, 2002). At present, psychology in few sub-Saharan countries has reached the indigenization stage of development.

Psychological services in most sub-Saharan countries are scarce and primarily available in urban areas. Kenya, for example, with a population of about 30.5 million, has only about 3,000 psychologists and counselors (Koinange, 2004). Estimates for Nigeria vary, but there are probably no more than a few thousand psychologists serving a population of 120 million (Gire, 2004). Furthermore, psychology in this region has an image problem, that is, it is not seen as strongly relevant to the needs of the public. As a result, it is ignored by many.

The history and current status of psychology in South Africa is unique in the sub-Saharan region. Psychology was introduced relatively early in this country. Intelligence tests were first used as early as 1916, and the discipline was established at the University of Stellenbosch the following year (Stead, 2004). Unfortunately, the development of South African psychology has been closely tied to apartheid politics. Intelligence tests, in particular, were used extensively to justify racial segregation. Furthermore, South Africa's first national psychology association, founded in 1948, was divided into two separate organizations for more than two decades due to disagreements regarding non-White membership. Compared to other sub-Saharan countries, psychology is well established as a science and profession in South Africa. Currently, 79% of South African psychologists are White, but the proportion of non-White psychologists has increased dramatically since the advent of Black majority rule in the 1990s.

Psychology in sub-Saharan Africa is mostly in the early stages of development. Future challenges common to many countries in this region include developing ethical guidelines and legislation regulating the activities of psychologists and creating a psychology of greater relevance to the indigenous culture. Furthermore, some commentators have called for an African psychological association to promote collaborative efforts across the continent and to represent African psychology abroad (Mpofu, 2002).

Psychology in Latin America

The pace and extent to which modern psychology has developed in Latin America varies across the countries of that region. Generally, psychology is more firmly established as a science and a profession in Latin-American countries with a higher socioeconomic level of development, such as Argentina, Brazil, and Mexico (Sosa & Valderrama-Iturbe, 2001). Historically, European and U.S. influences as well as the political and economic conditions in Latin America have markedly affected the course of the development of psychology in this region.

As in Europe, where it originated, Latin-American psychology had its beginnings as a subfield of philosophy, although some of the first psychology courses in Latin America were established to train teachers, lawyers, and physicians (Ardila, 1982b). Experimental psychology began relatively early in Argentina, which was the leading Latin-American country during the pioneer period of psychology. Rodolfo Rivarola taught the first psychology course in Latin America at the University of Buenos

Aires in 1896 (Klappenbach, 2004; Sosa & Valderrama-Iturbe, 2001). Horacio Piñero, who replaced Rivarola for that course, founded the first experimental laboratory in Latin America in 1898 (Ardila, 1982b). In Mexico, plans were made for a psychology laboratory in 1902, but were not fully realized until Enrique Aragón founded one at Mexico's National University in 1916. Manoel Bomfim established the first laboratory in Brazil in 1906 in Rio de Janeiro with assistance from Alfred Binet to replicate his laboratory in La Sorbonne (Hutz, McCarthy, & Gomes, 2004). These early laboratories were essentially demonstration laboratories established for training purposes.

Early psychology in Latin America was influenced by that of France and was, as such, oriented toward clinical as well as experimental psychology (Ardila, 1982b; Klappenbach, 2004). Psychoanalysis, often brought to Latin America by physicians trained in France, became highly influential in some countries, particularly Argentina. U.S. behaviorism became an important influence during the 1960s, particularly in Mexico and Brazil, which were visited by Fred S. Keller and B. F. Skinner, respectively (Sosa & Valderrama-Iturbe, 2001).

In most Latin American countries, programs for training professional psychologists were established during the 1960s (Ardila, 1982b). Such programs are usually 5-year undergraduate programs leading to licensure as a psychologist. Graduate programs leading to doctoral degrees are less common, especially in countries where economic resources devoted to research and education are scarce. Private practice has become increasingly common, but government agencies have traditionally employed most psychologists in this region.

As noted by Ardila (1982b), Latin-American culture has traditionally valued the humanities over science and technology. Consequently, psychology in this region has developed more as a clinical profession than a science. A future challenge for psychology in Latin America, therefore, is to develop more culturally relevant research programs.

INTERNATIONAL ASSOCIATIONS IN PSYCHOLOGY

One of the most effective ways to share information about psychology across nations has been through face-to-face encounters in forums provided by various international societies. These encounters include formal presentations at meetings as well as less formal social gatherings. Both types of situations present enormous opportunities for learning about psychology in other countries. In addition, these groups often provide publication outlets, as well as committees that address special issues. All in all, they have become one of the most effective venues for international communication in psychology (see chapters 3, 10, and 12 for more on the global mission and regulatory activities of psychological organizations as well as how to become involved in them).

IUPsyS remains the preeminent international organization in psychology. From its European beginnings as the original international congress, it has evolved into an association of a somewhat different sort. Only national organizations are permitted to join, with a limit of one per nation. Currently, there are 70 national members in the IUPsyS (the number varies as new members are added and others may be dropped for various infractions). The governing body of the IUPsyS is the General Assembly, which is made up of the Executive Committee and delegates from the member nations. The Executive Committee meets annually to conduct affairs of the organization (Sabourin, 2001).

The IUPsyS sponsors international meetings every 4 years (prior to 1972, the meetings were held every 3 years) and, since 1995, regional congresses in between. Since 1980, the congresses have been held in Leipzig (1980), Acapulco (1984), Sydney (1988), Brussels (1992), Montréal (1996), Stockholm (2000), and Beijing (2004). Recent congresses have attracted approximately 4,000 or more attendees (Pawlik & Rosenzweig, 2000). IUPsyS publishes the *International Journal of Psychology*, a membership directory, and a CD–ROM containing important sources on global psychology (Stevens & Wedding, 2006). Several standing committees are active and conduct business between meetings, such as the Committee on Communication and Publications, the Committee on Research, and Development of Psychology as a Science and as a Profession (Merenda, 1995).

A second organization of considerable importance to global psychology is the International Association of Applied Psychology (IAAP). Founded in 1920 by Edouard Claparède, a Swiss psychologist, the association also sponsors a major meeting, the International Congress of Applied Psychology. For most of their early history, congresses were held in Europe at irregular intervals, including a significant disruption during the years surrounding World War II. However, since 1974, the meetings have been held on a 4-year cycle, alternating with the IUPsyS, so that a major international congress of psychology is held somewhere in the world every two years. The only IAAP congress held in the United States took place in 1998 in San Francisco, with the APA as host.

2. HISTORY OF PSYCHOLOGY

Unlike the IUPsyS, the IAAP is an organization of individual members. Originally focused on work and organizational aspects of psychology, it now has a wide range of special interest sections available to members, including applied gerontology, health psychology, economic psychology, sport psychology, and traffic and transportation psychology, along with other traditional applied areas (Merenda, 1995). Its major publication is *Applied Psychology: An International Review* (formerly, *The International Review of Applied Psychology*). It also publishes a newsletter and a membership directory.

The third major international organization has a history that is notably different from those of the IUPsyS and IAAP. The International Council of Psychologists (ICP) began as the National Council of Women Psychologists, a group formed in the United States in 1941 to aid in the war effort. In 1946, after the war had ended, the organization voted to continue in existence, but with a revised agenda. It was now called the International Council of Women Psychologists, and its women-only membership had as its goal the understanding and promotion of psychology throughout the world. In 1959, men were admitted to the association and, in 1962, the organization adopted its present name.

The ICP has always devoted itself to psychology in all its forms, as opposed to the scientific or applied orientation of the other two major international organizations. It holds annual meetings and, unlike the IUPsyS and IAAP, has always had a strong representation of women among its leaders. Although the organization has had many international members, it has always been U.S.-based and, until the 1970s, all its presidents resided in the United States. In 1976, the office of Secretary General was created, and most of the day-to-day operations of the organization, formerly conducted by the President and Board, were transferred to that office. Subsequently, Lisette Fanchon (1978–1979) was elected ICP President, the first to reside outside of the U.S. In the years since her election, there have been many non-United States presidents. Most recently ICP has established a tandem affiliation with IAAP.

In addition to these three associations, there are many other important organizations concerned with international psychology.

The APA has not ignored the benefits of an international perspective in their organization. In 1944, the APA established a Committee on International Relations in Psychology whose initial mission was to advise the organization on the recovery and restoration efforts concerning the laboratories and libraries destroyed in Europe during World War II

(Fowler, 1998b). Later, the role of the committee was expanded to consult with the APA on a wider range of international issues. In 1974, a full-time Office of International Affairs was created to coordinate several international programs, including a journal-donation program, a travel-grant program, and a quarterly newsletter. Despite these efforts by the APA, a group of individuals felt that certain goals could be achieved only through the creation of a separate APA international division.

The effort to form a new division resulted in friction with individuals who felt that the division might duplicate activities and generate unnecessary tension with the Office of International Affairs. Some individuals, who later supported the division, were initially opposed to its formation. As a result of this opposition, the process of creating a new division was difficult, and an earlier proposal presented to the APA Council of Representatives was rejected. However, in 1997, the Council of Representatives approved the addition of a new division to their association: the Division of International Psychology.

The division has become an active part of the larger association, with eight regular committees and a large number of ad hoc committees. The division is primarily responsible for organizing international programs at the annual APA convention where it typically has representation from 40 or more countries. Among its other activities, the division sponsors a web-based clearinghouse that provides information on various aspects of international psychology and recognizes important contributors to international psychology through its awards committee. It also publishes a newsletter/journal, the *International Psychology Bulletin* (formerly *International Psychology Reporter*).

SUMMARY AND CONCLUSIONS

Mainstream psychology is being challenged now as it has never been challenged before. No longer can it ignore the evidence of its cultural embeddedness. Pedersen (1999) contends that psychology is undergoing a paradigm shift from monoculturalism to multiculturalism and has called for a "fourth force" in psychology, one based on a genuine appreciation of differences among cultures and the importance of context. Although basic mental and behavioral processes vary little across populations (e.g., memory), the content of such processes varies markedly because it is embedded in the matrix of culture (e.g., language-bound reasoning). He argues that we make assumptions about the world every day and these assumptions are embedded in our respective cultures. If we are to arrive at a psychology that is genuinely global, whether it be multiple indigenous psychologies or a unifying cultural psychology, we must first understand the assumptions that we make.

The role of the United States in global psychology continues to change. In its pioneer days, United States psychology was open to research and ideas from around the world, but particularly from Europe. As psychology in the United States matured and prospered, it became more driven by its own home-grown version of psychology and it relied less on input from other countries. That self-involvement reached its peak in the decades following World War II.

Now, U.S. psychology is being forced to make some adjustments. There is little doubt that its monolithic power over international psychology is being eroded through the strengthening of psychology in some nations and its emergence in others. The United States is likely to retain its influence over global psychology in the new century through the sheer size and breadth of its resources. Nonetheless, the psychology of the future is likely to see some significant international shifts in power and influence. One example can be seen in the trend toward regionalization. Psychologists in regions with political, geographical, or cultural commonalities have united through international psychological organizations representing the countries of those regions. The EFPA is a good example of this development, and similar organizations have been proposed for African, Arab, and Asian countries. It will be interesting to see whether such regional cooperation can advance the development of indigenous models of psychology and offset the U.S. dominance in the field.

Psychology has come a long way from its pioneering days in Leipzig where, for Wundt and several other early contributors, the application of psychology was of no particular interest. Nowadays, it is the application of psychology that frequently drives the science, and that application goes beyond the one-to-one clinical encounter or the evaluation of a group of school children. Sexton and Misiak (1976) posed a question several decades ago that is still relevant today: "What significance, if any, does this psychology, so energetically and ably pursued in so many countries of the world, have for the unity, peace, and happiness of this globe?" (p. 9). The answer to that question is still unclear. But, the hope of many psychologists working in the international arena is that its significance will be profound.

RECOMMENDED READINGS

Brock, A. C. (Ed.). (2007). *Internationalizing the history of psychology*. New York: New York University Press.

David, H. P., & Buchanan, J. (2003). International psychology. In D. K. Freedheim (Ed.), *Handbook of psychology: History of psychology* (Vol. 1, pp. 509–533). New York: Wiley.

Jing, Q. (2000). International psychology. In K. Pawlik & M. R. Rosenzweig (Eds.), *International handbook of psychology* (pp. 570–584). London: Sage.

Rosenzweig, M. R. (Ed.). (1992). *International psychological science: Progress, problems, and prospects*. Washington, DC: American Psychological Association.

Rosenzweig, M. R. (1999). Continuity and change in the development of psychology around the world. *American Psychologist, 53*, 252–259.

Russell, R. W. (1984). Psychology in its world context. *American Psychologist, 39*, 1017–1025.

Sexton, V. S., & Hogan, J. D. (Eds.). (1992). *International psychology: Views from around the world*. Lincoln: University of Nebraska Press.

Sexton, V. S., & Misiak, H. (Eds.). (1976). *Psychology around the world*. Monterey, CA: Brooks/Cole.

Sexton, V. S., & Misiak, H. (1984). American psychologists and psychology abroad. *American Psychologist, 39*, 1026–1031.

Stevens, M. J., & Wedding, D. (Eds.). (2004). *Handbook of international psychology*. New York: Brunner-Routledge.

Stevens, M. J., & Wedding, D. (Eds.). (2006). *Psychology: IUPsyS global resource* [CD-ROM]. (7th ed.). Hove, UK: Psychology Press.

REFERENCES

Adair, J. G., Coêlho, A. E. L., & Luna, J. R. (2002). How international is psychology? *International Journal of Psychology, 37*, 160–170.

Ahmed, R. A. (1998). Preface. In R. A. Ahmed & U. P. Gielen (Eds.), *Psychology in the Arab countries* (pp. xii–xiv). Menoufia, Egypt: Menoufia University Press.

Ahmed, R. A., & Gielen, U. P. (1998). Psychology in the Arab world. In R. A. Ahmed & U. P. Gielen (Eds.), *Psychology in the Arab countries* (pp. 3–48). Menoufia, Egypt: Menoufia University Press.

Ardila, R. (1982a). International psychology. *American Psychologist, 37*, 323–329.

Ardila, R. (1982b). Psychology in Latin America today. *Annual Review of Psychology, 33*, 103–122.

Ardila, R. (1993). Latin American psychology and world psychology: Is integration possible? In U. Kim & J. W. Berry, (Eds.), *Indigenous psychologies: Research and experience in cultural context* (pp. 170–176). Newbury Park, CA: Sage.

Bailey, D. S. (2004, July/August). Beyond our borders. *Monitor on Psychology, 35*(7), 58–59.

Barnes, B. (2004). Psychology in India. In M. J. Stevens & D. Wedding (Eds.), *Handbook of international psychology* (pp. 225–242). New York: Brunner-Routledge.

Bauserman, R. (1997). International representation in the psychological literature. *International Journal of Psychology, 32*, 107–112.

Blowers, G. H. (2000). Learning from others: Japan's role in bringing psychology to China. *American Psychologist, 55*, 1433–1436.

Blumenthal, A. L. (1985). A reappraisal of Wilhelm Wundt. *American Psychologist, 33*, 1081–1088.

Boring, E. G. (1929). *A history of experimental psychology.* New York: Appleton-Century.

Britt, S. H. (1942). European background (1600–1900) for American psychology. *Journal of General Psychology, 27*, 311–329.

Danziger, K. (1983). Origins and basic principles of Wundt's Völkerpsychologie. *British Journal of Social Psychology, 22*, 303–313.

David, H. P., & Buchanan, J. (2003). International psychology. In D. K. Freedheim (Ed.), *Handbook of psychology: History of psychology* (Vol. 1, pp. 509–533). New York: Wiley.

Draguns, J. G. (2001). Toward a truly international psychology: Beyond English only. *American Psychologist, 56*, 1019–1030.

Fowler, R. D. (1998a, May). Sample psychology's international flavor. *APA Monitor, 29*(5), 3.

Fowler, R. D. (1998b). International activities in the American Psychological Association. *International Psychology Reporter, 2*(1), 6–7.

Fowler, R. D., & Newman, R. (2004). Psychology in the United States. In M. J. Stevens & D. Wedding (Eds.), *Handbook of international psychology* (pp. 109–128). New York: Brunner-Routledge.

Gergen, K. J., Gulerce, A., Lock, A., & Misra, G. (1996). Psychological science in cultural context. *American Psychologist, 51*, 496–503.

Geuter, U. (1987). German psychology during the Nazi period. In M. G. Ash & W. R. Woodward (Eds.), *Psychology in twentieth-century thought and society* (pp. 165–187). New York: Cambridge University Press.

Gielen, U. P., & Pagan, M. (1993). International psychology and American mainstream psychology. *International Psychologist, 34*(1), 16–19; (2), 5.

Gire, J. T. (2004). Psychology in Nigeria: Origins, current status and future. In M. J. Stevens & D. Wedding (Eds.), *Handbook of international psychology* (pp. 43–58). New York: Brunner-Routledge.

Graumann, C. F. (1997). Psychology in postwar Germany: The vicissitudes of internationalization. *World Psychology, 3*(3–4), 253–277.

Groebel, J. (1992). Germany. In V. S. Sexton & J. D. Hogan (Eds.), *International psychology: Views from around the world* (pp. 159–181). Lincoln: University of Nebraska Press.

Hilgard, E. R. (1987). *Psychology in America: A historical survey.* Orlando, FL: Harcourt Brace.

Hogan, J. D. (1995). International psychology in the next century: Comment and speculation from a U.S. perspective. *World Psychology, 1*, 9–25.

Holdstock, T. L. (2000). *Re-examining psychology: Critical perspectives and African insights.* London: Routledge.

Hutz, C. S., McCarthy, S., & Gomes, W. (2004). Psychology in Brazil: The road behind and the road ahead. In M. J. Stevens & D. Wedding (Eds.), *Handbook of international psychology* (pp. 151–169). New York: Brunner-Routledge.

Jing, Q. (2000). International psychology. In K. Pawlik & M. R. Rosenzweig (Eds.), *International handbook of psychology* (pp. 570–584). London: Sage.

Jing, Q., & Fu, X. (2001). Modern Chinese psychology: Its indigenous roots and international influences. *International Journal of Psychology, 36*, 308–418.

Kim, U., & Berry, J. W. (1993). *Indigenous psychologies: Research and experience in cultural context.* Newbury Park, CA: Sage.

Klappenbach, H. (2004). Psychology in Argentina. In M. J. Stevens & D. Wedding (Eds.), *Handbook of international psychology* (pp. 129–150). New York: Brunner-Routledge.

Koinange, J. W. (2004). Psychology in Kenya. In M. J. Stevens & D. Wedding (Eds.), *Handbook of international psychology* (pp. 25–41). New York: Brunner-Routledge.

Lienert, G. A. (1977). Über Werner Traxel: Internationalität oder Provinzialismus zur Frage: Sollten Psychologen in Englisch publizieren? *Psychologische Beiträge, 19*, 487–492.

Lunt, I. (1996). The history and organization of the European Federation of Professional Psychologists' Associations (EFPPA). *European Psychologist, 1*, 60–64.

Lunt, I., & Poortinga, Y. H. (1996). Internationalizing psychology: The case of Europe. *American Psychologist, 51*, 504–508.

Merenda, P. F. (1995). International movements in psychology: The major international associations of psychology. *World Psychology, 1*, 27–48.

Misiak, H., & Sexton, V. S. (1966). *History of psychology: An overview.* New York: Grune and Stratton.

Moghaddam, F. (1987). Psychology in three worlds: As reflected by the crisis in social psychology and the move toward indigenous third-world psychology. *American Psychologist, 42*, 912–920.

Mpofu, E. (2002). Psychology in sub-Saharan Africa: Challenges, prospects and promises. *International Journal of Psychology, 37*, 179–186.

Pawlik, K., & Rosenzweig, M. R. (2000). Psychological science: Content, methodology, history, and profession. In K. Pawlik & M. R. Rosenzweig (Eds.), *International handbook of psychology* (pp. 3–19). London: Sage.

Pedersen, P. (Ed.). (1999). *Multiculturalism as a fourth force.* Philadelphia: Brunner.

Rosenzweig, M. R. (1999). Continuity and change in the development of psychology around the world. *American Psychologist, 53*, 252–259.

Sabourin, M. (2001). International psychology: Is the whole greater than the sum of its parts? *Canadian Psychology, 42*, 74–81.

Sexton, V. S. (1983, April). *Is American psychology xenophobic?* Presidential address presented at the meeting of the Eastern Psychological Association, Baltimore, MD.

Sexton, V. S., & Misiak, H. (1976). *Psychology around the world.* Monterey, CA: Brooks/Cole.

Sexton, V. S., & Misiak, H. (1984). American psychologists and psychology abroad. *American Psychologist, 39*, 1026–1031.

Sosa, J. J. S., & Valderrama-Iturbe, P. (2001). Psychology in Latin America: Historical reflections and perspectives. *International Journal of Psychology, 36*, 384–394.

Soueif, M. I., & Ahmed, R. A. (2001). Psychology in Arab countries: Past, present, and future. *International Journal of Group Tensions, 30*, 211–240.

Stead, G. B. (2004). Psychology in South Africa. In M. J. Stevens & D. Wedding (Eds.), *Handbook of international psychology* (pp. 59–73). New York: Brunner-Routledge.

Stevens, M. J., & Wedding, D. (Eds.). (2004). *Handbook of international psychology.* New York: Brunner-Routledge.

Stevens, M. J., & Wedding, D. (Eds.). (2006). *Psychology: IUPsyS global resource* (7th ed.). [CD-ROM]. Hove, UK: Psychology Press.

Tanaka-Matsumi, J., & Otsui, K. (2004). Psychology in Japan. In M. J. Stevens & D. Wedding (Eds.), *Handbook of international psychology* (pp. 193–210). New York: Brunner-Routledge.

Tikkanen, T. (2004). *The European Diploma in Psychology (EuroPsy) and the future of the profession in Europe*. Retrieved January 4, 2005, from http://www.efpa.be/start.php

Traxel, W. (1979). Publish or perish!—Auf Deutsch oder auf Englisch? *Psychologische Beiträge, 21*, 62–77.

Wundt, W. (1916). *Elements of folk psychology: Outlines of a psychological history of the development of mankind* (E. L. Schaub, Trans.). London: Allan and Unwin.

3

Current Trends in Global Psychology

Elizabeth Nair
Work and Health Psychologists

Rubén Ardila
National University of Colombia

Michael J. Stevens
Illinois State University

INTRODUCTION

State-of-the-art information technology and electronic communication have effectively condensed the geographical distances between countries around the globe. Although oceans and mountains still physically separate countries and states, psychologists across the world share databases, review the published research of their peers, and ask questions and receive answers from each other within minutes across continents. The one prerequisite is a shared language. Most often this is the English language because of its worldwide importance among scientists that evolved especially after World War II. French is also being used rather extensively as a means of communication between psychologists from France and various French-speaking nations and regions located in Europe, North and West Africa, and Canada (Québec). In addition, Spanish serves as an

important link among psychologists from many Latin-American countries and Spain. By contrast, German and Russian are now less often used
as means of communication between psychologists worldwide and other
social scientists than in earlier times.

This chapter will consider the current picture of psychology in the
world today, taking a global perspective. We review current trends
reflected in international and regional psychology conferences, worldwide trends shaping the future of psychology, and current trends predom-
inating within selected world regions (see chapters 2 and 12 for more on
international psychology organizations, their history and opportunities
for involvement).

CURRENT TRENDS REFLECTED IN INTERNATIONAL PSYCHOLOGY ORGANIZATIONS

The International Union of Psychological Science (IUPsyS) was founded
in 1951 with 11 charter members. In 2005, the membership comprised 70
countries with all continents represented. Notably, in the last decade,
national psychology associations from more African, Asian, eastern
European, and Latin-American countries have joined. These new members of the IUPsyS often seek to raise the bar within their own countries
and regions with regard to standards of training, professional accreditation and practice, implementation of professional codes of ethics, and
other discipline-related issues. At the General Assembly of the IUPsyS in
2004, it was recognized by members present that the manner in which the
discipline was practiced and evaluated in one country would impact the
way psychology was viewed in other parts of the world, given the present
scenario of a global marketplace. Accordingly, capacity-building has become
an important element of recent agendas of the IUPsyS, both at Board and
Assembly meetings.

In response to the need to strengthen psychology in various member
countries, the IUPsyS initiated a series of capacity-building workshops,
with the main objective of equipping national psychology associations
with the knowledge and skills to improve their structure, organization,
functioning, and contributions to civil society and nation-building.
Capacity-building has taken the form of a series of workshops organized
in conjunction with international and regional psychology congresses.
The first such focused workshop was held in Singapore in July 2002 in
conjunction with the International Congress of Applied Psychology
(ICAP), followed by a second in Dubai in December 2003 in conjunction
with the first Middle East and North Africa Regional Congress of

Psychology (MENA RCP), and a third in Beijing in August 2004 in conjunction with the International Congress of Psychology (ICP). The national associations of countries in which psychology as a discipline did not have a robust profile nominated participants. Office holders within these associations were identified as participants because they were deemed likely to initiate action through their membership to raise the standard of the discipline in their country. It was also believed that regional groupings of psychology associations could benefit from networking and a shared geography and cultural history upon which to expand opportunities for psychological contributions toward the development of civil society.

These national capacity-building workshops have become a co-existing partner with the Advanced Research and Training Seminars (ARTS), initiated in 1992 with Ype Poortinga as the first Coordinator (Adair, 2001). ARTS continue to be cosponsored by the IUPsyS, the International Association of Applied Psychology (IAAP), and the International Association of Cross-Cultural Psychology (IACCP). The objectives of ARTS are to help finance participation at international congresses by younger scholars from lower income countries. The most recent ARTS were held in Singapore in conjunction with the ICAP in July 2002, and in Beijing and Xian in August 2004 in conjunction with the ICP (Adair & Lunt, 2005).

On December 26, 2004, following an earthquake in Sumatra, countries around the Indian Ocean suffered casualties totaling more than 500,000 as a result of a giant tidal wave, known as a *tsunami*. The dead, injured, and bereft families included locals and several thousand vacationers from abroad. Many countries, groups, and individuals immediately made financial contributions, matched the donations of others, and provided professional support services. Medical personnel and engineers were among those who gave their time and expertise to help provide relief and physical reconstruction for the affected countries. In this regard, the IUPsyS organized a regional workshop in Singapore in May 2005, targeting psychologists in the countries that suffered the heaviest casualties, namely India, Indonesia, Sri Lanka, and Thailand. National psychology associations and senior psychologists and mental-health personnel nominated participants from their respective countries. Three participants were selected from each country on the basis of being directly involved in psychosocial rebuilding efforts in the wake of the tsunami, as well as being in positions in which they could impact policy and practice on a broader scale. Disaster management experts were identified and invited to serve as workshop trainers. The American

Psychological Association (APA) supported this initiative as a major donor with funds and with a disaster mental-health intervention consultant on the team of trainers and facilitators who delivered the workshop. Several other national and international organizations (the Australian Psychological Society, Chinese Association of Science and Technology, IAAP, International Society for the Study of Behavioral Development, and UNESCO) also contributed toward this initiative. Country participants reported that they found the training guidelines, intervention protocols, shared experiences, and networking opportunities to have been both enlightening and useful. In conjunction with the IAAP, a follow-up with participants of the May 2005 psychosocial rebuilding workshop was planned as a long-term action–research program, spanning over a 3-year period from May 2005 to April 2008. The second tsunami aftermath workshop was hosted by the IAAP in Bangkok in November 2005 in conjunction with a regional psychology conference cosponsored by the IUPsyS and IAAP.

Although the four countries affected by the tsunami are Asian, the diversity among them is striking. These countries have different predominant religions, with India being mainly Hindu, Indonesia mainly Muslim, and Sri Lanka and Thailand mainly Buddhist. In each of these countries, the families that suffered losses as a result of the tsunami were of these faiths as well as Christian. Contextual diversity notwithstanding, the shared disaster experience brought psychologists together from around the world, both as participants and trainers, to focus their attention and efforts on the unifying goal of psychosocial reconstruction, applying the most effective and culturally appropriate methods available based on needs analyses and impact evaluations. This workshop represents an increasingly evident trend in global psychology, namely collaboration across national boundaries and specialty lines, in order to craft and implement programs that establish a globally high standard of training and practice, which benefits the discipline and profession as well as those who are served.

The IUPsyS has continued to represent the discipline of psychology at various multidisciplinary forums, such as the International Council of Scientific Unions (ICSU), International Social Science Council (ISSC), and UNESCO. Recent years have seen contributions from various specialty areas, including cognitive science, environmental psychology, developmental psychology, and social psychology. An example of ongoing international multidisciplinary activity is the ICSU-sponsored 2004 project, Human Dimensions of Global Change: Human Perceptions and

Behavior in Sustainable Water Use. Project funding was received from UNESCO and the U.S. State Department (Ritchie, 2005). The International Geographic Union is the principal partner. Pilot work has been completed in France, India, Italy, and Mexico. The IUPsyS has also secured grants from these organizations to pursue research and training agendas, including grants from the ICSU, ISSC, and the U.S. National Academy of Science for activities supported by UNESCO and the U.S. State Department. These activities included ARTS seminars and a multidisciplinary project on Environmental Psychology in Developing Countries: A Multi-Method Approach (Ritchie, 2005).

The IAAP, founded in 1920, is the oldest international psychology association beginning more as a European-oriented organization, with most of the ICAP meetings held in French-speaking and German-speaking Europe, as is true for the ICP (Merenda, 1995). Membership is made up of individuals, who currently number about 1,600, from over 80 countries. Its official languages are English and French. There are 16 Divisions: Organizational Psychology (originally a core Division of the IAAP); Psychological Assessment and Evaluation; Psychology and National Development; Environmental Psychology; Educational, Instructional and School Psychology; Clinical and Community Psychology; Applied Gerontology; Health Psychology; Economic Psychology; Psychology and Law; Political Psychology; Sport Psychology; Traffic and Transportation Psychology; Applied Cognitive Psychology; Student Division; and Counseling Psychology. The Division on Traffic and Transportation Psychology encapsulates the shared aims of all IAAP Divisions (Traffic and Transportation Psychology, 2000). It paraphrases the twofold objective of Article 1 of the IAAP's Constitution: (a) to establish contact between people in different countries who are engaged in scientific work in the various fields of applied psychology, and (b) to advance the study and achievement of means likely to contribute to scientific and social development in these fields. Examples of research investigations studied by this Division include driver fatigue and safety, attitude change toward speeding, and implicit construction of the consequences of accidents. The accomplishments of various IAAP Divisions often appear as publications in scientific journals, papers delivered at specialty congresses, workshops, and divisional newsletters.

There has been a concerted effort and consistent, persuasive communication in recent issues of the IAAP Newsletter to move the divisional leadership and members toward engagement in policy-impacting initiatives in their respective countries as well as toward dialogue with international,

multidisciplinary organizations with wide-ranging potential for impacting
policy. One manifestation of this movement is the 2004 entry of the IAAP
as a U.N.-affiliated non-governmental organization (NGO). The message
reiterated by IAAP President Michael Frese (2004) has been that research
findings in psychology have much to offer policy makers in guiding them
toward better informed decision making that would affect the quality of life
of many people in different countries. In the same communication,
President Frese announced the formation of 12 subgroups, charged to produce memoranda about their policy-making agendas by the 2006 ICAP in
Athens. These subgroups include Active Aging, Entrepreneurship,
Ethnopolitical Violence, Environmental Psychology, HIV/AIDS
Prevention, Human Capital, Immigration, Indigenous People, Quality of
Life, Role of Women, Stress and Health, and Unemployment.

In the last two decades, both the IUPsyS and IAAP have held their quadrennial congresses in Asian countries. The ICP was just held in Beijing in
2004 and the ICAP convened in Kyoto in 1990 and in Singapore in 2002.
The quadrennial congresses of the two organizations are a critical nexus of
their functions and charter. For example, Article 3 of the IAAP's
Constitution (2004) has as its first priority the periodic convening of international and regional congresses as well as workshops. Similarly, Article 2
of the IUPsyS's *Statutes* (International Union of Psychological Science,
2004) states that the primary goal of the organization is the exchange of
ideas and scientific information between psychologists of different countries and the organization of international congresses and other meetings
on subjects of general or special interest. The geographical move from
Europe and North America to Asia is reflective of the growth and development of the discipline in Asian countries, which will be discussed in
greater detail later. China and India comprise 37% of the world's population. The need for applied psychology to contribute toward a better quality
of life in these countries has been acknowledged and is being addressed by
national associations of psychology, not only in these countries, but in
other Asian nations as well (Stevens & Wedding, 2004a, 2004b).

In tandem, the IUPsyS and IAAP have sponsored regional congresses
in recent years in Asia and the Middle East, namely in Mumbai in 2000,
Dubai in 2002, and Bangkok in 2005. The follow-up to the May 2005
Psychosocial Rebuilding Workshop in the Aftermath of the Tsunami will
be hosted by the IUPsyS and IAAP in conjunction with the Bangkok
regional conference, and will involve participants from the four tsunami-
affected countries. This is an example of a larger trend that reflects a pragmatic approach in collaboration between the two oldest and largest

international psychology associations, designed to maximize the impact on the discipline and region. It is a change in modus operandi, rather than a change in statutes or rules of governance.

The IUPsyS and IAAP have intensified the sharing of information, collaboration, and support in order to "give psychology away," and to work in tandem with other disciplines to improve the quality of life globally, not just provincially. A symbolic watershed was the establishment of the World Forum by Bernhard Wilpert, the then IAAP President, on the occasion of the ICAP in San Francisco in 1998. The understanding was that the World Forum would be co-chaired by the respective Presidents of the IUPsyS and IAAP and serve as a co-ordinating mechanism for the discipline across regional groupings and specialty areas at the international level. The World Forum has since become institutionalized at the ICAP and ICP. How much this venue will benefit the advancement of global psychology depends on the agendas and outcomes of future meetings.

The composition of the executive boards of IUPsyS and IAAP has seen an increase in the number of women, although the majority of board members are men and the positions of President and Secretary-General continue to be filled by men. There is a school of thought that this increase in female board membership may have helped in shaping the direction of both organizations toward more concerted efforts to engage psychologists from less advantaged countries into the network of global psychology. For example, over the past three decades, Çiğdem Kağitçibaşi of Turkey has been the most actively profiled female board member in both the IUPsyS and IAAP. More recently, Ingrid Lunt of the United Kingdom and Elizabeth Nair of Singapore were elected in the same cohorts to the Boards of the IAAP and IUPsyS in 1998 and 2000, respectively. Lunt took on the mantle of ARTS from John Adair in 2005, after co-coordinating the seminar series with him for 2 years, and now shares responsibility for ARTS with Heidi Keller of Germany. Nair became editor of the IAAP *Newsletter* in 2002, succeeding Lunt. With Ype Poortinga, she inaugurated the IUPsyS' national capacity-building workshop series, and was responsible for initiating and organizing the IUPsyS' Psychosocial Rebuilding in the Tsunami Aftermath Workshop in May 2005. These activities reflect the globally impactful contributions of a small but increasing number of women who hold leadership positions in international psychology organizations.

The size and physical barriers across the vast African continent have meant that the development of the discipline and profession of psychology has proceeded at a different pace and path depending on economic problems as well as conditions prevailing in specific countries. Studies of African populations that receive the most attention continue to be those published by visiting scholars whose main institutional affiliations are in countries outside of Africa. The MENA RCP, organized by the IUPsyS in 2003 in Dubai, was an initiative to facilitate the scientific development of the discipline and profession within the region; it grew out of a similar regional congress in Durban, South Africa that was organized by the IUPsyS in 1999. The IUPsyS, IAAP, and IACCP co-sponsored the MENA RCP. One of the much-lauded outcomes of this regional meeting was the decision by participants to establish a formal regional grouping of national psychology associations. The 2012 ICP, to be held in Capetown, South Africa, is likely to become a focus for national psychology associations across the African continent to collaborate. In the years leading up to this congress, there will be an impetus for African psychologists and national psychology associations to attend in order to have a say in the development of the discipline in their region of the world.

Two other international psychology organizations are worth mentioning at least briefly: the IACCP and the International Society for the study of Behavioral Development (ISSBD). The IACCP was founded in 1972 and has as its aim to facilitate communication among those interested in issues involving the intersection of culture and psychology. It has worked in close cooperation with the IUPsyS and IAAP over the years, holding its congresses in geographic and temporal contiguity so that its approximately 800 members could attend both congresses more conveniently if they wished to do so. The IACCP has also been a primary actor in the formation and support of ARTS workshops. The ISSBD aims to promote scientific research on human development throughout the life span. It publishes a journal six times a year as well as a substantial newsletter, and convenes a congress every other year. Membership, currently at about 1,500, is open to researchers from any scientific discipline who are interested in human development.

CURRENT TRENDS REFLECTED IN REGIONAL PSYCHOLOGY ORGANIZATIONS

Europe

The European Federation of Psychologists' Associations (EFPA) comprises 31 member associations and represents about 200,000 psychologists (Tikkanen, 2005b). Countries with the largest number of psychologists are Germany with 45,000, followed by Italy with 41,000, and France with 35,000 (Tikkanen, 2005b). The ratio of psychologists per inhabitant among EFPA member countries is 1:1,850, with Belgium, Croatia, Denmark, Iceland, and the Netherlands having a higher proportion of psychologists to population.

Contemporary trends in European psychology are reflected in documents that have been ratified and adopted by EFPA member countries, such as:

1. The EFPA Review Model for the description and evaluation of psychological tests.
2. A charter of professional ethics for psychologists.
3. Standards for professional training in psychology.
4. Training standards for psychologists specializing in psychotherapy.

The EFPA regional grouping could serve as a template for the Asia-Oceania Psychological Association and, possibly, other regional organizations in Africa and the Middle East. Each region is likely to have shared features as well as diversity. This duality is a product of historical events and processes that influence a region's orientation and cultural emphases, and has implications for the development of regionally homogeneous, yet richly varied research and application in clinical, personality, and social psychology. As a template for regional psychology groupings, the EFPA offers several elements that can be replicated elsewhere, such as the equivalence of professional qualifications and minimum standards for educational attainment and skills acquisition across countries. The rationale for professional equivalence and minimal competencies as a means of ensuring occupational mobility across countries should be highly persuasive. Furthermore, the process of broad-based consultation, collaboration, and active involvement among EFPA member states serves as a model for countries in other regions that seems likely to elicit participation.

North America

The APA, which had 82,190 full members and fellows, 2,414 high school and community college affiliates, 3,878 international affiliates, and 51,897 student affiliates in 2004, is currently the largest national association of psychologists in the world. With a full-time chief executive officer, offices, and permanent staff to provide membership services, the APA has acquired experience and expertise in public-policy advocacy protocols. For example, the APA's Council of Representatives has compiled a policy manual oriented toward global concerns and issues that includes actions taken over 40 years on such topics as human rights, psychiatric diagnosis and political dissent, and violence. The *Publication Manual* (American Psychological Association, 2001) is used in many countries around the world as the accepted standard for the preparation and formatting of manuscripts, research reports, books, theses and dissertations, and all manner of psychology publications. Over the years, the APA has been generous in its outreach to help develop the discipline and profession of psychology worldwide. Such generosity has included offering free access to its electronic database of published research (PsycINFO) and the provision of expert consultants (Editorial Mentor Program).

The APA has 54 Divisions (Divisions are labeled 1–56, but Divisions 4 and 11 no longer exist). Division 52 is International Psychology. Membership of Division 52 includes affiliate members, who pay divisional fees, but need not be full dues-paying members of the APA. Such affiliate members are likely to be psychologists from other countries, who have full membership in their respective national psychology associations. Affiliate membership enables the Division, and the APA, to globalize its orientation and agenda, with international colleagues eligible to join divisional committees and task forces and to collaborate on research presented at annual congresses. Division membership reached 1,000 in 2006.

One of the newest Divisions of the APA is the American Society for the Advancement of Pharmacotherapy. An impetus for launching this Division was the movement for training and legislation that would permit clinical psychologists to have limited prescriptive rights for patients under their care. There are currently 11 training programs in psychopharmacology for psychologists in the United States. In 2002, New Mexico became the first U.S. state to grant prescriptive privileges to specially trained psychologists. In 2004, Louisiana became the second such state to pass a similar law (Holloway, 2004). This parallels a slowly emerging global trend toward the authorization of psychologists as primary-care providers (Stevens & Wedding, 2004a). Although the exception, psychologists in such countries as China and Iran are loosely authorized as primary-care providers with limited prescription privileges. In these countries, psychologists are recognized as expert treatment providers, whose services are integral to illness prevention and health promotion.

Other Divisions of the APA that have a rich global agenda include the Society for the Psychological Study of Social Issues (SPSSI) and the Society for the Study of Peace, Conflict, and Violence (Peace Psychology). The SPSSI is an international group of over 3,500 psychologists, allied scientists, and students who share an interest in research on the psychological aspects of important social issues. The SPSSI brings theory and practice to bear on human problems of the group, community, and nation, as well as on the increasingly urgent global problems. Its activities include publication of the *Journal of Social Issues, Analysis of Social Issues and Public Policy*, and the SPSSI *Newsletter* as well as annual programming at the APA convention and SPSSI convention. Research on social issues is fostered through several award and grant programs. With NGO status, the SPSSI serves as consultant to the Economic and Social Council of the United Nations.

Peace Psychology works to promote peace throughout the world and within nations, communities, and families. It encourages psychological and multidisciplinary research, education, and training on issues concerning peace, nonviolent conflict resolution, reconciliation, and the causes, consequences, and prevention of violence and destructive conflict. Peace Psychology fosters communication among researchers, teachers, and practitioners who are applying psychological knowledge and methods not only to resolve and prevent conflict, but also to create positive social conditions that promote human well-being. A Division journal, *Peace and Conflict: Journal of Peace Psychology*, and newsletter are published regularly, and a web site has been established that contains syllabi, class assignments, and other instructional resources for those interested in promoting peace education through the curriculum (http://www. webster.edu/peacepsychology/ppresourceproject).

The Canadian Psychological Association (CPA) engages its membership in discussions of issues of general and specific interest by posting Discussion Documents on its web site. One example is the document posted by the Task Force on Empirically Supported Treatments in May 1998, an issue that has come to the forefront of professional psychology in North America. The CPA alerts its members by posting web links to government and policy reports that have a bearing on psychology-related topics. Thus, there is a web link to the Standing Senate Committee on Social Affairs, Science, and Technology (http://www.cpa.ca/SocialAffairs/) where one can find scientific reports and professional opinions that have been presented to legislators in an effort to inform them on such matters as national health-care policy.

The APA and CPA practice of deliberately seeking out and creating opportunities to impact public policy is the model that IAAP President

Michael Frese (2004) would like to see in operation on a global platform, including the presentation of relevant psychological research to policy-making bodies, such as the U.N. and World Health Organization. This niche is being addressed at present by North American psychology organizations, but the IUPsyS and IAAP are bidding to make available their own empirical research which is more globally representative in terms of sampling, data-gathering methods, and practical recommendations (see chapters 9 and 12 on the interface of psychology organizations and policy-making entities). This is important for face, content, and criterion validity, especially when the implementation of decisions made by governments and policy-making bodies might impact critically on end-users in developing countries (see chapters 4 and 9 on psychology and macro-level interventions in the majority world, respectively).

Latin America

The Interamerican Society of Psychology (SIP) is the largest and one of the most active psychology associations representing Central and South America, as well as the Caribbean. It includes members from the countries of this region, as well as from Canada and the United States, essentially, the entire Western hemisphere. SIP was founded in Mexico City in 1951, and has been influential in the development of psychology as a science and as a profession in the region.

Over the years, SIP has organized 30 congresses of psychology, which have convened in a majority of Latin-American countries, with each drawing several thousand participants. The most recent congress took place in Buenos Aires in 2005, and the next one will be in Mexico City in 2007. SIP publishes a scientific journal, *Revista Interamericana de Psicología/Interamerican Journal of Psychology*, with articles in Spanish, Portuguese, and English intended to promote the interface of psychologies and collaboration among psychologists of different countries in the Americas, along with a newsletter, *Psicologo Interamericano/Interamerican Psychologist*.

SIP has provided Latin-American psychologists with directions and guidelines for training in the science and practice of psychology as well as in capacity-building. SIP has also organized task forces that have exerted considerable influence on the evolution of specific areas of psychology in Latin America, including developmental psychology, educational psychology, experimental psychology, environmental psychology, health psychology, the history of psychology, I/O psychology, neuropsychology, and social/community psychology, among others. Noteworthy are recent efforts of the work group to establish a psychology of the Americas.

The Middle East

The Middle East Psychologists Network (MEPN) is a small, but promising organization for psychologists and mental-health professionals who are interested, hail from, and work in this distinct and diverse cultural region. The MEPN is endorsed and sponsored by the Association for Humanistic Psychology and Common Bond Institute. At present, the MEPN coordinates efforts to provide continuing education opportunities for its members. Periodically, announcements are posted on the MEPN's web site (http:// ahpweb.org/cbi/middle_psych.html) about research opportunities, employment, conferences, and specialized training. The MEPN is currently engaged in creating a set of by-laws as well as a regional code of ethics, standards for licensure, accreditation of psychology programs, and conferences. Although ambitious, the MEPN is likely to achieve its goals and grow in significance given the expectation that an indigenous Islamic psychology will become more firmly established in the region and across the Muslim world (Stevens & Wedding, 2004b). Furthermore, with the co-sponsorship of the MENA RCP, the MEPN is poised to provide national psychology organizations with a regional structure and organization for promoting capacity-building and addressing shared concerns (e.g., intergroup conflict).

CURRENT GLOBAL TRENDS

Several resources capture in different ways the contemporary trends in psychology manifested at global and regional levels. The first is the *Handbook of International Psychology* (Stevens & Wedding, 2004a), which examines the history of psychology, the education and training of psychologists, the scope of scientific and professional activity, and future challenges and prospects of the discipline in 27 countries across six continents. Another valuable resource is *Psychology: IUPsyS Global Resource* (Stevens & Wedding, 2006), a CD–ROM that contains not only articles on the origins and development of psychology in different parts of the world, but also numerous databases, including a global bibliography of psychological research and sets of abstracts and proceedings of research presented at past ICAPs and ICPs. Periodically, there are special issues of the *International Journal of Psychology* devoted to a review of national and regional trends in the discipline and in specialty fields. These resources are of enormous value to readers who wish to pursue in greater detail the general trends we outline later.

We now turn to four major global trends in psychology: the growth of psychology, the specialization of psychology, the feminization of psychology, and the emergence of contextually sensitive paradigms.

Growth of Psychology

Evidence for the growth of psychology around the world can be seen vis-à-vis two main indicators: the number of psychologists and psychology students and the number of psychology programs (Stevens & Wedding, 2004b).

Sexton and Hogan (1992) reported a massive increase in the number of psychologists throughout the world in the early 1990s. This trend continues (Stevens & Wedding, 2004b). For example, approximately 7,000 psychologists are listed in the registry of Israeli psychologists, a rise of more than 100% since the late 1990s. In South Africa, there are about 120 psychologists per million citizens, a 45% increase in over 10 years. Brazil predicts that 10,000 psychologists will enter the workforce annually. Even in industrialized countries, the growth of psychology continues. In the United Kingdom, the number of applicants admitted to psychology programs rose by 20% from the 2002 to 2003. However, the proportion of psychology graduates who find positions in the field can be quite low in some countries, reflecting the oversupply of graduates relative to those countries' needs and resources. This is especially evident in developing countries where psychology lags behind other disciplines seen as having greater value to society (Stevens & Wedding, 2004b; see chapter 4).

In developing countries in particular, the number of universities with psychology programs is growing. Thirty-two percent of the Philippines' 249 psychology programs were inaugurated in the last decade alone. In eastern Europe, many private universities have opened to meet the growing demand for training in psychology. In Russia, there are about 50 such institutions in Moscow and 30 in St. Petersburg, many of which seek to become accredited by the state.

Specialization in Psychology

Sexton and Hogan (1992) noted a trend toward psychological specialization, with each country's path toward specialization mirroring its own national needs and goals. Specialization in psychology can best be seen in the proliferation of and growing diversity within psychology organizations, formalized opportunities for training in disciplinary specialties, and access to advanced telecommunications (Stevens & Wedding, 2004b).

Japan has seen a rise in the number of specialties, with 38 psychological organizations attesting to the vigor of specialization, and a growing tendency toward dialogue among specialties, as manifested by joint membership within organizational divisions (e.g., clinical-forensics-personality-rehabilitation). The Chinese Psychological Society now has 15 committees, each representing a distinct field of psychology. Even in underdeveloped countries, psychological associations convene professionals from various specialties (e.g., Nigerian Association of Clinical Psychologists, Nigerian Association of Industrial-Organizational Psychologists).

Growing specialization is also reflected in the formalization of specialty training. In Russia, there are 15 paths to specialization accredited by the Ministry of Education (e.g., social adaptation management training). In 2002, the Indonesian Alliance of Psychologists established an agency to regulate training in psychological specialties. As specialization in psychology continues, so too has the codification of practice standards for specialists, particularly in instances in which a specialty is fairly well-established (Stevens & Wedding, 2004b).

Innovations in telecommunications have had a significant impact on specialization in psychology. Leading universities in most countries, including those in the majority world, are digitally wired, as are hospitals and psychology organizations, although to a lesser degree. The benefits of advanced telecommunications to psychologists include opportunities for specialization via distance-learning, access to recent scholarship in scientific and applied specialties (e.g., cognitive science and capacity-building), and avenues for networking with psychology organizations that represent specialized fields. Communications technology has its detractors, however. For example, Mexican psychologists are concerned that the Internet and World Wide Web are not equally accessible to psychologists around the world and that the gap in knowledge and skills between psychologists in industrialized countries versus less developed countries will widen (Sánchez-Sosa, 2004).

Feminization of Psychology

Consistent with Sexton and Hogan (1992), "psychology around the world tends to be a female occupation, in some cases dramatically so"

(p. 469). The feminization of psychology is reflected in a growing gender imbalance in the workforce, the higher proportion of female to male psychology students, and certain fields of specialization that have become increasingly dominated by women (Stevens & Wedding, 2004b).

In industrialized nations, women have become dominant in most, but not all settings in which psychologists work. In South Africa and Israel, women represent 60% and 70% of working psychologists, respectively. In Spain, 75% of registered psychologists are female. In the majority world, women also constitute the majority of psychologists; for example, women make up 60–70% of psychologists in Colombia. In fact, since the 1990s, the number of female psychologists has overtaken that of male psychologists in both Australia and South Africa. However, there are several nations in less developed and more culturally conservative regions (e.g., Africa, the Middle East) where psychologists tend to be male. For instance, 95% of psychologists in Nigeria are male and 65% of Egyptian psychologists are male.

In Western countries, the proportion of female undergraduates ranges from approximately 66% in the United States to 80% in Spain and 84% in the United Kingdom. Likewise, women comprise the vast majority of psychology students in developing countries, such as India. Even in the conservative Middle East, the number of women pursuing an undergraduate degree in psychology has risen. For example, in Egypt women earn two thirds of the baccalaureates in psychology. In Kuwait as well, a large percentage of the psychology majors are women. There, most female students consider psychology to be a good preparation for their later roles as wives and mothers, and they often do not wish to pursue graduate studies. Their B.A. degree already qualifies them for some professional positions.

Turning to graduate programs in psychology, women have been the majority for some time in the United Kingdom and recently became the majority in the United States. However, in spite of the number of female baccalaureates in various industrialized and less developed countries, relatively few women advance to graduate study. In Japan, 80% of the doctorates in psychology are awarded to men.

Although women hold a broad spectrum of jobs in diverse employment settings, traditional gender differences in specialization remain. More women work in clinics and schools, whereas more men fill positions in academia and in business and industry. This demarcation reflects the employment status of female psychologists in many countries, regardless of cultural affiliation or degree of industrialization. For example, in Australia, where the composition of the Australian Psychological Society is 72% female, far more men than women have attained the status of

Fellow, suggesting that men continue to be more dominant in academia. A similar pattern exists for male and female psychologists in Colombia. Such trends may also reflect cohort effects related to the increasing feminization of psychology. Whereas in previous generations, male psychologists were more likely to be elected to Fellow status, the chances for women in the current generation of psychologists to be elected as Fellows will increase in coming years.

Furthermore, female psychologists tend to earn less than their male counterparts, and are more likely to be employed part-time, as is the case in India and Spain. The preservation of traditional gender roles across culture and level of national development, characterized by an uneven division of domestic labor, makes it difficult for women to pursue careers in the same unfettered manner as men. Likewise, workplace discrimination is problematic for many female psychologists, who often cannot rely on institutionalized protections (Metzner, Rajecki, & Lauer, 1994).

Although psychology as an undergraduate and post-graduate major continues to attract more women than men, the glass ceiling in terms of the leadership of academic departments and schools of psychology remains firmly in place, with few exceptions (Heckel, 1972; Madden, 2005). The highest professional, administrative, and management positions in various fields of applied psychology are disproportionately filled by men. The cohorts of female psychologists in academic, research, and practice settings have to be content with being in second place. Unfortunately, the disproportionate underrepresentation of qualified women in top-level positions remains a low priority.

Contextually Sensitive Paradigms

Recognition of the culture-bound nature of Western psychology has led to paradigmatic shifts in many parts of the world. Psychologists representing many specialties have responded to calls for greater sensitivity, knowledge, and competence in studying and working with culturally diverse peoples. Two contemporary trends that are leading toward more culturally sensitive paradigms can be summarized as multiculturalism and indigenization (Stevens & Wedding, 2004b).

Psychologists, especially in heterogeneous and industrialized countries, increasingly realize that their activities are imprinted by a Western *emic* and, hence, have limited meaning and utility. Thus, in the United Kingdom psychology students study social constructionism, and in Germany psychologists are pressing for ethics codes that explicitly address the cultural context in which psychology is practiced. Canadian psychologists have begun to offer nontraditional interventions to diverse populations in novel settings. They draw upon strategies for problem resolution found in First Nations' cultures in designing and implementing interventions to help indigenous communities cope with changes in family life, the workplace, and the larger community as the ethnic and racial face of Canada evolves. Because Singapore is becoming more heterogeneous due to its commercial infrastructure and strategic location, the Singapore Psychological Society has been called upon to develop programs to orient practitioners to the needs of residents from distinct cultural and religious backgrounds.

Indigenous approaches to psychology have a rich history, especially in Asia and Mexico (see chapters 5 and 8 for more on the development of indigenous psychologies and their expression in psychotherapeutic methods, respectively). For decades, the National Association for Filipino Psychology has sought to indigenize conceptual, methodological, and applied dimensions of psychology. South African psychologists struggle to balance Western theories and techniques with indigenous knowledge and methods. For example, given the prevalence of Black-African healing traditions (e.g., divination, herbal remedies) and the dearth of rural practitioners, South African psychologists are considering the merits of including indigenous healers in the health care system. In research, qualitative inquiry has gained a foothold, as it does not require proficiency in English or familiarity with objective assessment.

Evidence for the indigenization of psychology can also be found in the less developed world (Stevens & Wedding, 2004b). For more than 15 years, the Society for the Advancement of Muslim Psychology in Pakistan has sought to develop an Islamic psychology based on the Koran and religious treatises. A course in Islamic Studies is now mandatory for undergraduates. Graduate courses on Islamic psychology have also been crafted that synthesize Islamic values with Western psychotherapies. For example, *Zikr Allah* is a meditative technique based on Sufi mysticism designed to alleviate stress. Indian psychology is also becoming more grounded in indigenous religious scripture. The psychology curriculum includes coursework on parapsychology and indigenous therapeutic methods (e.g., Yoga Nidra).

CURRENT REGIONAL TRENDS

We now examine significant trends in psychological science and practice that are taking place in four distinct regions of the world: Asia, Europe, Latin America, and Oceania.

Asia

The diversity of ethnicity and historical evolution in Asian countries is paralleled also by differences in the traditions in psychology that have become more entrenched in these distinct countries, perhaps reflecting a certain reaction toward the intrusion of globalization. The development of psychology in Japan and China has followed mainly the route of a laboratory tradition in cognitive and physiological psychology (Stevens & Wedding, 2005; Tanaka-Matsumi & Otsui, 2004; Yang, 2004). In other Asian countries, like India, Indonesia, and Thailand, the emphasis has been on more culturally based community and clinical intervention (Stevens & Wedding, 2004a). With more opportunities for collaboration across Asian countries, it is anticipated that there will be a concerted move toward empirically supported psychological research and practice.

East Asia.   Because of China's emerging dominance and the critical roles that China plays on the world stage, we have chosen to focus this section primarily, but not exclusively, on current trends in Chinese psychology. Chinese psychology is adopting a multifaceted approach to meet the demands of economic modernization and global interdependence. Since 1981, government support has created favorable conditions for education, research, and practice in psychology. Rather than applying Western models and interventions, Chinese psychologists embrace a multidisciplinary perspective and collaborate with economists, historians, and political scientists (Yang, 2004).

Researchers in organizational management examine how massive corporate transformation in China is influencing interorganizational relationships, opportunity structures and social processes, and individual behavior within companies (Tsui, Schoonhoven, Meyer, Lau, & Milkovich, 2004). Additional applied work is being carried out on three dimensions of managerial competency modeling that emphasizes a distinctly Chinese approach to theory development, methodology, human resources and management practices, socioeconomic perspectives around the world, the assessment of leadership qualities, person—job—organization fit, and organizational capacity for modernization and cultural adaptation (Wang, 2003). A wide range of studies in biopsychology is being conducted in China (Lin & Sui, 2004) on behavioral and physiological stress, the effects of conditioning on immunity, and long-term aspects of drug addiction. Similarly, cognitive neuroscientists in China are investigating neural mechanisms of perception, patterns of neural activity in selective attention, separating universal and language-specific aspects of linguistic processes, neural substrates of memory formation and learning, and disorders in cognitive brain functions (Zhou & Luo, 2003). Over the last 2 decades, developmental psychologists in China have focused heavily on studies of the cognitive development, language development, and socialization of children—only children—and aging, with trends toward greater indigenization in research methods and applications (Miao & Wang, 2003).

From Academia Sinica in Taiwan, Yang Kuo-Shu, Hwang Kwang-Kuo, and others (Yang, 1998, 2000; Yang, Hwang, & Yang, 2005) have been engaged for more than 3 decades in conceptual and empirical approaches to answering questions regarding the traditionalist–modernist evolution of the Chinese people. They argue for different theoretical approaches to be distinguished, and make a case for using quantitative methods with data collected from individuals, rather than adopting thematic, social constructionist methods (see Yang et al., 2005). Yang (2003) also persuades psychologists from other developing countries to heed the dynamic evolutionary aspect of their indigenous cultures.

Japan, with its 100-year history of scientific psychology, has the largest contingent of psychologists in East Asia. Over the last few decades, the number of Japanese psychologists has risen sharply—estimated at present to be 20,000—and research in and applications of all branches of psychology have widened (Oyama, Sato, & Suzuki, 2001). The Japanese Union of Psychological Associations, founded in 1999, coordinates the myriad activities of the nation's 38 diverse psychology organizations, the largest of which is the Association of Japanese Clinical Psychology (Oyama et al., 2001). Approximately one-third of Japanese universities have departments of psychology that educate students at least to the bachelor's degree (Tanaka-Matsumi & Otsui, 2004). In view of psychology's popularity among students and the general public, along with the need for more advanced degree holders, efforts are underway to expand and diversify the country's doctoral training programs. The scientist–practitioner model of training has been successfully imported to Japan from the United States, as has a growing call for evidence-based treatment. Although Japan has yet to establish a mechanism for licensing psychologists, psychologists follow the ethical guidelines crafted by the national organizations to which they belong; the growing specialization of Japanese psychology will likely generate more formal systems of credentialing (Tanaka-Matsumi & Otsui, 2004).

In academic research, Japanese developmental psychologists have produced a cornucopia of research, a substantial proportion of which is cross-cultural in design (Shwalb, Nakazawa, & Shwalb, 2005) and includes: patterns of mother–child interaction, language and concept development, leadership, and longevity and successful aging. Japanese comparative psychologists have collected laboratory and field data for over 50 years on chimpanzees at Kyoto University's Primate Research Institute that has shed light on the origins of human cognition and behavior as well as on the cultural transmission of knowledge (Tanaka-Matsumi & Otsui, 2004). Other strong research traditions are in cognitive neuroscience, engineering psychology, forensic psychology, the history of psychology, and learning.

Applied psychology in Japan has often developed in response to societal needs. For example, to combat school-refusal behavior and peer bullying, the Japanese Ministry of Education, Culture, Sports, Science, and Technology now places clinical psychologists in schools to counsel students and consult with teachers and parents (Tanaka-Matsumi & Otsui, 2004). Naikan and Morita therapies remain popular indigenous methods, with studies attesting to their suitability in remediating cultural manifestations of psychopathology, especially the social anxieties that seem to attend modern urban life in Japan.

South Asia. As already noted, Indian psychology today features a growing movement toward indigenization, based on religious scripture, which offers an alternative approach to understanding and implementing change at the individual and social levels (Stevens & Wedding, 2004b). Psychology has become popular among university students. The core curriculum is being standardized, indigenous topics integrated (e.g., parapsychology), and specialty training vocationalized. A wide range of specialties, whose research and practice agendas reflect the country's pressing social needs, increasingly characterizes psychology in India. These have been comprehensively reviewed in three volumes edited by Pandey (2000, 2001, 2004). There are two factors, however, that continue to limit the advancement of Indian psychology: (a) psychology organizations are often short-lived and ineffectual due to internal conflict and external competition, and (b) many female psychologists are so burdened by multiple roles that they lack time and energy for their careers.

Europe

Gilgen and Gilgen (1987) wrote about the gradual stagnation of European psychology by the late 1970s. The current revitalization of European psychology takes two forms: the renewal of psychology in western European countries that are member states of the European Union, and in eastern European countries that have transitioned from communism to alternative economic and political systems. Although the EFPA represents 200,000 professional psychologists via its member associations, the number of persons with training in psychology in the 31 EFPA nations (excluding Russia, Ukraine, and some other nations) is estimated to be 293,000, and throughout Europe is thought to be 310,000, making Europe the region with the largest number of psychologists worldwide (Tikkanen, 2005b).

Before proceeding, it is important to mention the significant contemporary trend toward the Europeanization of education and training in psychology. This trend extends across the East–West "divide," and reveals the extent to which the continent's identity is becoming more distant from U.S. influence as the European Community slowly, but surely expands (see chapter 10, this volume). More specifically, the Leonardo da Vinci program consists of 12 states that are homogenizing curricular requirements within and between countries into a common core curriculum, leading to the European Diploma (Tikkanen, 2005a). The program will be 6 years in duration and involve 3 years of undergraduate study, a 2-year post-graduate certificate, and 1 year of supervised practice. The intent is to make the requirements for licensure in psychology equivalent across Europe.

West Europe. Given that many developments and traditions in modern psychology originated in the German-speaking countries of Germany, Austria, and Switzerland (Gielen & Bredenkamp, 1997/2004; Plath & Eckensberger, 2004), it is fitting to emphasize the current status and future direction of the discipline and profession in these countries.

Cognitive psychology has long held the interest of German-speaking psychologists. Most research in this area has centered on the forms and functions of mental representations, memory, cognitive biases, the nature and separation of conscious and unconscious mental processes, intentional and goal-directed behavior, and decision making in complex situations (Hussy & Echterhoff, 1997/2004). Developmental psychology also has a rich tradition in German-speaking countries, with much prospective research on cognitive, moral, social, and self-concept development; developmental psychopathology; and cross-cultural comparisons

(Pinquart & Silbereisen, 1997/2004). All major stages of life have been investigated, including a number of groundbreaking studies of the cognitive and physical changes associated with normal aging. Social psychology in the German-speaking world has become rejuvenated, perhaps owing to the contributions of North American social psychologists. Topics on which German-speaking social psychologists have made internationally recognized contributions include attribution theory, conceptions of justice, processes of social interaction, and the formation of social judgements (Hormuth & Mathy, 1997/2004). Finally, in spite of diverse legal and regulatory procedures, clinical psychology remains the main professional field for psychologists in Germany, Austria, and Switzerland, with behavioral medicine and health psychology having had a significant impact on the practice of this specialty (Baumann, 1997/2004).

In sum, psychology in German-speaking countries is proceeding along two main lines: an orientation toward basic, multidisciplinary research that recognizes the complexity and situated nature of psychological phenomena and a growing orientation toward service in evermore broadly conceived domains of practice (Plath & Eckensberger, 2004; Stevens & Wedding, 2005).

The Scandinavian countries of Denmark, Norway, Sweden, and Finland are often seen as homogeneous, unified not only by their geographical proximity in North Europe, but also by similar languages (except for Finnish), shared historical and cultural traditions, similar political systems, and the high priorities placed on social welfare and egalitarian ideals (Lundberg, 2001). However, there are noteworthy variations in many disciplines, including psychology, in which subtle cultural differences, academic traditions, and strong personalities have determined the national course of psychology. The burgeoning research in Scandinavia reflects the demand for useful applications of psychological science in rapidly evolving societies. However, the focus and form of research in specific Scandinavian countries have differed. The strong experimental, cognitive, and neurobiological orientation of Finnish and Swedish psychology contrasts with the more phenomenologically and psychotherapeutically oriented psychology of Denmark and Norway (Lundberg, 2001).

Eastern Europe.   Since the fall of communism, eastern Europe has undergone unprecedented transformation, leading to the re-awakening of psychology. In Russia, there is rekindled interest in Pavlov, Bekhterev, and Vygotsky and the establishment of distinct academic departments that mirror the social needs of Russia today, as noted previously. During the period of *perestroika*, new regional psychology associations were established that had applied foci, mirroring the interest of psychologists in such areas as organizational consulting and psychotherapy. Some of these associations currently work with the government, NGOs, and the Orthodox Church to foster alternative approaches to the delivery of health-related services as well as the privatization of such services (Balachova, Isurina, Levy, Tsvetkova, & Wasserman, 2004). Russian psychologists are increasingly engaged in collaborative research with social scientists from other countries in such multidisciplinary areas as cognitive neuroscience. In addition to these lines of inquiry, Russian psychologists are conducting more applied research, including epidemiological studies, treatment–outcome studies, and prospective studies on the effectiveness of primary and secondary prevention programs, given the country's high incidence of alcoholism, delinquency, divorce, and suicide (Balachova et al., 2004).

Societal transformation in eastern Europe involves the interplay between economic and political forces and normative systems that regulate daily life. Following this perspective, social scientists and systems analysts at the University of Warsaw have developed computer simulations that map the slow, radiating course of macro-social change. Polish psychologists are conducting other socially relevant studies of the transitional process to a democratic free-market system (e.g., Korzeniowski, 2002). Predictions based on classical theories of authoritarianism have been confirmed through observations of an increased intensity of authoritarianism within Polish society, including demands for state benefits, which reflect the difficulty experienced by Poles in adjusting to rapid global change. Interest in the impact of societal transformation has also led German researchers to examine whether such change has weakened the social networks of families in the former German Democratic Republic (Nauck & Schwenk, 2001).

Latin America

In Latin America there are approximately 178,000 professional psychologists. In sheer numbers, this group forms a large portion of world's psychologists (Ardila, 2002). The leading countries are Brazil and Mexico, but important developments can also be seen in Argentina, Chile, Colombia, Peru, and Venezuela. Doctoral training programs have been established in several Latin-American countries, mainly in Brazil and Mexico, but also in other nations. The majority of psychologists are women, approximately 70%, although the male-to-female ratio varies from one nation to another.

Significant events in Latin-American psychology have taken place within the last 10 years (Pereira, 2005; Sánchez-Sosa, 2001). Beyond the safeguarding of the profession, Latin America has seen the rejuvenation of scientific and applied psychology, particularly in countries with healthy economies and political institutions (Stevens & Wedding, 2004b). Brazilian and Colombian psychologists are pioneering creative ways of unifying science and practice within the curriculum. Psychology textbooks published by Latin-American authors now balance national and international research. Brazilian psychologists are also leaders in translating and adapting psychometric measures into equivalent versions suited to Brazilian culture.

The current trends in Latin-American psychology are:

1. Scientific orientation. There is a great interest among psychologists in the scientific method. The pioneers of psychology in Latin America founded laboratories, did experimental research, and tried to organize psychology following the standards of the natural sciences. Today, psychology in Latin America is becoming significantly more empirical, objective, and quantitative, particularly in Brazil, Colombia, Mexico, and more recently, Argentina. For several decades, psychology in Argentina and Uruguay was based on psychoanalysis, and only recently have other orientations to psychology become part of training programs and professional practice.

2. Dependency. The use of imported models has characterized Latin-American psychology, especially in its early stages. Rationalism (Descartes), empiricism (Locke), and vitalism (Bergson) were the main doctrines imported by Latin-American psychologists.

3. Lack of originality. During the formative period, a number of imported theories, instruments, measures, and practices were at the core of Latin-American psychology. In recent decades, Latin-American psychologists have produced original work synthesizing history and culture into the mainstream biopsychosocial model of human functioning (Díaz-Guerrero, 1972).

4. Between social relevance and political activism. Psychologists are very aware of social issues, work on relevant social topics, and, in some cases, have proposed politically oriented alternatives (see Aron & Corne [1994] on Martin-Baró's liberation psychology).

5. Emphasis on applied psychology. Latin-American psychology gives special importance to practical work, particularly useful short-term applications in the educational and social fields.

6. Human beings at the center. Psychologists in Latin America work more with human participants than with animals. They are interested in describing, understanding, and predicting human behavior. Although there is important work being conducted in comparative psychology and psychobiology, the emphasis is on human participants.

These characteristics of psychology in Latin America are indicative of current trends. Applied research, using quantitative methods, is more frequent than basic research, or studies that involve qualitative methodology. Socially relevant work is highly valued. Although all areas of psychology are valued—from neuropsychology to community psychology and from the experimental analysis of behavior to cognitive science— probably clinical work in various settings is a more strongly established specialty than any other.

Psychology is a firmly grounded discipline and the work done by psychologists is highly esteemed within Latin-American countries. One of the negative aspects of Latin-American psychology is its isolation, its limited participation in international congresses, and the scarcity of publications in English. At the present time, worldwide participation is improving, but there is still a long way to go. Latin-American psychologists will eventually attain that delicate balance between *etic* and *emic*, between universal validity and local relevance. This will be a very important end result of the current trends just described.

Oceania

Physically distanced from Europe and North America, yet as part of the Commonwealth, psychology in Australia and New Zealand has followed essentially British traditions. As in the United States, licensing and registration of psychologists is state-based, rather than centralized, though there is a single Australian Psychological Society and a New Zealand Psychological Society, which are the national bodies representing the psychologists of these countries.

In 1988, the ICP was hosted in Sydney, Australia. The ICAP is scheduled to convene in Melbourne, Australia in 2010. Australian psychologists have registered their intention to be part of a regional network of psychologists, together with Asian psychologists. The Australian Psychological Society has participated at Asia–Oceania meetings held in Singapore in 1992, Guangzhou in 1993, Montréal in 1996, and again in Singapore in 2004. The Asia–Oceania Psychological Association is a regional grouping of national psychology associations from Australia, Hong Kong, India, Indonesia, Korea, Malaysia, New Zealand, Philippines, Singapore, and Taiwan, with other national psychology associations having recently expressed a desire to join. This association is still in its formative stage, and requires strong and focused leadership to become established as a formal and functional organization.

Psychology in Australia and New Zealand does not have a unique identity. As is true for all of Oceania, theory and practice derive from Europe and the United States (Stevens & Wedding, 2004b, 2006). However, in Australia, recent work with indigenous peoples has focused on community development, in which psychologists work with communities to enhance the skills and capabilities needed for the self-assessment of needs and for the development and delivery of services by the community to the community. A holistic model of wellness is viewed as best suited to this individual-within-community culture. In a related vein, Australian psychologists see themselves as having a regional if not a global active role. The Australian Psychological Society has had a long-standing interest group, Psychologists for the Promotion of World Peace, whose large membership remains involved in seeking to understand and resolve intergroup conflict.

Since the 1970s, academic departments in New Zealand have expanded typically to some 30 or more full-time faculty, representing all disciplinary specialties. Psychology departments at the Universities of Auckland, Canterbury, Otago, and the Victoria University of Wellington are known for conducting research on behavioral and cognitive neuroscience, clinical psychology, cognitive psychology, developmental psychology, sensation and perception, and social and cultural psychology, much like mainstream departments in other English-speaking countries (i.e., Canada, the United Kingdom, the United States). Massey University and the University of Waikato tend to emphasize more applied areas of psychology. Critical psychology and discourse theory have also developed strongly in some departments, especially at Auckland and Massey, and research based on Maori perspectives has emerged as a distinctive focus in some departments, notably at Waikato and Massey.

It is important to note that psychologists in Oceania have taken greater interest in the indigenous peoples, cultures, and psychologies of the neighboring South Pacific (Bolitho, Carr, & O'Reilly, 2002). In particular, psychologists are studying: the social issues promulgated by the unstoppable advance of globalization (e.g., the loss of cultural identity, urbanization, and disempowerment), the development of local psychologies based on a reactionary revival of group and cultural identity and reassertion of traditional values, and the construction and practice of both global and local repertoires whereby a melding of distinct yet complementary normative systems offer adaptive solutions to the complex realities of 21st century living.

CONCLUSION

A number of threads are discernable in the tapestry of current trends in global psychology. These include:

1. The popularity of psychology as a subject of choice in undergraduate programs continues to proliferate.
2. A majority of psychology undergraduates are female, with a few exceptions in African and Asian countries.
3. Positions of leadership in academic departments, research institutions, and international psychology associations continue to be held, with little exception, by males.
4. Psychologists in countries with a past or present Communist political regime (e.g., Poland and China) are beginning to publish their research more widely, with the rest of the world showing interest in their work.
5. Asian countries are beginning to take center stage in organizing large-scale international psychology congresses (e.g., China, Japan, Singapore).
6. Psychologists in the large Spanish-speaking world, most notably in Latin America, seek entry to the global arena of international dialogue in psychology. Their intent is constrained by the fact that English is the main language of international discourse.
7. The EFPA has provided a useful template for regional psychology groupings around the world. Africa and Asia–Oceania could use this model, emphasizing the membership and collaboration of all participating countries, with the objectives of establishing or maintaining high academic and professional standards as well as occupational mobility across countries in the region.
8. The U.S. has the largest financial resources of all national psychology associations. The APA has been generous in sharing knowledge, skills, and expertise with colleagues around the world.

As national psychology associations across the world move toward more collaborative work with each other, certain cautions must be remembered. Issues of cultural relativism in the interpretation of behavior, expression of emotions, and the case of the "ungrateful recipient of help" are points about which psychologists must be reminded, even in the very act of being collaborative across countries. Psychological reactivity and a response to perceived patronizing might lead to resentment and, eventually, rejection by recipient countries. The likelihood of such resentment would be especially likely when the offer is linked to research directives and practice agendas set outside of the country and not viewed as a priority by recipient countries. In the process of collaborating globally, there is a need for sensitivity to cultural differences and nuances. Drawing upon studies of effective intergroup relations, the importance of egalitarian patterns of communication and a valuing by all parties of the interaction itself cannot be overstated (van Dick et al., 2004).

Over generations, humankind has made many technological advances, ventured into outer space, plumbed the oceans, and studied microorganisms invisible to the eye, but it has not yet learned how to live amicably and at peace. The magnitude of this problem of coexistence ranges from the nuclear and extended family units to internal conflicts within nations and wars raged across geographic, ethnic, linguistic, and religious boundaries. With global networking across national psychology associations and regional psychology groupings, perhaps psychologists may yet be able to fashion and put to good use a template for facilitating and enhancing effective communication and interaction on a global scale. The workgroups under the aegis of IUPsyS and IAAP, given the composition of their membership and terms of reference, are well-positioned to take the lead in forging new collaborative global ventures.

RECOMMENDED READINGS

Ardila, R. (2002). *Psicología en América Latina, pasado, presente y futuro* [Psychology in Latin America, past, present, and future]. Mexico City: Siglo XXI.

Gielen, U. P., & Bredenkamp, J. (Eds.). (1997/2004). *World psychology: Special issue. Psychology in the German-speaking countries.* Online book available at http://www.iiccp.freeservers.com

Sexton, V. S., & Hogan, J. D. (Eds.). (1992). *International psychology: Views from around the world.* Lincoln: University of Nebraska Press.

Stevens, M. J., & Wedding, D. (Eds.). (2004). *Handbook of international psychology.* New York: Brunner-Routledge.

Stevens, M. J., & Wedding, D. (Eds.). (2006). *Psychology: IUPsyS global resource* [CD–ROM] (7th ed.). Hove, UK: Psychology Press.

REFERENCES

Adair, J. G. (2001). The first decade of ARTS: The Congress years 1992–2000. *International Journal of Psychology, 36*, 202–204.

Adair, J. G., & Lunt, I. (2005). Report on the Advanced Research and Training Seminars (ARTS) 2004. *International Journal of Psychology, 40*, 132–139.

American Psychological Association. (2001). *Publication manual* (5th ed.). Washington, DC: Author.

Ardila, R. (2002). *Psicología en América Latina, pasado, presente y futuro* [Psychology in Latin America, past, present, and future]. Mexico City: Siglo XXI.

Aron, A., & Corne, S. (Eds.). (1994). *Ignacio Martín-Baró: Writings for a liberation psychology*. Cambridge, MA: Harvard University Press.

Balachova, T., Isurina, G., Levy, S., Tsvetkova, L., & Wasserman, L. I. (2004). Psychology in Russia. In M. J. Stevens & D. Wedding (Eds.), *Handbook of international psychology* (pp. 293–309). New York: Brunner-Routledge.

Baumann, U. (1997/2004). Clinical psychology in the German-speaking countries. In U. P. Gielen & J. Bredenkamp (Eds.), *World psychology: Special issue. Psychology in the German-speaking countries* (pp. 146–165). Brooklyn, NY: St. Francis College, Institute for International and Cross-Cultural Psychology. Online book available at http://www.iiccp.freeservers.com

Bolitho, F. H., Carr, S. C., & O'Reilly, B. M. (Eds.). (2002). *Psychology in the South Pacific: Global, local and glocal applications. South Pacific Journal of Psychology* online book available at http://spjp.massey.ac.nz/books/bolitho/contents.shtml

Díaz-Guerrero, R. (1972). *Hacia una teoría histórico-bio-psico-socio-cultural del comportamiento humano* [Toward a historical-bio-psycho-socio-cultural theory of human behavior]. Mexico City: Trillas.

Frese, M. (2004). The President's report on the years 2002–2004. *International Association of Applied Psychology Newsletter, 16*(4), 1–8.

Gielen, U. P., & Bredenkamp, J. (Eds.). (1997/2004). *World psychology: Special issue. Psychology in the German-speaking countries*. Online book available at http://www.iiccp.freeservers.com

Gilgen, A. R., & Gilgen, C. K. (Eds.). (1987). *International handbook of psychology*. New York: Greenwood.

Heckel, R. V. (1972). Trends in the selection of psychology heads: 1946–1970. *American Psychologist, 27*, 226–230.

Holloway, J. R. (2004). Louisiana grants psychologists prescriptive authority [Electronic version]. *Monitor on Psychology, 35*(5). Retrieved July 11, 2005, from http://www.apa.org/monitor/may04/louisianarx.html

Hormuth, S. F., & Mathy, M. (1997/2004). Social psychology in Germany. In U. P. Gielen & J. Bredenkamp (Eds.), *World psychology: Special issue. Psychology in the German-speaking countries* (pp. 130–145). Brooklyn, NY: St. Francis College, Institute for International and Cross-Cultural Psychology. Online book available at http://www.iiccp.freeservers.com

Hussy, W., & Echterhoff, G. (1997/2004). Cognitive psychology in the German-speaking countries. In U. P. Gielen & J. Bredenkamp (Eds.), *World psychology: Special issue. Psychology in the German-speaking countries* (pp. 64–102). Brooklyn, NY: St. Francis College, Institute for International and Cross-Cultural Psychology. Online book available at http://www/iiccp.freeservers.com

International Association of Applied Psychology. (2004). *Constitution of the International Association*. Retrieved July 10, 2005, from http://www.iaapsy.org/

International Union of Psychological Science. (2004). *Statues and rules of procedure*. Retrieved July 10, 2005, from http://www.am.org/iupsys/information/statuteseng.html#rules

Korzeniowski, K. (2002). Authoritarianism in Poland in the years of transformation 1990–1997 [Abstract]. *Polish Psychological Bulletin, 33*, 31–38.

Lin, W., & Sui, N. (2004). Biopsychology research in China. *International Journal of Psychology, 38*, 311–322.

Lundberg, I. (2001). Zeitgeist, Ortgeist, and personalities in the development of Scandinavian psychology. *International Journal of Psychology, 36*, 356–362.

Madden, M. E. (2005). 2004 Division 35 Presidential Address: Gender and leadership in higher education. *Psychology of Women Quarterly, 29*, 3–14.

Merenda, P. F. (1995). International movements in psychology: The major international associations of psychology. *World Psychology, 1*, 27–48.

Metzner, B. S., Rajecki, D. W., & Lauer, J. B. (1994). New majors and the feminization of psychology: Testing and extending the Rajecki-Metzner model. *Teaching of Psychology, 21*, 5–11.

Miao, X., & Wang, W. (2003). A century of Chinese developmental psychology. *International Journal of Psychology, 38*, 258–273.

Nauck, B., & Schwenk, O. G. (2001). Did societal transformation destroy the social networks of families in East Germany? *American Behavioral Scientist, 44*, 1864–1878.

Oyama, T., Sato, T., & Suzuki, Y. (2001). Shaping of scientific psychology in Japan. *International Journal of Psychology, 36*, 396–406.

Pandey, J. (Eds.). (2000). *Psychology in India revisited — Developments in the discipline: Vol. 1. Physiological foundation and human cognition*. Delhi, India: Sage.

Pandey, J. (Eds.). (2001). *Psychology in India revisited — Developments in the discipline: Vol. 2. Personality and health psychology*. Delhi, India: Sage.

Pandey, J. (Eds.). (2004). *Psychology in India revisited — Developments in the discipline: Vol. 3. Applied social and organizational psychology*. Delhi, India: Sage.

Pereira, M. E. (2005). A timeline of psychological ideas. In M. J. Stevens & D. Wedding (Eds.), *Psychology: IUPsyS global resource* [CD–ROM] (6th ed.). Hove, UK: Psychology Press.

Pinquart, M., & Silbereisen, R. K. (1997/2004). Current research in German developmental psychology. In U. P. Gielen & J. Bredenkamp (Eds.), *World psychology: Special issue. Psychology in the German-speaking countries* (pp. 103–118). Brooklyn, NY: St. Francis College, Institute for International and Cross-Cultural Psychology. Online book available at http://www.iiccp.freeservers.com

Plath, I., & Eckensberger, L. H. (2004). Psychology in Germany. In M. J. Stevens & D. Wedding (Eds.), *Handbook of international psychology* (pp. 331–349). New York: Brunner-Routledge.

Ritchie, P. L.-J. (2005). *Annual Report of the International Union of Psychological Science (IUPsyS) to the International Council for Science (ICSU)*. Retrieved July 10, 2005, from http://www.am.org/iupsys/archive/2004-anrep.pdf

Sánchez-Sosa, J. J. (2001). Psychology in Latin America: Historical reflections and perspectives. *International Journal of Psychology, 36*, 384–394.

Sánchez-Sosa, J. J. (2004). Psychology in Mexico: Recent developments and perspective. In M. J. Stevens & D. Wedding (Eds.), *Handbook of international psychology* (pp. 93–107). New York: Brunner-Routledge.

Sexton, V. S., & Hogan, J. D. (Eds.). (1992). *International psychology: Views from around the world.* Lincoln: University of Nebraska Press.

Shwalb, D. W., Nakazawa, J., & Shwalb, B. J. (2005). *Applied developmental psychology: Theory, practice, and research from Japan.* Greenwich, CT: Information Age Publishing.

Stevens, M. J., & Wedding, D. (Eds.). (2004a). *Handbook of international psychology.* New York: Brunner-Routledge.

Stevens, M. J., & Wedding, D. (2004b). International psychology: A synthesis. In M. J. Stevens & D. Wedding (Eds.), *Handbook of international psychology* (pp. 481–500). New York: Brunner-Routledge.

Stevens, M. J., & Wedding, D. (Eds.). (2006). *Psychology: IUPsyS global resource* [CD-ROM] (7th ed.). Hove, UK: Psychology Press.

Tanaka-Matsumi, J., & Otsui, K. (2004). Psychology in Japan. In M. J. Stevens & D. Wedding (Eds.), *Handbook of international psychology* (pp. 193–210). New York: Brunner-Routledge.

Tikkanen, T. (2005a). *Report on the European Diploma (EuroPsy) and the future of the profession in Europe.* Retrieved June 2, 2005, from http://www.efpa.be/start.php

Tikkanen, T. (2005b). *The present status and future prospects of the profession of psychologists in Europe.* Retrieved July 5, 2005, from http://www.efpa.be/news.php?ID=12

Traffic and Transportation Psychology: Division XIII. (2000). *Traffic and Transportation Division: Aims and rules.* Retrieved July 10, 2005, from http://www.surrey.ac.uk/Psychology/ Traffic_Psychology/#G

Tsui, A. S., Schoonhoven, C. B., Meyer, M. W., Lau, C. M., & Milkovich, G. T. (2004). Organization and management in the midst of societal transformation: The People's Republic of China. *Organization Science, 15,* 133–144.

van Dick, R., Wagner, U., Pettigrew, T. F., Christ, O., Wolf, C., Petzel, T., Castro, V. S., & Jackson, J. S. (2004). Role of perceived importance of intergroup contact. *Journal of Personality and Social Psychology, 87,* 211–227.

Wang, Z.-M. (2003). Managerial competency modeling and the development of organizational psychology: A Chinese approach. *International Journal of Psychology, 38,* 323–334.

Yang, K.-S. (1998). Chinese responses to modernization: A psychological analysis. *Asian Journal of Social Psychology, 1,* 75–97.

Yang, K.-S. (2000). Monocultural and cross-cultural indigenous approaches: The royal road to the development of a balanced global psychology. *Asian Journal of Social Psychology, 3,* 241–263.

Yang, K.-S. (2003). Methodological and theoretical issues on psychological traditionality and modernity research in an Asian society: In response to Kwang-Kuo Hwang and beyond. *Asian Journal of Social Psychology, 6,* 263–285.

Yang, K.-S., Hwang, K.-K., & Yang, C.-F. (Eds.). (2005). [Chinese indigenous psychology] (Vols. 1–2). Taipei: Yuanliu Publishing.

Yang, Y. (2004). Advances in psychology in China. In M. J. Stevens & D. Wedding (Eds.), *Handbook of international psychology* (pp. 179–191). New York: Brunner-Routledge.

Zhou, X., & Luo, Y. J. (2003). Cognitive neuroscience in China. *International Journal of Psychology, 38,* 299–310.

4

Theory, Research, and Practice in Psychology in the Developing (Majority) World

Juan José Sánchez-Sosa and Angélica Riveros
National Autonomous University of Mexico

INTRODUCTION

The purpose of this chapter is to explore the current conditions in developing countries that mediate the activities performed by psychologists, as such conditions intersect with the overarching process of globalization. The chapter first addresses conventions regarding such terms as *developing* or *underdeveloped*. We then review some of the implications of globalization for the development of psychology in countries, and we describe the effects of national underdevelopment on the main activities by psychologists, including research, education and training, and professional practice, among others. We also present a set of descriptive data on the areas of the discipline and profession that are addressed by psychologists in developing countries, as reflected in publications generated during the last five years. The chapter concludes with a list of recommendations for psychologists from developed nations aimed at supporting the progress of psychology in less developed countries.

GLOBALIZATION OF PSYCHOLOGY

Although academic psychologists have long valued the benefits of maintaining international ties with colleagues at universities and research institutions (e.g., Holtzman, 1970), it is perhaps only in the last 20 years that most psychology organizations have expressly adopted initiatives to establish systematic communication with psychologists and associations in other countries in order to pursue common goals (Friedlander, Carranza, & Guzman, 2002; see chapters 2 and 3). This relatively recent interest seems to have grown not only from the attention given by the media to the general phenomenon of globalization (initially linked to trade relations and digital communications), but also from a perceived need that psychology as a discipline and profession would benefit from integrating theories, research methods, and applications used in other countries, including those in the so-called developing world.

Some psychology organizations have, from their very foundation, adopted a core global scope of action, as is true of the International Union of Psychological Science, the International Society of Clinical Psychology, the Interamerican Society of Psychology, and the International Association of Applied Psychology, to cite a few. In practically all organizations of this kind, a key purpose is the promotion of mutual knowledge and collaboration on research and, to a lesser extent, practical applications as well as the education and training of future psychologists. It was perhaps the proliferation of regional trade agreements during the 1990s that paved the way for further attention to the potential benefits of establishing or strengthening communication and exchange among various professionals, including psychologists, as was the case with the North America Free Trade Agreement (Sánchez-Sosa, 2002).

How is Globalization Beneficial for Psychology?

Human psychological functioning, including its key components— behavior, cognition, affect, and to a lesser extent physiology—receive constant and strong influences from learning and culture through interaction with other human beings and with the surrounding environment. Such interaction has a wide variety of modalities and, therefore, ways to affect human functioning, depending upon such factors as geography, language, culture, etc. (Mays, Rubin, Sabourin, & Walker, 1996; see chapter 5, in this volume for more on indigenous approaches to understanding the person-in-context). The effect of human interaction is an outgrowth of exchanges that take place in the context of specific social norms and regulations (e.g., childrearing) (chapter 6 in this volume offers a more complete analysis of the normative bases of behavior and experience). Thus, behavior becomes the main instrument through which humans negotiate life at every level, from minimal daily chores and routines to life's major challenges, threats, and transitions. Since the principles and mechanisms involved in the regulation of human behavior are germane to both the natural and social sciences, psychologists have become the leading authority on human functioning and experience. Psychologists worldwide carry out two main tasks: discovering and understanding the principles and mechanisms of human behavior, and modifying human interaction in order to solve socially relevant problems in such areas as health, education, and work (Connolly, 1985). On the one hand, psychology will be hard pressed to achieve these aims within an ever growing global context unless psychologists strive for a more systematic and multidirectional dialogue ranging from the natural principles and mechanisms thought to affect human functioning to the regulation of professional practice. On the other hand, no one discipline or profession can become truly global if it ignores its status, progress, and challenges in what currently constitutes the majority of nations in the world, known as developing countries.

Mere knowledge of the scientific and professional advances of psychology worldwide, however, is not likely to generate the dynamic and productive exchanges needed for the mutual benefit of psychologists from diverse world regions. Psychologists outside the developed world publish thousands of articles and books every year, and there are numerous psychology journals with the word *international* in their title. More collaborative training and research by psychologists from both developed and developing countries that target areas of shared interest and concern would lead to a genuine transnational cross-fertilization of psychological ideas and methods—a point repeated throughout this book. In fact, one additional challenge to the globalizing of psychology lies in the establishment of comparable education and training curricula that would eventually expand geographic mobility, be it academic or professional (Ardila, 2004; Landerholm, Gehrie, & Hao, 2004; see chapter 10 of this volume).

WHAT IS A "DEVELOPING" COUNTRY?

There are probably as many ways to define *developing* or *underdeveloped* as there are conceptions of national development within such disciplines as economics, political science, and sociology. In terms of national development and the advancement of psychology as science or profession, at least two general ideas might help in categorizing countries as either *developed* or *developing*. One stems from the formal classification scheme used by international organizations as the U.N. For instance, the World Health Organization (WHO) uses epidemiological data on mortality rates to divide countries into *developed* (i.e., with low mortality rates) or *developing* (i.e., having high mortality rates). This classification allows for some in-between and transitional groupings, like "developing with low rates," such as Cuba or Mexico (World Health Organization, 2004). Although this definition of *developing* may have limitations, it may also decrease the conceptual risks of adopting other more commonplace definitions, such as Domestic Product (GDP) or Annual Per-Capita Income. The main problem with these definitions is that they convey little more than gross averages, which hardly characterize the actual conditions experienced by a vast majority of the inhabitants of a nation. A country with a relatively high GDP may still have profound inequalities in socioeconomic conditions (e.g., access to basic services).

A second way to establish a distinction regarding the progress of psychology might involve an inspection of psychologists' scholarly productivity vis-à-vis international databases. Although somewhat more arbitrary, this second option would help to estimate the national and regional outlines of scientific and applied activities by psychologists. An examination of the specific characteristics of full-text publications by psychologists from all or most developing countries would prove a daunting data-collection task that could well take years, in addition to requiring a well-funded multilingual team. There is, however, an excellent update on contemporary developments and challenges to the future of psychology in a recent book edited by Stevens and Wedding (2004), which contains contributions by distinguished psychologists from 27 countries representing all levels of social and economic development.

In this chapter we adopt a combination of the two options just described by first using the WHO classification, then grouping countries along agreed upon geographical regions of the world, and finally examining the titles and abstracts of publications in psychology in the PsycINFO database maintained by the American Psychological Association (APA). This exploratory data set is presented in Tables 4.1 through 4.6. From the outset, it is clear that this approach may hold the risk of overlooking some potentially significant contributions by psychologists in developing countries. However, the use of finer-grained strategies would demand considerable time and resources, and would be more appropriate for projects aimed at analyses of specific lines of contemporary scientific and applied research. Finally, since the scope of the present chapter does not include a long-term historical perspective, the published literature included in the exploratory data covers only the last five years.

A broad spectrum of countries might be viewed as *developing*, we wish to emphasize. This may explain why some of them evince more scientific and professional activity than others. Clearly, the socioeconomic conditions that affect the work of psychologists in China and Turkey are more nearly those of many industrialized countries, as opposed to the conditions that exist in the poorer countries of Africa and Southeast Asia. But, economic and social conditions explain only part of the variance in psychology's presence in the majority world. An argument can be made for a relationship between cultural factors (e.g., ethnicity, language, and religion) and the state of psychology in developing countries. That is, some countries, although poor, are culturally European or semi-European (e.g., Argentina, some former Soviet republics); this has implications for the cultural acceptance of psychology, how long psychology has existed as a discipline and profession, and its future prospects. In a nutshell, psychology's ability to thrive in the developing world is determined by a complex network of interacting variables, including economics, culture, and many others yet to be identified.

WHAT DOES "DEVELOPING" MEAN IN TERMS OF PSYCHOLOGISTS' WORK?

Attempting to establish formal agreement on all of the elements that comprise a definition of *developing* and *underdeveloped* may prove far more difficult than actually describing the typical conditions under which psychologists work in such countries and the ways in which varying levels of national development affect their scientific or professional output. Scarcity of resources, facilities, and suitable working conditions are the most obvious characteristics of national underdevelopment (Leung & Zhang, 1995). Other limitations to the advancement of psychology in developing countries stem more from peculiarities of their political or administrative systems than from a lack of basic resources. For example, the statutory structure and policies of some universities include such conditions as heavy teaching loads with no sabbatical leave and administrative committees that give little or no credit for research when considering salary and promotions. In other cases, there are more pervasive conditions that impede psychologists' work. For example, inadequate networking among psychologists may result in continued dependence on psychology from developed countries even when there are scholars and practitioners in the same region working on topics of shared interest (e.g., health). There also may be a certain degree of self-imposed disciplinary isolation among psychologists who reject outside influence in the name of indigenization (e.g., the Philippines) or operate under invasive political or religious ideologies (e.g., Cuba; Stevens & Wedding, 2004).

Given these realities, we attempt in the following section to describe some of the most frequent problems as identified through numerous informal accounts by colleagues from developing countries at conferences of psychology.

Access to Information

One of the most direct effects of limited resources is restricted access to scientific or professional information, which in turn decreases the visibility of the scientific and social problems in developing countries and the potential solution to those problems (Sluzki, 2004). For decades, it has been rare to find in a department or school of psychology at a university outside of the developed world a periodical section of a library with complete collections of diverse journals. Finding complete collections and a continuous subscription to such journals remains almost unheard of and represents a serious obstacle to the dissemination of psychological knowledge. One of the most common experiences of a faculty member working on a research study or a student working toward a thesis is to search a journal issue only to find that the library's subscription has been cancelled due to budgetary problems. Furthermore, the availability of specialized books in university libraries is frequently limited to titles that pertain to specific courses or projects. Faculty and students at many public universities are left with few options other than pooling their resources to purchase books themselves. Professors who are financially able to pay for journal subscriptions from their own pockets remain a very small minority.

Sometimes the only choice open to faculty, students, and practitioners is to use what is available, which usually means relying on incomplete and outdated conceptual, empirical, and applied literature as the basis of a research proposal or professional project (Gopal, 1995). Another possibility is to resort to locally published or unpublished sources, which were produced under the same adverse conditions. Perhaps the most creative option, although not necessarily the most frequent, is to contact a colleague from a developed country and request support or assistance. In such cases, the professor or student must be relatively fluent in a foreign language, most likely English. Usually such contacts receive attention and a good response. In the best of circumstances, the exchange could lead to joint projects or the launching of a new program at the university in the developing country. In other cases, the exchange might provide useful feedback in updating the curriculum, thus strengthening a training program, provided that the initiative receives ongoing support by an enthusiastic benefactor with resources.

As can easily be imagined, poor access to scientific or professional information is likely to affect both the quality and quantity of the research or professional activity carried out by psychologists in developing countries. One additional complication of this situation is that it contributes to a vicious cycle. If psychological research and practice in a country are not of good quality, then they are not likely to solve pressing social problems in that country. Thus, psychology and psychologists are liable to be seen as ineffective by governmental agencies or NGOs, by the media, and by the general public. In time, this may lead to smaller allocations of resources and fewer employment opportunities. In addition, the chances that research produced under such conditions will make significant contributions to the global body of psychological knowledge are slim, further diminishing interest and attention from abroad.

The digital communications and Internet boom of the 1980s and 1990s was expected to alleviate many of the aforementioned deficits in developing countries. Although this has been the case to some degree, thanks in part to access to full-text publications in some databases, recent top-flight publications are still extremely expensive and difficult to obtain by academicians, students, and practitioners in many developing countries, especially at public universities and institutions (Sánchez-Sosa, 2004). Some have argued that the digital divide between the industrialized and developing worlds has actually widened, and that advanced telecommunications have encouraged the further Americanization of psychology worldwide (Stevens & Wedding, 2004). In addition, the benefits of having access to specialized information assumes that the user has command of the language in which is it written—typically English. It should be remembered that widespread low levels of formal education, including facility with foreign languages, is a characteristic of national underdevelopment, except perhaps in countries where foreign tourism has long represented such a vital source of income that learning a foreign language is relatively commonplace.

Equipment and Facilities

Another aspect of national underdevelopment with direct implications for the work of psychologists, be it scientific or applied, is the availability of basic equipment, facilities, and work conditions, usually taken for granted in developed countries. Equipment and facilities have an obvious bearing on the possibility of conducting high quality work, particularly if psychologists are not expected or able to invest the effort in finding alternate means to carry out their work. Some examples of much-needed items include laboratory equipment, measurement devices, photocopiers, computers, printing facilities, and audiovisual aids (Agboola & Lee, 2000). Some office or teaching settings even grapple with the lack of such basic supplies as printing paper, ink or toner, pens and pencils, rulers, paper clips, and staplers. Frequent interruptions in electricity and the lack of running water in labs and rest rooms are among the conditions that tend to occur only occasionally outside the developing world, but can be chronic in countries with very depressed economies.

Conditions in applied settings, such as health care facilities, also serve to exemplify the specific demands encountered by psychologists (Crane & Carswell, 1992). A frequent difficulty encountered by researchers, interns, and practicum students in public and sometimes in private hospitals stems from limited space, leading to uncomfortable or even unsafe occupancy ratios. Since psychologists have not yet achieved the same level of professional recognition as physicians, it is rare to find psychologists who have been assigned specific, let alone exclusive, space to administer interventions, collect data, or supervise trainees. It is safe to assume that at least some published research by psychologists in developing countries conducted in such settings involved collecting data in hallways and waiting rooms. In addition, if data collection involves taking measures of such variables as blood pressure, the number of available sphygmomanometers (or any other sophisticated measuring device) is likely to extend or delay data-collection schedules (Mariko, 2003). Thus, a data set, which was to be completed in a reasonable amount of time, may well take much longer to obtain. By the same token, similar conditions are likely to prevail in schools, factories, and other research or applied settings where psychologists in developing countries work (Ahasan, Campbell, Salmoni, & Lewko, 2001). Imaginative readers will probably have little difficulty visualizing examples of how shortages of resources and an inadequate infrastructure affect the work of psychologists in these and other settings.

Research Funding

There is wide variability in the developing world in terms of the sources and the amount of funding for research in psychology. A detailed account of specific sources, criteria for the approval of grant proposals, and the current status of research funding within specific areas of psychology in over 40 so-called less developed countries is beyond the scope of this chapter. However, there seem to be commonalities regarding the socioeconomic conditions that give rise to certain research priorities and trends in organizational policies and procedures that characterize the interaction between funding agencies and research-oriented institutions, such as universities (Bauserman, 1997).

One characteristic of funding for scientific research in developing countries is the narrow array of funding agencies. Developing countries frequently have rather centralized governments with cabinet-level administrators in charge of education, science, and professional practice. Typically, a branch of the Ministry of Education administers nationwide research policies and funding programs. Since most governmental decisions in these countries are usually made within an economic reality of limited wealth and small budgets, scientific research is rarely high among national priorities (Fouche & Louw, 2002).

Most developing countries share such problems as: uneven and incomplete educational coverage (sometimes even at the elementary level), low agricultural and industrial capacity and production, the need to import goods produced abroad (which must be paid for with hard currencies), a highly uneven distribution of wealth, unacceptable levels of poverty, deteriorating or obsolete infrastructure, widespread and pressing health concerns, and varied levels of political and social unrest. In addition, some countries face disadvantageous conditions linked directly to their geographical location, such as widespread desert in portions of North Africa and the Middle East, relatively infertile or hard-to-work mountainous land in the South American Andes, or disaster-vulnerable coastlines in some countries of Southeast Asia.

In this context, even when research becomes an acknowledged national necessity, priorities tend to revolve around topics that are closely related to economic growth and production and the fulfillment of immediate social needs. In principle, when health and education are considered part of a developing country's research priorities, psychologists in such a country would stand a chance to compete successfully for funding. As it frequently occurs, however, in many developing countries psychology is a relatively new discipline and profession. Since psychologists tend to be fewer in number and have lower status than physicians or educators in both governmental and academic institutions, research funds earmarked for the social sciences may be channeled to support projects in other disciplines (Swartz, Tomlinson, & Landman, 2004). In addition, it is only in the last two decades that some developing countries—for instance Greece, South Africa, Turkey, and a few others in Latin America, Asia, and the Middle East, include at least one psychologist on committees that review grant proposals in the social sciences. Finally, there is always the possibility, though rare, that final decisions on funding will be made by officials with overriding political agendas, sometimes in contradiction to the terms outlined by the call for grant proposals.

Another typical characteristic of research grants in developing countries is their small size. A formally established ceiling for grant proposals is often stated from the outset in calls for proposals. For example, in Latin America it is customary at the two largest public research-funding institutions in Mexico—the National Council for Science and Technology and the National Autonomous University—to establish a ceiling equivalent to $19,000 USD per year. Larger grants are considered "special," and tend to be awarded to projects in certain areas or lines of research. Also, depending on the incidence of periods of severe financial hardship, researchers sometimes obtain official responses from funding agencies stating that, although the review committee approved a grant proposal based on the significance and methodological rigor of the project, monies were deferred because of a scarcity of resources generally. These times of severe hardship are usually declared by governments through their ministries as soon as the economy's relevant indices signal further constraints in resources, thus pointing to the need to fund only programs that directly address pressing national priorities.

Thus, public funding for research in psychology in developing countries is another potential source for a vicious cycle. Since funds for research are especially tight and tend to go to other disciplines, the possibilities that sound research projects by psychologists will lead to solid and well recognized publications are slim. In turn, this will likely slow the rate at which psychology as a science and profession grows and receives recognition in the public and private sectors, both within a given country and internationally (Díaz-Loving, Reyes-Lagunes, & Díaz-Guerrero, 1995). This outcome, then, will further diminish the chances that new grant proposals will receive funding. And, so on.

Other funding options for psychological research in developing countries include grants from international foundations and programs (see chapter 12, this volume, for other sources of funding for international work in psychology). Several branches of the U.N., such as UNESCO, UNICEF, and WHO, and organizations like the International Social Sciences Council, among many others, regularly publish calls for grant proposals within their domain of activity. One interesting feature of many such calls is that they emphasize research in developing countries. Also, some private foundations such as the Ford Foundation, McArthur Foundation, the German Volkswagen Stiftung, and the Dutch Bernard van Leer Foundation, reserve space for proposals from social scientists, including psychologists from the developing world. Most private foundations have specific provisions in their charters regarding the type of areas or projects that are eligible for funding (e.g., child development projects in poor countries). It is frequently up to the creativity of psychologists from developing countries to draft proposals that intersect with at least one of these areas without giving the impression of forcing "a square peg into a round hole."

One additional possibility through which psychologists from developing countries can sometimes obtain research funding stems from personal exchange arrangements, in which a researcher from a developed country spends, for instance, a sabbatical leave at an institution in a developing country as part of an already-funded project. The choice of country by the recognized scientist may be based on reasons other than the development of psychology in the host country or a specific line of inquiry. The visit might be related to an agreed upon project that grows out of a long-standing personal relationship between colleagues. Sometimes this type of arrangement nets an improvement in the status and scientific progress of psychology in a developing country, provided that the stay entails some systematic effort at scientific capacity building.

Education and Training

University programs that train professional psychologists are probably as varied in the developing world as those in more developed countries (Burgess et al., 2004). However, although diversified by historical and socioeconomic conditions, the professional education and training of psychologists in the developing world shows some commonalities, probably attributable to two circumstances. First, the link between research and application has made its way into most professional training programs. Indeed, there are very few psychologists today who would contest the notion that applied interventions designed to solve socially relevant problems are effective to the degree that they are grounded in natural principles and mechanisms discovered and reconfirmed through basic psychological research.

Second, the types of socially relevant problems, which often involve human behavior as a key ingredient, tend to be very similar in most developing countries because many of them reflect a common scarcity of resources and inadequate infrastructure. Three examples follow: health, education, and business and industry. Although these topics are also of major interest to researchers and practitioners in industrialized nations, the foci differ (e.g., in the case of health, psychologists in developing countries are concerned more about arresting the spread of communicable diseases than in promoting healthy lifestyles).

Health. In the area of health, many developing countries still suffer the economic and social consequences of high incidences of communicable diseases, especially among young children and the elderly. Although it has been known for a long time that these diseases are related to the availability of sanitary conditions, psychological research has also shown that human behavior can be modified to compensate, to a degree, for the lack of such conditions. Thus, such behaviors as hand washing before eating and after contact with contaminated materials, thoroughly cooking food, and proper waste disposal have been targeted for modification by campaigns throughout the developing world, and psychologists often participate in designing or conducting such behavior-modification programs. The widespread dissemination of information about proven interventions, however, remains problematic in developing countries (Edejer, 2000). This, however, is likely to change in developing countries where psychologists are using modern telecommunications in creative ways to educate the public through such modalities as radio and television serials (e.g., Tanzania and Mexico, respectively).

Some nations, however, have reached levels of progress which, although not enough to exclude them from the category of *developing countries*, have generated living conditions associated with epidemiological levels of disease that are more typical of developed countries, including cancer (Vijayan, Esser, & Steigerwald, 2003), diabetes (Chacko, 2003), heart disease (Levine & Bartlett, 1984; Steer, Carapetis, Nolan, & Shann, 2002), and the medical sequelae of substance abuse (Abdul-Quader, DesJarlais, Chatterjee, Hirky, & Friedman, 1999; Westermeyer, 2004). These trends most likely stem from a combined effect of improved economies and education, among others. In Brazil and Mexico, for example, the incidence and prevalence of communicable diseases have been in decline for at least two decades. This is due to both economic development and the promotion of health in elementary and/or high school curricula, as well as via media campaigns. On the other hand, factors such as the aging of the population and increase in life expectancy, growing urbanization, and lifestyle changes linked to modernization have led to an acceleration in chronic degenerative diseases more typical of developed nations.

In developing nations psychologists design and administer several forms of health-care interventions. These are usually aimed at changing behavioral patterns in order to establish better lifestyles and promote self-help skills in patients and their families. Occasionally, psychologists in these settings train other health-care professionals in the knowledge and skills required to educate and facilitate the improved health of their patients (De los Ríos & Sánchez-Sosa, 2002).

Mental health continues to be a source for concern because it constitutes a significant burden for individuals and families in general and in developing societies in particular. One aspect of mental health that demands closer attention is the type of professional training required by psychologists who will work under different economic, social, and cultural conditions (Sriram, 1990). In developing countries, the curricula for psychologists expected to work in mental health tends to overlap, sometimes excessively, with that of psychiatrists, psychiatric nurses, and social workers. Such overlap rarely endows psychologists with competencies specifically related to psychological research-based knowledge. Furthermore, these curricula often provide little more than skills aimed at supporting other professionals and, hence, delay the formation of a professional identity and reduce professional opportunities. Finally, prevailing approaches to training seldom provide psychologists with competencies needed to solve the myriad of social problems from which low-income populations suffer. Thus, reorienting and strengthening curricula, including pedagogies that raise social awareness and nurture social action, is in urgent need of further development (see chapter 11 for more on education and training for a global psychology).

Education. In terms of education, many developing countries face common problems, such as poorly developed curricula at all levels of instruction, a scarcity of textbooks and other study materials, ineffectively trained teachers, inadequately endowed libraries and laboratories, antiquated and invalid instruments and measures, few computers, decaying facilities, marginally paid teachers, and the lack of competent school administrators and support personnel (O'Sullivan, 2003; Serpell, 1993; Simkins, 2003). Again, although not much can be achieved under such conditions, educational psychologists can help improve several aspects of the educational environment. Some examples include adopting a low-cost approach in designing materials, evaluating the effectiveness of curricula and retooling their content and organization, improving pedagogical skills, and enhancing study behavior.

Business and Industry.   A third cluster of shared problems encountered by developing countries can be found in the areas of production, work environments, and organizational structure and climate (Robertson, 2003). These problems usually occur in the larger context of decaying industrial facilities and equipment (including agricultural tools), low salaries, and minimal benefits. Among the most glaring problems are: a poorly trained workforce, inadequate personnel-selection procedures, high absenteeism, and alarming rates of accidents in the workplace. Because human behavior constitutes a main causal factor of many of these problems, psychologists can and do contribute to their solution.

Although the problems in business and industry cited above are common to developing countries and are tied to social needs, the conditions that prevail in different countries have varying effects on the demand for psychological research and services. Thus, professional training in psychology in developing countries tends to reflect national realities, which in turn are mirrored in the applied research conducted by psychologists. Just one example is the relatively high proportion of studies on street-children in Brazil (Abadia-Barrero, 2002; DeSouza, Koller, Hutz, & Forster, 1995; Filho & Neder, 2001; Huggins & Rodrigues, 2004).

Except for the conceptual orientation and methodological and technical preferences derived from their complex and challenging national conditions, training programs for psychologists in the developing world share a number of commonalities, due more to the history of psychology as a discipline than to widespread agreement on matters pertaining to theory, research, and practice. Thus, most professional programs include at least three components. The first consists of a core of knowledge related to the basic principles and mechanisms that regulate behavior. This knowledge is presented in such courses as sensation and perception, cognitive processes, language, and the biological bases of behavior. The second component consists of coursework in measurement and experimental methodology, and includes psychological testing, interviewing, research design, and statistics.

The third component involves coursework and practica (sometimes with supervision) in diagnostic systems and the selection and implementation of psychotherapeutic interventions. Depending on the theoretical orientations and historical traditions in specific countries, programs may favor the practice of having students become familiar with a specific literature or set of authors, rather than providing for more diverse exposure. One example is professional training in Argentina, in which the vast majority of psychologists undergo psychoanalytic training of some sort (Brignardello, 1975; Neuburger, 2002).

This suggests that professional training programs in developing countries are far from homogeneous. There is probably less uniformity in programs within the developing world than among those taught in Canadian, U.S., and European universities. In fact, the history of psychology in some developing countries was determined more by groups of psychologists adhering to relatively distinct theoretical perspectives than to the steady evolution of research or practical applications emanating from academia (see chapter 2, this volume). Sometimes the prevailing approach to the training of psychologists stems from accidental historical conditions. This occurs, for example, when a group of faculty with a specific theoretical viewpoint develops political clout to such an extent that it is able to determine most of the modalities of training, application, and sometimes even the regulatory aspects of professional practice. Let us also remember that psychology in some countries developed around the extraordinary impact of the scholarship and mentoring provided by academic psychologists, who contributed to or solidified the national identity of their psychology (chapter 5 provides an in-depth perspective on the indigenization of psychology in the developing world). Some better known examples are Arrigo Angelini and Carolina Martuscelli-Bori in Brazil, Qicheng Jing in China, Janak Pandey and Durganand Sinha in India, Rogélio Díaz-Guerrero and Luis Lara-Tapia in Mexico, Michael Durojaiye in Nigeria, Virgilio Enriquez in the Philippines, and Çiğdem Kağitçibaşi and Muzafer Sherif in Turkey.

The teaching methods used to train psychologists in developing countries are as varied as the course content in psychology in these countries. A growing trend is to exploit more advanced and technologically supported methods of pedagogy as departments or schools become more affluent. The basic format still widely used is in vivo lecturing and, as access to other options increases, one is likely to find updated readings, audio-visually supported demonstrations (e.g., overheads, audio recordings), digital projections, and real time Internet-based video conferencing. It should be clear, however, that the quality of professional training depends only partially on resources and technology. In principle, one can probably find excellent training programs that rest primarily on the presentation of up-to-date information by competent and experienced faculty, in vivo supervised training in applied settings, and reliable and valid methods for evaluating the acquisition of knowledge and skills.

There are additional aspects of institutions of higher education in the developing world that contribute to their being distinct from most of those in the developed world. For instance, the limited resources and infrastructure capabilities that characterize developing countries appear related to levels of social unrest. One more or less specific source for such instability stems from the fact that the population growth in some developing countries is not commensurate with the availability of services or social benefits, of which access to higher education is one of the most problematic. At least two conditions appear to contribute to this situation. The first is the large number of young people who seek admission to universities, which are usually already overcrowded. Politicians, journalists, and university administrators themselves unwittingly contribute to this dilemma by voicing the opinion that education in general and higher education in particular is the single most important determinant of upward social mobility. Secondly, political parties occasionally take advantage of this perceived hope among youth by making all sorts of promises about greater access to and support for a university education in order to gain adherents. The politicization of higher education sometimes results in pressures on governments and university presidents to admit far more students than even the physical infrastructure can functionally hold. When this happens, universities experience severe problems beyond those related to underdevelopment per se (Aluede & Imhanlahimi, 2004; Hirsch, 1990; Veeraraghavan & Samantaray, 1988). Just to mention a few, classes end up having unwieldy numbers of students. At times, the political pressure intensifies to the point of orienting the curricula to suit certain ideological tenets (often disguised as theoretical conceptions in psychology) and relegating the acquisition of genuine professional competencies to a lesser priority.

Professional Practice

To the extent that psychology in a given developing country has a definite or at least an identifiable historical development, leading to well-established training programs at recognized universities, professional practice by psychologists in that country will tend to be formally recognized. Under these circumstances, legal provisions that cover the professional practice of psychologists have been in place in many developing countries for decades. Most such countries have legal stipulations in their national or local laws that protect the title of *psychologist*. On the other hand, the specificity of education and training and the legal responsibilities and limits associated with professional practice are not always as clearly articulated. The training requirements for psychologists and the legislative regulation of the profession in some developing countries often depend on idiosyncrasies in national or local educational systems and/or the perceptions of the profession held by government officials.

It should be remembered that, depending on certain forces of history, psychology has experienced varying levels of advancement in different countries and, hence, varying degrees to which it is established as a profession in those countries (Sánchez-Sosa & Valderrama-Iturbe, 2001; see chapter 10, this volume). Some developing countries have enjoyed formal university-based coursework in psychology as well as organizations for psychologists since the first decade of the 20th century. At present, these countries also tend to have numerous university-based professional training programs, relatively well-established journals, and public agencies that fund research. Other countries have achieved similar levels of development only in the last two or three decades, or are currently making progress toward those goals. In addition to economic factors, the differential outcomes for psychology in developing countries stem from other events and forces, including cultural, geographical, historical, and religious. For example, the colonial occupation of India by Great Britain or that of more than 20 countries in Latin America by Spain and Portugal sometimes included governmental policies that promoted university education and, hence, the development of such disciplines as psychology. By contrast, the decades-long virtual isolation of China due to ideologically based educational policies kept the discipline and profession of psychology relatively dormant; it is only recently that we witness an enthusiastic and well-supported renaissance of psychology in China (Stevens & Wedding, 2004).

One problem that psychologists in developing countries face in terms of professional practice stems from the historical fact that psychology often first developed in academic settings where psychologists shared disciplinary territory with other scholars, in particular philosophers, lawyers, and physicians. Philosophy, law, and medicine are much more established disciplines; some were instituted at universities hundreds of years earlier than was psychology. Thus, it is only natural that these disciplines and professions, often acting formally or informally as guilds, have had more opportunity to create institutional strongholds, which constitute formidable political competition for psychologists in terms of institutional decision making. This status differential exists both within and outside of academic settings and can be seen operating in governmental agencies, NGOs, and private corporations. Because the public also perceives other disciplines and professions to have dominion over psychology, psychologists must invest extraordinary effort to have their discipline and profession viewed with respect, as having potential value for individual and collective well-being.

In developing countries, individuals from many occupations may claim to have the authority to understand and solve problems that involve human behavior, although they are careful not to label themselves as psychologists. The services that these persons offer range from entirely baseless forms of psychotherapy, to "specialized teaching," to personnel selection, etc. Perhaps, the most ironic aspect of this phenomenon lies in the fact that psychologists in developing countries rarely face professional obstacles as a result of the lack of competence, but they are at a disadvantage relative to other occupations whose image has been unrealistically enhanced due to the unique social history of their countries (Boratav, 2004; Rahman, 2004). Comparatively smaller salaries and reduced access to positions of greater responsibility and privilege are but two indications of psychologists' disadvantageous position (Sánchez-Sosa, 2004).

It is in this context that scientific and professional psychology organizations can exert their greatest influence. Even a superficial analysis of the current realities for psychologists in developing countries reveals that there is still a long road ahead if psychology associations are to attain the legal stature and political power of such large and well led organizations as the APA. It should also be clear that the education of politicians and the general public is an all-important priority for psychologists regardless of a country's level of development (DeLeon, O'Keefe, VandenBos, & Kraut, 1982).

SOME EXPLORATORY DATA

In order to convey a general sense of the activities of psychologists in the developing world, descriptive data were collected that summarized the frequencies of published literature in different professional interest areas (see Tables 4.1 through 4.6). The search tool used was the "Ovid" version of the APA's PsycINFO database. After entering a developing country's name and selecting the "Use as Keyword" option, data were collected based on the way in which the descriptors of titles and abstracts produced themes or lines of research in the database's secondary search page. This methodology, then, served to identify the type of work of psychologists in terms of theory, research, and practice, at least as evidenced by published literature that presumably is work-related. As explained at the beginning of the chapter, a combination of the WHO's epidemiological conception of *developing* and agreed upon geographical regions of the world were used to create a list of developing countries by region. We remind readers that drawing on published literature appearing in the PsycINFO database does not provide an entirely accurate or thoroughly exhaustive index of the work activities of psychologists in the developing world. Therefore, the data that we offer should be viewed as providing a general characterization of psychology in these countries.

Three readers, two of them psychologists fluent in English, participated in the analysis and classification of titles and abstracts. After the first reader completed a search of the database, working lists, and eventually the tables themselves, were revised on the basis of a subsequent examination of the predominant features of each title and abstract. If the first reader had any doubt about the main category to which a citation belonged, a second reader examined the title and abstract. In cases of disagreement between the first and second readers, a third reader (the principal author) analyzed the pertinent information and, in consultation with the other readers, reached consensus on a given classification. During the initial planning that preceded the collection of data, all readers agreed on the importance of keeping personal biases to a minimum. At the end of data collection, all three readers checked the tables for inaccuracies and inconsistencies.

The analysis emphasized the activity of national authors by including only titles with at least one author from the developing country in question. One exception to this procedure arose from the impossibility of distinguishing national authors from collaborators in developed countries when all authors' last names belonged to the same linguistic family (e.g., English surnames in English-speaking Caribbean nations). In these cases the institutional affiliation was used as the country locator.

The data recorded for some developing countries required a more sensitive approach to their classification due to the amount and diversity of scholarly productivity. The topics listed in the leftmost column of the

TABLE 4.1

Research Activity by Psychologists in the Developing Countries of North and Central America

Topic	Belize	Costa Rica	El Salvador	Guatemala	Honduras	Mexico	Nicaragua	Panama
Social factors	TR	RA	R	TR	R	TR***A	R	R
Culture/Ethnography	R	R		R		TR***		R
Gender issues	R		R			TR**		
Sexuality	R		R			TR**		
Risky health behavior						TR*A		
Substance abuse		R				TR**A		R
Abuse/Violence	R	R				R*A		
Crime related								
Marriage/Family						TR*		R
Children		R				TR**A	R	R
Adolescents						R*A		
Elderly						R*A		
Learning processes				R		TR*		
Curricula/Professors		R		TR		TRA*	TRA	
College students						R*A		
Natural disaster	TR						R	
Effects of war			R				TR	
Animal research	R	R				TRA		TR
Quality of life						TRA		
HIV/AIDS					TR	R*A		
Physical health	TRA			TR	R	TR**A	T	
Mental health	TRA				R	TR**A		
Health care services		R		R	R	TR*A	R	
Stress/Anxiety/PTSD					R	R*	RA	
Epidemiology						TR**		
I/O-Human resources						R		A
Conceptual analysis				T		TRA	T	T
Psychometrics		R	R			T***A		R
Foreigners	17	44	11	33	10	261	15	22
Total	20	64	23	60	17	733	26	32

Note. T = Theory; R = Research; A = Application.
* ≥ 10-19 articles. ** ≥ 20-29 articles. *** ≥ 30 articles.

TABLE 4.2

Research Activity by Psychologists in the Developing Countries of the Caribbean

Topic	Bahamas	Barbados	Cuba	Dominica	Dominican Republic	Grenada	Haiti	Jamaica	Santa Lucia	Trinidad & Tobago
Social factors	R	R	R	R	R	T	T	R		R
Culture/Ethnography	R	R	R				T	R		RA
Gender issues	R	R		R	R		R	R		R
Sexuality			TR	R			R	R		R
Risky health behavior					R		R	R		
Substance abuse										RA
Abuse/Violence		R					T	R		
Crime related		R								
Marriage/Family		R	R					R		
Children		R						R		R
Adolescents						A		RA		R
Elderly										
Learning processes		R						A		R
Curricula/Professors		R				A		A		R
College students								A		
Natural disaster										
Effects of war	R		R				T			
Animal research	R									
Quality of life	R	R						R		
HIV/AIDS	R	R	R			A	T	RA		R
Physical health		R						R		R
Mental health	R						T			R
Health care services			TRA				TR			
Stress/Anxiety/PTSD		R	T							R
Epidemiology							R	R		
I/O-Human resources					TR					
Conceptual analysis			TR							RA
Psychometrics			R							
Foreigners	4	8	18	5	27	2	24	26	1	9
Total	11	19	44	6	31	4	30	43	1	20

Note. T = Theory; R = Research; A = Application.

* ≥ 10-19 articles. ** ≥ 20-29 articles. *** ≥ 30 articles.

121

TABLE 4.3A
Research Activity by Psychologists in the Developing Countries of South America

Topic	Argentina	Bolivia	Brazil	Chile	Colombia	Ecuador
Social factors	TR*		T*R***A	TRA	TRA	TR
Culture/Ethnography		R	TR***	R**A	R*	TR
Gender issues	R	R	TR***A	RA	R	TR
Sexuality	TR	R	TR	R*A*	A	R
Risky health behavior	TR	R	TR*A	TRA	RA	T
Substance abuse	R		TR***A*	RA	RA	R
Abuse/Violence	R		TR**A	TR*A	RA	R
Crime related			TRA		R	
Marriage/Family	R	R	TR*A	RA	R	R
Children	TRA			RA	TR	TR
Adolescents	R*		TR*A	RA	R	TR
Elderly	R		TR**	R	R	
Learning processes	TR*A		TR***A*	TRA	TR	
Curricula/Professors			TR*A*	RA		
College students	TR		TR*A	R		
Basic processes	R		R*			
Animal research	TR*A	R		R		R
Quality of life	R			R		
HIV/AIDS	TR	R	TR**A	R	RA	T
Physical health	TR	R	TR***A	RA	R	R
Mental health	R*	R	TR**A	R*A	R	R
Health care services	TRA		TR*R*A	TR	TRA	
Stress/Anxiety/PTSD			TRA	R	R	TR
Epidemiology	TR		TR***	T*R*	R	
I/O-Human resources	R		TR*A	TRA	R	R
Psychoanalysis	TRA		TRA	R	R	
Conceptual analysis	TRA		T*R*A	TRA	T	T
Psychometrics	R*		T***	R*	R	R
Foreigners	49	17	104	50	31	23
Total	210	29	812	160	107	40

Note. T = Theory; R = Research; A = Application.
* ≥ 10-19 articles. ** ≥ 20-29 articles. *** ≥ 30 articles.

TABLE 4.3B
Research Activity by Psychologists in the Developing Countries of South America

Topic	French Guiana	Guyana	Paraguay	Peru	South Georgia	Suriname	Venezuela	Uruguay
Social factors		R	R	TRA			R	R
Culture/Ethnography		R	R	TR*				
Gender issues				TR			R	
Sexuality				TRA			R	
Risky health behavior				R			R	
Substance abuse				TR			T	
Abuse/Violence				R			R	R
Marriage/Family				R				R
Children		R		R				
Adolescents							R	
Elderly								TR
Learning processes				TR			R	
Curricula/Professors				TR			R	
College students							R	
Basic processes								
Animal research				R				R
Quality of life								
HIV/AIDS				TR				
Physical health		R	R	R			TR	R
Mental health			R	R*				R
Health care services				TRA			TR	R
Stress/Anxiety/PTSD				R			TR	R
Epidemiology				TR				R
I/O-Human resources								TR
Psychoanalysis				TR			T	
Conceptual analysis				R			T	
Psychometrics							TR	
Foreigners	4	7	4	26	3	6	12	4
Total	4	10	8	77	3	6	46	15

Note. T = Theory; R = Research; A = Application.
* ≥ 10-19 articles.   ** ≥ 20-29 articles.   *** ≥ 30 articles.

123

TABLE 4.4A

Research Activity by Psychologists in the Developing Countries of Asia and the Pacific

Topic	Afghani stan	Bangladesh	Bhutan	Cambodia	China	East Timor	Fiji	India	Indon-esia	Laos	Malaysia	Maldives	Micro-nesia	Mongolia
Social factors	R*A				TR**			TR**	R		TR			
Culture/Ethnography		R			TR***A			TR**	TR	R	TR*			
Gender issues		TR		R	TR***A		TR	TR**	R		R	R		
Sexuality		R			TR***A		R	R*			R			
Risky health behavior		TR		R	R*A			R*						
Substance abuse		R		T	TR***A			TR*A	RA					
Abuse/Violence/Crime		R			TR*A			TR*						
Religion/Islam										R				
Marriage/Family					TR***			TR*						
Pregnancy														
Parental practice		R		R	R***A			R*						
Children		R			TR***A			R*						
Adolescents		R			TR***A			R						
Elderly		R			TR***A			TR*	R		R			
Technology/Media Tools					TR*A			TR			TRA		A	
Learning processes					TR***A			TR**		R	TRA			
Curricula/Professors					TR***A			TR			TRA			
Students/Peers		R			TR***A			TR			TR			
Basic processes					R***			R*			R			
Animal research				R	TR**			R*	R					
Quality of life		R			R***A			TR						
HIV/AIDS		TRA		TRA	TR*A			TR*A	R	R	R			
Physical health		R		R	TR***A			TR***A	RA		R			
Mental health		R		R	TR***A		R	TR***			TRA			R
Health care services		TR		TA	TR*A		R	TR*A	RA		TR		A	

(Continued)

TABLE 4.4A (Continued)
Research Activity by Psychologists in the Developing Countries of Asia and the Pacific

Topic	Afghanistan	Bangladesh	Bhutan	Cambodia	China	East Timor	Fiji	India	Indonesia	Laos	Malaysia	Maldives	Micronesia	Mongolia
Depression														
Stress/Anxiety/PTSD	R			AR	TR**A			TR		R	R			R
Suicide					TR***A		R	TR						
Epidemiology	R			R	R**		R	TR*	R	R	R			R
Politics/Government	R				TR*			TR	R	R	T			
Effects/Military														
Marketing/Consumerism					TR***A			R			TR			
I/O-Human resources								TR***A						
Interventions					TR**A			TRA		T	T			
Psychometrics					TR***A			R**			R			
Foreigners	64	3		25	269	5	28	403	93	5	62	2	11	7
Total	103	3		43	1917	5	34	835	112	10	136	2	13	10

Note. T = Theory; R = Research; A = Application.
* ≥ 10-19 articles. ** ≥ 20-29 articles. *** ≥ 30 articles.

TABLE 4.4B

Research Activity by Psychologists in the Developing Countries of Asia and the Pacific

Topic	Myanmar	Nepal	North Korea	Pakistan	Palau	Papua	Philippines	Solomon Islands	South Korea	Sri Lanka	Thailand	Vietnam
Social factors		R		R			R		R		RA	
Culture/Ethnography	TR		R	RA		TR	TR'A		TR'''	R	TR*	R
Gender issues	T			R			TRA		R'A	R		
Sexuality							R		R'A			
Risky health behavior				R			R		R		RA	
Substance abuse	R			R							TRA	R
Abuse/Violence/Crime							R		TRA	R		
Religion/Islam				R								
Marriage/Family				RA			RA		R*			
Pregnancy				TA								
Parenting				RA		T	TR		R	R	R	
Children			R	RA		T	R		R'A	R	R	
Adolescents			R	R					R			R
Elderly	TRA								TR*		RA	
Technology/Media tools									TRA			
Learning processes	R						TR	T	TR			R
Curricula/Professors			T	RA		T	TR		TR'A		TR	TR
Students/Peers				RA					R*			
Basic processes	R			R								
Animal research						T	R					
Quality of life									R*			
HIV/AIDS	T						RA		R*		R	
Physical health		RA		RA	R	T	RA		R''A	RA	TR'A	R

TABLE 4.4B (Continued)
Research Activity by Psychologists in the Developing Countries of Asia and the Pacific

Topic	Myanmar	Nepal	North Korea	Pakistan	Palau	Papua	Philippines	Solomon Islands	South Korea	Sri Lanka	Thailand	Vietnam
Mental health		R		RA	TR	T	R		R*	TR	TRA	
Health care services	R	T		TRA			RA		TR*A	RA	TR*A	
Depression				R								
Stress/Anxiety/PTSD		R	R	R		T	R		RA	R	R	TR
Suicide				TR					TR	R		
Epidemiology	TR			R			R		TR	R	R	
Politics/Government		T		R			TR		TR*	TR	TR	
Effects/Military				R								
Marketing/Consumerism									TR*			
I/O-Human resources		R					R		R**		R	
Interventions		T		R			TAR		RA	TR	TRA	
Psychometrics				R			R		R	R	R*	
Foreigners	8	56	1	62	3	41	44	5	173	39	116	0
Total	10	83	4	109	5	49	118	6	550	61	222	6

Note. T = Theory; R = Research; A = Application.
* ≥ 10-19 articles. ** ≥ 20-29 articles. *** ≥ 30 articles.

127

TABLE 4.5A

Research Activity by Psychologists in the Developing Countries of the Middle East and North Africa

Topic	Algeria	Bahrain	Djibouti	Egypt	Ethiopia	Iran	Iraq	Jordan	Kuwait	Lebanon	Libya	Morocco
Social factors				R	TR	R		R	R	R		R
Culture/Ethnography	R	R		TR	T	TR	R	R*	R*	R		R
Gender issues				TR		R		R*	R	R		
Risky health behavior		R		R		R		R	R	R		
Substance abuse		R		R	R	TR*		R	R	R		
Abuse/Violence/Crime		R		TR				R	R			R
Religion/Islam				TR	R	TR		R	R	R		
Marriage and family				R		R		R	R*	R		R
Pregnancy/Contraception				R		R		R	R	R		
Parenting				R		R		R	R			
Children				R	R	RA		R	R	R		
Adolescents				R		R		R	R	R		
Elderly		R						R	R	R		
Technology/Media tools					T							
Learning processes				R		R		R	R	RA		
Basic processes		R		R		T		R	R	R		
Curricula/Professors				RA		TR	T	R	R	RA		
Students/Peers					R	TR*A		TR*	R*	R		
Animal research									R			
Quality of life				R	R	R		R	R	R		R
HIV/AIDS		R		R	R	R*A	R	R	R*			
Physical Health	TR	R		R	R	R*A	R	R	R	R		R
Mental health		R		TR	TR	TR		R	R	R		R
Health care services		RA		TRA		R	TR	TR	R			R

(Continued)

128

TABLE 4.5A (Continued)
Research Activity by Psychologists in the Developing Countries of the Middle East and North Africa

Topic	Algeria	Bahrain	Djibouti	Egypt	Ethiopia	Iran	Iraq	Jordan	Kuwait	Lebanon	Libya	Morocco
Depression	R	R		R		R		R	R			
Stress/Anxiety/PTSD				R		TR		R	R*	R		
Suicide					R	R			R			
Epidemiology				TR	R	R	R		R	R		R
Politics/Government		R		T	R	R		R	R	R		R
Effects of war/military				R	A	R	TR	R	R*	R		
I/O-Human resources	T			R	R	TA	R	R*		R		R
Interventions				R		R		R	R			
Psychometrics		R				R		R	R*			
Foreigners	11	1	2	58	41	53	94	59	16	34	3	31
Total	13	17	2	92	60	72	98	138	77	73	3	40

Note. T = Theory; R = Research; A = Application.
* ≥ 10-19 articles. ** ≥ 20-29 articles. *** ≥ 30 articles.

TABLE 4.5B

Research Activity by Psychologists in the Developing Countries of the Middle East and North Africa

Topic	Oman	Qatar	Saudi Arabia	Somalia	Sudan	Syria	Tunisia	UAE	Yemen
Social factors	R		TR		R			R	
Culture/Ethnography	R		R				R	TR	R
Gender issues		R				R			R
Risky health behavior			TRA					R	
Substance abuse			R					R	
Abuse/Violence/Crime			R		R		R		R
Religion/Islam			R					R	
Marriage/Family			R				R		R
Pregnancy/Contraception			R			R			
Parenting							R	R	
Children			R		R			R	
Adolescents	R		R					R	
Elderly			R					R	
Technology/Media tools								R	
Learning processes			R					R*	
Basic processes	T		R		T		R	R	
Curricula/Professors	T		TR					R	
Students/Peers	R		R*				R	R*	
Animal research	R								
Quality of life	R		R				R		
HIV/AIDS	R						R		
Physical health	R	R	TRA				R	RA	
Mental health	R		R*				R	R	
Health care services	R		R		T	R		TR	

TABLE 4.5B (Continued)

Research Activity by Psychologists in the Developing Countries of the Middle East and North Africa

Topic	Oman	Qatar	Saudi Arabia	Somalia	Sudan	Syria	Tunisia	UAE	Yemen
Depression			R					R	
Stress/Anxiety/PTSD			R						
Suicide			R						
Epidemiology			R						R
Politics/Government			R					A	
Effects of war/military									
I/O-Human resources	R		R					TRA	
Interventions			R					A	
Psychometrics			R			R	R	R	
Foreigners	9	9	20	13	16	13	6	23	7
Total	25	10	63	13	19	15	12	78	10

Note. T = Theory; R = Research; A = Application.
* ≥ 10-19 articles. ** ≥ 20-29 articles. *** ≥ 30 articles.

131

TABLE 4.6A
Research Activity by Psychologists in the Developing Countries of Central and Southern Africa

Topic	Angola	Benin	Botswana	Burkina	Burundi	Cameroon	Central African Republic	Chad	Congo	Côte d'Ivoire	Gabon
Social factors	R		TR	R		TR		R	R	R	R
Culture/Ethnography			R	R					R	R	
Gender issues											
Risky health behavior	R					R				T	
Substance abuse											
Abuse/Violence/Crime	R		R								
Marriage/Family			R								
Pregnancy/Contraception											
Parenting			RA								
Children			R			R			R		
Adolescents						RA			R		
Elderly			R								
Technology/Media tools			R								
Learning processes			R								
Basic processes											
Curricula/Professors			TRA			R					
Students/Peers	R		R	R							
Animal research						R	RA		TR		R
Quality of life	R		R								
HIV/AIDS	R		RA	A		RA		R	R	T	
Physical health	R		RA	R	R	RA				R	
Mental health	R								R	R	
Health care services	A		T	R						R	

(Continued)

TABLE 4.6A (Continued)

Research Activity by Psychologists in the Developing Countries of Central and Southern Africa

Topic	Angola	Benin	Botswana	Burkina	Burundi	Cameroon	Central African Republic	Chad	Congo	Côte d'Ivoire	Gabon
Depression											
Stress/Anxiety/PTSD									R		
Suicide											
Epidemiology		R		A							
Politics/Government			R						R		
Effects of War/Military			TRA								
I/O-Human resources											R
Interventions	A										
Psychometrics				R							
Foreigners	7		20	4	5	37	4	8	35	27	4
Total	8		28	11	6	47	7	9	40	32	8

Note. T = Theory; R = Research; A = Application.

* ≥ 10-19 articles. ** ≥ 20-29 articles. *** ≥ 30 articles.

TABLE 4.6B
Research Activity by Psychologists in the Developing Countries of Central and Southern Africa

Topic	Gambia	Ghana	Guinea Bissau	Kenya	Lesotho	Liberia	Madagascar	Malawi	Mali	Mauritius	Mozambique	Namibia	Niger	Nigeria
Social factors	R	TRA	R	TR*	T			R			R	R	R	TR*
Culture/Ethnography				R										TR
Gender issues										R				TR*
Risky health behavior								R						R'A
Substance abuse				R										A
Abuse/Violence/Crime		R												TR
Marriage/Family		TR		R	T									TR
Pregnancy/Contraception				RA							T			R
Parenting		R		R				R						
Children	R	R		TR				R			T			RA
Adolescents		R		RA				A						R'A
Elderly		R		R										TR
Technology/Media tools				A										
Learning processes					RA									TR
Basic processes				R										T'
Curricula/Professors		R		TR	A			T				R		TR
Students/Peers				R	RA			T				R		TRA
Animal research				RA			R							
Quality of life														R
HIV/AIDS	R	RA		TRA			R	RA				R		TRA
Physical health	R	RA		TRA		R	R	R		A	T	R		TRA
Mental health		R		T'				T						TR'A
Health care services		TRA		TR		R	R	TRA		A	T	R		TR'A

(Continued)

TABLE 4.6B (Continued)
Research Activity by Psychologists in the Developing Countries of Central and Southern Africa

Topic	Gambia	Ghana	Guinea Bissau	Kenya	Lesotho	Liberia	Madagascar	Malawi	Mali	Mauritius	Mozambique	Namibia	Niger	Nigeria
Depression														
Stress/Anxiety/PTSD	RA			R						R				R
Suicide														
Epidemiology	R			T				R						R
Politics/Government		R		T										TR
War Effects/military														
I/O-Human resources	R			T						R				R*A
Interventions	A			A					A	A				
Psychometrics				R								R		R*
Foreigners	82	4		108	11	6	41	22	14	5	17	11	24	76
Total	114	7		155	14	7	47	31	16	8	19	17	25	214

Note. T = Theory; R = Research; A = Application.
* ≥ 10-19 articles. ** ≥ 20-29 articles. *** ≥ 30 articles.

135

TABLE 4.6C
Research Activity by Psychologists in the Developing Countries of Central and Southern Africa

Topic	Rwanda	Senegal	Seychelles	South Africa	Sudan	Swaziland	Tanzania	Togo	Uganda	Zambia	Zimbabwe
Social factors	RA		R	R**			R		R	R	R
Culture/Ethnography		R	R	TR***A	TR		T'R*		R**A	TRA	TRA
Gender issues											
Risky health behavior	R			RA		R	R		TR	R	R
Substance Abuse	R			R*			R			R	R
Abuse/Violence/Crime	R			R***			R		TR	R	
Marriage/Family				R			R				R
Pregnancy/Contraception											
Parenting				R*		R					
Children	A			R'A	R		RA		R	R	R
Adolescents				R**A	R				RA	R	R
Elderly											
Technology/Media tools				R							
Learning processes				R							
Basic processes				TR							
Curricula/Professors				TR**A			R				TR
Students/Peers				R***A			RA		R		TR
Animal Research				R			R	R	R		R
Quality of life								R			R
HIV/AIDS	R			R**A***		R	R'A	T	TRA	R	RA
Physical health	R			R***A			TRA	R	RA	A	R
Mental health	R			R**A			R	R	R	R	R
Health care services	R			TR***A		R	TRA	T	R	R	RA

TABLE 4.6C (Continued)
Research Activity by Psychologists in the Developing Countries of Central and Southern Africa

Topic	Rwanda	Senegal	Seychelles	South Africa	Sudan	Swaziland	Tanzania	Togo	Uganda	Zambia	Zimbabwe
Depression											
Stress/Anxiety/PTSD				R*A					R		R
Suicide				R							
Epidemiology				R			R		R		R
Politics/Government				A	T				TR		T
Effects of war/military									R		
I/O-Human resources				R			A				R
Interventions				TRA*					A		A
Psychometrics				R*			R		R	R	R
Foreigners	33	19	5	185	16	6	82	3	93	48	58
Total	35	26	7	738	18	8	118	6	156	60	96

Note. T = Theory; R = Research; A = Application.
* ≥ 10-19 articles. ** ≥ 20-29 articles. *** ≥ 30 articles.

tables are not always identical because searches of the database did not always yield the same set of topics. In some instances, listing all possible topics in a search would have produced tables of unmanageable size. If a topic appeared on a country's list, but upon further analysis the citations did not justify a separate category (e.g., an ambiguous contribution), it was provisionally held aside until the entire analysis for the country was completed. At the conclusion of the analysis, the citation in question was re-examined and assigned to the next pertinent category based on the problem addressed or methodology used, whichever seemed the more dominant feature. If, on second examination, a topic re-appeared in a given country's list, but the database did not display a distinct category for it, the topic was, again, provisionally held aside, re-examined, and eventually added to the next most inclusive category. The few instances in which such classification difficulties arose tended to reflect the unique sociohistorical circumstances associated with a given country or region. Two examples are the effects of war in Pakistan and patterns of alcohol and/or drug use in certain Asian countries.

Regarding the type of contribution, as opposed to a topic's specific content, criteria were added to those implicit in the labels that appeared in the initial database search. For example, citations were categorized as theoretical if they included mainly meta-analytic considerations or comments, were clearly reflective in purpose, and/or did not entail the collection of data or manipulation of experimental variables. Citations were categorized as applied if they involved the evaluation of interventions directed toward a clinically or socially relevant problem or the correlation of variables relevant to such a problem. If a citation contained elements of both sets of features just described, it was classified as both "theoretical" and "applied."

Once the list of topics for a country was completed, another procedure was used to refine the list and to maintain reasonably sized tables. For example, Asia generally produces many publications on broad topics. In this case, a small number of citations on specific topics did not justify additional categories, but rather were subsumed under the next most appropriate general category. In the case of China, topics with very few entries, and therefore not presented in Table 4.4, include publications on language, natural disasters, sudden acute respiratory syndrome (SARS), immigrants, human resources in industry, and single-child adaptive behaviors; animal research included mainly panda conservation efforts. The same approach was used to accommodate the publications by Cambodian psychologists on the effects of war, survivors of war, military veterans, and refugees, all of which were incorporated into the Stress/Anxiety/PTSD category.

We wish to state, however, that we preferred specific topics to general ones in order to achieve greater precision in characterizing the research productivity of a developing country. In a contrasting example, the relatively low level of research productivity in Africa permitted greater specificity in the topics listed. This is the main reason why, for instance, the topic "Effects of War/Military" appears in the tables for Central and Southern Africa, rather than being integrated within other categories, such as Anxiety/PTSD, as was the case for studies published in other regions. We even retained topics that emerged from our PsycINFO search for which no literature was published during the last 5 years in order to identify significant areas that had not captured the interest of psychologists in certain developing nations (e.g., "Gender Issues" in Central and Southern Africa, "Quality of Life" in South America).

Thus, Tables 4.1 through 4.6 include exploratory data on the research productivity of psychologists from developing countries within the following world regions: North and Central America, the Caribbean, South America, Asia and the Pacific, the Middle East and North Africa, and Central and Southern Africa. Each table shows in the first column the list of topics covered by the database search. The names of the developing country appears directly beneath the title, with each column containing frequency data corresponding to the type of entry as follows: T designates citations with a predominantly theoretical content or conceptual analysis, R stands for empirical articles, and A represents practical applications. As we already mentioned, if a publication was related to more than one topic, it was recorded in a maximum of three topics. A category represented by a letter stands for up to 10 citations, one represented by a letter with a single asterisk indicates 10 to 19 citations, a letter plus two asterisks represents 20 to 29 citations, and a letter with three asterisks stands for 30 or more citations. Thus, for example, in Table 4.4, the intersection of China (second country column) and the "Sexuality" (fourth topic row) contains data for less than 10 theoretical/conceptual publications, over 30 empirical studies, and fewer than 10 articles on practical applications.

Generally speaking, the tables reflect two main outcomes. First, there is considerable variability in the productivity of different developing countries and in the types of articles published. Second, columns that appear to be more "full" tend to be associated with larger and more affluent developing countries. As noted earlier, the strength of a developing country's publishing tradition and the preparedness of its authors to publish in internationally indexed database journals also reflect historical factors that must be considered in any interpretation of the level of scholarly output. Careful inspection of tabular columns will give readers a sense of the main lines of work in which psychologists in a particular developing country are engaged and their level of productivity within those lines of work.

Although the exploratory dataset does not allow for definitive conclusions about the status and trends of psychological work in developing nations, some interpretations seem plausible. Higher publication rates tend to reflect an emphasis on applied research. The main areas for such studies include education, health, I/O settings, and community and social well-being. In many developing countries, basic research is perceived by government officials and psychologists alike as an expendable luxury given pressing social issues and scarce resources. It is also possible that developing countries with higher research productivity have managed to establish ways of coordinating the activities of higher educational institutions and agencies and organizations that provide social services. If so, policies may be in place in these countries that directly or indirectly support the development of psychology through the channeling of resources for applied research to both higher education and social services.

There also seems to be a positive association between the geographical, historical, and/or political proximity of developing to developed countries or regions and higher rates of published research. Beyond the increasing numbers of psychologists from developing countries who receive university degrees in nearby developed nations, these psychologists serve a key role in shaping the character of psychology in their home countries, sometimes independently or through ongoing scholarly relations with colleagues and mentors from their host country.

We want to issue a word of caution. A high rate of publication by psychologists in a given country does not necessarily translate into the systematic use of widely accepted scientific methods in the furtherance of programmatic research. In countries where it is customary to publish virtually everything stemming from academic work (e.g., Argentina), vast numbers of articles are devoted to theoretical reconsiderations of classic theories or to revised reflections on the philosophical or ideological underpinnings of psychotherapeutic approaches. It is not common in developing countries to find the level of teamwork and organization needed for the establishment and maintenance of high quality peer-reviewed journals. Even well-respected journals adopt relatively lenient criteria in evaluating manuscripts which, in turn, fail to promote or improve sound scholarship.

Another finding in the present study was that foreign psychologists from developed countries appear to spend time collecting data in a developing country, but invest little or no effort in promoting the development of psychology in the host country or in collaborating with a colleague from that country. It is regrettable that local psychology and psychologists do not benefit from such potentially productive and, perhaps, seminal interaction. Some examples include psychologists from Australia, the United Kingdom, and the United States who conduct studies in such small, developing countries as Morocco, Somalia, East Timor, and the Maldives.

RECOMMENDATIONS

Although the aims of this chapter did not include derivation of specific recommendations to further the development of psychology in countries of the majority world, it is only natural that some relatively concrete ideas emerged from the themes discussed above. The support of psychologists from developed countries could take any one or more of these forms. It must be emphasized that, although these recommendations may be worth implementing, they do not necessarily follow from the empirical data presented in this chapter.

Psychologists from developed nations might facilitate the progress of psychology in developing countries by:

1. Learning a foreign language, especially one spoken in various countries where psychology has been established and is continuing to advance.
2. Subscribing to one or more journals published in developing countries, particularly since subscription rates tend to be comparatively low.
3. Attending and participating in national conventions in developing countries and regional conferences in the developing world.
4. Searching for academic or professional exchanges and inviting psychologists from a developing country for a stay at a host academic or professional institution (during their visit, it would help to offer capacity-building activities in the teaching, research, and application of psychology).
5. Inviting psychologists from developing countries to contribute papers to a journal with which you are affiliated and/or to participate as editorial board members or reviewers for manuscripts (it is important to provide thoughtful and sensitive feedback).

6. Choosing developing countries for sabbatical leaves or shorter academic or professional stays.
7. Inviting psychologists from developing countries to participate in boards, committees, and task forces of professional psychology organizations in your country.
8. Inviting psychologists from developing countries to co-author articles or papers for journals or for conference presentations.
9. Visiting colleagues while vacationing in developing countries and learning about and providing encouragement for their activities.
10. Thinking about how else psychology might be strengthened in developing countries and following through with corresponding action.

In a final note, institutional or organizational support from the developed world can take many different approaches, and is limited only by the imagination. The strongest psychology organizations, national and international, would do a profound service to the discipline and profession by supporting psychology in less fortunate areas of the world (as in the capacity-building workshops described in chapter 3 and the macro-level interventions presented in chapter 9). We must not forget that psychology is alive and well in many developing countries, and its current value and future promise deserve nurturing.

RECOMMENDED READINGS

Adair, J. G., Coelho, A. E. L., & Luna, J. R. (2002). How international is psychology? *International Journal of Psychology, 37,* 160–170.

Adair, J. G., & Kağitçibaşi, Ç. (Eds.). (1995). Development of psychology in developing countries [Special issue]. *International Journal of Psychology, 30*(6).

Bauserman, R. (1997). International representation of the psychological literature. *International Journal of Psychology, 32,* 107–112.

Burgess, G. H., Sternberger, L. G., Sánchez-Sosa, J. J., Lunt, I., Shealy, C. N., & Ritchie, P. (2004). Development of a global curriculum for professional psychology: Implications of the combined-integrated model of doctoral training. *Journal of Clinical Psychology, 60,* 1027–1049.

Connolly, K. (1985). Can there be a psychology for the third world? *Bulletin of the British Psychological Society, 38,* 249–257.

Díaz-Loving, R., Reyes-Lagunes, I., & Díaz-Guerrero, R. (1995). Some cultural facilitators and deterrents for the development of psychology: The role of graduate research training. *International Journal of Psychology, 30,* 681–692.

Elder, J. P. (2001). *Behavior change and public health in the developing world.* Thousand Oaks, CA: Sage.

Leung, K., & Zhang, J. (1995). Systemic considerations: Factors facilitating and impeding the development of psychology in developing countries. *International Journal of Psychology, 30,* 693–706.

McMinn, M. R., & Voytenko, V. L. (2004). Investing the wealth: Intentional strategies for psychology training in developing countries. *Professional Psychology: Research and Practice, 35,* 302–305.

Stevens, M., & Wedding, D. (Eds.). (2004). *Handbook of international psychology.* New York: Brunner-Routledge.

ACKNOWLEDGEMENTS

The author is gratefully indebted to Karla Suárez, Brenda Fuentes, and Carlos G. Castro for assisting in the collection and organization of database information. This chapter was made possible in part by grant IN-309705 from the National Autonomous University of Mexico and additional support from the International Union of Psychological Science.

REFERENCES

Abadia-Barrero, C. E. (2002). Growing up in a world with AIDS: Social advantages of having AIDS in Brazil. *AIDS Care, 14,* 417–423.

Abdul-Quader, A. S., DesJarlais, D. C., Chatterjee, A., Hirky, A. E., & Friedman, S. R. (1999). Interventions for injecting drug users. In L. Gibney, R. J. DiClemente, & S. Vermund (Eds.), *Preventing HIV in developing countries: Biomedical and behavioral approaches. AIDS prevention and mental health* (pp. 283–312). Dordrecht, Netherlands: Kluwer.

Agboola, I. O., & Lee, A. C. (2000). Computer and information technology access for deaf individuals in developed and developing countries. *Journal of Deaf Studies and Deaf Education, 5,* 286–289.

Ahasan, M., Campbell, D., Salmoni, A., & Lewko, J. (2001). Some intervening and local factors among shift workers in a developing country: Bangladesh. *Journal of Workplace Learning, 13,* 164–172.

Aluede, O. O., & Imhamlahimi, J. E. (2004). Towards a psychological frame for explaining student unrest in Nigerian universities. *College Student Journal, 38,* 135–142.

Ardila, R. (2004). Psychology in Colombia: Development and current status. In M. J. Stevens & D. Wedding (Eds.), *Handbook of international psychology* (pp. 169–178). New York: Brunner-Routledge.

Bauserman, R. (1997). International representation of the psychological literature. *International Journal of Psychology, 32,* 107–112.

Boratav, H. B. (2004). Psychology at the crossroads: The view from Turkey. In M. J. Stevens & D. Wedding (Eds.), *Handbook of international psychology* (pp. 311–330). New York: Brunner-Routledge.

Brignardello, L. A. (1975). Psicoterapia y psicoterapeutas en la Argentina [Psychotherapy and psychotherapists in Argentina]. *Revista Interamericana de Psicología, 9*(1–2), 187–211.

Burgess, G. H., Sternberger, L. G., Sánchez-Sosa, J. J., Lunt, I., Shealy, C. N., & Ritchie, P. (2004). Development of a global curriculum for professional psychology: Implications of the combined-integrated model of doctoral training. *Journal of Clinical Psychology*, 60, 1027–1049.

Chacko, E. (2003). Culture and therapy: Complementary strategies for the treatment of type-2 diabetes in an urban setting in Kerala, India. *Social Science and Medicine*, 56, 1087–1098.

Connolly, K. (1985). Can there be a psychology for the third world? *Bulletin of the British Psychological Society*, 38, 249–257.

Crane, S. F., & Carswell, J. W. (1992). A review and assessment of non-governmental organization-based STD/AIDS education and prevention projects for marginalized groups. *Health Education Research*, 7, 175–193.

DeLeon, P. H., O'Keefe, A. M., VandenBos, G. R., & Kraut, A. G. (1982). How to influence public policy: A blueprint for activism. *American Psychologist*, 37, 476–485.

De los Ríos, J. L., & Sánchez-Sosa, J. J. (2002). Well-being and medical recovery in the critical care unit: The role of the nurse–patient interaction. *Salud Mental*, 25, 21–31.

DeSouza, E., Koller, S., Hutz, C., & Forster, L. (1995). Preventing depression among Brazilian street children. *Revista Interamericana de Psicología*, 29, 261–265.

Díaz-Loving, R., Reyes-Lagunes, I., & Díaz-Guerrero, R. (1995). Some cultural facilitators and deterrents for the development of psychology: The role of graduate research training. *International Journal of Psychology*, 30, 681–692.

Edejer, T. T. (2000). Disseminating health information in developing countries: The role of the Internet. *British Medical Journal*, 321, 797–800.

Filho, G. C., & Neder, G. (2001). Social and historical approaches regarding street children in Rio de Janeiro (Brazil) in the context of the transition to democracy. *Childhood: A Global Journal of Child Research*, 8, 11–29.

Fouche, J. B., & Louw, D. A. (2002). A profile of academics, non-academics and graduate students in South African psychology. *Journal of Psychology in Africa, South of the Sahara, the Caribbean, and Afro-Latin America*, 12, 19–39.

Friedlander, M. L., Carranza, V. E., & Guzman, M. (2002). International exchanges in family therapy: Training, research, and practice in Spain and the United States. *Counseling Psychologist*, 30, 314–329.

Gopal, M. (1995). Teaching psychology in a third world setting. *Psychology and Developing Societies*, 7, 21–45.

Hirsch, E. L. (1990). Sacrifice for the cause: Group processes, recruitment, and commitment in a student social movement. *American Sociological Review*, 55, 243–254.

Holtzman, W. H. (1970). Los seminarios internacionales de psicología en Texas: Un experimento continúo de intercambio transcultural en psicología [Texas international psychological seminars: A progress experiment in intercultural exchange in psychology]. *Revista Interamericana de Psicología*, 4(3–4), 279–282.

Huggins, M. A., & Rodrigues, S. (2004). Kids working on Paulista Avenue. *Childhood: A Global Journal of Child Research*, 11, 495–514.

Landerholm, E., Gehrie, C., & Hao, Y. (2004). Educating early childhood teachers for the global world. *Early Child Development and Care*, 174(7–8), 593–606.

Leung, K., & Zhang, J. (1995). Systemic considerations: Factors facilitating and impeding the development of psychology in developing countries. *International Journal of Psychology*, 30, 693–706.

Levine, R. V., & Bartlett, K. (1984). Pace of life, punctuality and coronary heart disease in six countries. *Journal of Cross-Cultural Psychology, 15*, 233–255.

Mariko, M. (2003). Quality of care and the demand for health services in Bamako, Mali: The specific roles of structural, process, and outcome components. *Social Science and Medicine, 56*, 1183–1196.

Mays, V. M., Rubin, J., Sabourin, M., & Walker, L. (1996). Moving toward a global psychology: Changing theories and practice to meet the needs of a changing world. *American Psychologist, 51*, 485–487.

Neuburger, R. P. (2002). Liaison-psychoanalysis in Argentina. *Journal of European Psychoanalysis, 15*, 53–69.

O'Sullivan, M. (2003). The development of effective strategies to teach reading among unqualified primary teachers in a developing country context. *International Journal of Early Years Education, 11*, 129–140.

Rahman, N. K. (2004). Psychology in Pakistan. In M. J. Stevens & D. Wedding (Eds.), *Handbook of international psychology* (pp. 243–260). New York: Brunner-Routledge.

Robertson, P. L. (2003). The role of training and skilled labor in the success of SMEs in developing economies. *Education and Training, 45*(8–9), 461–473.

Sánchez-Sosa, J. J. (2002). Globalizacion, practica profesional transnacional y certificacion [Globalization, transnational professional practice and certification]. In G. Vazquez (Ed.), *Ensenanza, ejercició y regulación de la profesión: Psicología* [Teaching, practice and professional regulation: Psychology] (pp. 43–64). Mexico City: National College of Psychologists and UNAM School of Psychology.

Sánchez-Sosa, J. J. (2004). Psychology in Mexico: Recent developments and perspective. In M. J. Stevens & D. Wedding (Eds.), *Handbook of international psychology* (pp. 93–107). New York: Brunner-Routledge.

Sánchez-Sosa, J. J., & Valderrama-Iturbe, P. (2001). Psychology in Latin America: Historical reflections and perspectives. *International Journal of Psychology, 36*, 384–394.

Serpell, R. (1993). *The significance of schooling: Life journeys in an African society.* New York: Cambridge University Press.

Simkins, T. (2003). School leadership in Pakistan: Exploring the head teacher's role. *School Effectiveness and School Improvement, 14*, 275–291.

Sluzki, C. E. (2004). Editorial: The World Health Organization, the *American Journal of Orthopsychiatry*, and Third World countries. *American Journal of Orthopsychiatry, 74*, 99–101.

Sriram, T. G. (1990). Psychotherapy in developing countries: A public health perspective. *Indian Journal of Psychiatry, 32*, 138–144.

Steer, A. C., Carapetis, J. R., Nolan, T. M., & Shann, F. (2002). Systematic review of rheumatic heart disease prevalence in children in developing countries: The role of environmental factors. *Journal of Pediatrics and Child Health, 38*, 229–234.

Stevens, M., & Wedding, D. (Eds.). (2004). *Handbook of international psychology.* New York: Brunner-Routledge.

Swartz, L., Tomlinson, M., & Landman, M. (2004). Evidence, policies and practices: Continuities and discontinuities in mental health promotion in a developing country. *International Journal of Mental Health Promotion, 6*, 33–38.

Veeraraghavan, V., & Samantaray, S. K. (1988). A comparative study of student unrest in two different years in Utkal University. *Indian Psychologist, 5*, 39–48.

Vijayan, R., Esser, S., & Steigerwald, I. (2003). Low-tech, high-touch: Pain management with simple methods. *Pain Practice, 3*, 88–91.

Westermeyer, J. (2004). The importance and difficulty of drug research in developing countries: A report from Kabul as timely reminder. *Addiction, 99*, 802–804.

World Health Organization. (2004). *List of member states by WHO region and mortality stratum.* Retrieved April 19, 2005, from http://www.who.int/whr/2004/annex/topic/en/annex_member_en.pdf

5

Development of Indigenous Psychologies: Understanding People in a Global Context[1]

Uichol Kim
Young-Shin Park
Inha University

INTRODUCTION

We are living in a global era in which our lives are closely intertwined with each another. Our environment, economy, welfare, security, and future are closely interconnected. Although many people feel that globalization is a recent phenomenon, various forms of it have been with us for thousands of years. Two types of globalization can be identified in terms of its nature, process, and goal: unilateral and enlightened globalization. Unilateral globalization is based on the belief in the superiority of its own culture, values, and ideals and the imposition of a single standard on all cultures. Historically unilateral globalization has been the typical mode, with one culture dominating and subjugating other cultures.

Enlightened globalization is based on understanding, dialogue, respect, and integrating knowledge to foster cultural development. It recognizes that each culture has a different set of values, belief, skills, and resources and integrates diverse information to transform the world. In medieval

---

[1]This chapter is based on the state-of the-art address provided at the 28th International Congress of Psychology, Beijing, August 8–13, 2004.

Europe, for example, enlightened globalization freed Europeans from the grip of superstition, fear, and famines. During this time, civilization in other parts of the world flourished. Europeans were able to integrate this information to launch a new era known as the Renaissance.

With Marco Polo's travel to Asia, Europeans awoke to new possibilities of wealth, knowledge, and technology. The West learned from China how to cultivate raw materials such as cotton, tea, spices, and paper. Paper allowed cheap and efficient distribution of information, which facilitated the rapid spread of knowledge. Cultivation of cotton, tea, and spices improved the quality of life. The desire to find a shorter route to the East led to the discovery of the Americas. Europeans came into contact with Muslim cultures and learned about Greek philosophy, democracy, mathematics, medicine, and science. The Enlightenment in Europe made modernization, democracy, and science possible, which in turn was made possible by the knowledge, technology, and resources obtained from the Middle East, Far East, Africa, and the New World (Kim, Aasen, & Ebadi, 2003).

The discovery and integration of knowledge during the Renaissance served as the foundation for the development of science, technology, and civil societies (Kim, Helgesen, & Ahn, 2002). The physical sciences (e.g., astronomy, chemistry, physics) were first to develop. Newtonian physics provided a simple, elegant, and mechanical explanation of the physical world. Chemists discovered the basic elements, and these elements serve as building blocks for explaining the structure and formation of complex objects. Science provides the most accurate and universal understanding of the natural world, and this knowledge has been used to control and shape our environment.

Psychology developed in the late 19th century, attempting to emulate the success of the natural sciences. Psychology flourished as a discipline and became highly successful in terms of number of students, faculty members, research projects, funding, and professional organizations (Koch & Leary, 1985). In terms of its scientific status, however, U.S. psychology experienced a crisis in the early 1970s (Elms, 1975; Koch & Leary, 1985). During this time, scholars around the world questioned the universality of psychological theories, and many called for the development of indigenous psychologies (Kim & Berry, 1993; see chapter 2, this volume, for a review of the international history of psychology).

LIMITATIONS OF GENERAL PSYCHOLOGY

Scholars criticize general psychology as an example of unilateral globalization that has been imposed in Africa, Latin America, Asia, Oceania, and on peoples native to North America (Azuma, 1984; Enriquez, 1993; Kim & Berry, 1993; Nsamenang, 1995; Sánchez-Sosa, in press; Sinha, 1997; Yang, 2000; Yang, Hwang, & Yang, 2005; see chapter 4, this volume, on psychology in developing countries). Indigenous psychologists argue that each culture should be understood from its own frame of reference, including its own ecological, historical, philosophical, and religious context. They also point out that general psychology has ignored the rich academic and cultural traditions of non-Western countries that could have enriched and advanced the field. Indigenous psychologists reject the unilateral imposition of U.S. psychology and argue for the adoption of the enlightened approach in which psychological knowledge is generated based on dialogue, understanding, and scientific rigor (Kim & Berry, 1993; Kim, Yang, & Hwang, 2006).

Although psychological theories have been assumed to be objective, value-free, and universal, they are criticized for being limited in external validity (Kim & Berry, 1993; Shweder, 1991; see chapter 6, this volume, for a critique of the assumptions underlying Western psychology). Many scholars point out that psychological theories reflect the values, goals, and issues of the United States and Western Europe, and they are not universal (Azuma, 1984; Kim & Berry, 1993; Sinha, 1997). In Canada, Berry (1974) was critical of the culture-bound and culture-blind nature of psychology. In France, Moscovici (1972) pointed out that U.S. psychologists adopted "for its themes of research and for the contents of its theories, the issues of its own society" (p. 19). Even in the United States, psychologists recognize that psychological theories reflect the cultural values and goals of the United States (Koch & Leary, 1985; Sampson, 1977).

Scholars have pointed out the need to go beyond the focus on intra-individual processes and systematically analyze phenomena that are influenced by context, relationship, society, and culture (Azuma, 1984; Ho, 1986; Sinha, 1997; Yang, 2000; Yang et al., 2005). Psychologists around the world have contributed to the development of indigenous psychology and expansion of the domain and methodology of psychological research (see chapter 7, this volume, for a discussion of qualitative research methods). Table 5.1 lists psychologists who have contributed to the development of indigenous knowledge and to the theoretical, methodological, and empirical advancement of psychology.

Other scholars have questioned the internal validity of general psychology (Bandura, 1997; Harré, 1999; Kim, 1999; Koch & Leary, 1985). Psychology modeled after Newtonian physics was an attempt to develop objective, abstract, and universal theories, and it excluded the subjective aspects of human functioning (i.e., consciousness, agency, meaning, and

TABLE 5.1
Contributors to Indigenous Psychology

Researcher	Nationality	Topic
John Adair	Canada	Process of indigenization
Carl Marin Allwood	Sweden	Meta-analysis
Hiroshi Azuma	Japan	Socialization, child development, educational achievement
John Berry	Canada	Intelligence, ecological influence
Pawel Boski	Poland	Humanist values
Sang-Chin Choi	Korea	Indigenous concepts
Pierre Dasen	Switzerland	Cognitive development, intelligence
Padmal de Silva	United Kingdom	Buddhist psychology
Rogélio Díaz-Gurrero	Mexico	Ethnopsychology, personality
Rolando Díaz-Loving	Mexico	Ethnopsychology, conception of the self
Michael Durojaiye	Nigeria	Social intelligence
Carolyn Pope Edwards	United States	Parental ethnotheories
Lutz Eckensberger	Germany	Moral development
Virgilio Enriquez	Philippines	Language, indigenous concepts
James Georgas	Greece	Ecological psychology, family
Heidi Fung	Taiwan	Child development
David Ho	Hong Kong	Child development, counseling, methodological relationalism
Kwang-Kuo Hwang	Taiwan	Confucianism, relationalism
Denise Jodelet	France	Social representation of body and self
Çiğdem Kağitçibaşi	Turkey	Socialization and parent-child relationship
Boris Lomov	Russia	Physiological psychology
Ramesh Mishra	India	Indigenous cognition
Bame Nsamenang	Cameroon	Child development
Young-Shin Park	Korea	Achievement, delinquency, quality of life
Kai-Ping Peng	United States	Taoist thought
Rogelia Pe-Pua	Australia	Indigenous methodology
José Miguel Salazar	Venezuela	National identity
Durganand Sinha	India	Hindu philosophy
Jai B. P. Sinha	India	Leadership
Joseph Trimble	United States	Mental health, ethnic identity of native peoples
Susumu Yamaguchi	Japan	Attachment, concept of control, indigenous concepts
Chung-Fang Yang	Hong Kong	Chinese conception of the self
Kuo-Shu Yang	Taiwan	Personality, social psychology

beliefs). Although the concepts of agency and consciousness were central in theories developed by Wilhelm Wundt and William James, subsequent theorists have expunged them. Although psychology was founded and developed in Europe, it became indigenized and institutionalized in the United States (Kim & Park, 2005; Koch & Leary, 1985).

INDIGENOUS PSYCHOLOGIES

Kim and Berry (1993) define indigenous psychology as "the scientific study of human behavior or mind that is native, that is not transported from other regions and that is designed for its people" (p. 2). Indigenous psychology advocates examining knowledge, skills, and beliefs people have about themselves and how they function in their cultural context. It represents a descriptive approach in which the goal of psychology is first to provide documentation of how human beings function in their ecological and cultural context. With this decriptive understanding as a foundation, theories, concepts, and methods are then developed and tested. The goal is to create a more rigorous, systematic, and universal science that can be theoretically and empirically verified (see chapter 6, this volume, for more on how emic description can lead to the discovery of etic constructs).

First, indigenous psychology emphasizes contextualized understanding rooted in a particular setting (e.g., ecological, political, historical, or cultural context). It emphasizes the discovery and use of natural taxonomies in search of regularities, general principles, and universal laws. It examines how people view themselves, relate to others, and manage their environment.

Second, contrary to popular misconception, indigenous psychologies are not limited to the study of native peoples, ethnic groups, or people living in distant lands. Indigenous research has often been equated with the anthropological analysis of "exotic" people living in distant lands. Although such studies are necessary, indigenous psychology is needed for all cultural, native, and ethnic groups, including economically developed countries (Kim & Berry, 1993; Kim et al., 2006).

Third, acceptance of indigenous psychology does not affirm or preclude the use of a particular method. Indigenous psychology is part of the scientific tradition in which an important aspect of the scientific endeavor is the discovery of appropriate methods for the phenomenon under investigation. Scientists should not and cannot be bound to a particular method (Boulding, 1980). The use of qualitative, quantitative, and multiple methods are recommended to increase our confidence that a particular finding is valid and not an artifact of research methodology (Enriquez, 1993; see chapter 7, this volume). Results from multiple methods should be integrated to provide a more comprehensive and robust understanding of psychological phenomena.

Fourth, it has been assumed that insiders have a better understanding of indigenous phenomena and that outsiders can have only a limited understanding. Although a person who has been born and raised in a particular community may have insights and understanding of indigenous phenomena, this may not be true in all instances. An outsider with an external point of view can call to attention what is assumed to be natural, but is actually cultural. Although an outsider may have a superficial understanding of indigenous phenomena found in other cultures, he or she may point out peculiarities, inconsistencies, and blind spots that insiders may have overlooked. Both internal and external points of view are necessary in providing a comprehensive and integrated understanding of psychological phenomena.

Also, with globalization many scholars from non-Western countries receive their training in the West. Although most psychologists continued to replicate Western theories (Sinha, 1997), the most vocal criticism comes from psychologists who have been trained in the West and have worked to establish psychology in their own country (e.g., Hiroshi Azuma in Japan, Sang-Chin Choi in South Korea, Rogélio Díaz-Guerrero in Mexico, Michael Durojaiye in Nigeria, Virgilio Enriquez and Alfred Lagmay of the Philippines, David Ho in Hong Kong, Bame Nsamenang in Cameroon, José Miguel Salazar in Venezuela, Durganand Sinha and Jai B. P. Sinha in India, and Kuo-Shu Yang and Kwang-Kuo Hwang in Taiwan). Bicultural psychologists, who have insights from two or more cultures, can point out bias in psychological research and contribute to the development of a truly universal psychology (Ho, 1995).

Fifth, many indigenous psychologists search philosophical and religious texts for explanations of indigenous phenomena. Too often, they use philosophical treatises (e.g., the Confucian classics) or religious texts (e.g., the Koran or Vedas) as an explanation of psychological phenomena. We need to distinguish indigenous philosophies and religions from indigenous psychology. Philosophical and religious texts were developed for specific purposes several thousand years ago. In order to utilize these texts, we must first translate these philosophical or religious ideas into psychological concepts and empirically verify their validity. We cannot assume that, because a person is Chinese, he or she will necessarily live by Confucian values or that Hindu Dharma can explain the behavior of an individual because he or she is Indian. Psychologists have used these texts to develop psychological concepts (Paranjpe, 1998), but these analyses are more appropriately viewed as speculative philosophy and have yet to be supported by empirical evidence.

Sixth, as with other scientific traditions, one of the goals of indigenous psychology is the discovery of universal facts, principles, and laws. Psychological universals, however, must be theoretically and empirically verified, rather than assumed a priori.

Seventh, indigenous psychology represents a transactional scientific paradigm in which individuals are viewed as agents of their own action and collective agents through their culture (Bandura, 1997; Harré, 1999; Kim, 2000; Kim & Berry, 1993). In human sciences, we are both the subject and the object of investigation, and we communicate our understanding to other people. Although the objective, third-person viewpoint is necessary in psychology, it is not sufficient. We need to supplement it with a first-person perspective (i.e., incorporating agency, meaning, and intention, Bandura, 1997) and a second-person analysis (e.g., discourse analysis, Harré, 1999). We need to derive an integrated understanding of first-person, second-person, and third-person perspectives in order to construct a complete picture of human functioning. Research is a creative and generative enterprise in search of a probabilistic understanding of human action, rather than a deterministic search for objective knowledge (Bandura, 1997). Research topics and stimuli must be meaningful and contextualized.

Eighth, psychologists have criticized indigenous psychologies for accumulating idiosyncratic data, fragmentation, reverse ethnocentrism, and moving against the trend of globalization (Hermans & Kempen, 1998; Ho, Peng, Lai, & Chan, 2001; Triandis, 2000). Speculative analysis of indigenous concepts has been presented as a prime example of indigenous psychology. The concepts of *amae* in Japan (indulgent dependence; Doi, 1973) and *kapwa* in the Philippines (shared identity with other; Enriquez, 1993) have been introduced. It is difficult to evaluate the scientific merit of these indigenous concepts since very little empirical evidence exists to support the anecdotal accounts of how they operate. This has been among the main criticisms of indigenous psychology.

The Japanese concept of *amae* has been a focus of international attention; it was first described by Doi (1973). Yamaguchi and Ariizumi (2006) pointed out that both Japanese and U.S. scholars have erroneously interpreted the concept of *amae* as an example of dependence (Doi, 1973; Johnson, 1993; Rothbaum, Weisz, Pott, Miyake, & Morelli, 2000). This assertion was made without a clear definition of *amae* or empirical evidence to support the underlying assumption. Kim and Yamaguchi (1995) administered an open-ended questionnaire to 841 respondents living in various parts of Japan (237 middle-school students, 224 high-school students, 243 university students, and 137 adults) to explore various facets of *amae*. The results indicated that *amae* involves an exchange between two people: one person who requests a specific favor and another person who grants the request. *Amae* occurs in close relationships, and the special request, which is often demanding and unreasonable, is granted because of the close relationship.

Yamaguchi and Ariizumi (2006) conducted a series of experiments to analyze different facets of *amae*. They defined *amae* as the "presumed acceptance of one's inappropriate behavior or request" (pp. 164–165). They developed scenarios containing instances of *amae* and carried out studies with a sample of Japanese, U.S., and Taiwanese students. They found that respondents engage in *amae* in order to obtain a desired goal through the help of a powerful other (i.e., proxy control) as well as to affirm the close relationship. They found that the U.S. and Taiwanese respondents were more likely than Japanese respondents to engage in *amae*. They concluded that although *amae* is an indigenous Japanese concept, the psychological features of *amae* can be found in other cultures. Thus, a series of empirical studies have helped to clarify the confusion that was initially created by Japanese and U.S. scholars. These studies outline key features of *amae*, which could potentially challenge some of the precepts of attachment theory (Yamaguchi & Ariizumi, 2006).

A TRANSACTIONAL MODEL OF SCIENCE

Human behavior is shaped by the goals people set for themselves, the skills that they develop, and the outcomes that shape their actions. Similar to indigenous psychology, Bandura (1997) pointed out that people are agents of their own action, motivated to control their lives in order to attain desirable goals and attach meaning to them. Although our body and brain provide the basis for our behavior, they do not determine them. They are used to control the environment and to realize our goals. Bandura pointed out that the human mind and behavior are not just reactive, but they are generative, creative, and proactive.

The method by which we exert control over the environment can be direct or indirect and exerted by an individual or in concert with other people (Bandura, 1997; Kim & Park, 2005). Two types of direct control can be identified: *primary control* and *collective control*. If a person exerts direct control over the environment, it is an example of primary control. If people work together in concert to manage their environment, it is an example of collective control (e.g., democracy). Two types of indirect control can be identified: *secondary control* and *proxy control*. If a person obtains assistance from another person in managing the environment, it is an example of proxy control. If a person adjusts to a given environment and regulates himself or herself in order to adapt to the environment, it is an example of secondary control. Western theories have emphasized direct control over the environment through the use of primary and collective control. As will be shown subsequently, East Asian cultures emphasize the maintenance of harmony and use of indirect control (i.e., secondary control through self-regulation and proxy control by obtaining social support).

Bandura (1997, 2004) has applied social cognitive theory to help people take control of their lives and to change their lifestyles. This theory forms the basis for interventions to teach diabetic children to manage their health, workers to reduce their cholesterol levels, patients with coronary artery disease to implement lifestyle changes, and patients with arthritis to manage their pain. The theory has also been used to develop radio and television dramas that promote society-wide changes in health and AIDS prevention in India, Mexico, and Tanzania and to reduce the birth rate and elevate the rights of women in China. Consistent with the position advocated by indigenous psychology, Bandura (1997, 2004) has demonstrated that a more rigorous and universal general theory of human functioning can be developed if researchers are willing to integrate human agency, intention, meaning, and context into their research designs.

A STARTING POINT FOR RESEARCH

Enriquez (1993) identified two approaches to indigenous psychology: *indigenization from without* and *indigenization from within*. Indigenization from without involves taking existing psychological theories and methods, and modifying them to fit the local cultural context. The approaches advocated by some cultural and cross-cultural psychologists are examples of indigenization from without (e.g., Triandis, 2000). Rather than assuming that a particular theory is universal a priori, researchers modify and adapt psychological theories and integrate them with the local cultural knowledge. Those aspects that can be verified across cultures are retained as possible cultural universals.

In indigenization from within, theories and methods are developed internally and local information is considered to be a primary source of knowledge (Enriquez, 1993). For example, one of the core values and assumptions that psychologists from East Asia are questioning is that of individualism (Ho et al., 2001). In East Asia, human relationships occupy center stage in defining interactions within family, school, work settings, and society (Azuma, 1986; Ho et al., 2001; Kim & Park, 2005). Recently, both cross-sectional and longitudinal studies have yielded results that confirm the importance of close relationships in South Korea that are highly reliable, valid, and applicable (Kim & Park, 2005; Park & Kim, 2004). Although psychological theories have emphasized individualism, research indicates that relationships are central to understanding human development and functioning in different parts of the world (Helgesen & Kim, 2002; House, Landis, & Umberson, 1988; Kim et al., 1994).

CULTURE

Culture is not a variable, quasi-independent variable, category, or mere sum of individual characteristics. Culture represents the collective utilization of natural and human resources to achieve desired outcomes (Kim, 2001b). Differences in cultures can exist if we pursue different collective goals, utilize different methods and resources to realize these goals, and attach different meaning and values to them. Researchers have found that the majority of Americans and Europeans emphasize the values of individual rights, personal freedom, and open debate, whereas the majority of East Asians are likely to emphasize an orderly society, harmony, and self-discipline (Hofstede, 1991).

Although our physiology is the basis for all our actions, it is culture that shapes, directs, and modifies our actions. To use an analogy, computers consist of hardware and software. Our physiology is like the hardware of a computer and culture is like the software (Hofstede, 1991). A computer operates differently depending of the type of software that is downloaded. When children are born, although they have the potential to learn any language, they usually learn one language. Language represents symbolic knowledge that provides a cultural community with the collective ability to organize, express, communicate, and manage ideas.

People have a capacity for self-reflection and creativity that computers do not possess. Computers must be programmed to operate. Human beings have the capability of changing themselves, others, and their environment. Without culture, human beings would be like other animals, reduced to basic instincts. Culture allows us to know who we are, define what is meaningful, communicate with others, and manage our environment. It is *through* culture that we think, feel, behave, and manage our reality (Shweder, 1991). Just as we use our eyes to see the world, we use our culture to understand our world. For a person born and raised in a particular culture, his or her own culture feels supremely natural. Because we filter events and experience through our culture, it is difficult, but not impossible to recognize our own culture (Shweder, 1991).

Cultures undergo dramatic transformations. At the turn of the century, East Asian societies were far behind in science and technology, lacking in educational, economic, and political infrastructure and experiencing national turmoil. Despite limited natural resources, East Asian governments and companies were able to design appropriate educational, political, and economic systems to transform latent human resources into powerful nations. Currently, Japan is the second largest economy in the world. South Korea (abbreviated hereafter as Korea) and Taiwan have two of the fastest growing economies in the past 30 years. China is emerging as a major international player with a rapidly expanding economy. The purpose of the following section is to provide an indigenous analysis of educational and economic achievement in East Asia.

UNDERSTANDING ACHIEVEMENT IN EAST ASIA: AN INDIGENOUS AND CULTURAL ANALYSIS

The phenomenal economic growth in East Asia has been spurred by educational transformations (Kim & Park, 2005). In Korea, for example, high-school enrollment is at 99%, and more than 80% of students enroll in a college or university (Park & Kim, 2004). The economic miracle of East Asia is closely tied to the educational aspirations and investment made by adolescents and their parents.

In international comparisons of academic achievement of middle-school students (National Center for Educational Statistics [NCES], 2000; Organization for Economic Cooperation and Development [OECD], 2003), East Asian students are the top achievers in mathematics, science, and reading literacy. Students from Singapore are the top performers in mathematics, followed by those from Korea, Taiwan, Hong Kong, and Japan (NCES, 2000). In the sciences, Taiwanese students are the top performers, followed by students from Singapore, Hungary, Korea, and Japan.

According to the OECD (2003), Japanese students are at the top in mathematics, Korean students are at the top in sciences, and both are near the top in reading literacy (Korea is ranked 6th and Japan 8th). U.S. students are ranked 19th in mathematics and 18th in sciences (NCES, 2000). According to the OECD (2003) survey, they are ranked 15th in reading literacy, 19th in mathematical literacy, and 14th in scientific literacy.

In Western countries, there are significant variations. In Europe, Finnish students do as well as East-Asian students and German students perform as poorly as American students. In North America, Canadian students perform much better than American students. Follow-up studies conducted in 2003 indicate a similar pattern of results (NCES, 2004; OECD, 2004). These findings baffle many psychologists since they are inconsistent with existing psychological theories. Traditional psychological and educational theories that emphasize biology (e.g., innate ability, IQ), individualistic values (e.g., intrinsic motivation, ability attribution, self-esteem), and structural features (e.g., high educational spending, small class size, individualized instruction) cannot explain the relatively poor performance of American students and high performance of East-Asian students.

First, although the U.S. government spends more money per student than its East-Asian counterparts, and although Americans schools have smaller classes, American students perform far below their East Asian counterparts. Second, although students in the United States perform poorly in mathematics and science, they have high self-esteem for these subjects. They are ranked first in self-esteem for science and fourth for mathematics (NCES, 2000). By contrast, East-Asian students have relatively low self-esteem: Korean students are ranked 32nd in self-esteem for mathematics and 21st for self-esteem in science, Japanese students are ranked 34th and 16th, respectively, and Taiwanese students 30th and 18th. A similar pattern of results has been found in follow-up studies (NCES, 2004; OCED, 2004), forcing researchers to question current conceptions of self-esteem and the validity of self-esteem measurements.

Third, as to the motivation for studying math, 41% of U.S. students strongly agreed with the statement that it is "to get the desired job." However, only 10% of Korean students and 12% of Japanese students strongly agreed with this motivation (NCES, 2000). For Korean students, 85% agreed that it is to "enter a desired university" (social motivation) and 62% agreed that it is "to please their parents" (relational motivation). For Korean students, relational and social motivations outweighed personal motivation.

Fourth, in developmental psychology, Freudian, Piagetian, behavioral, and humanistic theories do not adequately examine the role played by parents. Attachment theory does examine the role of parents, with separation and individuation seen as necessary for the emergence of secure attachment (Rothbaum et al., 2000). In East Asia, parents play a central role in child development by defining the goals of socialization, teaching children the necessary cognitive, linguistic, relational, and social skills, and providing them with a supportive family environment. Parents play an important role throughout a child's life, and maintenance of strong familial relationships is the key to education, economic success, and quality of life.

Fifth, concepts such as guilt have quite a different connotation and use in East Asia (Azuma, 1986; Park & Kim, 2004). In many, but not all Western psychological theories, guilt is presumed to reflect irrational beliefs, neurotic fears, or forbidden wishes. The extensive experience of guilt is believed to cause developmental problems in adolescence. In East Asia, it is considered appropriate for children to feel guilty or indebted to their parents for all of the devotion, indulgence, sacrifice, and love that they have received (Azuma, 1986; Ho, 1986; Park & Kim, 2004). Children feel indebted to their parents because they cannot repay their parents for what their parents have bestowed upon them. Guilt in East Asia is viewed as an important interpersonal emotion that promotes filial piety, achievement motivation, and relational closeness.

Educational Achievement

The phenomenal educational attainment in East-Asian societies has been systematically documented (Park & Kim, 2004; Stevenson, Azuma, & Hakuta, 1986; Stevenson & Lee, 1990). The main factor responsible for high academic performance lies in socialization practices that promote and maintain a strong relational and emotional bond between parents and children. It is the role of parents to provide a positive family environment for children and to pressure children to succeed. Children learn to discipline themselves and to develop their academic skills with the help of their parents. This type of socialization facilitates the development of proxy control. A second major factor is the emphasis on self-regulation, especially the belief in the importance of persistent effort. The third major factor is the compatibility of values between familial and school environment that promotes collective efficacy.

Interdependence and Proxy Control.   The parent–child relationship provides the basis for the development of the self. Parental devotion, sacrifice, and support are important features of the traditional socialization that still operates in modern East Asia (Azuma, 1986; Ho, 1986; Park & Kim, 2004). In East Asia, a mother remains close to her child to make the child feel secure, to set a minimal boundary between herself and the child, and to meet all the needs of the child. Children's strong dependency needs, both emotional and physical, are satisfied by their mother's indulgent devotion, even if that involves tremendous sacrifice on her own part.

A mother's job is to use the close relationship with her children to encourage them to discipline themselves and to succeed in school. She becomes a mediator between the home environment and the school environment by socializing appropriate values and normative behavior. As children mature, they are expected to extend and transfer their interdependent identification and loyalty from their mothers to their teachers.

In East Asia, the relationship between teachers and their students is seen as an extension of the parent–child relationship. The typical climate in schools pressures the student to strive for personal excellence and encourages students to cooperate in a group. Children are motivated to please the teacher, and their attention is focused on the teacher. Even in a class size as large as 40 to 60, East-Asian students are more attentive, less disruptive, and more dedicated to their schoolwork than are students in the West (Park & Kim, 2004; Stevenson & Lee, 1990).

Self-Regulation   The second important value is that of *self-regulation*, especially the emphasis on persistent effort. Excellence in performance provides evidence that a child has developed moral character through perseverance. It is a visible demonstration that a child has deeper abilities to become a virtuous adult. Holloway, Kasgiwagi, and Azuma (1986) pointed out that "the emphasis on individual effort includes a sense of responsibility to the group to which one belongs" (p. 272). In Confucian-heritage societies, individuals are pressured to contribute to the group through hard work, and success is collectively defined and shared. Whereas natural talent and ability are emphasized in parts of the West, in East Asia effort and self-cultivation are highly valued.

Lebra (1976) found in a free-association task that over 70% of Japanese respondents, both young and old, men and women, attributed success to diligence, effort, and endurance whereas only 1% attributed it to ability. Other researchers (Holloway et al., 1986; Park & Kim, 2004;

Stevenson & Lee, 1990) also found that East-Asian students, parents, and teachers attribute poor performance in school to a lack of effort rather than ability. European-American students, parents, and teachers are most likely to attribute failure to innate ability.

Collective Control. In East Asia, there is a greater congruence of achievement values in the family, school, and society than in the West. In the West, individualistic values are often in conflict with a relatively hierarchical classroom structure, curriculum, and teacher–student relationship (White & LeVine, 1986). In the West, development of one's talent, whether in sports, music, or the arts is emphasized, and academic achievement may not be considered a primary goal (White & LeVine, 1986). The diversity of viewpoints is considered to be a strength of individualistic societies, but it can lead to conflict among the students, parents, and teachers when manifested in academic settings.

In East Asia, students, parents, and teachers unanimously agree that academic achievement is the primary goal for children and adolescents, and they work together toward this goal. There is considerable agreement among all parties concerning the goals of education and the methods for realizing academic achievement. This collective agreement among family, school, and society promotes collective efficacy and is a key factor in motivating students to attain a high level of achievement (Park & Kim, 2004).

The importance of self-regulation, parental support, and collective control is not unique to East-Asian students. In the U.S., Asian-American students are high achievers since they possess the above characteristics (Farkas, Grobe, Sheehan, & Shuan, 1990; Kim & Chun, 1994). Similarly, socialization practices and the emphasis on education in Finland closely parallel those values found in East Asia, which may be partially responsible for the high level of educational achievement among Finnish students (Helgesen & Kim, 2002).

Delinquency and School Violence. Although East Asian students are high achievers, there are costs. When Korean students were asked in 1996 to describe the most stressful aspect of their lives, 28% report pressure to achieve academically, followed by a personal relationship (20%), and family life (15%; Park & Kim, 2004). During the economic crisis of 1999, 44% of students reported pressure to achieve academically as being the most stressful, followed by a personal relationship (16%), and family life (14%; Park & Kim, 2004). The pressure to succeed academically is the main source of stress, interpersonal problems, and delinquency for East-Asian students (Park & Kim, 2004; Tsuneyoshi, 2001). Even with this pressure and stress, when East-Asian students succeed academically, it brings economic, relational, and social rewards.

East-Asian societies have not successfully dealt with those students who cannot adjust to the rigid school system, cope with the pressures to achieve, those who fail to do well academically, or engage in delinquent behavior (Park & Kim, 2004; Tsuneyoshi, 2001). The rate of students who refuse to attend school and the level of delinquency and school violence have been increasing rapidly in recent years. In Korea, nearly half of the teachers and students report that teachers and administrators have to some degree lost the leadership and authority to teach and regulate students, and more than half of primary-, middle-, and high-school students reported experiencing school violence (Park & Kim, 2004). Similar findings have been found in Japan (Tsuneyoshi, 2001).

East-Asian students, teachers, and parents have low efficacy when responding to delinquency and school violence, perhaps explaining why they appear unable to stem the rising tide of these twin social problems (Park & Kim, 2004; Tsuneyoshi, 2001). Although East-Asian societies have been able to foster the development of self-, proxy, and collective control in promoting high academic achievement, they have yet to develop the necessary control needed to slow the dropout rate, delinquency, and school violence.

Organizational Culture.   In East Asia, researchers note that capitalism, industrialization, and urbanization have not significantly altered the underlying cultural value system that emphasizes human-relatedness (Hwang, 1998; Kim, 1998; Misumi, 1985). The phenomenal economic progress of East-Asian countries has been achieved in part due to the maintenance of human-relatedness. Capitalism itself became modified to fit underlying East-Asian cultural values that emphasize human-relatedness (Kim, 1994; Misumi, 1985).

Contrary to the Western emphasis on individual rights, competition, and contractual relationship between employees and employers, many organizations in East Asia are managed as an extension of a family (Kim, 1998; Hwang, 1998). In these societies, companies and governments encourage paternalism, cooperation, and contribution to the group. Employees in a company are looked after like parents look after their children. In turn, employees are expected to be loyal, committed, and hard-working. In a national survey of personnel managers from mining and manufacturing firms in Korea, over 80% strongly endorsed the ideas of paternalism and collectivism (Kim, 1994). These companies provide occupational and welfare services to their employees to foster paternalism, in-group solidarity, and collectivism, which were found to increase production, efficiency, solidarity, loyalty, job satisfaction, and social control (Kim, 1994).

In comparative studies of U.S. and Japanese managers, the nature and role of a group are viewed very differently (Sullivan, Suzuki, & Kondo, 1986). Managers in the United States tend to give rewards based on individual performance and provide greater rewards when an employee works alone. For American managers, the successful person working alone should receive the highest reward. Japanese managers, by contrast, tend to distribute rewards equally and give greater rewards to individuals who worked in a group and who had been influenced by the group. Japanese managers see groups as facilitating the enhancement of productivity. Consistent with this belief, Japanese managers reward individuals who work with their group in an interdependent manner and are highly influenced by the group's attitudes and advice, regardless of their level of performance. Similarly, Gabrenya, Wang, and Latané (1985) found that for meaningful, skill-related tasks, U.S. students who worked in a group tended to loaf (i.e., engage in social loafing), whereas Chinese students tended to work harder in a group (i.e., engage in social striving).

Justice and Organizational Effectiveness. In decision-making and negotiation theories developed in the West, a quid pro quo strategy is considered to be the most effective (Axelrod & Hamilton, 1981). In other words, if your partner cooperates, then you cooperate with your partner. If your partner does not cooperative, then you are not expected to cooperate (i.e., lex talionis, or "an eye for an eye, a tooth for a tooth"). Systematic research suggests that this is the most effective strategy in inducing cooperation and positive outcomes in the West, and that this model has been widely used in economic, political, and social arenas (Axelrod & Hamilton, 1981).

The quid pro quo strategy and equity theory are effective in individualistic cultures. In East Asia, the norm of seniority prevails. Within this framework, reward is not based on individual performance, but rather how long a person has been with the group. In a typical university in Japan, Korea, and Taiwan, senior professors are paid much more than junior professors. They have the largest offices and have access to the greatest amount of resources, although a junior professor may be much more productive than his or her senior counterparts. Moreover, a junior professor is expected to show respect, serve a senior professor, and handle much of the administrative burdens. It creates a temporal imbalance, with senior professors receiving larger and more numerous benefits than junior professors. Equity can only be achieved when junior professors become senior professors, since they are then eligible for all benefits, including junior professors who will serve them. From a long-term relational perspective, justice and equity are maintained. This phenomenon is not unique to East Asia, and has been documented in different parts of the world (Aycan, 2006).

In the relational perspective, individuals are motivated to maintain the group. Since senior professors receive benefits beyond their contribution, they are motivated to remain in the group and maintain the group. Junior professors will receive more substantial benefits only if they remain in the group long enough to become senior professors. As a result, they are motivated to preserve the group. Empirical studies indicate that the seniority norm enhances group solidarity, commitment, and loyalty, and it has been widely adopted in East Asia (Kim, 1994; Kim, 1998; Yuki & Yamaguchi, 1996). However, since the reward is not directly linked to performance, it could also lead to incompetence, corruption, and nepotism (Kim, 1998, 2001a).

In addition to the norm of seniority, East Asians interact with others differently depending on the nature of the partner. If Person A contributes 70% to the overall outcome and Person B contributes 30%, an equitable distribution would be to give $70 to Person A and $30 to Person B. In the West, this type of distribution is considered fair and just (Kim, Park, & Suzuki, 1990; Leung & Bond, 1984). In East Asia, if Person A contributes 70% and Person B contributes 30%, the reward is distributed equitably if the partner is an outgroup member. If, however, the partner is an in-group member, the high performer will divide the reward equally (i.e., 50/50; Kim et al., 1990; Leung & Bond, 1984). In other words, the high performer will share his or her own reward with a less achieving in-group member. The sacrificial behavior of the high performer can promote a sense of gratitude, loyalty, and harmony. Although there is a temporary imbalance, the high performer can expect future benefits from the friend or from the group (Yamagishi, Jin, & Miller, 1998). This type of distribution is based on the indigenous parent–child model, in which it is the role of parents to sacrifice for their children and for children to feel indebted to their parents (Park & Kim, 2004).

East-Asian parents willingly sacrifice for their children since their own parents cared for them unconditionally when they were young (Park & Kim, 2004). Children are expected to return their sense of gratitude to the parents, but not the favor. They are expected to raise their own children with the same degree of sacrifice, devotion, and love as did their parents. This flow of sacrifice, devotion, and love is what binds family members together through generations and keeps them strong. What is valued in East Asia is the flow of obligation from one generation to another, not a quid pro quo exchange.

This long-term relational perspective among in-group members, rather than the short-term quid pro quo strategy, is accepted as being just, fair, and effective in East Asia since it promotes group solidarity, loyalty, and harmony. The long-term relational perspective is a cultural norm and it is widely expressed in East-Asian schools, organizations, and companies since it promotes harmony and group solidarity. This principle is behind the Sunshine Policy that president Kim Dae-jung has pursued with North Korea (Kim, 2001a). It is, however, not without its problems.

There are two possible outcomes for organizations adopting the long-term relational perspective. As noted, in East Asia a low-performing employee will receive the same benefits as a high-performing employee. In the ideal situation, the low-performing employee should feel a sense of shame, indebtedness, and gratitude and work harder to contribute to the group. This will create synergy and organizational dynamism that appears to be responsible for the high level of productivity in East Asia. If, however, the low-performing employee simply accepts a reward without the intention or motivation to contribute to the group, then it will lead to organizational ineffectiveness and discontent (Yamagishi et al., 1998).

High-performing employees expect to be rewarded in the long run. If they are not so rewarded, they will leave the organization (Kim, 1998; Yamagishi et al., 1998). Thus, if the long-term contingency is not fulfilled, high-performing employees will leave a company and the fate of that company is left to low-performing "free riders" who do not contribute. As a result, such a company will face financial and moral bankruptcy. This is one reason for the Asian economic crisis that has plagued Japan, Korea, and Taiwan (Kim, 1998, 2001a).

The long-term relational perspective has contributed to phenomenal educational and economic progress in East Asia. It has, however, also contributed to incompetence, nepotism, and corruption. Strong leaders like Park Chung-hee, Lee Kwan Yew, and Mohamad Mahathir used the long-term relational perspective to justify their policies. In order for the long-term relational perspective to be effective in companies, organizations, and society, people must trust the specific system in which it operates. Institutions in East-Asia are not trusted because they lack accountability, integrity, and transparency (Helgesen & Kim, 2002). Although East-Asian countries have developed economically, they are ranked low in transparency: Japan was ranked 24th, Korea 47th, Taiwan 35th, and China 71st in 2004 (Transparency International, 2004).

The problem can be resolved when the system becomes transparent and everyone knows who the high and low performers are (Kim, 1998). The low performer will be compelled to work harder or leave the group since he or she will experience a sense of shame. The high performer will be rewarded equitably in the long run. Transparency is also necessary to ensure that every member of the group will behave with integrity. Finally, individuals need to be held accountable for their behavior. Without accountability, integrity, and transparency, individuals and groups will not be motivated to work hard and contribute to the group, and corruption and conflict could emerge.

Many East Asians criticize the long-term relational perspective and advocate for the adoption of a Western system in which rewards are allocated on the basis of individual performance (Kim, 1988). The optimal solution has been neither the short-term or long-term perspective, since each approach has its merits and weaknesses. Many East-Asian companies have opted to blend both strategies, rewarding individual performance in order to enhance self-efficacy, while at the same time rewarding group performance in order to enhance collective efficacy (Kim, 1988). The key to organizational management and effectiveness in East Asia is to provide accurate feedback based on transparency and to allocate reward based on both short-term and long term perspectives (Kim, 1988).

CONCLUSION

Indigenous psychology represents a transactional model of science in which agency, meaning, intentions, and goals are incorporated into research design. It advocates examining the knowledge, skills, and beliefs people have about themselves and how they function in their cultural context. It represents an approach in which the content (i.e., agency, meaning, beliefs) and context (i.e., family, society, culture, ecology) are explicitly incorporated into the research design. With theoretical, conceptual, and empirical descriptions, ideas are developed and tested to explain observed regularities. The goal is to achieve a more rigorous, systematic, and universal science that can be theoretically and empirically verified. The goal of indigenous psychology is similar to general psychology, but the means to realizing this goal differ markedly.

We must be cautious of external impositions that may distort our understanding of human beings. Initially, many psychologists imposed the natural-sciences paradigm to study human beings. In the rush to become an independent branch of science, early psychologists tailored the discipline to fit the natural-sciences paradigm. Although psychologists were able to achieve a modest degree of methodological sophistication, psychological knowledge became distorted. Psychologists have discarded central constructs (e.g., agency, consciousness, intentions, meaning) in the quest for an objective science.

The second imposition is the a priori assumption of the universality of psychological theories. With very little conceptual development and empirical testing, psychological theories have been assumed to be universal. This assumption is particularly troublesome since most theories are developed in the United States and tested mainly on university students in laboratory settings. We do not know very much about people in other cultures, and erroneous conclusions have been drawn about other cultures because psychologists have assumed that their theories were universal.

Third, experts have imposed their views on the lay public. Psychologists have been premature in developing theories and methods without fully understanding the phenomena in question. Psychology has largely failed to describe psychological phenomena from the inside, that is, from the perspective of the experiencing person. Instead, psychologists have dissected the world into behavior, cognition, emotion, and motivation, whereas in reality these elements are interlaced components of experience rather than units of experience. Psychology can best be described as the *psychology of psychologists*. It represents the way psychologists have come to understand people and not necessarily the way in which people understand themselves and the world.

Finally, indigenous psychology advocates for the development of more rigorous theories based on epistemological and scientific grounds. We have focused most of our attention on internal or external validity, and not on practical validity (Kim, 2001b). In a practical sense, perhaps the greatest psychologist was William Shakespeare. He was not an analyst like Freud or Piaget, and he did not conduct experiments like Skinner, but he was able to capture human drama on paper and stage. His dramas have been performed over the past centuries in many cultures and are loved throughout the world. In a similar vein, the greatest therapists may have been composers, such as Ludwig van Beethoven or Wolfgang Amadeus Mozart, whose music is able to soothe frazzled nerves and ease the frustrations of daily life. Walt Disney could be considered the most notable developmental psychologist. He was able to capture the hearts and minds of children and the young-at-heart. We may not think of these people as psychologists, but they have captured and reproduced human psychology on stage, film, tapes, and paper for centuries and across cultures. We need to learn from them and to translate their phenomenological knowledge into systematic conceptual and empirical forms. Psychology is a discipline that can link humanities (which focus on human experience and creativity) with social sciences (which focus on analysis and verification).

RECOMMENDED READINGS

Allwood, C. A., & Berry, J. W. (Eds.). (2006). Origins and development of indigenous psychologies: An international analysis [Special issue]. *International Journal of Psychology, 41*(4).

Cheung. F. M., Cheung, S. F., Wada, S., & Zhang, J. X. (2003). Indigenous measures of personality assessment in Asian countries: A review. *Psychological Assessment, 15*, 280–289.

Enriquez, V. G. (Ed.). (1990). *Indigenous psychology: A book of readings.* Quezon City, Philippines: Philippine Psychology Research and Training House.

Hwang, K. K., & Yang, K. S. (Eds.). (2000). Indigenous, cultural and cross-cultural psychology [Special issue]. *Asian Journal of Social Psychology, 3*(3).

Kim, U., Aasen, H. S., & Ebadi, S. (2003). *Democracy, human rights, and Islam in modern Iran: Psychological, social and cultural perspectives.* Bergen, Norway: Fagbokforlaget.

Kim, U., & Berry, J. W. (Eds.). (1993). *Indigenous psychologies: Experience and research in cultural context.* Newbury Park, CA: Sage.

Kim, U., Yang, K. S., & Hwang, K. K. (2006). *Indigenous and cultural psychology: Understanding people in context.* New York: Springer.

Nsamenang, A. B. (2004). *Cultures of human development and education: Challenge to growing up African.* Hauppauge, NY: Nova Science Publishers.

Sánchez-Sosa, J. J. (in press). Rogélio Díaz-Guerrero, father of Mexican ethnopsychology: A conversation. In U. P. Gielen (Ed.), *Conversations with international psychologists.* Greenwich, CT: Information Age Publishing.

Sinha, D. (1997). Indigenizing psychology. In J. W. Berry, Y. H. Poortinga, & J. Pandey (Eds.), *Handbook of cross-cultural psychology: Vol. 1. Theory and method* (pp. 129–169). Boston: Allyn and Bacon.

Yang, K. S., Hwang, K. K., & Yang, C. F. (Eds.). (2005). *Chinese indigenous psychology* (Vols. 1–2). Taipei: Yuanliu Publishing. [in Chinese]

REFERENCES

Axelrod, R., & Hamilton, W. D. (1981). The evolution of cooperation. *Science, 211*, 1390–1396.

Aycan, Z. (2006). Paternalism: Towards conceptual refinement and operationalization. In U. Kim, K. S. Yang, & K. K. Hwang (Eds.), *Indigenous and cultural psychology: Understanding people in context* (pp. 445–466). New York: Springer.

Azuma, H. (1984). Psychology in a non-Western country. *International Journal of Psychology, 19,* 145–155.

Azuma, H. (1986). Why study child development in Japan? In H. Stevenson, H. Azuma, & K. Hakuta (Eds.), *Child development and education in Japan* (pp. 3–12). New York: Freeman.

Bandura, A. (1997). *Self-efficacy: The exercise of control.* New York: Freeman.

Bandura, A. (2004). Swimming against the mainstream: The early years from chilly tributary to transformative mainstream. *Behavior Research and Therapy, 42,* 613–630.

Berry, J. W. (1974). Canadian psychology: Some social and applied emphasis. *Canadian Psychologist, 15,* 132–139.

Boulding, K. (1980). Science: Our common heritage. *Science, 207,* 821–826.

Doi, T. (1973). *The anatomy of dependence.* Tokyo: Kodansha.

Elms, A. C. (1975). The crisis of confidence in social psychology. *American Psychologist, 30,* 967–976.

Enriquez, V. G. (1993). Developing a Filipino psychology. In U. Kim & J. W. Berry (Eds.), *Indigenous psychologies: Research and experience in cultural context* (pp. 152–169). Newbury Park, CA: Sage.

Farkas, G., Grobe, R. P., Sheehan, D., & Shuan, Y. (1990). Cultural resources and school success: Gender, ethnicity and poverty groups within an urban school district. *American Sociological Review, 55,* 127–142.

Gabrenya, W. K., Jr., Wang, Y. E., & Latané, B. (1985). Social loafing on an optimizing task: Cross-cultural differences among Chinese and Americans. *Journal of Cross-Cultural Psychology, 16*(2), 223–242.

Harré, R. (1999). The rediscovery of the human mind: The discursive approach. *Asian Journal of Social Psychology, 2,* 43–62.

Helgesen, G., & Kim, U. (2002). *Good government: Nordic and East Asian perspectives.* Copenhagen: Danish Institute of International Affairs.

Hermans, J. M., & Kempen, J. G. (1998). Moving cultures: The perilous problem of cultural dichotomy in a globalized society. *American Psychologist, 53*(10), 1111–1120.

Ho, D. Y. F. (1986). Chinese patterns of socialization: A critical review. In M. H. Bond (Ed.), *The psychology of the Chinese people* (pp. 1–37). Oxford, UK: Oxford University Press.

Ho, D. Y. F. (1995). Internalized culture, culturocentrism, and transcendence. *Counseling Psychologist, 23,* 4–24.

Ho, D. Y. F., Peng, S. Q., Lai, A. C., & Chan, S. F. (2001). Indigenization and beyond: Methodological relationalism in the study of personality across cultural traditions. *Journal of Personality, 69*(6), 925–953.

Hofstede, G. (1991). *Cultures and organizations: Software of the mind.* New York: McGraw-Hill.

Holloway, S., Kasgiwagi, K., & Azuma, H. (1986). Causal attributions by Japanese and American mothers and children about performance in mathematics. *International Journal of Psychology, 21,* 269–286.

House, J. S., Landis, K. R., & Umberson, D. (1988). Social relationships and health. *Science, 241,* 540–545.

Hwang, K. K. (1998). Two moralities: Reinterpreting the findings of empirical research in Taiwan. *Asian Journal of Social Psychology, 1,* 211–238.

Johnson, F. A. (1993). *Dependency and Japanese socialization.* New York: New York University Press.

Kim, K., Park, H. J., & Suzuki, N. (1990). Reward allocations in the United States, Japan and Korea: A comparison of individualistic and collectivistic cultures. *Academy of Management Journal, 33,* 188–198.

Kim, U. (1998). Understanding Korean corporate culture: Analysis of transformative human resource management. *Strategic Human Resource Development Review, 2,* 68–101.

Kim, U. (1999). After the "crisis" in social psychology: Development of the transactional model of science. *Asian Journal of Social Psychology, 2,* 1–19.

Kim, U. (2000). Indigenous, cultural and cross-cultural psychology: Theoretical, philosophical and epistemological analysis. *Asian Journal of Social Psychology, 3,* 265–287.

Kim, U. (2001a). Analysis of democracy and human rights in cultural context: Psychological and comparative perspectives. In H. S. Aasen, U. Kim, & G. Helgesen (Eds.), *Democracy, human rights and peace in Korea: Psychological, political and cultural perspectives* (pp. 53–94). Seoul: Kyoyook Kwahasa.

Kim, U. (2001b). Culture, science and indigenous psychologies: An integrated analysis. In D. Matsumoto (Ed.), *Handbook of culture and psychology* (pp. 51–76). Oxford. UK: Oxford University Press.

Kim, U., Aasen, H. S., & Ebadi, S. (2003). *Democracy, human rights, and Islam in modern Iran: Psychological, social and cultural perspectives.* Bergen: Fagbokforlaget.

Kim, U., & Berry, J. W. (Eds.). (1993). *Indigenous psychologies: Experience and research in cultural context.* Newbury Park, CA: Sage.

Kim, U., & Chun, M. (1994). Educational "success" of Asian Americans: An indigenous perspective. *Applied Behavioral Development, 15,* 329–341.

Kim, U., Helgesen, & Ahn, B. M. (2002). Democracy, trust and political efficacy: Comparative analysis of Danish and Korean political culture. *Applied Psychology: An International Review, 51*(2), 317–352.

Kim, U., & Park, Y. S. (2005). Integrated analysis of indigenous psychologies: Comments and extensions of ideas presented by Shams, Jackson, Hwang and Kashima. *Asian Journal of Social Psychology, 8*(1), 75–95.

Kim, U., & Yamaguchi, S. (1995). Conceptual and empirical analysis of *amae:* Exploration into Japanese psycho-social space. *Proceedings of the Japanese Group Dynamics Association, 43,* 158–159.

Kim, U., Yang, K. S., & Hwang, K. K. (Eds.). (2006). *Indigenous and cultural psychology: Understanding people in context.* New York: Springer.

Kim, U. M. (1994). Significance of paternalism and communalism in the occupational welfare system of Korean firms: A national survey. In U. Kim, H. C. Triandis, Ç. Kağitçibaşi, S. C. Choi, & G. Yoon (Eds.), *Individualism and collectivism: Theory, method and application* (pp. 265–285).Thousand Oaks, CA: Sage.

Koch, S., & Leary, D. E. (1985). *A century of psychology as science.* New York: McGraw Hill.

Lebra, T. S. (1976). *Japanese patterns of behavior*. Honolulu: East–West Center.

Leung, K., & Bond, M. H. (1984). The impact of cultural collectivism on reward allocation. *Journal of Personality and Social Psychology, 47*, 793–804.

Misumi, J. (1985). *The behavioral science of leadership*. Ann Arbor, MI: University of Michigan Press.

Moscovici, S. (1972). Society and theory in social psychology. In J. Israel & H. Tajfel (Eds.), *The context of social psychology* (pp. 17–68). London: Academic Press.

National Center for Educational Statistics. (2000). *Mathematics and science in eighth grade: Findings from the Third International Mathematics and Science Study*. Washington, DC: U.S. Department of Education.

National Center for Educational Statistics. (2004). *Highlights from trends in the mathematics and science study*. Washington, DC: U.S. Department of Education.

Nsamenang, A. B. (1995). Factors influencing the development of psychology in sub-Saharan Africa. *International Journal of Psychology, 30*, 729–738.

Organization for Economic Cooperation and Development. (2003). *Education at a glance: OECD indicators*. Paris: OECD.

Organization for Economic Cooperation and Development. (2004). *ELearning for tomorrow's world: First results from OECD 2003*. Paris: OECD.

Paranjpe, A. (1998). *Self and identity in modern psychology and Indian thought*. New York: Plenum.

Park, Y. S., & Kim, U. (2004). *Adolescent culture and parent–child relationship in Korea: Indigenous psychological analysis* [in Korean]. Seoul: Kyoyook Kwahaksa. [in Korean]

Rothbaum, F., Weisz, J., Pott, M., Miyake, K., & Morelli, G. (2000). Attachment and culture: Security in the United States and Japan. *American Psychologist, 55*, 1093–1104.

Sampson, E. E. (1977). Psychology and the American ideal. *Journal of Personality and Social Psychology, 35*, 767–782.

Sánchez-Sosa, J. J. (in press). Rogélio Díaz-Gerrero, father of Mexican ethnopsychology: A conversation. In U. P. Gielen (Ed.), *Conversations with international psychologists*. Greenwich, CT: Information Age Publishing.

Shweder, R. A. (1991). *Thinking through cultures: Expeditions in cultural psychology*. Cambridge, MA: Harvard University Press.

Sinha, D. (1997). Indigenizing psychology. In J. W. Berry, Y. H. Poortinga, & J. Pandey (Eds.), *Handbook of cross-cultural psychology: Vol. 1. Theory and method* (pp. 129–169). Boston: Allyn and Bacon.

Stevenson, H., Azuma, H., & Hakuta, K. (Eds.). (1986). *Child development and education in Japan*. New York: Freeman.

Stevenson, H., & Lee, S. Y. (1990). Context of achievement: A study of American, Chinese and Japanese children. *Monographs of the Society for Research in Child Development, 55*(1–2).

Sullivan, J. J., Suzuki, T., & Kondo, Y. (1986). Managerial perceptions of performance: A comparison of Japanese and American work groups. *Journal of Cross-Cultural Psychology, 17*, 379–398.

Transparency International. (2004, October 22). Corruption perceptions index. In *Corruption surveys and indices*. Retrieved March, 2005, from http://www.transparency.org/cpi/2004/cpi2004.en.html#cpi2004

Triandis, H. C. (2000). Dialectics between cultural and cross-cultural psychology. *Asian Journal of Social Psychology, 3*, 185–196.

Tsuneyoshi, R. (2001). *The Japanese model of schooling: Comparisons with the United States*. New York: Falmer Routledge.

White, M. I., & LeVine, R. A. (1986). What is an *li ko* (Good child)? In H. Stevenson, H. Azuma, & K. Hakuta (Eds.), *Child development and education in Japan* (pp. 55–62). New York: Freeman.

Yamagishi, T., Jin, N., & Miller, A. S. (1998). In-group favoritism and culture of collectivism. *Asian Journal of Social Psychology, 1*, 315–328.

Yamaguchi, S., & Ariizumi, Y. (2006). Close interpersonal relationships among Japanese: Amae as distinguished from attachment and dependence. In U. Kim, K. S. Yang, & K. K. Hwang (Eds.), *Indigenous and cultural psychology: Understanding people in context* (pp. 163–174). New York: Springer.

Yang, K. S. (2000). Monocultural and cross-cultural indigenous approaches: The royal road to the development of a balanced global psychology. *Asian Journal of Social Psychology, 3*, 241–263.

Yang, K. S., Hwang, K. K., & Yang, C. F. (Eds.). (2005). *Chinese indigenous psychology* (Vols. 1–2). Taipei: Yuanliu Publishing. [in Chinese]

Yuki, M., & Yamaguchi, S. (1996). Long-term equity within a group: An application of the seniority norm in Japan. In H. Grad, A. Blanco, & J. Georgas (Eds.), *Key issues in cross-cultural psychology* (pp. 288–297). Lisse, Netherlands: Swets and Zeitlinger.

III

THEORY, RESEARCH, PRACTICE, AND TRAINING IN GLOBAL PSYCHOLOGY

Part III of *Toward a Global Psychology: Theory, Research, Intervention, and Pedagogy* contains six chapters: Toward a Conceptual Foundation for a Global Psychology by Fathali M. Moghaddam, Christina E. Erneling, Maritza Montero, and Naomi Lee; Qualitative Research Methods for a Global Psychology by Graham B. Stead and Richard A. Young; Psychotherapeutic and Related Interventions for a Global Psychology by Juris P. Draguns; Macro-Social Interventions: Psychology, Social Policy, and Societal Influence Processes by Michael G. Wessells and Andrew Dawes; Toward a Global Professionalization of Psychology by Jean L. Pettifor; and Education and Training for a Global Psychology: Foundations, Issues, and Actions by Anthony J. Marsella. These chapters underscore the global economic, political, social, and technological forces that continue to exert a profound influence, not necessarily benign, on psychology as a discipline and a profession. In addition, they address the growing needs for alternative conceptual models, investigative methods, interventions both small and large, regulatory legislation and ethical guidelines, and approaches to the preparation of psychologists that are relevant to the unsolved and emerging problems of an interdependent world.

Chapter 6 builds upon the historical perspective on psychology portrayed in chapter 2 and the descriptions of psychology in the majority world and the indigenization movement in psychology presented in chapters 5 and 6, respectively. Moghaddam, Erneling, Montero, and Lee trace psychology's roots to Western European thought and its long-time home base in the United States. Although internal debate has existed within the field since its earliest years, today's fragmentation reflects the progress that the Second and Third Worlds of psychology have made in challenging mainstream U.S. psychology to expand its theoretical and cultural horizons, also noted in chapter 1. A variety of alternative psychology movements have taken hold, and some have gained in international influence. The alternative psychologies share a conceptual core, which postulates that psychology should focus upon: (a) processes of collective meaning-making, (b) the collective nature of primary psychological reality, (c) time-dependent psychological processes, and (d) normative explanations based on rules and conventions of correctness. The authors contend that alternative psychologies, with their cultural inclusiveness and sensitivity, represent the best promise for discovering universals in thought and action, which has a multitude of significant implications for research methodologies (chapter 7), psychotherapies (chapter 8), macro-level interventions (chapter 9), professional ethics (chapter 10), and education and training (chapter 11). This core chapter further holds that the universals which are discovered will not be the causal mechanisms of mainstream psychology, but rather patterns of social practices that imbue psychological activity with everyday meaning. The authors conclude with a hopeful vision for the future in which alternative and traditional psychologies will partner effectively to better understand the biological enabling conditions and normative meaning systems that guide and give significance to human psychological activity.

In chapter 7, Stead and Young reflect on qualitative research methods suited to a global psychology. They examine the philosophical assumptions that underlie quantitative and qualitative methods, and emphasize the importance of adopting culturally appropriate research methods, rather than ones rooted in a monolithic science. The issues and perspective which they articulate agree closely with what is presented in the opening chapter of this book, the chapters in part II that describe the emergence of indigenous psychologies and, of course, the other chapters of part III, especially those which speak to the need for alternative conceptual foundations in psychology, interventions that better fit problems-in-context, and new curricula with which to prepare culturally competent psychologists. Stead and Young construe psychology as a cultural enterprise and, hence, they view research methods as cultural tools in scientific research rather than as ways of transcending normative practices. They also advocate for the development and application of investigative approaches that are capable of capturing the cultural manifestations of human action and interaction—a most appropriate vision for a global psychology. Within this framework, they describe four qualitative methods, which owing to their different theoretical and procedural bases, contribute in unique ways to the definition and extension of a richly diverse global psychology. These methods are action theory, discourse analysis, grounded theory, and focus groups. Stead and Young illustrate how these methods offer possibilities for studying psychological phenomena-in-context and for recognizing distinctly local knowledge.

From its inception to the present day, psychotherapy has been a global enterprise. In chapter 8, Juris Draguns describes the variety of current theories and practices in psychotherapy around the world, both within the currently dominant psychodynamic, humanistic, and cognitive behavioral frameworks as well as outside of them. Draguns also explains how research on psychotherapy process and outcome has evolved into a global undertaking, highlighting the growing trend toward multidisciplinary efforts to unify the field, themes which appear throughout this book, especially in chapters 1, 5, and 6. Draguns also considers psychotherapy in its various sociocultural and political contexts and in the course of rapid societal transformation. All of the chapters contained in part III of *Toward a Global Psychology* are germane to the role of culture in shaping psychotherapeutic interventions and responses to them, which Draguns reviews in great detail; his contribution is especially valuable because he reviews the non-English language literature, which is unfamiliar to many readers. Draguns marshals evidence to support the claim that traditional healing techniques are beneficial in their respective cultural milieus, and summarizes accumulated clinical wisdom on the importance of recognizing culturally relevant beliefs and practices in one's clients. Beyond this, Draguns offers new lines of inquiry for psychotherapy process and outcome research, noting that further progress in enhancing the effectiveness and efficiency of psychotherapy is in part predicated on pooling information, knowledge, and skill from around the world. To this end, the barriers that still stand in the way of a free flow of communication across languages, cultures, and nations must be removed.

In chapter 9, Michael Wessells and Andrew Dawes analyze how psychology can go beyond its traditional focus on micro-level processes (see chapter 8) to address contemporary macro-level problems, such as armed conflict, racism, and HIV/AIDS (and other pressing concerns identified in chapter 1). The authors argue that psychological work on macro-level issues requires a systems-analytic framework, avoidance of reductionism, and sensitivity to issues of ethics, culture, and power (this viewpoint is repeated throughout the book, but nowhere more eloquently than in chapters 6, 7, 10, and 11 of part III). Broadly speaking, psychology can help to address macro-level issues through a mixture of top–down, bottom–up, and middle–out strategies. Top–down strategies are illustrated through national policy advocacy and changes on such issues as racial segregation in the United States and the deinstitutionalization of orphans in Angola. Bottom–up strategies are exemplified by community-based programs to reintegrate former child soldiers in Democratic Republic of Congo and to prevent and mitigate HIV/AIDS in Malawi. Middle–out strategies are captured by interactive problem-solving workshops that, in the context of the Israeli–Palestinian conflict, improve relations between ascending leaders, who can then influence their respective communities. The chapter also shows how psychologists influence macro-level processes by serving in advisory and support roles for national efforts, such as the Truth and Reconciliation Commission in South Africa. Wessells and Dawes conclude that, although psychology has much to contribute in the wider social arena, it makes its fullest contribution through a multidisciplinary approach and careful attention to program outcomes.

Professional psychology is increasingly global in its sharing of information, the form and scope of practice, and the development of standards for competent and ethical practice. In chapter 10, Jean Pettifor charts the march toward globalization in the regulation of professional psychology. Efforts to establish a morally grounded set of ethical principles for professional practice demonstrate a high level of commonality across disciplines from a historical perspective as well as in today's world, as traced in chapters 2 and 3, respectively. Consistent with chapter 8, Pettifor notes that differences in cultural values are often perceived as challenges to the globalization of professional psychology, such as issues of individualism and collectivism, science and folklore, secular and theocratic societies, and democratic and authoritarian regimes. These challenges may be met by facilitating a greater understanding of humanitarian values across different cultures, as advocated in chapter 11, by the growing movement for the indigenization of psychology to meet local needs, as described in chapter 5, and by the industrialized nations that so far have dominated the psychology agenda, listening, sharing, and making efforts to understand the needs of the majority world, as presented in chapter 4. The present chapter centers mainly on the role that professional regulation and ethical guidelines play in the internationalization and potential globalization of psychology. In so doing, Pettifor extends the worldwide and regional perspectives on the history of psychology provided by chapter 2 and focuses on contemporary developments in professional psychology that are reviewed in a more general way in chapters 3 and 12.

Chapter 11, Education and Training for a Global Psychology: Foundations, Issues, and Actions, builds upon Anthony Marsella's landmark 1998 publication in the *American Psychologist*, in which he argued for and delineated a curriculum that would educate and train future global psychologists. In the present chapter, Marsella examines with passion and vision what is needed for psychologists to engage the world, and its many pressing contemporary challenges, in a culturally competent and socially responsible manner. After reviewing the psychosocial impact of contemporary global events and forces, as in chapters 1, 8, and 9, along with mainstream psychology's limited usefulness in understanding and responding to those forces and events, as in chapters 1, 2, 5, and 6, Marsella maps out three core elements of education and training in global psychology: characteristics of the student, a philosophy of education, and the process and content of training, which includes recommendations for learning about and researching different cultures. The latter element provides a segue to the many pedagogical resources and suggestions contained in chapter 12. Of overarching importance, however, is Marsella's call to psychologists worldwide to advance psychology to a higher level of global relevance through a value-based fusion of the person and the discipline (i.e., a full-capacity global citizen). His emphasis on the need for alternative models, methods, interventions, and standards of practice echoes the positions taken by the authors of chapters 6, 7, 9, and 10, respectively.

6

Toward a Conceptual Foundation for a Global Psychology

Fathali M. Moghaddam
Georgetown University

Christina E. Erneling
Lunds University

Maritza Montero
Central University of Venezuela

Naomi Lee
Georgetown University

INTRODUCTION

> As a European scientist, I could not help but be disappointed, and often frustrated, that the neuroscience literature from outside the United States was frequently overlooked ... Had I delved into the book without any prior knowledge of the field, I would have concluded that brain research has been restricted to a small corner of Southern California.
> —Emery (2003, pp. 585–586)

This comment by Emery, in a generally positive book review, serves as a point of departure for our discussion of conceptual perspectives in global psychology. This review appeared not in a cultural, critical, or fringe journal, but in *Science*, the flagship scientific research journal, and the reviewed book focuses not on culture or ideology, but on neuroscience, purportedly the most objective domain of "cutting-edge" psychological research in the 21st century. We begin by pointing out that the enormous volume of research in the United States, even in "a small corner of Southern California," means that it is now a challenge for U.S. researchers to see beyond their borders. Even before the collapse of the Soviet Union, the United States already was the sole superpower of psychology (Moghaddam, 1987), exporting traditional U.S. psychology to the rest of the world. Since the 1990s, the global influence of the U.S. has in some ways increased, and traditional U.S. psychology has become traditional world psychology.

But a second, in some ways competing, trend also exists and appears to be growing in strength in different parts of the global village now taking shape. This is the development of *alternative psychologies*, which have evolved primarily in Second- and Third-World societies, but for the most part are as yet less known among mainstream U.S. psychologists.[1] The alternative psychologies are in fundamental ways distinct and different from both traditional U.S. psychology and traditional cross-cultural psychology, which share the same underlying positivist assumptions (Moghaddam & Studer, 1997). The main objective of this discussion is to critically articulate the view of the person put forward by the alternative psychologies, highlighting differences with the traditional causal model of behavior. In contrast to the belief that forms of argumentation create disorganization and disunity in psychology (Katzko, 2002), we assert that psychology is fragmented because of fundamental, real, and growing conceptual differences between traditional psychology and the emerging alternatives.

Although conceptual fragmentation existed early in the history of psychology (Bühler, 1927), today's disunity reflects two interrelated developments. First, as psychology in the Second and Third Worlds has matured, it has broadened its field of inquiry to tackle questions left unaddressed by mainstream U.S. psychology. At the same time, growing numbers of psychologists have directed their theoretical and empirical endeavors toward defining the cultural processes by which individuals make sense of their lives. The objection might be raised here that given the thousands of different cultures and normative systems in the world, the normative approach would only produce an epistemological nightmare of thousands of different psychologies.

---

[1]We wish to distinguish our definition of *alternative psychologies* from those which refer to the alternative mental-health movement.

On the contrary, we propose that the best strategy for discovering universals in thought and action is to be found by exploring across the rich diversity of human cultures (this theme appears in many other chapters, most notably, chapter 5, this volume, on indigenous psychologies). Turn-taking, reciprocity, and the consequences of social categorization are examples of domains in which universals are probable (Moghaddam, 2002). Moreover, we propose that the alternative psychologies represent the best promise for discovering universals in thought and action. Mainstream psychological research and practice to date has, in spite of its presumed culture-free conceptual framework, been fundamentally shaped by local and regional cultural experiences in the majority populations of Western Europe and North America. Alternative psychologies, in bringing forth a variety of meaning systems, widen the field of known psychological experience. Thus, in supplementing mainstream with alternative approaches, the possibility of discovering universals is improved rather than diminished. In this spirit, the first part of this chapter briefly reviews recent developments in the alternative psychologies, mostly outside the United States. In the second part, we identify shared features of the alternative psychologies. In a brief conclusion, we point to possible scenarios for future developments in global psychology.

ALTERNATIVE PSYCHOLOGIES

The forms that alternative psychologies have taken through the history of psychology tell the story of a discipline shaped by philosophical debate, shifts in international power, and increasingly organized counter-movements critical of traditional psychology (see chapter 2, this volume). The youngest of the critical voices come from the Third World; they are answering the call to generate locally relevant knowledge rather than re-fashion imported knowledge (Moghaddam, 1990). In so doing, Third-World countries are more effectively promoting national development (see chapters 3 and 4 in this volume on current trends and psychology in the majority world, respectively). Indeed, the Third World is not alone in needing contextually relevant knowledge. Even a denizen of the First World makes sense of her life through frameworks molded and re-molded by her dynamic surroundings. In taking a holistic view of human psychology, whereby single phenomena are situated within larger historical, cultural, and political processes, alternative psychologies attempt to achieve greater contextual sensitivity to address the diverse needs of continually changing societies.

Alternative Psychologies in Historical Context

The history of psychology reveals that there has always been some diversity in the approaches adopted by researchers (Hergenhahn, 2001). This was signaled early on by Wundt's (1916) "two psychologies"—an experimental laboratory-based branch and a more qualitative field-based *Völkerpsychologie* (Folk Psychology)—as well as by Dilthey's (1914–1936/1985) *Geisteswissenschaften* (The Human Sciences) and Stern's *Kritischer Personalismus* (Critical Personalism; Lamiell, 2003). Even in the heyday of behaviorism in the 1930s and 1940s, Gestalt and psychoanalytic orientations provided influential alternatives.

Since the rise to preeminence of cognitive psychology in the second half of the 20th century, various alternative approaches, most recently evolutionary psychology (Moghaddam, 2005), have exerted considerable influence. These alternatives have co-existed with more traditional approaches and have received greater attention in recent discussions (for example, in cognitive psychology, see Erneling & Johnson [2005] and Johnson & Erneling [1997], and in developmental psychology see Bruner [1983, 1990, 1996], Rogoff [1990, 2003], Shanker & Greenspan [2004], and Tomasello [1999]. Language and culture have been central themes in the alternative psychologies. McCrone (1990, 1999) argues for the crucial role of language to make possible and shape the human higher mental abilities, such as memory and self-awareness. Johnson (2003) discusses the role of cultural inventions, particularly language and logic, in constituting human rationality as it has emerged in history. Danziger (1997) shows how psychological categorizations vary with culture, but also within (Western) culture over time. As these examples indicate, alternative approaches have always been integral to international psychology. But, there is something rather unique about the contemporary international situation, in that one country, the United States, has gained supreme influence on the world stage. Not since the supremacy of Germany for several decades in the second part of the 19th century has one country so completely dominated global psychology.

It was perhaps inevitable, given the growth of European social psychological centers and the critical social tradition in Europe, that the movement to develop alternatives to traditional U.S. psychology should first evolve in Western Europe and in the domain of social psychology (Israel & Tajfel, 1972), with a focus on collective processes as a move away from the perceived reductionism of traditional U.S. psychology (Moscovici, 1988; Tajfel, 1984). The ideological roots of this movement are found in the writings of Hegel, Marx, and the Frankfurt tradition (Adorno, 1967; Horkheimer, 1972). This movement broadened in Europe to include developmental, personality, and health-related research (Drenth, Sergeant, & Takens, 1990). More specific topics addressed by Europeans turning away from a traditional U.S. perspective have been: memory (Middleton & Edwards, 1990), adolescence (Nurmi, 2001), social and clinical aspects of identity (Weinreich & Saunderson, 2003), learning disabilities (Mehan, 1996), the self (Benson, 2001), human development (Burman, 1994), cognition in everyday life (Smedslund, 1997), reasoning and arguing (Billig, 1987), and cognitive science (Harré, 2002).

In non-Western societies, the attempt to develop alternative psychologies has been mainly associated with national development and also, experiences arising out of colonization and imperialism. This includes attempts to identify: Arab (Ahmed & Gielen, 1998) and Asian (Kao & Sinha, 1997; Yang, Hwang, Pedersen, & Daibo, 2003) voices in psychology; liberation psychology in South America (e.g., Lira, 2000; Montero, 1994b, 2000a); explorations of the psychology of oppression in Africa (Nicholas, 1993); issues of national development in lower income regions in Africa and elsewhere (Okpara, 1985); schooling and child development in low-income societies (Nsamenang, 1992; Serpell, 1993); and the psychology of colonized peoples (Riley, 1997; Taylor, 2002). Recent reviews of the major journals in low-income societies reveal that despite the continued influence of traditional U.S. psychology, some distinct indigenous psychological research is being conducted in key areas, such as poverty and child development, national identity, and health and family relations (Reyes-Lagunes, 2002; Salazar, 2002). These trends, then, reflect a concern to develop indigenous psychologies outside the U.S. (Kim & Berry, 1993; see chapter 5, this volume). Besides dealing with topics not found in traditional psychology, a number of indigenous psychologies are developing alternative theories and methods. We now turn to a closer look at Latin-American liberation psychology as an example of a relatively mature, theoretically grounded alternative psychology that provides lessons for psychologists worldwide.

Liberation Psychology

The avowed goal of liberation psychology is to fight against oppression and poverty. This battle is waged in collaboration with and through the empowerment of people suffering from exclusion and inequality (Martín-Baró, 1986, 1990; Montero, 2000b). Its roots are in Paolo Freire's adult education, particularly in his seminal 1972 and 1973 works (English publication dates), as well as in the theology of liberation movement underway throughout Latin America at the same time. Marx's *Economic and Philosophical Manuscripts* as well as Antonio Gramsci's ideas about the role of intellectuals in guiding the people influenced critical sociology as developed by Fals Borda (1959, 2001), which in turn helped shape liberation psychology. Liberation psychology has also been influenced by Vygotsky's (1978) formulation of mind evolved through and in social interactions, as reflected particularly by his much discussed concept of the zone of proximal development—the difference between the level at which the child can achieve independently and the level at which the child can achieve with the support of others. Liberation psychology, as part of a broader intellectual and political movement, is attracting attention outside Latin America, and its proponents have encouraged increased dialogue with critical, community, and applied social psychologists around the world (Burton & Kagan, 2005).

Unlike traditional psychology's embracing of impartiality, liberation psychology grounds itself in a particular ethics, one that gives priority to collective over individual rights and duties (Moghaddam, 1998; see chapter 10, this volume on how professional and ethics bear on this issue). Psychologists who identify with this tradition explicitly aim to end injustices by confronting societal problems (Denzin & Lincoln, 1998; Parker 2005). Toward this goal, liberation psychology studies the daily psychosocial means by which ideology is produced and reproduced (Montero, 1984), and in its concern with construction and reconstruction of social reality, liberation psychology is similar to narrative psychology emerging in Europe (Crossley, 2000). Liberation psychology links people's material conditions to discourse practices in that it encourages *problematization, conscientization,* and *de-ideologization* (Freire, 1973/1988) of those conditions. Problematization is the process through which critical examination reveals a seemingly acceptable situation as problematic, triggering transformational reflection and actions. An example is when a group of women come to see it as a problem that they are underpaid at the factory and mistreated at home. Conscientization is the mobilizing and liberating means by which a person becomes aware of her social relatedness and her capacity for critical thought and change. De-ideologizing involves breaking down discourse that serves to disguise and distort social injustices, such as language about the "natural role" of mothers that justifies mistreatment of women. Conscientization is attained by problematizing and de-ideologizing the status quo.

A number of philosophical concepts underpin liberation psychology and are echoed in the broader themes of alternative psychologies. First is an *epistemology of relatedness*, which describes a mode of knowing based in relationships, whereby all individuals are drawn into relationships of some sort, be they with other people or with objects. Echoes of Vygotsky (1978) are evident in this concept and in the proposition of Brazilian educator Paulo Freire (1973/1988) that we are "beings of relationships in a world of relationships" (p. 41). That is, we gain knowledge by establishing relationships with other people, as well as with the things we create and use. Interpersonal relationships include I and You, We and They, He and She (Dussel, 1977, 1988, 1998; Moreno, 1993; Montero, 2000b, 2002). The emotions that arise within these relationships provide an additional path to knowledge (Sawaia, 1999, 2004). Thus, human knowledge does not exist in isolation, but rather it is generated and transmitted relationally.

A second philosophical guidepost for liberation psychology is the concept of *analectics* or *ana-dialectics* (from the Greek word *ana*, meaning "through" or "beyond"), as distinguished from dialectics. *Dialectics* is the interrelation of a thesis and its antithesis that produces new knowledge. This new knowledge is a synthesis of elements taken from both thesis and antithesis. In dialectics, thesis and antithesis are complementary and form a unity or totality in the sense that what is present in one is lacking in the other. The symbolic representation of *yin* and *yang* in Chinese philosophy is a well-recognized visual depiction of a dialectic. Analectics widens the totality circumscribed by a dialectic. Through analectics, the Other can be brought into the thesis–antithesis relationship (Dussel, 1988, 1998). Analectics provides a philosophical foundation for intelligible dialogue between vastly different peoples. An example of such dialogue is that which took place between American Indians and Europeans in the 15th and 16th centuries. To each, the Other appeared outside its frame of reference and was thus seen as fantastical and super-human (Europeans perceived by American Indians as gods) or inhuman (American Indians seen by Europeans as animals). Liberation psychology applies a positive connotation of analectics to promote diversity and inclusion (Montero, 2002), and to learn about the Other through this inclusion (Freire, 1973/1988). Analectics is transferred into practice through participatory action research (see chapter 7, this volume, for more on this and other qualitative research methods).

Originating in the ideas sketched by Lewin (1947) and further developed particularly in Latin America (Montero, 1994a, 2000b; Rodríguez Gabarrón & Hernández-Landa, 1994), participatory action research is an alternative means of producing psychosocial knowledge that has attracted a range of proponents. It combines research, intervention, and participation of the targeted population. This action-oriented research is particularly sensitive to the distance between researchers and participants (referred to as "epistemology of distance" by Fernández Christlieb, 1994, 1995 and as "cultural distance" by Moghaddam, Walker, & Harré, 2002). A greater role for research participants has led to the redefinition of concepts, processes, and practices in community and political psychology (Montero, 2003, 2004; Sánchez, 2004; Sawaia, 1999; Serrano-García, Bravo-Vick, Rosario-Collazo, & Gorrin-Peralta, 1998; Serrano-García & López-Sánchez, 1994).

A good example of the impact of liberation psychology is Ignacio Martín-Baró's (1994a) unconventional use of public opinion polling during El Salvador's Civil War. State discourse (the "Official Discourse") falsely portrayed the Salvadoran people as eagerly supporting the government's actions, such as condoning U.S. intervention, barring social democrats from the 1984 elections, and rejecting dialogue between the insurgents and the government. Martín-Baró used traditional survey methods to shape a counter-propaganda that reflected back to the Salvadoran people their true opinions about the civil war underway. In this manner, the public opinion poll was employed as a "de-ideologizing instrument" that brought lived experience into harmony with collective sentiment, and in doing so unmasked Official Discourse as propaganda.

A second example of empirical research in liberation psychology comes from work with slum neighborhoods in Caracas, Venezuela (Montero, 1994c). Using participatory action research methods, researchers performed needs assessments with 346 neighborhood residents. Discussions with residents revealed that problems, such as unreliable running water and free-flowing sewage, had become naturalized, or part of an acceptable norm. Community members perceived running water and sewage control as unmet needs, but they took no action to change their conditions. The study showed that only when unmet needs are brought into conscious awareness and carry strong emotional valence are people capable of acting to change the situation. The needs assessment process, a discursive act between community members and researchers, sets off a process of conscientization, whereby what was once considered acceptable is de-ideologized. Rather than impose their own value systems onto community members, researchers engaged in dialogue with members to bring to surface the community's own needs. This type of research empowers a community to transform in ways that are more relevant and lasting than if change is directed by the research team.

Further applications of this alternative psychology include: psychosocial effects of disease control programs (Briceño-León, Gonzales, & Phelan, 1990), the study of religion in psychosocial warfare (Martín-Baró, 1990), war and mental health (see Martín-Baró, 1994b), and therapy for victims of political repression (Becker, Lira, Castillo, Gómez, & Kovalskys, 1990). This brief introduction to liberation psychology exemplifies how alternative psychologies, in constructing contextually compatible theory and practices, address key issues of global interest (see chapter 9, this volume, for additional material on psychologically grounded macro-level interventions).

International Alternative Movements

The movements toward alternative psychologies in the Second and Third Worlds are reflected in several broader, more international movements. These include the emergence of ethogenics (Harré & Secord, 1972), discursive psychology (Billig, 1992; Edwards & Potter, 1992), narrative psychology (Crossley, 2000), as well as alternative research methods (Hayes, 1997). Although these new movements have had some influence in the United States, particularly through the work of Bruner (1990) and Gergen (1991), they are far better known in other parts of the world. Nevertheless, the most important themes of these new movements are shared by cultural psychology, which is gaining ground in the United States (Cole, 1996; Ratner, 2002; Stigler, Shweder, & Herdt, 1990). Also, both the narrative-discursive tradition and cultural psychology share the earlier influence of symbolic interactionism (Blumer, 1969; Goffman, 1959), ethnomethodology (Garfinkel, 1967), and activity psychology (Pearce & Cronen, 1981).

Thus, at the same time that the exportation of psychological conventions from the United States to the Second and Third Worlds has continued and in some ways increased, there have also been growing movements toward alternative psychologies, and these have become increasingly influential, particularly outside the United States. Although the alternative psychologies have their differences, they also have important common themes, and it is to these that we turn next.

CONCEPTUAL CORE OF THE ALTERNATIVE PSYCHOLOGIES

In the alternative psychologies, the person is the fundamental unit of analysis. Persons are not clusters of causal systems, but active beings interacting together with others using tools (such as one's brain or voice) to achieve goals in accordance with local rules and norms. Rules and norms are not causes of behavior, but rather criteria by which correctness and incorrectness, rightness and wrongness are judged. Both are collectively shared and collectively upheld by the community and need not have individual representations. Rules are more prescriptive than norms and may be upheld by laws. In contrast, norms are more flexible, and the sanctions for violating norms are less punitive than those for breaking a rule. Neither rules nor norms causally determine one's behavior, that is, one is free to defy either.

Although there are enabling conditions for mental activity that are causal systems, like the brain, alternative psychologies do not reduce psychological activity to such causal systems. Instead, the paradigmatic elements of mental activity are symbolic interactions among persons. Symbolic interactions, or discourses, organize the enabling conditions as in the case of learning a language, wherein speech sounds (the enabling condition) are given meaning and communicative use in a socio-linguistic setting (Erneling, 1993).

To engage in discursive activity is to engage in joint meaningful and normative psychological activity using symbols, which are any mutually recognizable representation of meaning such as words, pictures, gestures, or signs. Discursive acts include more than just verbal conversations. They encompass publicly recorded and publicly displayed cognitive activities in linguistic forms like books and dissertations, as well as *carriers* of meaning and rules of conduct, like flags, attire, and buildings (Moghaddam, 2002). Discourse also occurs in teachings, sports, arts, and the like. In discursive acts, norms and rules emerge in historical and cultural circumstances and make something not only meaningful, but also inform persons of the correct or incorrect thing to do, learn, think, or feel. People's behavior and beliefs also change through discursive acts. Examples include how the rules for tennis have changed over time or how art is different in ancient Egypt compared to that of late 19th century Paris.

The relationship between the alternative psychologies and traditional psychology can be further clarified by exploring a number of propositions that are shared by the alternative psychologies, which postulate that the science of psychology should give primacy to:

1. Processes of collective meaning making over patterns of individual behavior.
2. Primary psychological reality as a collective phenomenon rather than states or dispositions of the individual mind.

3. Time-dependent processes through which episodes unfold over individual states as an outcome of personal or public processes.
4. Normative explanations based on rules and conventions of correctness as opposed to causal explanations centered on hidden mechanisms, cognitive or neural.

Meaning Making

Alternative psychologies give priority to meaning-making over behavior. They are primarily concerned with how human actions, as well as events and objects in the world, are ascribed meaning. The focus is on processes of sense-making and interpretations of what is taking place, with less importance given to actions and events as "objectively measured" from the outside. For example, the alternative psychologies consider the central research question to be the meaning of a remembered event, rather than remembering empty of meaning, such as the attempt to identify a location in the brain for a neural representation of a memory.

From this alternative perspective, human development involves individuals becoming active participants in the process of appropriating, manipulating, and manufacturing meaning. This process is intimately tied to the learning of language and its use in "language games," practical activities in which words and other symbols play a crucial part. In this respect, a common influence on the alternative psychologies has been Wittgenstein's (1998) studies on the philosophy of psychology. He proposed the centrality of conceptual innovation over experimental study in psychology, stating: "For in psychology there are experimental methods and conceptual confusion" (Wittgenstein, 1953, p. 232). Alternative psychologies have re-directed the focus of psychology from individual causal mechanisms to collective meaning-making processes, thereby advancing the conceptual foundation of the discipline.

Wittgenstein (1953, 1998) stressed the priority of everyday language activities or language games to human activity. Everyday language demarcates the psychological activities that are important to people in given sociolinguistic contexts. Psychological activities, such as remembering Mother's Day or calculating a gratuity, are learned or appropriated in different language games. Furthermore, Wittgenstein argued that rules and norms are not causes of behavior; rather, they order the discursive activities by which people make sense of what is taking place. They are also criteria for judging the correctness or incorrectness of a psychological activity. Psychological activities, such as remembering or thinking, and linguistic activities, like reading, are not manifestations or the result of hidden, private psychological mechanisms that cause actual remembering, thinking, or reading. We need not study the brain to decide if a person can read.

Language allows for communicating and learning more sophisticated cultural practices, as well as influencing such practices and even constructing new ones. Thus, for example, the young in England learn to talk about a "Royal Family" (Billig, 1992) and to know what "royalty" means as part of English culture. Similarly, in the United States people learn the meaning of "Old Glory," and such carriers serve to transfer from one generation to another values central to a culture (Moghaddam, 2002). The process of meaning-making is ongoing in everyday life and is related to local contexts.

The contention that meaning-making is foundational to the science of psychology implies that humans should be studied in relation to context. The claim that the ascription of meaning is context dependent does not negate the possibility that laboratory studies can serve a very useful purpose in psychological research (Moghaddam & Harré, 1992). Participants in laboratory experiments ascribe meaning to events, persons, and objects in the laboratory, as they do outside the laboratory. A major difference typically is that in laboratory studies participants are isolated, whereas in the world outside the laboratory people usually engage in sense-making through active collaboration with others. Thus, in everyday life, meaning-making is derived through social interaction—not in isolation from others—unless a person is living in long-term solitary confinement or some other unusual situation; but even then, there are often imagined others involved. Of course, in most laboratory contexts participants engage in meaning-making through interactions with experimenters, starting with questions such as "What is this study about?" and "What am I supposed to do?" Because of this, the alternative psychologies give priority to collective rather than individual construction of psychological reality (Moghaddam, 2005).

The Collective Construction of Psychological Reality

The meaning-making that characterizes humans is not a private endeavor, involving isolated minds. The alternative psychologies view psychological reality as a collective rather than individual construction. This is in some respects a reflection of the Gestalt motto, "the whole is more than the sum of its parts," but it is also more than that. The focus is no longer on assumed mental mechanisms within isolated individuals, but rather collective processes outside individual minds—on norms, rules, conventions, and, in short, cultural practices and meaning systems collectively shared and jointly upheld. Of course, even within a single community, considerable heterogeneity will exist. The fact that people engage in arguments reflects the diversity of perspectives at people's disposal. It is in this respect that we can best understand the idea of intersubjectivity arising out of interobjectivity: Psychological experiences at the individual and interpersonal levels emerge from collectively constructed experiences (Moghaddam, 2003). This is akin to Vygotsky's (1978) idea of appropriation by the individual from the common social reality.

From the perspective of the alternative psychologies, primary psychological reality is not dependent on any individual and is not a product of individual characteristics, but arises out of collective characteristics and is collectively maintained. For example, stereotypes about minority groups are not a product of any isolated individual minds nor are they dependent on any particular individuals. Such stereotypes are present "out there" in the discourse of society, including the contents of the mass media, which often strengthen the role of carriers in transporting stereotypes forward (Moghaddam, 2002).

In this regard, the alternative psychologies have been particularly influenced by Vygotsky (1978), who viewed the developing child in networks of interactions and supportive scaffoldings provided by others. Vygotsky's concept of the zone of proximal development has important implications for how psychologists should assess the abilities of all individuals (Moghaddam, 2005). This is because in everyday life individuals typically carry out tasks through interactions with others, and an arguably more realistic way to measure their abilities is by assessing them in the course of such interactions. Of course, in some situations others can detrimentally influence individual performance (Steele, 1997).

According to Vygotsky (1978), individual minds come into being as words. Other symbolic devices are acquired in the public domain, which then come to be used by the individual in private ways. "Every function in the child's cultural development appears twice: first, on the social level, and later, on the individual level" (p. 57). His idea of appropriating the collective public to become the individual and private, as in the case of social speech turning into egocentric speech and eventually into private thinking, is an account of how psychological being comes into existence. Initially, public language is used in interactions in which the adult functions to order and interpret the child's behaviors and reactions. Later, the child uses learned speech to control others. Then, with egocentric speech (i.e., talking aloud to oneself) and internalized speech (i.e., thinking), the child controls her own actions. In this way, concepts like the self are culturally and socially transmitted, forming the child's own actions and the ordering of her subjective experiences.

This process can be understood in terms of symbiosis (see Erneling, 1993, and Shotter, 1974). By symbiosis, we mean a relationship in which the infant is dependent on the adult not only for the satisfaction of its physical needs, but also for social, linguistic, and mental activity. The adult actively transmits language by emitting language, correcting the infant's speech, and engaging in conversations with infants. These conversations are initially based on the infant's natural expressions and behaviors, and later on its limited repertoire of linguistic utterances. Parents speak for infants, as in "Is baby tired?," "Oh, we're so tired," "Does baby want to go sleepies?," "We want to take our nap now, don't we?," and so on. Parents thus pretend to have a two-way conversation with the infant (see Hoff-Ginsberg, 1997, and Sachs, 1993). In this way, parents help infants express themselves by supplementing infants' limited linguistic ability. These supplements eventually serve as models for later linguistic achievements. They are ultimately internalized or, in Vygotsky's terms, "appropriated" as part of the child's private psychological activity. Thus, the infant's expressions of innate, idiosyncratic (relative to specific language) speech-sounds are incorporated into a social and symbolic–communicative context.

An example of early social–communicative interactions based on natural and innate behaviors are different kinds of games, for example, "peekaboo" (Bruner, 1983). Playing peekaboo seems to occur in most cultures (Erneling, 1993), though its meaning is not necessarily universal. Differential meanings can be ascribed to common acts, as in the case of crying. In Western cultures, crying is often seen as a sign of hunger, but for mothers among !Kung speaking Bushmen, where the infant is carried on the mother's back most of the time, certain movements are taken to be the usual signs for hunger (Konner, 1972). The same point is illustrated by the so-called Baby X experiments. In these experiments, adults are shown videos of infants labeled as girls or boys and asked to describe the behavior of the infant (e.g., its reaction to the sudden appearance of a Jack-in-the-Box doll). If the adult thinks the child is a girl, the adult typically describes the infant as reacting with different feelings (e.g., fear) than if the adult thinks the infant is a boy (e.g., anger; Vasta, Haith, & Miller, 1995). Thus, a single activity can carry a range of meanings, allowing for enormous cultural and contextual variation.

However, the ascription of different meanings to behavior is not completely arbitrary. In the case of infant behavior, some limited spectrum of meanings is ascribed. If such were not the case, the infant would never be satisfied or would not even survive (Gray, 1978; Lock, 1978). Hence, infants' behaviors are from the beginning combined and coordinated with others based on local social norms. This symbiotic process continues throughout life, as children and adults learn, for example, to talk about what royalty means as part of an English culture (Billig, 1992).

Time-Dependent Processes

The alternative psychologies focus primarily on psychological processes rather than on selected outcomes. The focus on process has direct implications for research methods. In particular, the alternative psychologies rely heavily on discourse to explore the interactive processes associated with psychological experience. It is taken for granted that any demarcation of particular points in discourse, as in the "beginning" or "end" of a given psychological experience, are likely to be arbitrary or culture-bound, rather than objective and culture-free. Although categorization of discourse from the outside may be culture-bound, the meaning of discourse and its categorization can reach some level of objectivity by looking at the speaker's point of view.

The issue of the role of discourse provides another opportunity for us to further clarify the difference between the alternative psychologies and traditional U.S. psychology. From the perspective of traditional U.S. psychology, reliance on discourse in order to get at psychological processes is problematic. Although much progress has been made in qualitative methods and discourse analysis in particular (Edwards & Potter, 1992; Hayes, 1997), critics would argue that it is not clear what the requirements and limitations are for studies on processes. For example, when accounts are gathered of past events and behavior, to what extent do such accounts reflect reconstructive memory as opposed to ongoing psychological processes? When discourse is assessed, to what extent should researchers question the integrity of the participants, such as when participants have political motives to deceive or social motives to present the self as positive (Billig, 1987)? But, from the perspective of the alternative psychologies, these questions and concerns are misplaced because the alternative psychologies do not take discourse to be a product of underlying psychological processes; rather, they propose that discourse *is* the psychological processes. That is, discourse is not treated as a window through which to peer into one's motives. Rather, it is the most appropriate plane at which to understand the meaning of a psychological process.

Normative Explanations

A common feature of the alternative psychologies, and perhaps their most important shared characteristic that differs from traditional U.S. psychology, is their emphasis on normative rather than causal explanations of human behavior. The alternative models turn away from logical positivism and determinism; they tend to reject, or are guided much less by the assumption that human behavior is causally determined and that the task of psychologists is to discover the causes of behavior. Consequently, alternative psychologies often abandon the traditional research design based on variables, whereby independent variables (assumed causes) are manipulated in order to measure their impact on dependent variables (assumed effects).

This does not mean that the alternative psychologies have abandoned prediction as a major goal in psychological research. However, the alternative psychologies postulate that regularities and predictability in human behavior arise through individuals adopting particular normative systems as guides; normative systems being "out there" in society in the shape of norms, rules, values, and so on. Styles of individual thinking and behavior are regulated by the wider culture in which persons are socialized and live. Such regulation means that patterns emerge in thinking and acting, and future behavior is frequently highly predictable on the basis of such patterns. Consequently, the alternative psychologies reject the idea that the predictability of behavior is evidence of causation; rather, they take it to be evidence of shared normative systems (Moghaddam, 2002). Nevertheless, a key feature of this paradigm is that individuals can choose to reject traditional normative systems, accepted ways of thinking and doing, and to travel down paths less taken.

According to the core assumptions of alternative psychologies, it is persons in a shared form of life that create the psychological sphere for one another. Psychological activity, like remembering, is not a mere biological process; rather, it is also a sociocultural process of interaction and negotiation. It is in these shared symbolic practices that the individual becomes and functions as a psychological being. Thus, there are no preestablished universal foundations except for some biological enabling conditions, like the brain. And, even the brain is shaped by cultural forces. From this perspective, cognitive, linguistic, and emotional activity cannot be extricated from social processes. The individual is part of the social from the start, and psychological activities like remembering and using language are, given certain biological enabling conditions, the product of social interactions in culturally and historically varied systems. This brings power and politics into psychology.

It becomes impossible to study psychological activities without regard for the institutions, interactional patterns, and values existing in the society where people develop and act as competent psychological beings. In this vein, alternative psychologies view individual identity as intimately bound up with the larger social groupings that have traditionally been the subject matter of sociologists. Moving beyond the individual and small groups, alternative psychologies recognize the complex macro-identities that people possess. This term has evolved to (a) account for broader categories of social identity (e.g., national, religious, political, ethnic), and to (b) explain how aspects of one's identity can simultaneously carry both positive and negative valence (Montero, 1984, 1996; Salazar, 1983). This second point contrasts with various traditional theories that assume a need for balance and symmetry in cognition and social relationships, examples being cognitive dissonance theory and equity theory (Moghaddam, 1998).

The unit of analysis in studying psychological activities like remembering, thinking, imagining, and talking is not mental schemas, representations and rules, grammar, or the individual learner's achievement in different laboratory situations, but rather persons engaged in public and shared conversational interactions. If concepts like mental rules, representations, or schemas are to have any explanatory value, they must be seen as being grounded in actual social practices, not the other way around (Harré, 2001).

The alternative psychologies also reject the argument underlying traditional U.S. psychology to the effect that human behavior will be causally explained when we have gathered all there is to know about situational and dispositional factors. One viewpoint is that we do not yet have enough data; the best scientific way forward is to gather more and more data about cause–effect relations. In contrast, the alternative psychologies argue that the most important "real sciences" tend to be theory driven, rather than data-accumulation efforts, an important example being physics. Rather than accumulating data in the hope of arriving at grand theories, Einstein and other physicists developed general theories as a first step and launching point for empirical research. Thought experiments are the dominant tool at the cutting-edge of research in physics.

Earlier, we provided examples of the strength of theory-driven alternatives. The theoretical premise of participatory-action research, in which so-called "research subjects" transform their contexts and themselves through collaborative participation, has been highly influential in the social sciences. Adult education, community psychology, and liberation psychology showcase this influence.

CONCLUDING DISCUSSION

We discuss two main issues in this final section: first, the impact of the alternative critical and normative approaches outside the United States and, second, the future of psychology and the question of whether there will be greater unity or fragmentation.

The Impact of Alternative Approaches

It would be misleading to assess the impact of the alternative psychologies in Africa, Asia, and Latin America by examining publications in the traditional outlets. On the one hand, the editorial boards of traditional outlets act as screeners, excluding works that do not meet traditional standards. On the other hand, ideological, cultural, and professional factors mean that many African, Asian, and Latin-American psychologists either are unable or unwilling to prepare research reports that meet traditional criteria. The result is that much of the activity in applied and research psychology taking place outside the West remains unknown to the West (see chapters 1 and 8, this volume). Even research reported at conferences suffers the same fate. Adair, Coêlho, and Luna (2000) reported a zero correlation between the frequencies of topics reported at applied psychology congresses in Asia and Asian research topics abstracted in PsycLIT. In reviewing applied and research psychology in Africa, Asia, and Latin America, our assessment is that the greatest impact of alternative approaches has been in community psychology in Latin America (Lira, 2001; Montero, 1994b, 2004). Interesting efforts are underway in Asia to integrate indigenous and imported psychology (Kim, 2000), but these are at a preliminary stage. The work of Vygotsky is influencing research and education in Africa (Gilbert, 1997; Serpell, 1993, 2004), but again this work has only begun to reach a wider audience.

The clearest evidence of the influence of the alternative psychologies in publications is in journals such as *Culture & Psychology*, *Theory & Psychology*, and *Theory of Social Behavior*. The *British Journal of Social*

Psychology included narrative psychology papers for a time into the first decade of the new millennium, but it has more recently reinstated traditional criteria. On the applied front, community interventions, primary and secondary prevention programs, and health and citizen-development projects have been proven successful not only in Australia, South Africa, and South America, but also in the United States, where the web pages of the University of Kansas (especially their Community Tool Box, which can be found at http://ctb.ku.edu/) and Vanderbilt University (http://www.vanderbilt.edu/) are good examples.

Fusion or Greater Divergence in the Future?

On the one hand, the growth of the alternative psychologies in association with the expansion of psychological research in the Second and Third Worlds might be indicative of a schism in international psychology. The alternative psychologies and traditional U.S. psychology might be seen as something akin to the two different psychologies proposed by Wundt (1916). From this perspective, there might evolve splits and separations, so that psychology as a cultural, discursive, or normative science branches away from psychology as a causal science. Signs of this split are apparent in some major universities in the U.S. and elsewhere.

On the other hand, new developments in research are creating unexpected and exciting possibilities for increased dialogue and collaboration between the alternative psychologies and traditional U.S. psychology. Perhaps surprisingly, these developments include new discoveries in cognitive neuroscience. Consider, for example, research since the mid-1990s on aging and memory, using newly available brain-imaging techniques (Reuter-Lorenz, 2002). This research suggests that even when seniors do as well as younger adults on memory tasks, they often do so by using different parts of their brains to do the same tasks. There are strong indications that seniors can compensate for certain types of neural decline by adopting alternative thinking strategies: "Engaging in elaborative encoding … improves aging memory and can sometimes reduce age differences in performance. Moreover, providing this kind of 'environmental support' for aging memory can … sometimes reduce age differences in performance" (Reuter-Lorenz, 2002, p. 395). The implication is that both memory behavior and associated neural activity are influenced by "environmental" support, in particular the kinds of strategies available in the cultural context. This cognitive neuroscience research dovetails in interesting ways with memory research in the new tradition of the alternative psychologies (Dixon, 1996). Findings suggest that, although seniors do not do as well as younger adults when tested in isolation, they can be just as accurate when tested on how well they remember collectively. That is, seniors seem to have adopted certain strategies for remembering that only come into effect through and in social interactions. Research on aging and memory in both cognitive neuroscience and the alternative psychologies suggests individual memory performance in some ways evolves from the scaffolding available in the larger context, again reflecting the broader theme of intersubjectivity arising out of interobjectivity.

Increased dialogue is needed in order to build and take advantage of connections between research in the alternative psychologies and more traditional research, such as in neuroscience. For example, since Hebb's (1949) conceptualization of cell assemblies, emphasizing learning in perception and other fundamental areas, and more fine-grained subsequent discussions illuminating brain plasticity (Pribram, 1971), the idea has emerged of the brain as a holistic system that changes in fundamental ways in relation to context (Pribram, 1991). The brain as a biochemical communication and decision-making system becomes in important ways transformed through contextual experiences. Rather than trying to link such changes to assumed cognitive mechanisms inside individual minds, the alternative psychologies suggest that the link should be to the wider social context and collective meaning-making. This and other possible links (Deaux & Philogène, 2001) need to be explored further through strengthened international and interdisciplinary dialogue.

We propose that the seemingly dichotomous alternative and traditional psychologies can complement each other to offer a fuller understanding of human psychology. Although the traditional paradigm is equipped to detail biological enabling conditions, alternative approaches shed light on the meaning and patterning of psychological activities. The former is well suited to studies of *performance capacity*—the quantifiable measure of abilities—whereas the latter addresses *performance style*—the manner in which behavior is carried out and given meaning (see Moghaddam, 2002). The strength of the alternative psychologies lies in their attention to cultural and historical context, processes of socially mediated change, and the importance of local meaning systems.

Critics may charge that alternative methods produce nonreplicable findings, but we respond that the criteria of reproducibility needs to allow space for individual agency and development as well as the contextual uniqueness of each lived experience. Although a person may not behave the same way in every similar situation, alternative psychologies expect that behavior is not arbitrary; rather, some significant patterns can be found, even across cultures. And in response to the critique that the qualitative methods employed by alternative psychologies lack the precision of quantitative methods, we respond that analytical precision need not only be represented interms of standard error, which is itself a cultural invention. In the case of discourse analysis, an analyst's interpretation may well reflect her particular cultural history, but this does not mean she cannot engage with others (including the "subjects" themselves) to arrive at a collaboratively constructed meaning of a particular event. Interobjectivity is not precluded by intersubjectivity. We believe that as the alternative psychologies gain ground, we may come closer to realizing Wundt's vision of a laboratory-based experimental psychology and a field-based *Völkerpsychologie*, coexisting and collaborating to make sense of both the enabling conditions and discursive acts that together comprise human psychological life.

RECOMMENDED READINGS

Burman, E. (1994). *Deconstructing developmental psychology*. London: Routledge.

Dussel, E. (1998). *La ética de la liberación* [Ethics of liberation]. México City: National Autonomous University of México.

Fals Borda, O. (2001) Participatory (action) research and social theory: Origins and challenges. In P. Reason & H. Bradbury (Eds.), *Handbook of action research* (pp. 27–37). London: Sage.

Freire, P. (1972). *Pedagogy of the oppressed*. Harmondsworth, UK: Penguin.

Harré, R. (1994). *The discursive mind*. Thousand Oaks, CA: Sage.

Ibáñez, T. (1998). Why a critical social psychology? In T. Ibañez & L. Iñiguez (Eds.), *Critical social psychology* (pp. 27–41). London: Sage.

Moghaddam, F. (1990). Modulative and generative interpretations to psychology: Implications for psychology in the three worlds. *Journal of Social Issues, 46,* 21–41.

Moghaddam, F. M. (2002). *The individual and society: A cultural integration*. New York: Worth.

Sawaia, B. B. (2004). Affectivity as an ethical-political phenomenon and locus of critical-epistemological reflection in social psychology. *International Journal of Critical Psychology, 9,* 167–210.

Vygotsky, L. (1978). *Mind in society: The development of higher psychological processes*. Cambridge, MA: Harvard University Press.

ACKNOWLEDGMENTS

We are grateful to Rom Harré and Karl H. Pribram for comments made on earlier drafts of this chapter.

REFERENCES

Adair, J. G., Coêlho, A. E. L., & Luna, J. R. (2000, July). Indigenous psychology in Asia: A view from abroad. In K. Leung (Chair), *Asian contributions to indigenous psychology*. Symposium conducted at the meeting of the International Association for Cross-Cultural Psychology, Putusk, Poland.

Adorno, T. W. (1967). Sociology and psychology. *New Left Review, November–December*, 67–80.

Ahmed, R. A., & Gielen, U. P. (Eds.). (1998). *Psychology in the Arab countries*. Menoufia, Egypt: Menoufia University Press.

Becker, D., Lira, E., Castillo, M., Gómez, E., & Kovalskys, J. (1990). Therapy with victims of political repression in Chile: The challenge of social reparation. *Journal of Social Issues, 46*, 133–150.

Benson, C. (2001). *The cultural psychology of self: Place, morality and art in human worlds*. London: Routledge.

Billig, M. (1987). *Arguing and thinking: A rhetorical approach to social psychology*. Cambridge, UK: Cambridge University Press.

Billig, M. (1992). *Talking of the Royal Family*. London: Routledge.

Blumer, H. (1969). *Symbolic interactionism: Perspective and method*. Englewood Cliffs, NJ: Prentice Hall.

Briceño-León, R., Gonzales, S., & Phelan, M. (1990). Housing and health: psychosocial and situational effects in a rural disease control program. *Journal of Social Issues, 46*, 109–119.

Bruner, J. (1983). *Child's talk*. New York: Norton.

Bruner, J. (1990). *Acts of meaning*. Cambridge, MA: Harvard University Press.

Bruner, J. (1996). *The culture of education*. Cambridge, MA: Harvard University Press.

Bühler, K. (1927). *Die Krise der Psychologie* [The crisis of psychology]. Jena, Germany: Fischer.

Burman, E. (1994). *Deconstructing developmental psychology*. London: Routledge.

Burton, M., & Kagan, C. (2005). Liberation social psychology: Learning from Latin America. *Journal of Community and Applied Social Psychology, 15*, 63–78.

Cole, M. (1996). *Cultural psychology: A once and future discipline*. Cambridge, MA: Harvard University Press.

Crossley, M. L. (2000). *Introducing narrative psychology: Self, trauma and the construction of meaning*. Buckingham, UK: Open University Press.

Danziger, K. (1997). *Naming the mind: How psychology found its language*. London: Sage.

Deaux, K., & Philogène, G. (Eds.). (2001). *Representations of the social*. Oxford, UK: Blackwell.

Denzin, N., & Lincoln, Y. (1998). Entering the field of qualitative research. In N. Denzin & Y. Lincoln (Eds.), *The landscape of qualitative research: Theories and issues* (pp. 1–33). Thousand Oaks, CA: Sage.

Dilthey, W. (1985). *Introduction to the human sciences: Vol 1. Wilhelm Dilthey. Selected Works* (R. A. Makkreel & F. Rodi, Trans.). Princeton, NJ: Princeton University Press. (Original work published from 1914–1936)

Dixon, R. A. (1996). *Compensating for psychological deficit and decline*. Hillsdale, NJ: Lawrence Erlbaum Associates.

Drenth, P. J. D., Sergeant J. A., & Takens, R. J. (Eds.). (1990). *European perspectives in psychology*. Chichester, UK: Wiley.

Dussel, E. (1977). *Introducción a la filosofía de la liberación latinoamericana* [Introduction to the Latin American philosophy of liberation]. Bogotá: Nueva América.

Dussel, E. (1988). *Accesos hacia una filosofía de la liberación* [Gateways to a philosophy of liberation]. Buenos Aires: La Aurora.

Dussel, E. (1998). *La ética de la liberación* [Ethics of liberation]. México City: UNAM.

Edwards, D., & Potter, J. (1992). *Discursive psychology*. London: Sage.

Emery, N. J. (2003). A user's guide to life. *Science, 300,* 585–586.

Erneling, C. E. (1993). *Understanding language acquisition: The framework of learning.* Albany, NY: SUNY Press.

Erneling, C. E., & Johnson, D. M. (Eds.). (2005). *The mind as a scientific object: Between brain and culture.* New York: Oxford University Press.

Fals Borda, O. (1959). *Desarrollo comunal en una vereda colombiana* [Communal development in a Colombian hamlet]. Bogotá: Universidad Nacional.

Fals Borda, O. (2001). Participatory (action) research and social theory: Origins and challenges. In P. Reason & H. Bradbury (Eds.), *Handbook of action research* (pp. 27–37). London: Sage.

Fernández Christlieb, P. (1994). La lógica epistémica de la invención de la realidad [Epistemic logic of reality invention]. In M. Montero (Ed.), *Conocimiento, realidad e ideología* (Vol. 6, pp. 19–36). Caracas: AVEPSO.

Fernández Christlieb, P. (1995). *La psicología colectiva un fin de siglo más tarde* [Collective psychology an end of the century later]. Barcelona: Anthropos.

Freire, P. (1972). *Pedagogy of the oppressed.* Harmondsworth, UK: Penguin.

Freire, P. (1973). *Education as critical consciousness.* New York: Seabury Press.

Freire, P. (1988). *Extensión o comunicación?* [Extension or communication]. México City: Siglo XXI. (Original work published 1973)

Garfinkel, H. (1967). *Studies in ethnomethodology.* Englewood Cliffs, NJ: Prentice Hall.

Gergen, K. (1991). *The saturated self: Dilemmas of identity in contemporary life.* New York: Basic Books.

Gilbert, A. (1997). Small voices against the wind: Local knowledge and social transformation. *Peace and Conflict: Journal of Peace Psychology, 3,* 275–292.

Goffman, E. (1959). *The presentation of the self in everyday life.* Garden City, NY: Doubleday.

Gray, H. (1978). Learning to take an object from the mother. In A. Lock (Ed.), *Action, gesture, and symbol: The emergence of language* (pp. 159–182). New York: Academic Press.

Harré, R. (2001). Norms in life: Problems in the representation of rules. In D. Bakhurst & S. Shanker (Eds.), *Jerome Bruner: Language, culture, and self* (pp. 150–166). London: Sage.

Harré. R. (2002). *Cognitive science: Philosophical introduction.* London: Sage.

Harré, R., & Secord, P. (1972). *The explanation of social behavior.* Oxford: Blackwell.

Hayes, N. (Ed.). (1997). *Doing qualitative analysis in psychology.* Hove, UK: Taylor & Francis.

Hebb, D. O. (1949). *Organization of behavior.* New York: Wiley.

Hergenhahn, B. R. (2001). *An introduction to the history of psychology* (4th ed.). Belmont, CA: Wadsworth.

Hoff-Ginsberg, E. (1997). *Language development.* New York: Brooks/Cole.

Horkheimer, M. (1972). *Critical theory.* New York: Seabury Press.

Israel, J., & Tajfel, H. (Eds.). (1972). *The context of social psychology.* London: Academic Press.

Johnson, D. M. (2003). *How history made the mind: The cultural origins of objective thinking.* Chicago: Open Court.

Johnson, D. M., & Erneling, C. E. (Eds.). (1997). *Reassessing the cognitive revolution: Alternative futures.* New York: Oxford University Press.

Kao, H. S. R., & Sinha, D. (Eds.). (1997). *Asian perspectives in psychology.* New Delhi: Sage.

Katzko, M. W. (2002). The rhetoric of psychological research and the problem of unification in psychology. *American Psychologist, 57,* 262–270.

Kim, U. (2000). Indigenous, cultural, and cross-cultural psychology: A theoretical, conceptual, and epistemological analysis. *Asian Journal of Social Psychology, 3,* 265–287.

Kim, U., & Berry, J. W. (Eds.). (1993). *Indigenous psychologies: Research and experience in cultural context.* Newbury Park, NJ: Sage.

Konner, M. J. (1972). Aspects of the developmental ethology of a foraging people. In N. B. Jones (Ed.), *Ethological studies of child behavior* (pp. 285–304). London: Cambridge University Press.

Lamiell, J. (2003). *Beyond individual and group differences: Human individuality, scientific psychology, and William Stern's critical personalism.* Thousand Oaks, CA: Sage.

Lewin, K. (1947). Action research and minority problems. In G. Weiss Lewin (Ed.), *Resolving social problems* (pp. 201–216). London: Souvenir Press.

Lira, E. (2001). Reflections on critical psychology: The psychology of memory and forgetting (T. Sloan, Trans.). In T. Sloan (Ed.), *Critical psychology: Voices for change* (pp. 82–90). New York: St. Martin's Press.

Lock, A. (Ed.). (1978). *Action, gesture, and symbol: The emergence of language.* New York: Academic Press.

Martín-Baró, I. (1986). Hacia una psicología de la liberación [Toward a psychology of liberation]. *Boletín de Psicología* (Universidad Centroamericana "José Simeón Cañas"), *22,* 219–231.

Martín-Baró, I. (1990). Retos y perspectivas de la psicología latinoamericana [Challenges and perspectives of Latin American psychology]. In G. Pacheco & B. Jiménez-Domínguez (Eds.), *Ignacio Martín-Baró (1942–1989). Psicología de la liberación para América Latina* (pp. 51–80). Guadalajara: Universidad de Guadalajara.

Martín-Baró, I. (1994a). Public opinion research as a de-ideologizing instrument (J. Carrol & A. Aron, Trans.). In A. Aron & S. Corne (Eds.), *Writings for a liberation psychology* (pp. 186–198). Cambridge, MA: Harvard University Press.

Martín-Baró, I. (1994b). *Writings for a liberation psychology* (A. Aron & S. Corne, Eds.). Cambridge, MA: Harvard University Press.

McCrone, J. (1990). *The ape that spoke language and evolution of the human mind.* London: Macmillan.

McCrone, J. (1999). *Going inside: A tour round a single moment of consciousness.* London: Faber and Faber.

Mehan, H. (1996). The construction of an LD student: A case study in the politics of representation. In M. Silverstein & G. Urban (Eds.), *Natural histories of discourse* (pp. 253–276). Chicago: University of Chicago Press.

Middleton, D., & Edwards, D. (Eds.). (1990). *Collective remembering.* London: Sage.

Moghaddam, F. M. (1987). Psychology in the Three Worlds: As reflected by the "crises" in social psychology and the move toward indigenous Third World psychology. *American Psychologist, 47,* 912–920.

Moghaddam, F. (1990). Modulative and generative interpretations to psychology: Implications for psychology in the three worlds. *Journal of Social Issues, 46,* 21–41.

Moghaddam, F. M. (1998). *Social psychology: Exploring universals across cultures.* New York: Freeman.

Moghaddam, F. M. (2002). *The individual and society: A cultural integration.* New York: Worth.

Moghaddam, F. M. (2003). Interobjectivity and culture. *Culture and Psychology, 9,* 221–232.

Moghaddam, F. M. (2005). *Great ideas in psychology: A cultural and historical introduction.* Oxford, UK: Oneworld.

Moghaddam, F. M., & Harré, R. (1992). Rethinking the laboratory experiment. *American Behavioral Scientist, 36,* 22–38.

Moghaddam, F. M., & Studer, C. (1997). Cross-cultural psychology: The frustrated gadfly's promises, potentialities, and failures. In D. Fox & I. Prilleltensky (Eds.), *Critical psychology* (pp. 185–201). Thousand Oaks, CA: Sage.

Moghaddam, F. M., Walker, B. R., & Harré, R. (2002). Cultural distance, levels of abstraction, and the advantages of mixed methods. In A. Tashakkori & C. Teddie (Eds.), *Handbook of mixed methods in social and behavioral research* (pp. 201–216). Hampshire, UK: Macmillan Press.

Montero, M. (1984). *Ideología, alienación e identidad nacional* [Ideology, alienation and national identity]. Caracas: EBUC.

Montero, M. (1994a). Investigación-acción participante. La unión entre conocimiento popular y conocimiento científico [Participatory action research: The union between ordinary and scientific knowledge]. *Revista de Psicología Univ. Ricardo Palma, 6,* 31–45.

Montero, M. (Ed.). (1994b). *Psicología Social Communitaria* [Social-community psychology]. Guadalajara: Universidad de Guadalajara.

Montero, M. (1994c). Consciousness raising, conversion, and de-ideologization in community psychosocial work. *Journal of Community Psychology, 22,* 3–11.

Montero, M. (1996). *Identidad social negativa. Un concepto en busca de teoría* [Negative social identity: A concept in search of a theory]. In J. F. Morales, D. Páez, J. C. Deschamps, & S. Worchel (Eds.), *Identidad social* (pp. 395–415). Valencia, Spain: Promolibro.

Montero, M. (2000a). El sujeto, el Otro, la identidad [Subject, other, identity]. *Akademos, 2,* 11–30.

Montero, M. (2000b). Participation in participatory action-research. *Annual Review of Critical Psychology, 2,* 131–143.

Montero, M. (2000c). Perspectivas y retos de la psicología de la liberación [Perspectives and challenges of liberation psychology]. In J. J. Vásquez (Ed.), *Psicología social y liberación en América Latina* (pp. 9–26). México City: Universidad Autónoma Metropolitana-Iztapalapa.

Montero, M. (2002). Construcción del Otro, liberación de si mismo [Constructing the other, liberating oneself]. *Utopía y Praxis Latinoamericana, 7,* 41–51.

Montero, M. (2003). *Teoría y práctica de la psicología comunitaria. La tensión entre comunidad y sociedad* [Theory and practice of community psychology: The tension between community and society]. Buenos Aires: Paidos.

Montero, M. (2004). *Introducción a la psicología comunitaria. Orígenes, conceptos y procesos* [Introduction to community psychology: Origins, concepts, and processes]. Buenos Aires: Paidós.

Moreno, A. (1993). *El aro y la trama* [The hoop and the weave]. Caracas: CIP.

Moscovici, S. (1988). Notes toward a description of social representations. *European Journal of Social Psychology, 18,* 211–250.

Nicholas, J. (Ed.). (1993). *Psychology and oppression: Critiques and proposals.* Johannesburg: Skottaville Publishers.

Nsamenang, A. B. (1992). *Human development in cultural context: A Third World perspective.* Newbury Park, CA: Sage.

Nurmi, J. E. (Ed.). (2001). *Navigating through adolescence: European perspectives.* New York: Routledge.

Okpara, E. (Ed.). (1985). *Psychological strategies for national development.* Benin, Nigeria: Nigerian Psychological Association.

Parker, I. (2005). *Qualitative psychology. Introducing radical research.* Buckingham, UK: Open University.

Pearce, W. B., & Cronen, V. E. (1981). *Communication, action, and meaning.* New York: Praeger.

Pribram, K. H. (1971). *Languages of the brain: Experimental paradoxes and principles of neuropsychology.* Englewood Cliffs, NJ: Prentice Hall.

Pribram, K. H. (1991). *Brain and perception: Holonomy and structure in figural processing.* Mahwah, NJ: Lawrence Erlbaum Associates.

Ratner, C. (2002). *Cultural psychology: Theory and method.* New York: Academic Press/Plenum.

Reuter-Lorenz, P. A. (2002). New visions of the aging mind and brain. *TRENDS in Cognitive Sciences, 6,* 394–400.

Reyes-Lagunes, I. (2002). Social psychology in Mexico: A fifteen-year review. *International Journal of Group Tensions, 31,* 339–363.

Riley, R. (1997). *From inclusion to negotiation: The role of psychology in Aboriginal social justice.* Perth: Curtin Indigenous Research Center.

Rodríguez Gabarrón, L., & Hernández-Landa, L. (1994). *Investigación participativa* [Participatory research]. Madrid: Centro de Investigaciones Sociológicas.

Rogoff, B. (1990). *Apprenticeship in thinking.* Oxford, UK: Oxford University Press.

Rogoff, B. (2003). *The cultural nature of human development.* New York: Oxford University Press.

Sachs, J. (1993). The emergence of intentional communication. In J. B. Gleason (Ed.), *The development of language* (pp. 39–64). New York: Macmillan.

Salazar, J. M. (1983). *Bases psicológicas del nacionalismo* [Psychological bases of nationalism]. México City: Trillas.

Salazar, J. M. (2002). Latin American psychology in the *Interamerican Journal of Psychology* in the 1990s. *International Journal of Group Tensions, 31,* 295–316.

Sánchez, E. (2004). Organization and leadership in the participatory community. In M. Montero (Ed.), *Leadership and organization for community prevention and intervention in Venezuela* (pp. 13–30). Binghamton, NY: Haworth Press.

Sawaia, B. B. (1999). Psicolog a social: Uma ciencia sem fronteira na modernidade [Social psychology: A science without boundaries within modernity]. In E. Wiesenfeld & M. Montero (Eds.), *La psicología al fin del siglo* (pp. 323–336). Caracas: USB-SIP-Fundación Polar.

Sawaia, B. B. (2004). Affectivity as an ethical-political phenomenon and locus of critical-epistemological reflection in social psychology. *International Journal of Critical Psychology, 9,* 167–210.

Serpell, R. (1993). *The significance of schooling: Life-journeys in an African society.* Cambridge, MA: Cambridge University Press.

Serpell, R. (2004, June 11). *Nurturing the spirit of inquiry.* Commencement address delivered at the University of Zambia, Lusaka, Zambia.

Serrano-García, I., Bravo-Vick, M., Rosario-Collazo, W., & Gorrin-Peralta, J. J. (1998). *La psicología social comunitaria y la salud* [Community social psychology and health]. San Juan, Puerto Rico: University of Puerto Rico.

Serrano-García, I., & López-Sánchez, G. (1994). *Una perspectiva diferente del poder y el cambio social para la psicología social comunitaria* [A different perspective of power and social change for community social psychology]. In M. Montero (Ed.), *Psicología social comunitaria. Teoría, método y experiencia* (pp. 167–210). Guadalajara: Universidad de Guadalajara.

Shanker, S. S. I., & Greenspan, G. (2004). *The first idea.* Cambridge, MA: Da Capo Press.

Shotter, J. (1974). The development of personal powers. In M. Richards (Ed.), *The integration of a child into a social world* (pp. 25–43). Cambridge, MA: Cambridge University Press.

Smedslund, J. (1997). *The structure of psychological common sense.* Mahwah, NJ: Lawrence Erlbaum Associates.

Steele, C. (1997). A threat in the air: How stereotypes shape intellectual identity and performance. *American Psychologist, 52,* 613–629.

Stigler, J., Shweder, R. A., & Herdt, G. (Eds.). (1990). *Cultural psychology: Essays in comparative human development.* New York: Cambridge University Press.

Tajfel, H. (Ed.). (1984). *The social dimension.* Cambridge, UK: Cambridge University Press.

Taylor, D. M. (2002). *The quest for identity.* Westport, CT: Praeger.

Tomasello, M. (1999). *The cultural origins of human cognition.* Cambridge, MA: Harvard University Press.

Vasta, R., Haith, M., & Miller, S. (1995). *Child psychology: The modern science* (2nd ed.). New York: Wiley.

Vygotsky, L. (1978). *Mind in society: The development of higher psychological processes.* Cambridge, MA: Harvard University Press.

Weinreich, P., & Saunderson, W. (Eds.). (2003). *Analyzing identity: Cross-cultural, societal and clinical contexts*. London: Routledge.

Wittgenstein, L. (1953). *Philosophical investigations*. Oxford, UK: Blackwell.

Wittgenstein, L. (1998). *Tractatus* (D. Kolak, Trans.). Mountainview, CA: Mayfield Publishing.

Wundt, W. (1916). *Elements of folk psychology: Outlines of a psychological history of the development of mankind*. London: Allan and Unwin.

Yang, K. S., Hwang, K. K., Pedersen, P. B., & Daibo, I. (Eds.). (2003). *Progress in Asian social psychology: Conceptual and empirical contributions*. Westport, CT: Praeger.

7

Qualitative Research Methods for a Global Psychology

Graham B. Stead
Cleveland State University

Richard A. Young
University of British Columbia

INTRODUCTION

In order to describe some research methods that we believe are appropriate for a global psychology, it is important to state what we believe global psychology to mean. Marsella (1998) refers to a global community psychology as "concerned with understanding, assessing, and addressing the individual and collective psychological consequences of global events and forces by encouraging and using multicultural, multidisciplinary, multisectoral, and multinational knowledge, methods, and interventions" (p. 1284). He sees global events as affecting most people throughout the world. How nations and people interpret and react to these events can vary considerably and therefore a global psychology should be attuned to diversity rather than a monolithic psychology providing universal principles for all cultures (see chapter 11, this volume, for a more complete description of global community psychology).

Marsella (1998) refers to 25 major global events ranging from telecommunications, knowledge, poverty, urban life, and war, to terrorism, health, human rights violations, and substance abuse, among others. He adds that a global psychology values diverse psychologies. Therefore, a global psychology supports indigenous psychologies (i.e., developed within a culture) and indigenization (i.e., adapting psychological tools imported from another culture) (see chapter 5, this volume, for more on the indigenization movement in psychology). Although the utilization of Western psychologies may be appealing to some non-Western psychologists, researchers have become increasingly aware of how psychological theories, research methods, and assessment techniques from one culture are not necessarily useful in another culture (Stead & Watson, 1998). In order to provide our rationale for including certain qualitative research methods, it is apposite to reflect briefly on the nature of quantitative and qualitative research methods.

QUANTITATIVE AND QUALITATIVE TRADITIONS: PHILOSOPHICAL ASSUMPTIONS

Quantitative research methodology is undoubtedly the most prevalent methodological approach in psychology and has relied heavily on positivistic philosophical assumptions. The term "positivism" was coined by Auguste Comte (1798–1857) and developed by Henri Saint-Simon (1760–1825) and Emile Durkheim (1858–1917), although its roots can be traced to earlier philosophers, such as Francis Bacon (1561–1626). Positivism was further advanced by the Vienna Circle, a group of scientists and philosophers who met in Vienna in the 1920s and 1930s (e.g., Rudolph Carnap, Otto Neurath). Positivism is strongly aligned to the natural sciences approach of obtaining scientific knowledge. It rests on the notion that legitimate knowledge can only be obtained through direct experience and verification and also draws on natural science research methods. Positivism is concerned with: causality, prediction, and control; reductionism (i.e., studying the smallest components of an organism); internal and external validity; the denial of the impact of the researcher's values on the research project; researcher objectivity (i.e., the unbiased or neutral researcher); the belief that there is a single reality; and commensurability (i.e., the accretion of knowledge; Guba & Lincoln, 1994; Mouton, 1993). Positivism has increasingly been criticized, particularly since the 1960s and 1970s, notably, some would suggest, through the work of Kuhn (1970), among others. However, it must be pointed out that most qualitative researchers do not see quantitative research methods as inappropriate per se. Qualitative researchers do not view quantitative methodology as universally relevant or applicable to all research questions, but only one of many useful methodological approaches. They argue that, instead of researchers automatically choosing quantitative techniques to research a problem, they should rather decide which of the numerous quantitative and qualitative methods are best suited to addressing their research questions.

For example, assume that students from a group- rather than an individual-oriented culture speak English as a second language and seldom have been asked to complete questionnaires. They are requested to complete a career indecision questionnaire developed in another country by people whose first language is English. The questionnaire focuses on individual problems thought to be associated with career indecision, such as lack of planning and an external locus of control. The questionnaire uses a Likert-type scale as its format. In this example, one would query whether any consideration was given to the respondents' context in terms of group-related questions, such as the family's role in career choice or whether planning and an external locus of control were factors associated with career indecision in that culture. One would wonder whether any attempt had been made to ensure that the items represented career indecision in that culture, whether the respondents understood the Likert-type scale, or the meanings of the words in each item. In this instance, a qualitative study using group discussions or individual interviews may provide a more culturally sensitive and fertile method for examining career indecision. Such data collection may enable the researcher to gain a better understanding of what is meant by career indecision in that culture, rather than relying on a questionnaire developed in a foreign context.

It is not possible to encapsulate qualitative methods in a pithy definition as they differ from each other in various ways. However, there are commonalities between these methods, some of which will be mentioned here (see Bryman, 1988; Stiles, 1993). Qualitative methods are concerned with understanding the meanings and processes of human action, generally through non-numerical ways that include, for example, text, videos, images, and material objects. Qualitative researchers generally view reality as perspectival and do not seek a universal or absolute reality, as positivists do. Therefore, the generalization of research findings is of limited interest. Context and culture are interrelated, with culture being important to understanding human action. People interact within cultural contexts, and psychological processes are cultural processes. In keeping with this line of thinking, research for a global psychology lends itself to qualitative research methods that do not align themselves with an objective, value-free, and reductionistic universal science, but with a science in which the arabesques of cultures and human relationships are underscored. Qualitative research is not seen as value-neutral or objective. The researcher is viewed as having preconceived ideas and theories (personal or literature-based) when approaching a problem. Also, the researcher's beliefs, scientific training, and personal background (e.g., gender, age, culture) arguably play a role in how the research is conducted and interpreted. Therefore, reflexivity is valued, that is, the critical self-reflections of one's own viewpoints and biases that may affect the methodological process. Researchers are interested in events that unfold over time rather than in static events situated only in the moment. Qualitative researchers do not seek linear causality between variables, but rather view people and systems that dynamically interact with each other. Viewing the research problem holistically and contextually is central to qualitative research, whereas reductionism (which is salient to positivism and reduces social totalities to the individual, or an organism to its smallest parts) is considered to blur a contextual understanding of what is being researched. Therefore, the researcher may seek to understand a topic in terms of various contexts such as history, family, organization, and school.

Many of the criticisms of qualitative research emanate from paradigmatic conflicts rooted in ontological and epistemological differences, and are therefore difficult to resolve. For example, positivists query the lack of operational definitions, the presence of multiple realities, and the lack of generalizability in qualitative studies. The value-laden subjective stance of the qualitative researcher and the lack of control of confounding variables in qualitative studies are also open to criticism. Questions regarding whether qualitative research is scientific and whether validity and reliability should be prominent in qualitative research are also raised (Smith, 1996; Woolgar, 1996). Perhaps, the most pertinent criticism is that, like quantitative research, qualitative research has been developed in Western countries. Methodologies in non-Western countries have yet to gain prominence in the broader academic literature. Seedat (1997) called for a liberatory psychology that views science as a cultural manifestation. He added that Western methodologies negate spiritual, intuitive, and humanistic ways of knowing and that researchers need to reconstruct their world using methods rooted in their cultures. His appeal for a liberatory psychology resonates with a call for diverse and global psychologies.

CHALLENGES OF DEVELOPING ALTERNATIVE, CULTURALLY APPROPRIATE RESEARCH METHODS

From a methodological perspective, one of the major challenges for global psychology, in which both research and practice are responsive to culture and cultural differences, is how psychologists are educated and socialized.

Modern psychology is based on a positivist paradigm, which is translated methodologically as experimental design and quantitative methods. Although there are emerging efforts in psychology to embrace methodological pluralism, "equally powerful forces of resistance—illiteracy and indifference—remain" (McMullen, 2002, p. 195). The methodological changes needed to address this illiteracy and indifference are precisely what global psychology and the chapters in this book have implicitly and explicitly pointed to, that is, the recognition of the "shared worlds" (p. 202) that construct the discipline of psychology. New, alternative research methods have the effect of not only expanding our view of what constitutes psychology, but also shifting it as well, akin to Kuhn's (1970) paradigm shift. Similarly a global worldview expects psychology to address issues such as social justice, social transformation, higher levels of awareness, and the integration of traditional beliefs and Western interventions, as well as reflect cultural integrity (see chapter 6 in this volume for a discussion of the normative foundation required for a global psychology, and chapters 8 and 9 on contextual sensitivity, knowledge, and skills needed for effective practice in the non-Western world). Research methods have to be able to speak to our capability to investigate these and similar issues.

The naming of alternative paradigms is another critical challenge as psychology moves to a broader global perspective. It is not an issue of either "quantitative and qualitative" or "quantitative or qualitative." Although this chapter addresses four "qualitative" research methods, the challenge is not to consider these in opposition to "quantitative" methods, as if these two terms could encapsulate the range of ontological and epistemological positions represented in research methods. Psychologists need to unpack the ontology and epistemology implicit in traditional and alternative research paradigms in light of the parameters of global psychology.

Another way in which alternative research methods can gain greater acceptance in psychology is for the discipline to develop its own methods. For example, with the exception of the action-theory method and discourse analysis, the specific methods described in this chapter have arisen in disciplines other than psychology. Although the use of research methods that have been developed in other disciplines may enhance cross-disciplinary knowledge, disciplinary specific methods may be more likely to address issues from a psychological perspective.

The research methods described in this chapter can generally be viewed as data-oriented methods. This proximity to psychology's empirical roots contributes to their attractiveness in a period of transition from a single, unified research framework in psychology to more pluralist methods. The challenge that psychology can anticipate, however, is how far the discipline can move from data-based methods without jeopardizing notions of validity, however broadly construed. At the same time, we recognize that more interpretative, and less data-oriented, methods, such as critical theory, are finding a place in psychology (e.g., Sloan, 2000).

The conceptual grounding of research and the level of abstraction that research results have reached are challenged by some data-oriented, qualitative methods. Psychology in the past century has been able to produce sophisticated conceptual work. Some alternative methods seem to prefer abandoning or ignoring this work in their effort to investigate phenomena from a "fresh" perspective. Moreover, without a conceptual foundation, many qualitative, data-based methods are not directed toward producing results at a high level of abstraction. For example, grounded theory aims at mid-range theory building, which has its usefulness in the global context, but does not represent the only goal of psychological research.

These challenges intersect in various ways with how psychology chooses to recognize and address culture. Stead (2004) observed that culture is often considered a nuisance variable in psychological research. Others have seen it as a variable, like others, to be controlled in research. Berry (2004) commented that often psychologists deconstruct culture into its constituent psychological processes in a kind of reductionism that belies its dynamic, ongoing nature. Boesch (1991) captured the complexity of culture and its relation to psychology in describing culture as the "field for action" (p. 29). He stated, "as an action field, culture not only induces and controls action, but is continuously transformed by it; ... culture is as much a process as a structure" (p. 29). This perspective brings culture to the forefront of psychological research, but not in the sense of taking an anthropological stance. Rather, culture is the ongoing intergenerationally shared processes that reflect the actions, projects, and careers of people. Psychology has access to the study of culture through methods that focus on human action, including behavior, cognition (i.e., the internal processes that guide action), and meaning (i.e., the goals or purpose of action) perspectives. Certainly the latter perspective relies on interpretation and hermeneutics as methods, but psychology should be cautioned not to let one perspective dominate its research agenda, and not be satisfied with research methods that are not able to integrate these perspectives.

Finally, from a methodological perspective, global psychology challenges researchers to seek collaborative research modalities between researchers and the "researched." It challenges researchers to unpack narrative and folk explanations as contributing to cultural understanding, to use naïve observations in local communities as beginning places for the research endeavor, and to recognize ongoing processes as critical aspects of human and cultural phenomena. As we address these challenges, the possibilities for an enhanced role for psychology in the global context become significant.

Marsella (1998) suggested a few qualitative methods that could be used in a global psychology, such as postmodern feminism, social constructionism, and hermeneutics. However, he did not provide a rationale for why these specific methods may be appropriate, but used them as exemplars of the need for research to focus on context, power, and meaning, all of which can be addressed by qualitative methodologies. There is a growing literature that argues for a substantial role for psychology in social transformation (e.g., Cajigas-Segredo, 2002). To some extent this argument has arisen in the particular social, political, and economic conditions of many Latin-American countries and is linked to both Freire's (1970) pedagogy of the oppressed and liberation theology. But, the distinctive liberation psychology that has emerged (Lira, 2000; Martín-Baró, 1994) asks psychologists to hear the voices of those they research in their own particular contexts of power and meaning. It is our purpose to articulate four methods, which could be used for research in a global psychology, that capture among global issues the place of psychology in social transformation. These methods are not exhaustive, but we believe that each can provide useful techniques for research in a global psychology.

SOME RESEARCH METHODS FOR A GLOBAL PSYCHOLOGY

Action Theory

As recently as 1994, Hoshmand observed that the study of meaningful and intentional action had not been distinguished by a unique methodology. Indeed, the lack of specific methods to understand action may reflect the inconsistent interest in action as a viable conceptual framework in psychology. However, since Hoshmand's comment, a promising qualitative method, the action-project method (Young, Valach, & Domene, 2005), has emerged. This method is explicitly based on action theory (e.g., von Cranach, Kalbermatten, Indermuehler, & Gugler, 1982), but action theory can be applied using a variety of research methods that incorporate an action-theory conceptualization (e.g., Valach, Young, & Lynam, 2002). Action theory itself emerged from perspectives ranging from Mead (1934) and Parsons (1937/1968) to Vygotsky (1986) and Weber (1949). It is part of recent efforts focusing on action (Brandtstätder & Lerner, 1999; Gollwitzer & Bargh, 1996; Hacker, 1994), notably in Latin America (Montero, 2000). In broad terms, action theory and the action-project method fall within a realist ontology and a constructivist epistemology (see Young & Valach, 2004, for further discussion). Action theory offers a distinct conceptual framework for research in psychology. It is directed toward understanding the intentional, goal-directed nature of human behavior. Its uniqueness is that it does not limit the explanation of behavior to causal antecedent conditions, as is the case with more traditional research approaches. Rather, research based on action theory takes an integrative perspective, that is, it brings together goal-directed, functional, and causal explanations, and at the same time captures context.

The importance of action theory for global psychology is that it can be used to research people in their everyday lives using a research frame and constructs that closely reflect how people live and make sense of their lives. At one level, action theory has a close connection to narrative and folk explanations of actions and sequences of actions. Bruner (1990) referred to *folk psychology* as "a system by which people organize their experiences in, knowledge about, and transactions with the social world" (p. 35). The content of narrative and folk-psychology data may vary across cultures, but it is generally held that, as human beings, we attribute intentions to agents irrespective of content (Lillard, 1998). In a global context, folk psychology and narrative are starting points, but a research method should be sufficiently robust to account for the multifaceted nature of human actions, which are linked over time and have complex goal structures.

The understanding of action and the bases for data collection are founded on three perspectives of action. Action can be seen from the perspective of manifest behavior, from the perspective of the internal cognitions (thoughts and feelings) that serve to direct and guide the action, and from the perspective of the social meaning that is attributed to it by the actors and others who share the language community. In using this approach as a research method, researchers attempt to gather data from all three perspectives. For example, Young and his colleagues (Young et al., 2001), in investigating the joint projects that parents and adolescents undertake that are directed toward the adolescent's future, gathered manifest behavior data by video, recording conversations between parents and adolescents. Internal cognitions were accessed through a procedure known as self-confrontation in which the video recording of the conversation (action) was immediately shown to participants individually after the conversation was completed. The video was stopped at 1-minute intervals and the participant was asked to recall his or her thoughts and feelings for the minute just seen on the video. Finally, data on the social meaning of the action were gathered from the participants during the self-confrontation as he or she commented on the meaning of the action. Social-meaning data were also gathered when participants were given the opportunity to comment broadly on the action in the introductory and exit interviews. Additional data from all three perspectives were gathered from self- and researcher-monitoring logs and reports, which were constructed to access information from these three perspectives. These allowed researchers "to construct rich, detailed descriptions of the nature and progress of goal-directed intentional behaviors, over time, with each data source contributing to the overall understanding" (Young et al., 2005).

The unit of analysis in action-theory research is the action, in contrast to the individual as the unit of analysis in much traditional psychological research. Many of the phenomena that are the subject of global psychology represent processes and can be conceptualized as goal-directed action. For example, violent conflict, human rights violations, and drug addiction, as worldwide phenomena, are not only amenable to investigation using the action-project method, but can be understood as significantly different through the lens of action theory.

Three levels of action contribute to this analysis. First, action is composed of a series of verbal and nonverbal elements. These elements are observable, and from a research perspective can be measured with specificity and precision. In the study cited above (Young et al., 2001), these elements were the words, phrases, and nonverbal behaviors used by the parents and adolescents in conversation, captured on video, and transcribed for purposes of analysis. When considered as a sequence, these elements contribute to the functional steps of an action, that is, how the elements serve to reach a goal and represent the flow and sequence of the action. Functional steps, in turn, contribute to the goal of action. They foster movement toward some type of goal, either as a process or desired end-state. Finally, goals represent the meaning of action processes. Their assessment is dependent on insight, actor-observer agreement, and social convention.

In the qualitative analysis of action data, the researchers initially identify the broadest goals or intentions for an action and then the goals for specific parts of the action. In attempting to describe what the participants are trying to do in the action, this analysis is subjective and social. This is followed by the detailed "bottom-up" analysis of the elements and functional steps, based on the coding of elements and the subsequent identification of functional steps. Finally, the "top-down" and the "bottom-up" coding are then brought together in a full understanding of the action in question. Throughout this analytic procedure, data from the self-confrontation interview serve as an adjunctive basis to understand goals, functional steps, and elements.

Action-theory research is well suited to investigate human processes, particularly processes across time. Individual and joint actions are relatively short-term phenomena, anchored cognitively, socially, and environmentally in our everyday lives. A sequence of individual and/or joint actions considered over time that contribute to a common goal is identified as a project. The study by Young et al. (2001), cited earlier, focused on the project system over an 8-month period and identified and described not only the joint project related to the adolescent's future, but also how this project was embedded in relationship, identity, parenting, and cultural projects. Finally, when projects coalesce over long periods of time or in highly significant domains of one's life, they are identified as careers. For example, Michel and Valach (1997, 2002) showed that suicide attempters often understand their attempt as a step in a suicide career. By identifying the action as the unit of analysis and recognizing that much of human action is social, action theory and, specifically, the action-project method circumvent the individual-social dichotomy in much of psychology. Both the conceptualization and the method are well attuned to collectivist as well as individualist cultures.

Action-theory research can make a particular contribution to global psychology in the framing of relevant research questions. Many of these questions can be framed as goal-directed action whether they reflect large-scale global concerns or issues pertinent to local groups and contexts. For example, in the global context, psychological knowledge and understanding should provide the basis for interventions. Most interventions reflect a goal-directed and intentional stance from the perspective of both the professional psychologist and the client. Having a conceptual framework and a research method that capture this system of goal-directed action is relevant in a global psychology. The importance of human relationships, and the means to understand them in the context of global psychology as broad political issues or specific interpersonal issues, are domains that action-theory research can address as well. Action theory also addresses the importance of communication in the development of joint goals.

Similarly, cultural and multicultural topics are central in a global psychology. Many cultural processes involve goals, functional steps, and elements. Indeed, action theory is particularly sensitive to the study of culture as cultures emerge from complex processes of construction in which the goal is to place the individual "within a world that appears ordered, 'transparent,' providing a space for the rules of action" (Boesch, 1991, p. 362). Thus, it is action (and project and career) that relates the individual to his or her culture. By focusing on the process characteristics of culture and not limiting it to ethnic or national parameters, action theory and its corresponding action-project method are sensitized to specific cultures within larger multicultural amalgams.

The goal of research using the qualitative action-project method is descriptive. It is to bring an understanding to the data that others can easily recognize. Findings can be reported in a variety of ways that are suited to the research questions. For example, Young et al. (2001) were able to describe the properties of projects across families and identify how the joint project about the adolescent's future contributed to a variety of goals within families and reflected the complexity of human action. Simultaneously, findings may also report discrepancies between elements, functional steps, and goals within and across participant dyads.

Among the strengths of the qualitative action-project method are its grounding in a conceptualization using language close to human experience, its comprehensive and systematic data gathering and analysis, and its ability to be readily used as part of mixed methods and quantitative studies. Users should be cautioned that there is not an easy "cookbook" approach to its use, that as a relatively new method, there are comparatively few published examples of its use at the moment, and that it can be adapted in various ways, but the full use of this method may require substantial resources. Finally, some may feel that this method is not sufficiently distinct from action theory itself to warrant its identification as a method. It is important to note, however, that action theory is an epistemology rather than a specific theory. It is a framework for examining human social action as meaningful and distinct from the movement of physical objects. This method, like all other qualitative and quantitative research methods, is based on significant assumptions about meaning, language, and knowledge. In the case of the action-project method, these assumptions are made explicit in action theory.

Discourse Analysis

Discourse analysis is well positioned to address global psychological issues. It is not an approach that focuses on reductionism or objectivity, but recognizes the embeddedness of human interaction in context. It does not focus on describing human behavior, but rather examines the role of power, politics, and ideology in human interactions. For example, discourse analysis has been used in the South African context to identify the role of power relations in interactions, the role of power in knowledge production, and whose interests are being served when interactions take place (de la Rey, 1997).

Discourse analysis emphasizes language usage and how language serves political and ideological interests. Words are not viewed as reflecting reality, as there are multiple realities depending on the discourse being employed. For example, assume a psychologist requests a client to describe his or her adjustment problems at work. There could be a relationship discourse in which interactions with the worker's peers and boss are discussed, a familial discourse in which the work role is described in relation to family functioning, and a psychological discourse where the client's emotional and motivational difficulties related to work are reflected upon within each of these discourses. Each of these discourses emphasizes a viewpoint and silences another, but multiple discourses enrich the story being told. Therefore, meaning inherent in these perspectives or realities is analyzed. Language and meaning are also socially shared. One's ideas are not situated in one's mind, but are created through a collective and public reality. Language is culturally embedded and therefore research is a cultural enterprise (Stead, 2004). According to Parker (1994), "Discourse analysis is concerned with the ways in which meaning is reproduced and transformed in texts, and when such reproduction and transformation concerns institutions and power relations we are led inevitably to consideration of the role of ideology" (p. 103). Discourse analysis serves to highlight how certain ideas or perspectives attain truth statuses, which are then seldom questioned. Therefore, a major purpose is to disrupt oppressive and exploitative discourse (Durrheim, 1997).

Meaning can only be understood within contexts, and cultural context is of special interest to discourse analysts and to a global psychology. Indeed, language cannot be divorced from culture and our thought processes are freed and constrained by the language we use. The discourse analyst does not objectively separate the text from the context, but seeks to understand communication as purveyors of ideological and political manipulation and persuasion (Parker, 1997). Function, construction, and variation are three major themes of discourse analysis, and text is examined with these themes in mind. Function refers to the purpose of the text. For example, the purpose of a request can be direct, "Could you please give me the ruler" or subtle, "It is so difficult to draw straight lines without a ruler." Construction emphasizes how cultural resources clarify the meaning of any symbolic activity. The meaning of text has its origin in cultural discourses and, therefore, discourses construct the nature of relationships between people. Variation is dependent on function, and how one describes something will depend on the context of communication. For example, an explanation of your feelings toward your workplace may vary considerably when talking to your boss, your partner, or a young child. Your accounts are therefore constructed as a version or perspective of events and do not reflect an absolute reality (Potter & Wetherell, 1987). So, a discourse analyst is interested in why you constructed your speech or writing in the way you did.

There are two major streams of thought, namely the Foucaultdian approach and the interpretive approach. The first stream adheres to the work of Michel Foucault (e.g., 1970, 1972). Foucault studied psychology and philosophy in Paris in the 1940s and 1950s. Although he initially taught at the University of Lille in France, he also taught in countries of Africa, Asia, Europe, and North and South America. Briefly, Foucault focused on discipline and confession (i.e., how we reveal ourselves to others) in his writings. His work on discipline is also present in his analyses of psychology. Here, he referred to the "psy–complex," which is the complex web of psychological practices that dictate how psychologists regulate and categorize people. It also dictates how people view themselves and others by using psychological words, some of which are now part of popular culture such as "Oedipus complex," "defense mechanisms," "schizophrenia," "conditioning," and so on. The discourse analyst would ask how these and other psychological terms came about, who benefits from these terms, and in what contexts they are used. When people accept such words, which become transformed into truths, they then participate in their own subjugation (Foucault, 1980).

The interpretive approach (Potter & Wetherell, 1987, 1994, 1995) has its focus on social psychological and sociological issues and aims to contribute "to our understanding of issues of identity, the nature of mind, constructions of self, other and the world and the conceptualization of social action and interaction" (Potter & Wetherell, 1995, p. 81). It examines how people construct their discourses to perform social actions. These discourses comprise linguistic resources and rhetorical devices to present alternative viewpoints to issues in question. The researcher is thus interested in how discourses are constructed to enable actions to be performed. For example, a woman considering whether to have an abortion may have competing discourses to contend with, namely, her religion's position on abortion, her parents' and partner's views, her medical doctor's advice, liberal and conservative positions on abortion, feminist discourse on the topic, and so on. How her discourse on whether to have an abortion competes with alternative discourses would be of interest to the discourse analyst. Although the interpretative approach includes an examination of ideology and power in its analyses, Parker (1997) states that it focuses more on the text than on locating it in sociopolitical contexts. He adds that the adherents of the interpretative approach are less critical of the political discourses in psychology than are Foucaultdian analysts.

There are no agreed upon methods by which to conduct discourse analysis. Discourse analysis is not theory-driven nor is it an attempt made to "fetishize" method (i.e., become obsessed with developing a detailed methodology of discourse analysis). Although this may be problematic to some, it may also reflect positivist expectations for detailed methodological designs and so-called "rigor." Here, one is reminded of Feyerabend (1975), a philosopher of science, who argued that there is no universal or "correct" scientific methodology and that scientists are methodological opportunists and science is an anarchistic enterprise. However, all discourse analytic methods focus on how language limits meaning. Guides to method can be found in Potter and Wetherell (1987), Parker (1992), and Burman and Parker (1993). One process of discourse analysis by Potter and Wetherell (1987) is briefly described below. The authors propose 10 stages of discourse analysis, namely: research questions (i.e., how text and writing are read, not merely descriptions of what happened as is often found in traditional research); sample selection (dependent on the research question and not on potential generalizability and random sample selection); collection of records and documents; interviews (in which the interviewer is an active participant); transcription (in which factors such timing, intonation, and silences may be included); coding (creating chunks of meaning from text that are inclusive); analysis (in which patterns in the data are examined in detail, rather than in terms of general trends); validation (the extent to which the discourse is coherent and why there may be inconsistencies in the text); the report (to present the analysis and conclusions so that the researcher's interpretations may be assessed); and application (how the research will be employed or applied).

Discourse analysis has also used quantitative indices in data analysis. Terre Blanche (1997) referred to the use of frequency counts, that is, how often certain words appear in text. As frequency counts provide a limited indication of which words are closely related to others, he suggested the employment of lexical nets. For example, he showed that in psychiatric reports he had analyzed, words such as "strange," "bizarre," "inappropriate," and "aggressive" were closely linked to the word "behavior." His analysis used a statistical formula indicating the degree of relationship between words. In so doing, he demonstrated how lexical nets provide insight into how word relationships provide evidence to admit a person to a psychiatric institution. He added that, "well rehearsed symptom checklists are recited over and over again with no necessary relation to actuality" (p. 154).

In South Africa, discourse analysis has been used to research many issues, such as the politicized discourses employed by the South African Truth and Reconciliation Commission that represented the old apartheid regime and the new regime (Hook & Harris, 2000), the arguably rhetorical and justificatory, rather than objective, nature of psychopathology (Hook & Parker, 2002), and the deconstruction of racialized discourses as manifestations of feeling threatened in the new democratic South Africa (Stevens, 1998). In the latter study, the sociohistorical context in which the discourses were embedded was examined by means of group interviews. In addition, participants' and researcher's interpretations of the contexts in which racialized discourses were nurtured and maintained were thematized. Such research, as mentioned above, does not seek "truth," which is seen as unobtainable, but attempts to unravel discourses that serve to maintain power and control. This is discourse analysis' strength, and one that is not easily realized through quantitative research methods.

Discourse analysis has been criticized for its relativity and its hesitancy to take any definitive political positions. The language of subjectivity and difference, as opposed to taking action against certain political issues, is sometimes seen as its major weakness (Burman, 1990). Its unraveling of cherished beliefs have a dispersive quality to them, and its perceived lack of attention to integrating the knowledge of a field can be disconcerting to some.

Discourse analysis views the social world as text (Parker, 1994), and it is a relatively radical form of social research. Through language, one begins to understand social interaction and, in so doing, the individual as decontextualized becomes less of a concern to the researcher than the larger context in which he or she dynamically interacts. It is the diversity of meaning and the contradictory routes to meaning within social contexts that interest discourse analysts. This approach is well suited to a global psychology because it examines the diversity of meaning in social and cultural contexts, with foci on social justice, social transformation, and power relations.

Grounded Theory

Grounded theory, with its emphasis on exploration, social action, sensitizing concepts, and qualitative method, resonates with the expectations of a global psychology. Equally, it includes features that are well accepted in the science of psychology, such as empiricism, data-based methods, and positivism. Grounded theory, which is one of the leading qualitative research methods in the social sciences today, arose from two strong influences in the 20th century—symbolic interactionism and positivism. In recent formulations it has shed its outward appearance of positivism. Nevertheless, its roots in traditional science are not only evident, but also attractive to psychologists.

Grounded theory, initially formulated by Glaser and Strauss (1967), is a research method whose purpose is to generate theory. These theories are usually produced by gathering qualitative data in the form of interviews and other documents, and subjecting these data to an analysis based on coding, constant comparison among parts of the data, the elaboration of more generalized categories, and the identification of a core category around which other categories revolve. Eventually, the delineation of a theory or explanation emerges not only from the identification of the core and other categories, but from the discursive memo-writing that accompanies the coding and the elaboration of categories.

In recent years, Glaser and Strauss (1967) have parted company in the development of grounded theory, with Glaser (1978) remaining close to the original version, whereas Strauss's reformulation (Strauss & Corbin, 1990) includes more methodological specification (see Heath & Cowley, 2004 for a discussion of the comparison between Glaser and Strauss). However, at their core, both versions share the same emphasis on the local, particular, and mid-range theory in contrast to the grand narratives of traditional science. Global psychology invites these types of theories.

For example, Morrow and Smith (1995) developed a theoretical model of coping and survival for women who have survived childhood sexual abuse. This study is based on a 10-week focus group of 11 women, documentation, follow-up participant interviews, and collaborative analysis between the researchers and the participants. The categories identified in this study were grouped as causal conditions, phenomena, context, intervening variables, strategies, and consequences and ordered in a linear, diagrammatic way, much like we would expect a structural or path analysis model to be presented. These groupings of categories revolved around the two core strategies: (a) keeping from being overwhelmed by threatening and dangerous feelings and (b) managing helplessness, powerlessness, and lack of control. The strengths of this theory, grounded in the experience of the women who had survived childhood sexual abuse, was that it pushed psychological understanding beyond the emotion- and problem-focused coping strategies that had been prevalent in the literature at the time of the study. From the perspective of global psychology it is important to note that the researchers and participants are engaged in the data analysis, potentially empowering activity for both groups.

To arrive at the research outcome, grounded theory researchers make certain assumptions and engage in particular practices. They assume that one's own culture, traditions, experiences, understandings, perceptions, and values are filters through which the data will be analyzed and, indeed, can contribute to the analysis. Grounded theory researchers assume that discovery is the heart of the research process. Discovery arises through an iterative process of data gathering and analysis that involves sensitivity to both what one brings to the analysis and what emerges in it. The practices that facilitate this discovery process include a sequence of coding and re-coding that proceeds from open or substantive coding to more complex coding that reflects and refines emerging categories. At both the early and later stages, the constant method of comparing data, instances, and later categories is used. These research steps are not sequential. They are inter-spersed with theoretical sampling, which is an effort to add new cases or data to the study based on promising ideas or the need to capture greater depth or variety because of what is emerging in the analysis. As researchers engage in this process, they are continually aware of moving the analysis from description to categories, concepts, and theories. In this pursuit, writing theoretical memoranda, which represent the researcher's exploration of emerging concepts and theories, is the critical practice. In recent works, Glaser (1992) emphasized the continual use of the constant comparative method, whereas Strauss and Corbin (1998) focused on developing the core and supporting categories that integrate socio-structural factors, personal action, and meaning to address the interaction of variables.

The Morrow and Smith (1995) example is oriented toward theory, but unlike traditional psychological research, its concern is with theory generation rather than theory validation. This focus on theory generation implies that where theories come from is important, particularly because these theories, as grounded in the everyday lives of people, capture and reflect different contexts and cultures. In the global context, grounded theory can support the development of indigenous theories rather than the importing of theories from other cultures.

Grounded theory's departure from theory validation as the purpose of research brings into question the place and value of the literature review as contributing to the formulation of the research questions. In grounded theory, the researcher is not to assume a particular theoretical position prior to the research. At the same time, the researcher cannot ignore the conceptual and theoretical contexts that surround the processes or phenomena being investigated. Cutliffe (2000) suggested that the literature review in a grounded-theory study allows the researcher to develop a degree of "conceptual density" (p. 1481) prior to launching the research. Henwood and Pidgeon (2003) recommend theoretical agnosticism over theoretical ignorance for the grounded-theory researcher. The issue of theory validation versus theory generation is one domain in which Glaser and Strauss, the originators of grounded theory, have recently disagreed, with Strauss (Strauss & Corbin, 1998) leaning more toward theory validation in the form of the construction of theory, rather than its discovery.

A number of salient issues in global psychology, such as the AIDS epidemic, poverty, and child-labor practices are embedded in such significant political rhetoric that the initial atheoretical perspective of grounded theory may serve to uncover more indigenous explanations. At the same time, without conceptual guides the grounded-theory researcher may unwittingly assume conceptualizations that are essentially political in purpose.

Some commentaries (e.g., Alvesson & Sköldberg, 2000) identify grounded theory as a data-oriented method because of its detailed use of empirical material. It is through data that grounded theory stays close to human action and establishes a link with traditional science. On the other hand, the reliance on empirical data has opened grounded theory to the criticism that it "finds itself shackled to surface structures" (Alvesson & Sköldberg, p. 33). However, the distinction Haig (1995) makes between data and phenomena with regard to grounded theory may serve to resolve the dilemma about the substance of possible outcomes of grounded theory studies. Haig suggested that grounded-theory studies should be based on the "relatively stable features of the world we seek to explain," that is, phenomena, rather than data idiosyncratic to particular investigative contexts.

Another aspect of grounded theory captured in the Morrow and Smith (1995) example is its focus on a social process—in this case, coping and surviving with childhood sexual abuse. Moreover, in focusing on this social process, the method undertakes to unearth the array of interactions that produce variation in that process. Gross (2004) illustrated the usefulness of grounded theory to investigate processes of interest to global psychology in her study of transnational migration and health. Specifically, in her grounded theory, refugees in Switzerland struggle with "imaginaries" of trauma and trust as they engage in the process of becoming "good" refugees. In other words, the medical and psychological identification of trauma fails to come to terms with the refugees' biographies, and, at the same time, is a diagnostic category that refugees must assume to acquire recognition and, perhaps, legal status in their new country.

The critical factor in appreciating grounded theory in the context of a global psychology is its commitment to both realism and relativism (Rennie, 2000). As it is currently formulated, it is open to being used to investigate a variety of contexts and issues and, at the same time, yields mid-range theories that are meaningful in particular local contexts as well as in the broader domain of psychological science. The roots of grounded theory in positivism can be seen as both an asset and a liability. Other liabilities include the lack of clarity in its relation to previous theories and extant literature, the "depth" of theories that emerge from grounded theory studies, and whether the largely interview-based data sources are reliable and valid for events that may have occurred some time earlier.

Focus Groups

Focus-group research has its origin in the 1920s, particularly in the development of survey questionnaires. In the 1970s market researchers employed focus groups to obtain participant opinions of products and to determine their needs. Focus-group interviews are now used for a variety of research projects and are an important qualitative research technique. The development of focus-group research has been slow, primarily due to positivism's emphasis on numerically based questionnaires and the control the researcher has traditionally wielded in determining the types of questions to be asked in questionnaires and interviews.

Focus-group research is an appropriate method to address global psychology issues. In focus groups, participants are encouraged to discuss issues with the researcher, facilitating but not directing or controlling the process to the same extent as would be found in quantitative methods. It is well positioned to research people's cultural perspectives and the normative understandings they employ to make their decisions (Bloor, Frankland, Thomas, & Robson, 2001). Normative understandings play an important role in people's actions, and yet researchers often view them as fundamental or taken-for-granted knowledge. These articulated and unarticulated assumptions of normative actions can be accessed in focus groups where participants explain the reasons for their views. The extent to which individual choice interacts with cultural beliefs may become more prominent in such discussions. Thus, focus-group research may be used to good effect in cultural and cross-cultural research where the function of group norms and the process and outcome of in-group conversations may become more apparent. In addition, research that examines local and indigenous perspectives may be well served through this approach.

The size of focus groups varies, but in general they are between 4 and 12 members (Kingry, Tiedje, & Friedman, 1990). Too large a group may result in too few participants contributing to discussions, and it also may be difficult to link the transcribed text to the speaker. The selection of participants also needs to be considered. Although there are no firm guidelines in this regard, it is desirable to keep the group members relatively homogenous in terms of gender, culture, socioeconomic status, and age, particularly when sensitive or potentially divisive topics are being discussed (Bloor et al., 2001). For example, focus groups comprising people with opposing views on topics such as abortion, military draft, HIV/AIDS, and gay marriage can elicit strong opinions from members that can be hurtful and emotionally upsetting to others in the group. Groups may be pre-existing or may be selected based on certain individual characteristics. This selection would depend on the research aims. It is also possible for a number of focus groups to be used in a particular study. For example, a study may examine high school students' perceptions of career barriers and the researcher may use three focus groups from grades 10 to 12. It is also important for participants to sign a statement of confidentiality. This may enable participants to disclose more fully.

There are various ways in which focus-group research may be employed and these include exploratory research, pretest focus-group research, and multi-method designs. Focus groups can be exploratory where limited research has been conducted in a field or in a particular context. For example, self-efficacy is well researched in the United States, although its meanings and relationship to cultural beliefs in other countries is not well documented. What is the meaning of self or selves and is efficacy inherent in the individual or deeply embedded in one's relationship to others and in one's culture? Does the meaning of self-efficacy vary in different contexts? Such research questions would lend themselves to exploratory focus-group research and the findings may then result in other research methods being employed, such as interviews or questionnaires.

Pretest focus-group research may be used to determine, for example, which questions need to be asked in the main study or whether certain questions for a future survey are understandable and relevant to participants. The pretest can also be useful in formulating hypotheses and for the researcher to get a sense of the participants' perceptions about a certain topic. In this way, focus-group research lends itself to indigenous research by researching issues rooted in context; it is thus suitable for a global psychology.

Focus groups are also used for triangulation in which multiple methods are used to confirm or validate findings (i.e., convergent validity), although it is debatable whether qualitative research methods can "validate" another method's findings. This is because responses from different qualitative methods can vary considerably in breadth and depth, making replication difficult. This is due to the fact that various methods are not necessarily directly comparable (Bloor et al., 2001). Perhaps, it is more appropriate to consider the focus group as providing alternative perspectives to the research findings. Hence, the focus group is useful as an additional method in a multi-method design.

Focus group research is a collectivistic approach that allows research participants to discuss issues in a group rather than in an individual environment. It also enables the researcher to observe collective human interaction (Madriz, 2000). The behavior of the facilitator, who is generally the researcher, is very important in all focus groups. The facilitator needs to develop rapport with and be trusted by the participants. He or she then introduces the topic to be discussed and may start the group discussions with a series of questions that are directly linked to the research aims. The interviewer's role is initially active, but it becomes more passive as the session continues. The facilitator tries to enable passive members to speak and moderates the output from very vocal members in the group. This is difficult, as restraining the output of vocal members may result in them being offended and limit their participation. In addition, the facilitator needs to enable individuals to discuss their feelings about the focus group deliberations should the need arise (i.e., be debriefed).

Interviews are usually tape recorded, with the permission of the participants, and the data are analyzed through coding, determining various themes, and analyzing linkages between themes. There is no specific analytic strategy to be used. However, Bloor et al. (2001) recommend conversation or discourse analysis (Silverman, 1993) as a possible analytic strategy. They emphasize the importance of transcribing all recorded speech including, for example, unfinished speech, interrupted speech, laughter, and length of silences. Speakers should also be identified in the transcription.

An example of focus-group interviews can be found in Hopa, Simbayi, and du Toit (1998). They studied the perceptions of psychiatrists, psychologists, traditional healers, and consumers, among others, toward traditional and Western healing in South Africa. They used 5 focus groups of between 6 and 9 participants. They analyzed the data using thematic content analysis and thereafter reported the frequencies of themes. They argued that the technique was flexible in its application and also had high face validity.

Focus-group research has various advantages. These include the observation of group processes with such interactions being more prominent than the research participant interaction characteristic of one-to-one interviewing. This method is useful when interviewing people who cannot read and write and also for people who dislike personal interviews (Kitzinger, 1995). Larger groups of people may be interviewed than is the case with individual interviews. This process may be suitable in certain cultures that prefer to discuss issues in groups rather than as individuals.

Focus research also has disadvantages. According to Morgan (1993) the facilitator needs to be more sensitive to group dynamics than is the case with individual interviewing. On occasion a research participant can dominate the conversation and influence the viewpoints of others in the groups, unless the researcher is skilled at enabling group, rather than individual, participation to prevail. Participants may also be hesitant to be completely open in their discussions due to the lack of privacy of the focus-group setting. The facilitator therefore needs to be adapt at in-group dynamics to overcome these possible disadvantages.

CONCLUSION

The methods described in this chapter are but four in a myriad of qualitative research approaches that reflect principles of pluralism and perspective, which are inherent in global psychology. These methods also give voice to the possibility of recognizing the unique and the local in the generation of new knowledge. Each method has the capacity to address a range of issues prompted by global psychology, generate findings that can be used in particular contexts, and contribute to discipline-based, inclusive knowledge in psychology. Global psychology invites change, including change in research methods, but more broadly change in the assumptions that undergird them. This change will inevitably be accompanied by tensions within psychology and within segments of the psychological community. It is important to stress, however, that psychology can contribute more directly to the personal and social fabric of the worlds in which it finds itself.

RECOMMENDED READINGS

Levett, A., Kottler, A., Burman, E., & Parker, I. (Eds). (1997). *Culture, power and difference: Discourse analysis in South Africa.* Cape Town: University of Cape Town Press.

Morrow, S. L., & Smith, M. L. (1995). Constructions of survival and coping in women who have survived sexual abuse. *Journal of Counseling Psychology, 42,* 24–33.

Parker, I. (2002). *Critical discursive psychology.* Houndsmills, UK: Palgrave Macmillan.

Richardson, J. T. E. (Ed.). (1996). *Handbook of qualitative research methods for psychology and the social sciences.* Leicester, UK: British Psychological Society.

Strauss, A., & Corbin, J. (1998). *Basics of qualitative research: Grounded theory procedures and techniques* (2nd ed.). Newbury Park, CA: Sage.

Valach, L., Young, R. A., & Lynam, M. J. (2002). *Action theory: A primer for applied research in the social sciences.* Westport, CT: Praeger.

Young, R. A., Valach, L., Ball, J., Paseluikho, M. A., Wong, Y. S., DeVries, R. J., McLean, H., & Turkel, H. (2001). Career development as a family project. *Journal of Counseling Psychology, 48,* 190–202.

Young, R. A., Valach, L., & Domene, J. F. (2005). The qualitative action–project method in counseling psychology. *Journal of Counseling Psychology, 52,* 215–223.

REFERENCES

Alvesson, M., & Sköldberg, K. (2000). *Reflexive methodology: New vistas for qualitative methodology.* London: Sage.

Berry, J. (2004). Review: *The psychological foundations of culture. Canadian Psychology, 45,* 315–316.

Bloor, M., Frankland, J., Thomas, M., & Robson, K. (2001). *Focus groups in social research.* London: Sage.

Boesch, E. E. (1991). *Symbolic action theory and cultural psychology.* New York: Springer-Verlag.

Brandtstädter, J., & Lerner, R. M. (Eds.). (1999). *Action and self-development: Theory and research through the life span.* Thousand Oaks, CA: Sage.

Bruner, J. (1990). *Acts of meaning.* Cambridge, MA: Harvard University Press.

Bryman, A. (1988). *Quantity and quality in social research.* London: Routledge.

Burman, E. (1990). Differing with deconstruction: A feminist critique. In I. Parker & J. Shotter (Eds.), *Deconstructing social psychology* (pp. 208–220). London: Routledge.

Burman, E., & Parker, I. (Eds.). (1993). *Discourse analytic research: Repertoires and readings of texts in action.* London: Routledge.

Cajigas-Segredo, N. (2002). Contributions of psychology to social transformation in Uruguay. *International Journal of Group Tensions, 31,* 53–77.

Cutliffe, J. R. (2000). Methodological issues in grounded theory. *Journal of Advanced Nursing, 31,* 1476–1488.

de la Rey, C. (1997). On political activism and discourse analysis in South Africa. In A. Levett, A. Kottler, E. Burman, & I. Parker (Eds.), *Culture, power, and difference: Discourse analysis in South Africa* (pp. 189–197). Cape Town: University of Cape Town Press.

Durrheim, K. (1997). Social constructionism, discourse, and psychology. *South African Journal of Psychology, 27,* 175–182.

Feyerabend, P. (1975). *Against method: Outline of an anarchistic theory of knowledge.* London: New-Left Books.

Foucault, M. (1970). *The order of things.* London: Tavistock.

Foucault, M. (1972). *The archaeology of knowledge.* London: Tavistock.

Foucault, M. (1980). *Power/knowledge: Selected interviews and other writings.* New York: Pantheon.

Freire, P. (1970). *Pedagogy of the oppressed* (M. Bergman Ramos, Trans.). New York: Seabury.

Glaser, B. (1978). *Theoretical sensitivity: Advances in the methodology of grounded theory.* Mill Valley, CA: Sociology Press.

Glaser, B. (1992). *Emergence versus forcing: Basics of grounded theory analysis.* Mill Valley, CA: Sociology Press.

Glaser, B., & Strauss, A. (1967). *The discovery of grounded theory.* Chicago: Aldine.

Gollwitzer, P. M., & Bargh, J. A. (Eds.). (1996). *The psychology of action.* New York: Guilford.

Gross, C. S. (2004). Struggling with imaginaries of trauma and trust: The refugee experience in Switzerland. *Culture, Medicine and Psychiatry, 28,* 151–167.

Guba, E. G., & Lincoln, Y. S. (1994). Competing paradigms in qualitative research. In N. K. Denzin & Y. S. Lincoln (Eds.), *Handbook of qualitative research* (pp. 105–117). Thousand Oaks, CA: Sage.

Hacker, W. (1994). Action regulation theory and occupational psychology: Review of German empirical research since 1987. *German Journal of Psychology, 18,* 91–120.

Haig, B. D. (1995). Grounded theory as scientific method. Retrieved September 30, 2004, from the University of Canterbury (Christchurch, New Zealand), Department of Psychology web site: http://www.ed.uiuc.edu/EPS/PES-Yearbook/95_docs/haig.html

Heath, H., & Cowley, S. (2004). Developing a grounded theory approach: A comparison of Glaser and Strauss. *International Journal of Nursing Studies, 41,* 141–150.

Henwood, K., & Pidgeon, N. (2003). Grounded theory in psychological research. In P. M. Camic, J. E. Rhodes, & L. Yardley (Eds.), *Qualitative research in psychology; Expanding perspectives in methodology and design* (pp. 131–156). Washington, DC: American Psychological Association.

Hook, D., & Harris, B. (2000). Discourses of order and their disruption: The texts of the South African Truth and Reconciliation Commission. *South African Journal of Psychology, 30,* 14–22.

Hook, D., & Parker, I. (2002). Deconstruction, psychopathology and dialectics. *South African Journal of Psychology, 32,* 49–54.

Hopa, M., Simbayi, L. C., & du Toit, C. D. (1998). Perceptions on integration of traditional and Western healing in the new South Africa. *South African Journal of Psychology, 28,* 8–14.

Hoshmand, L. L. T. (1994). *Orientation to inquiry in a reflective professional psychology.* Albany, NY: State University of New York Press.

Kingry, M. J., Tiedje, L. B., & Friedman, L. L. (1990). Focus groups: A research technique for nursing. *Nursing Research, 39,* 124–125.

Kitzinger, J. (1995). Introducing focus groups. *British Medical Journal, 311,* 299–302.

Kuhn, T. (1970). *The structure of scientific revolutions* (2nd ed.). Chicago: University of Chicago Press.

Lillard, A. (1998). Ethnopsychologies: Cultural variations in theories of mind. *Psychological Bulletin, 123,* 3–32.

Lira, E. (2001). Reflections on critical psychology: The psychology of memory and forgetting (T. Sloan, Trans.). In T. Sloan (Ed.), *Critical psychology: Voices for change* (pp. 82–90). New York: St. Martin's Press.

Madriz, E. (2000). Focus groups in feminist research. In N. K. Denzin & Y. S. Lincoln (Eds.), *Handbook of qualitative research* (2nd ed., pp. 835–850). Thousand Oaks, CA: Sage.

Marsella, A. J. (1998). Toward a "global-community psychology." Meeting the needs of a changing world. *American Psychologist, 53,* 1282–1291.

Martín-Baró, I. (1994). *Writings for a liberation psychology* (A. Aron & S. Corne, Eds.). Cambridge, MA: Harvard University Press.

McMullen, L. (2002). Learning the languages of research: Transcending illiteracy and indifference. *Canadian Psychology, 43,* 195–204.

Mead, G. H. (1934). *Mind, self, and society.* Chicago: University of Chicago Press.

Michel, K., & Valach, L. (1997). Suicide as goal-directed action. *Archives of Suicide Research, 3,* 213–221.

Michel, K., & Valach, L. (2002). Suicide as goal-directed action. In E. K. van Heeringen (Ed.), *Understanding suicidal behaviour: The suicidal process approach to research and treatment* (pp. 230–254). Chichester, UK: Wiley.

Montero, M. (2000). Participation in participatory action-research. *Annual Review of Critical Psychology, 2,* 131–143.

Morgan, D. L. (1993). *Successful focus groups. Advancing the state of the art.* Newbury Park, CA: Sage.

Morrow, S. L., & Smith, M. L. (1995). Constructions of survival and coping in women who have survived sexual abuse. *Journal of Counseling Psychology, 42,* 24–33.

Mouton, J. (1993). Positivism. In J. Snyman (Ed.), *Conceptions of social inquiry* (pp. 1–28). Pretoria: Human Sciences Research Council.

Parker, I. (1992). *Discourse dynamics: Critical analysis for social and individual psychology.* London: Routledge and Kegan Paul.

Parker, I. (1994). Discourse analysis. In P. Banister, E. Burman, I. Parker, M. Taylor, & C. Tindall (Eds.), *Qualitative methods in psychology: A research guide* (pp. 92–107). Buckingham, UK: Open University Press.

Parker, I. (1997). Discursive psychology. In D. Fox & I. Prillentensky (Eds.), *Critical psychology* (pp. 284–298). London: Sage.

Parsons, T. (1968). *The structure of social action.* New York: Free Press. (Original work published 1937)

Potter, J., & Wetherell, M. (1987). *Discourse and social psychology.* London: Sage.

Potter, J., & Wetherell, M. (1994). Analyzing discourse. In A. Bryman & R. G. Burgess (Eds.), *Analyzing qualitative data* (pp. 47–66). London: Routledge.

Potter, J., & Wetherell, M. (1995). Discourse analysis. In J. A. Smith, R. Harré, & L. Van Langenhove (Eds.), *Rethinking methods in psychology* (pp. 80–92). London: Sage.

Rennie, D. (2000). Grounded theory methodology as methodological hermeneutics: Reconciling realism and relativism. *Theory and Psychology, 10,* 481–502.

Seedat, M. (1997). The quest for liberatory psychology. *South African Journal of Psychology, 27,* 261–270.

Silverman, D. (1993). *Interpreting qualitative data: Strategies for analyzing talk, text and interaction.* London: Sage.

Sloan, T. S. (Ed.). (2000). *Critical psychology: Voices for change.* New York: St. Martin's Press.

Smith, J. A. (1996). Evolving issues for qualitative psychology. In J. T. E. Richardson (Ed.), *Handbook of qualitative research methods for psychology and the social sciences* (pp. 189–201). Leicester, UK: British Psychological Society.

Stead, G. B. (2004). Culture and career psychology: A social constructionist perspective. *Journal of Vocational Behavior, 64,* 389–406.

Stead, G. B., & Watson, M. B. (1998). Career research in South Africa: Challenges for the future. *Journal of Vocational Behavior, 52,* 289–299.

Stevens, G. (1998). "Racialized" discourses: Understanding perceptions of threat in post-apartheid South Africa. *South African Journal of Psychology, 28,* 204–214.

Stiles, W. B. (1993). Quality control in qualitative research. *Clinical Psychology Review, 13,* 593–618.

Strauss, A., & Corbin, J. (1990). *Basics of qualitative research: Grounded theory procedures and techniques.* Newbury Park, CA: Sage.

Strauss, A., & Corbin, J. (1998). *Basics of qualitative research: Grounded theory procedures and techniques* (2nd ed.). Newbury Park, CA: Sage.

Terre Blanche, M. (1997). "The knowledge that one seeks to disinter": Psychiatry and the discourse of discourse analysis. In A. Levett, A. Kottler, E. Burman, & I. Parker (Eds.), *Culture, power and difference: Discourse analysis in South Africa* (pp. 139–158). Cape Town: University of Cape Town Press.

Valach, L., Young, R. A., & Lynam, M. J. (2002). *Action theory: A primer for applied research in the social sciences.* Westport, CT: Praeger.

von Cranach, M., Kalbermatten, U., Indermuehler, K., & Gugler, B. (1982). *Goal-directed action.* London: Academic Press.

Vygotsky, L. S. (1986). *Thought and language.* Cambridge, MA: MIT Press.

Weber, M. (1949). *The methodology of the social sciences.* Glencoe, IL: Free Press.

Woolgar, S. (1996). Psychology, qualitative methods and the ideas of science. In J. T. E. Richardson (Ed.), *Handbook of qualitative research methods for psychology and the social sciences* (pp. 11–24). Leicester, UK: British Psychological Society.

Young, R. A., & Valach, L. (2004). The construction of career through goal-directed action. *Journal of Vocational Behavior, 64,* 499–514.

Young, R. A., Valach, L., Ball, J., Paseluikho, M. A., Wong, Y. S., DeVries, R. J., McLean, H., & Turkel, H. (2001). Career development as a family project. *Journal of Counseling Psychology, 48,* 190–202.

Young, R. A., Valach, L., & Domene, J. F. (2005). The qualitative action–project method in counseling psychology. *Journal of Counseling Psychology, 52,* 215–223.

8

Psychotherapeutic and Related Interventions for a Global Psychology

Juris G. Draguns
Pennsylvania State University

INTRODUCTION

The Scope of This Chapter

Psychotherapy in the modern sense of the term originated in Europe, then spread throughout most of the continent and expanded to the Americas. Its growth in the United States has been dramatic. By this time, psychotherapy is practiced in all regions of the world. Information about it has, however, been diffused in a highly asymmetrical manner. Over the last 50 years, innovations originating in North America have radiated rapidly across oceans and continents (see chapter 2, this volume, on international perspectives on the history of psychology). Specifically, this has been the case with the advent of behavioral and cognitive therapies, humanistic approaches, and psychoanalytic ego psychology. By contrast, only a few advances in theory or techniques from Europe or elsewhere have gained recognition and acceptance in the United States.

This chapter aspires to redress this imbalance. To this end, developments and innovations in psychotherapy proposed and implemented outside of the United States are introduced, both within the psychodynamic, humanistic–existential–phenomenological, and cognitive behavioral

233

frameworks as well as outside of them. The rapidly expanding non-U.S. contributions to the worldwide enterprise of psychotherapy research are described. Psychotherapists do not operate in a political vacuum, and a section of the chapter deals with the vicissitudes of psychotherapy under several political regimes and with the impact of rapid sociopolitical change and social transformation.

WHAT IS PSYCHOTHERAPY?

Psychotherapy is rooted in the arts of healing (Draguns, Gielen, & Fish, 2004) that have been practiced for millennia. Yet, contemporary psychotherapy aspires to a scientific status, as a mode of application of rational principles supported by systematically collected empirical data. For purposes of the present chapter, three defining criteria of psychotherapy are introduced. First, psychotherapy involves the encounter of at least two persons, one of whom is distressed. The other person brings to the situation his or her expertise, usually based on extensive and thorough professional training and experience. Second, psychotherapy involves communication and a relationship between two or more individuals. Third, the purpose of psychotherapy is to bring relief from suffering and/ or disability, accompanied by other beneficial changes such as a more effective use of the person's adaptive resources and a more realistic understanding of his or her motives, goals, and purposes (Draguns, 1975). Psychotherapy has been conceptualized as "a procedure that is sociocultural in its ends and interpersonal in its means" (Draguns, 1975, p. 273). The outward boundaries of psychotherapy are not sharply delineated, and psychotherapy overlaps with counseling and guidance and other procedures designed primarily to foster competence rather than to alleviate distress.

A GLOBAL PANORAMA OF PSYCHOTHERAPY: INNOVATIONS, MODIFICATIONS, AND ELABORATIONS

Psychoanalysis and Psychodynamic Therapies

The Challenge of Jacques Lacan. At the time of Freud's death in 1939, directions in development of psychoanalysis diverged. Whereas Hartmann, Kris, and Loewenstein (1946) inaugurated ego psychology, Jacques Lacan (1901–1981), a French psychoanalyst, embarked on a lifelong quest to preserve what he thought was the essence of Freud's contribution: his emphasis on the unconscious and on the primacy of desire. Whereas ego psychologists focused on the problem of adaptation, Lacan posited the centrality of emancipation from oppressive social and political constraint. He juxtaposed his rebellious stance toward the liberal capitalist political system in France and the French psychoanalytic establishment to the political pragmatism of U.S. ego psychologists. Lacan and his followers endeavored to construct a synthesis of Freud and Marx without, however, fully realizing their objective. Lacan's contributions are exceedingly difficult to summarize; his style is cryptic, aphoristic, and enigmatic, and his writings (Lacan, 1966, 1977) are based on transcripts of his lectures. Hill (2002) has distilled Lacan's five fundamental premises:

> Word meanings are not fixed and vary according to their use; Life is characterized by conflict and difficulty rather than harmony and ease; People tend to avoid acknowledging truth about themselves when such acknowledgement would imply the recognition of conflict and difficulty; People perceive and remember discontinuity and interruption a lot better than continuity and absence of change; and life and desire constitute the foundation of the human condition. (p. 24)

Hill (2002) and Lacan (1966, 1977) maintain that these five tenets are basic to Freud's formulation of psychoanalysis. On the technique level, Lacan pioneered the reduction in the number of weekly sessions in psychoanalysis from 4–6 to 1–3. He also introduced variations in the length of sessions in response to the needs of analysis at the moment, with some sessions being reduced to 15 minutes and others extended to 2 hours (Hill, 2002; Turkle, 1992). Lacan developed an elaborate theory concerning the end of analysis, and he emphasized the need for planning termination well in advance. Lacan also extended analysis to psychotics, which mainstream psychoanalysts tend to consider both impractical and undesirable. Lacan's career was mired in controversies with the International Psychoanalytic Association, several analytic organizations in France, as well as his opponents and former followers. Schisms in the organizations he created and then dissolved reverberate to this day. There is an imbalance between Lacan's theoretical contributions and his clinical observations, and the bases for his technical modifications are sometimes hard to derive from his theoretical formulations. Lacan remains a controversial figure, and his impact continues to be significant. Hill

(2002) estimates that about half of the 15,000 to 20,000 psychoanalysts active today use Lacanian ideas.

Argentina and Uruguay: Major, if Little Known, Centers of Psychoanalytic Activity.   For several decades, psychoanalysis has been a dominant influence on therapy and social thought in Argentina (Plotkin, 2001), even though theoretical pluralism has been slowly and gradually increasing. The reasons for the high concentration of psychoanalysts in Argentina and for the widespread acceptance of psychoanalysis by large segments of the educated urban Argentine middle class are complex. Plotkin estimated that the number of people who have undergone or are undergoing analysis may be, in proportion to population, one of the highest in the world. There are strong affinities between Argentine psychoanalysts and the British object–relations school. Perhaps in line with the sociocentric orientation of Argentine culture, psychoanalysts have emphasized interpersonal approaches and personal relationships. Pichon Rivière (1971) set out to bridge the gap between psychoanalysis and social psychology by concentrating on the group process. Angel Garma (1969) is internationally known, among other things, for developing novel approaches to the psychoanalytic treatment of psychosomatic disorders, especially ulcers. José Bleger (1967) differentiated ambiguity as a state of indeterminacy in perception, intention, and motivation and posited a link between the experience of ambiguity and symbiosis, harking back to the early stages of a person's development. Even before the political upheaval and terror that Argentina experienced in the 1960s and 1970s, some Argentine psychoanalysts were attracted to emancipatory therapies of Lacanian and/or Marxist inspiration, and these trends were exacerbated by the violent persecution unleashed by the military dictatorship (Plotkin, 2001). Apparently, however, an organic synthesis of these currents of thought and its integration into psychoanalytic practice has so far proved to be an ambitious but elusive goal.

Bernardi et al. (2001) offer glimpses of theoretical orientations, clinical services, and research projects within the Institute of Focal Psychotherapeutic Interventions in Montevideo, Uruguay. To a greater extent than their colleagues elsewhere, Uruguayan psychoanalyts appear to be committed to a continuous interchange between clinical observation and research findings. Not unlike their Argentine counterparts, they are shifting toward a more interpersonal and less intrapsychic orientation in their quest to maximize accessibility, effectiveness, and efficiency of psychoanalytic services.

Humanistic, Existential, and Phenomenological Approaches

The quest for personal meaning emerged as a major concern for psychotherapy in Europe in the first half of the 20th century (e.g., May, 1958). Pioneers of existential therapy concentrated on providing a philosophical rationale for psychotherapy. Techniques of intervention were regarded as distinctly subsidiary to promotion of genuine and spontaneous human encounters. However, Viktor Frankl (1905–1997) of Vienna, the founder of logotherapy, both propounded the metatheoretical and philosophical tenets of existentialism (e.g., Frankl, 1981) and proposed specific symptom-oriented interventions, such as paradoxical intention that invites the person to concentrate on the activity that he or she is trying to overcome. Thus, an insomniac is encouraged to try to stay awake and is thereby helped to achieve his or her purpose of falling asleep (Frankl, 1960). Swiss psychiatrist Medard Boss (1903–1990), best known for his integration of Heidegger's philosophy and psychodynamic psychotherapy, also formulated a nonreductionist approach to dream interpretation that seeks to discover the personal and unique symbolic meaning in dreams collaboratively with the dreamer (Boss, 1977). The dreamer is the principal seeker in this quest, and the therapist, a facilitator and catalyst. Kociunas (2003) in Lithuania concretized the basic existentialist conception of a human being as decision maker and active agent by inviting a person to take a series of steps, one at a time, as a metaphor for real-life dilemmas and choices.

A byproduct of phenomenological analysis, which is often a prominent component of existential psychotherapy, is the abundance and subtlety of terms referring to personal experience that are deeply embedded in its subjective culture and are exceedingly difficult to translate or apply in other sociocultural contexts. These words may constitute the pathways to implicit, yet basic, culturally shared assumptions.

From Behavioral to Cognitive Behavioral Therapy and Beyond: Making the Techniques and Mechanisms of Psychotherapy More Explicit

Behavior Therapy. Behavior therapy and behavior modification are regarded as prototypically U.S. movements. It was Wolpe (1958), however, who developed systematic desensitization in South Africa on an explicitly Pavlovian basis (Pavlov, 1941). Eysenck (1959) in England

introduced the term behavior therapy, and Yates (1970) in Australia and
Rachman (1969) in South Africa, the United Kingdom, and Canada
were prominent early contributors to behavioral interventions. Relaxa-
tion procedures, so prominent in the formative period of behavior therapy, go back to the introduction of autogenic training in Germany by
Oskar Vogt and Wilhelm Schütz early in the 20th century. As described by
Luthe (1969), this procedure aims to reduce bodily tensions on the basis
of self-directed verbal instructions. Autogenic training may result in
bringing autonomically regulated responses under voluntary, self-induced
control. Its byproduct is an altered state of consciousness in which a person's defenses may be lowered and the emergence of unconscious and
conflict-related material facilitated.

Öst (1989) in Sweden pioneered the removal of simple specific phobias, such as those of blood and flying, in a single session. Öst's technique
involves continuous exposure to the phobia-inducing stimulus. His
follow-up data indicate that the elimination of fear held for as long as four
years, and the procedure was found to be effective in 90% of cases, with
the average duration of treatment of little more than two hours. In the
Netherlands, Emmelkamp (1994) demonstrated the superiority of in vivo
over imaginal exposure in treating anxiety disorders. Because of its specificity and flexibility, functional analysis of behavior, as a prelude to
behavior therapy, has been extensively applied across ethnic and cultural
barriers without radically altering either its rationale or technique
(Tanaka-Matsumi, Higginbotham, & Chang, 2002).

Cognitive behavioral approaches have spread rapidly beyond their
North American origins. In the process, they have been revised, elaborated, and transformed. In the United Kingdom, Salkovskis (1996) greatly
expanded the scope of cognitive behavioral interventions by developing
evidence-based procedures for the treatment of panic states, suicidality,
hypochondriasis, and obsessions. Ehlers and Clark (2000) in England
extended these procedures to posttraumatic stress disorder (PTSD) and
Gillespie, Duffy, Hackmann, and Clark (2002) applied them to an unse-
lected sample of PTSD patients after a terrorist car bombing in Northern
Ireland, with high rates of symptom reduction. The gist of these interventions involved integrating traumatic memories into the totality of the person's experience, modifications in the appraisal of the traumatic event, and
elimination of dysfunctional behavioral and cognitive strategies. In
Australia, Ball, Mitchell, Malhi, Skillecorn, and Smith (2006) are applying
schema-focused cognitive therapy to reduce relapses in patients with bipolar disorder. Ladouceur (2002) in Quebec increased the effectiveness of

interventions in pathological gambling by designing and implementing focused cognitive behavioral treatment strategies. Liotti (1981) in Italy formulated an elaborate model of childhood experiences and beliefs that precede the onset of agoraphobia. Initially triggered by inhibition of environmental exploration, insecurity is amplified by separations, fear of solitude, a sense of vulnerability, avoidance of subjectively threatening situations, and an imperative need for a protector and companion. More recently, Liotti (2004) proposed a general model based on disruption of childhood attachment, dissociative processes, and vulnerability to disorders triggered by a traumatic experience. On the basis of this formulation, interpersonal difficulties should receive as much therapeutic attention as the more readily apparent traumatic recollections, dissociative experiences, and repressive defenses.

Extending the cognitive behavioral framework to ever more complex patterns of human experience, Guidano (1987), also of Italy, explicitly addressed the complexities of the self, described the distinctive cognitive organization in agoraphobia, depression, eating disorders, and obsessive–compulsive conditions, and proposed specific approaches for the investigation of life themes within the cognitive behavioral framework. Semerari (1999) has elaborated on applications of this framework to a wider range of even more intractable psychological disturbances.

Toyokawa and Nedate (1996) pinpointed three cognitive behavioral features that are congenial to Japanese culture: professionalism (an expert relationship with the client), self-disclosure through structured homework assignments, and a problem-focused approach. Which beliefs are considered irrational is, however, a matter of cultural determination. Thus, striving for acceptance by everyone is regarded as an irrational goal in the United States but is viewed in Japan as part of an understandable quest for social harmony. Moreover, according to Jun Sasaki (personal communication, January, 2005), some Japanese patients respond more readily to the technique of reframing, which involves detaching the patient's attention from the presenting symptom, than they do to standard cognitive behavioral techniques. Reframing has points of similarity with traditional Japanese therapeutic techniques, such as Morita therapy, that will be described later. Japanese therapists also advocate shifting the patient's focus from symptoms to positive motives and to the mundane tasks of living.

Feixas and Miró (1993) in Spain have pursued extensions of the cognitive behavioral framework to the subtler and more philosophical aspects of the therapeutic relationship and interaction. Miró (2000) addressed the challenge of overcoming the assumption that the other is but a reflection of one's own self. True mutuality or conviviality (i.e., interacting with the other as a genuine partner in a therapeutic or other dyad) can only be attained if the words designated by the pronouns *you, we,* and *I* are articulated and differentiated. This involves the recognition of the uniqueness of both the self and the other, as well as the similarity of their shared humanness.

With cognitive behavioral orientation as the point of departure, several German and Swiss psychotherapists have proceeded to extend the rationale and scope of interventions and also retain the explicitness and specificity characteristic of the cognitive behavioral approach. Butollo, Rosner, and Wentzel (1999) have introduced a multiphasic model of intervention for anxiety disorders that recognizes biological, psychological, and social aspects of the disturbance and targets in a focused manner its affective, cognitive, and interpersonal manifestations. Sachse (2002) introduced psychotherapy through clarification of the person's motives and goals. His objective is to identify and help change a person's schemas, especially those that underlie faulty problem-solving strategies. To that end, the therapist proceeds heuristically, by providing structure and asking searching questions. As Sachse (2002) put it, "clarification therapy begins where clarity ends" (p. 43). Caspar's (1989) practically oriented guide is focused on structured and solution-oriented psychotherapy centered on clients' life plans as they quickly emerge in the early stages of psychotherapy. These plans are not limited to instrumental activities for the attainment of immediate goals, but rather encompass implicit, hierarchically organized coping strategies.

A recent contribution by Grawe (2004) has bridged the gap between research-based cognitively oriented psychotherapy and recent advances in the neuropsychology of complex human behavior. Grawe believes that the ultimate goal of psychotherapy is to bring about neuronal change, and that advances in neuroimaging make it possible to monitor these changes in the course of psychotherapy and upon its conclusion. Grawe posits the primacy of a human striving for consistency that suffuses the four fundamental needs for: orientation and control, pleasure and avoidance of distress, bonding with others, and self-protection and self-enhancement. Therapy is commonly sought when inconsistency is experienced, and the therapist's modes of intervention, consonant with the current neuropsychological state of knowledge, include both symptom-oriented and experiential techniques. A prominent tool of psychotherapy is the activation and actualization of clients' resources, coupled with helping them cope with inconsistency. Grawe's volume represents both a major conceptual, integrative advance as well as a practically oriented, yet research based, manual that is applicable in clinical contexts.

Proceeding from a psychoanalytic rather than cognitive point of departure, Gilliéron (1997) in Switzerland made an important contribution to streamlining psychotherapy by introducing four sessions of pretherapy assessment and by describing specifically the techniques of brief psychotherapy and its indications. The common denominator of the contributions described in this section is the explicitness and clarity of the authors in translating their theoretical positions into specific and falsifiable modes of intervention.

Beyond Individual Therapy: Family Approaches

Interactions within the family differ across cultures and countries in nature and style. Consequently, national characteristics are potentially discernible in the manner in which family therapy is conducted in several countries. To work around the widespread Chinese inhibition against public airing of intrafamilial grievances, Gau and Chen (1998) in Taiwan developed a structured multistage model of therapeutically interviewing Chinese families, with systematic assessment shading off into focused, problem-centered interventions. In India, according to Rastogi and Wampler (1998), family members are reluctant to voice their feelings or conflicts directly. To circumvent this obstacle, therapists communicate through metaphors and story telling, and take note of nonverbal and indirect clues. Further descriptions of nationally characteristic modes of presenting family problems and culturally acceptable ways of correcting them are found in Gielen and Comunian (1999) and Ng (2003).

One of the most internationally visible schools of family psychotherapy is centered in Milan, Italy. As described by Mosconi, Gonzo, Sorgato, Tirelli, and Tomas (1999) and Selvini Palazzoli, Cirillo, Selvini, and Sorrentino (1989), the Milan approach is simultaneously geared toward therapy, assessment, and research. To this end, hypotheses about family functioning are formulated at the outset, based in part on the documented characteristics of families, especially those containing an anorexic or psychotic member. Information is sought about the way in which the strategies of individual family members and the rules by which the family as a group operates are connected. Parents are provisionally enlisted as cotherapists and information is gathered on children's reactions to the actions prescribed to parents by the therapist, such as temporary absences from the home. Hypotheses are examined not in light of their absolute truth-value, but on the basis of their acceptability to the family, and attempts to maintain the homeostasis of the family are initially reinforced. Selvini Palazzoli et al. (1989) maintained that, "whenever a fundamental rule is identified and changed, pathological behavior is quickly removed" (p. 12). Changes are further facilitated by feedback concerning relationships and changes therein. Therapeutic neutrality, or ambiguity or lack of expressiveness, is utilized to promote uncertainty in family members' minds as to with whom the therapist may side. Thus, the Milan approach is highly structured and features explicit rules about the therapist's role, interventions, and timing.

On the basis of accumulated experience of family therapists working across nations and cultures, Ng (2003) has offered the following seven generic suggestions:

1. Understanding culture's influence upon perception, in order to forestall succumbing to stereotypes and perceptual errors;
2. Avoiding the imputation of psychopathology to help-seeking families;
3. Identifying key family members and engaging them in group process;
4. Providing information and teaching in addition to addressing the family's problems;
5. Using action-oriented techniques by preference;
6. Responding to metaphoric communications and communicating in metaphors; and
7. Accepting the role of the therapist as a cultural mediator.

RESEARCH ON PSYCHOTHERAPY: AN EVOLVING GLOBAL ENTERPRISE

Systematic investigation of psychotherapy was sparked by the provocative challenge issued by Eysenck (1952) in the United Kingdom. For the ensuing 2 decades, psychotherapy research remained a predominantly U.S. endeavor. By now it is being carried out in all continents. The Society for Psychotherapy Research has evolved into a major international forum for psychotherapy investigators. Its journal, *Psychotherapy Research*, is simultaneously edited in the United States and Europe. Some of the current trends and recent conclusions from this dynamic and kaleidoscopic international enterprise are as follows:

1. European and U.S. researchers are in agreement that the effectiveness of psychotherapy has been substantially demonstrated.

The conclusions by Kaechele and Kordy (1992) in Germany, the Groupe d'Experts in France (2004), and Strupp (1996) in the United States coalesce on this point. Consequently, the focus of psychotherapy research has shifted from global outcome studies to the examination of more specific issues.

2. Several meta-analyses have been completed. In Germany, Wittmann and Matt (1986) included in their investigation all research reports on the effectiveness of psychotherapy that were published in German. Furthermore, Matt (1993) then compared the results of this analysis with those of the classical meta-analytic study conducted by Smith, Glass, and Miller (1980) in the United States. The results of these two research projects were more similar than different, and Matt cautiously and appropriately attributed the significant findings that emerged to artifactual sources. Grawe, Donati, and Bernauer (1994) undertook an extensive, international meta-analysis of 897 research investigations reported in the English and German languages. Most of the studies were conducted in Canada, Germany, the United Kingdom, and the United States. Grawe et al. concluded that cognitive behavioral therapy was significantly more effective than psychoanalytic or client-centered therapy. However, both of the above therapies produced demonstrable benefits, as did Gestalt therapy and family therapy. In a further meta-analysis of a carefully selected set of 42 studies, Grawe et al. sought to establish the respective advantages and disadvantages of five major varieties of psychotherapy: psychodynamic, humanistic, interpersonal, cognitive behavioral, and relaxation-based. Goal-oriented therapies that encourage autonomous problem solving were found to produce superior outcomes. The effects of interpersonal, cognitive behavioral, and reinforcement therapies for depression were on the whole comparable, although fitting the individual to intervention may enhance its effectiveness (Grawe, 2004). In a meta-analysis limited to the outcome of psychoanalysis and long-term psychodynamic therapy (Lamb, 2005a 2005b), 30 studies from 12 countries in the Americas, Australia, and Europe were examined. Findings indicated that psychoanalysis is an effective mode of treatment, with an averaged effect size of .73. A major international review of over 1,000 controlled psychotherapy research studies, including five meta-analyses, conducted under the auspices of the French Directorate of General Health (Groupe d'Experts, 2004), arrived at conclusions consonant

with those by Grawe et al. (1994), pointing to the greater effectiveness of cognitive behavioral therapy over psychoanalytic and family or couple treatments, but substantiating significant benefits produced by the other two modes of treatment. These views are amplified in a thorough review of empirically grounded treatments for anxiety by Salkovskis (2006) evaluated in Denmark, the United Kingdom, and the United States. Focused on negative interpretations of events and experiences and on the change of automatic and strategic reactions to them, cognitive behavioral interventons were superior to psychodynamic therapy and waitlist controls in symptom and distress reduction and in the persistence of therapeutic effects. These effects have been demonstrated for agoraphobia, panic state, obsessive-compulsive disorder, and PTSD, and are consonant with meta-analytic outcome studies in Australia of cognitive behavioral interventions for depression, panic, and generalized anxiety (Haiby, Donelly, Corry, & Vos, 2006).

3. Long-term programmatic and sequential research has been pursued at major research centers, for example in France (Ionescu, 1998), Germany (Dahl, Kachele, & Thoma, 1988; Kaechele, 1992), Italy (Liotti, 2004), Norway (Monsen, Odland, Faugli, Daae, & Eilertsen, 1995), Sweden (Blomberg, Lazor, & Sandell, 2001), Switzerland (Grawe, 2004), the United Kingdom (Salkovskis, 1996, 2006), and Uruguay (Bernardi et al., 2001). Kaechele (1992) has described the evolution of the Ulm Psychoanalytic Process Research from its initial concentration on case studies through its expansion to the large-scale intensive study of therapy process to the systematic study of the interplay of quantitative and qualitative approaches, all at the service of eventual integration of the totality of information thus acquired.

4. Researchers' shift of attention from global outcome studies to more specific objectives has been exemplified by investigations of promoting self-disclosure in Israel (Schechtman & Tsegahun, 2004) and the impact of treatment goals (Holtforth & Grawe, 2002) and gaze interaction in therapy dyads and triads (Fivaz-Depeursinge, de Roten, Carboz-Warnery, Metraux, & Ciola, 1994) in Switzerland. German investigators have explored personal conflict (Lauterbach, 1996, 2006), the predictive value of interpersonal problems in long-term therapy (Davies-Osterkamp, Strauss, & Schmitz, 1996), the role of verbalizing emotions in therapy outcome (Holzer, Pokorny, Kachele, & Luborsky, 1997), and the consequences of the wording of therapists' interventions (Sachse, 1998).

5. Maldavsky (2004) in Argentina constructed an elaborate lexicon of words and sentences that are expressive of fixations at the several Freudian stages of psychosexual development and of their corresponding defense mechanisms. This method represents the elaboration of an earlier scheme by another Argentine psychoanalyst, Liberman (1970), and is known as the David Liberman algorhythm (ADL). In its current version, ADL was applied to the transcripts of psychoanalytic sessions and related to progressions and developments at the case level and to the comparison of patients across diagnostic categories and levels of severity of the disorders experienced. Although a great many problems remain to be resolved, ADL is a major advance toward objectifying the study of psychoanalytic narration and making quantitative psychoanalytic research possible with an N of 1 (see chapter 7, this volume, for more on qualitative research methods). Independently, Ehlers (2004) in Germany developed a micro-measure of defense mechanisms, applicable across segments of psychoanalytic treatment and capable of being related to the vicissitudes of the analysand's experiences in treatment and in life.

6. Microanalytic studies of affect regulation were pioneered by a research team in Austria (Bänninger-Huber, Peham, & Juen, 2002; Juen & Bänninger-Huber, 2002; Peham, Ganzer, Bänninger-Huber, & Juen, 2002) who, working with therapy videotapes, differentiated prototypical interaction sequences from traps, the former fundamental for the maintenance of a working alliance and the latter indicative of reactivated conflictual affects. These two kinds of sequences were compared in mother–daughter and therapist–client dyads and were investigated as a function of the therapist's verbal and nonverbal behaviors.

7. The therapeutic alliance has emerged as a major topic in both U.S. and international investigations (Caspar, Grossmann, Unmussig, & Schramm, 2005; Hentschel & Bijlefeld, 1995; Hentschel, Kiessling, Heck, & Willoweit, 1992; Holtforth & Castonguay, 2005; Regli, Bieber, Mathier, & Grawe, 2001). The therapeutic alliance is fostered by attuning therapeutic interventions to the client's motivational goals. The importance of a therapeutic relationship has even been demonstrated to play an important role in cognitive behavioral interventions, a conclusion not often recognized in the pioneering stages of this therapeutic framework.

8. Two recent trends are discernible. First, the gap between research findings and clinical application has narrowed, but not disappeared (Kordy, 1995). Second, advances of neurological and neuropsychological research have opened a new area of contact between investigators and practitioners (Grawe, 2004). Advances in neuroimaging and neuroendocrinology have generated two interfaces: the use of neuroimaging techniques to gauge changes during psychotherapy and the extension of psychotherapeutic services to a wider range of somatic disorders.

9. Even though research standards tend toward global uniformity, national characteristics are apparent in researchers' modi operandi. Ionescu (1998) contrasted the epistemological emphasis of French researchers with the pragmatic approach prevalent among investigators in the United States. Rennie (2004) found that research on psychotherapy and counseling in Canada and the United States is influenced by positivism, whereas in the United Kingdom it exhibits an affinity to postmodernism and reflects a more skeptical and relativistic attitude. Strauss and Kaechele (1998) pointed to the long tradition of naturalistic and discovery-oriented research in Germany, so distinct from the hypothesis testing prevalent in English-speaking countries.

PSYCHOTHERAPY IN ITS
SOCIOCULTURAL CONTEXT

Psychotherapy is an encounter between client and therapist that occurs concretely and figuratively behind closed doors, protected from external intrusion by safeguards for confidentiality. Yet, therapists have also been construed as agents of their culture, and therapy, as a procedure concerned with a person's sociocultural integration (Draguns, 1975). Depending on the circumstances and needs in a particular case, bonds between the person and his or her cultural milieu are strengthened, loosened, or reexamined. Culture's impact is most directly evident in the ministrations of traditional healers in settings far removed from the familiar European-American cultural mainstream. However, culture's role is also observable, though less obtrusive, in the operation of modern, scientifically and academically trained therapists. (The chapters in part III are germane to the role of culture in scientific and applied domains of psychology, especially chapters 6, 7, 9, 10, and 11.)

Healers: Psychotherapists in Traditional Cultures?

Psychotherapy, as a secular, purportedly scientific procedure, has existed for less than two centuries. Healing, designed to make a person whole physically, mentally, and spiritually, has been practiced in all parts of the world for millennia. Healers' functions overlap, but do not coextend, with those of modern psychotherapists (Draguns, 1975; Tseng, 2001). Healers are also their societies' prophets, magicians, entertainers, tricksters, and often tolerated eccentrics (Krippner, 2002). Their activities include, but are not limited to, the induction of altered states of consciousness. Experience, magic, and tradition are intertwined in shaping healers' ministrations (Krippner, 2002). They rest on a foundation of culturally shared belief (Al-Issa & Al-Subaie, 2004; Nathan, 1994; Torrey, 1972) and are unlikely to evoke incomprehension or bafflement in the milieus where they are practiced.

Prince (1980), a Canadian psychiatrist who had worked in Nigeria, reported that nondirective and insight-oriented psychotherapy did not work with Yoruba psychiatric patients. Symptomatic and subjective relief was, however, brought about by direct, authoritative suggestions, not unlike divination as practiced by traditional healers. A prominent Nigerian psychiatrist, Lambo (1964) integrated Yoruba healing practices with Western psychiatric services, thereby initiating the transformation of healer's image from "a crazy witchdoctor to auxiliary psychotherapist" (Jilek, 1971, p. 200). In British Columbia, Jilek (1971, 1982, 2004) blended Salish Indian spirit dance-initiation ceremonies into treatment programs for young men who were experiencing alienation and depression, often with alcohol or drug abuse, suicidal behavior, and aggressive outbursts. These interventions were found to be more effective than modern, standard modes of treatment. Working with African individuals uprooted from their cultures of origin and thrust into a Western metropolis, Nathan (1994) in Paris espoused a radically emic approach. He exercised maximal flexibility in the format of therapy meetings, mode of intervention, and openness to participation by family and community members, including respected elders and healers. Nathan concluded that the crux of healing is a social bond in a shared framework of outlook and belief. Therapists must not impose their own conceptual grids or subject another culture's concepts and practices to analysis from an external perspective. This orientation has animated the description of traditional Yoruba healing encounters by Nathan and Hounkpatin (1996), who carefully refrained from commenting on these descriptions from an extraneous point of view.

Claver (1976), however, writing about Côte d'Ivoire in West Africa, decried the absence of quality standards for traditional health services and reported instances of manifest incompetence and ignorance of some healers, with far-reaching harmful results for persons treated. Both Claver (1976) and Scharfetter (1985), a Swiss psychiatrist, have also raised the question of the relevance of traditional healers' services in the context of rapid social change, especially in the burgeoning conglomerates in and around many of the major African cities. Peltzer (1995), a German clinical psychologist who inaugurated psychological services in several African countries, divided the population of contemporary Africa into three segments: traditional, transitional, and modern. Healers' interventions appear to be the avenue of choice for the first segment, may be partially applicable for the second, and are marginally relevant for the third, if at all.

Wessells and Monteiro (2004) demonstrated the usefulness of involving local healers in the rehabilitation of traumatized child soldiers who had been conscripted in Angolan civil war. Their results augur well for the inclusion of indigenous methods of psychological healing in responding to unanticipated disasters, natural or inflicted by humans. Relief programs after the tsunami that devastated coastal communities in South Asia in 2004, as described by Kalayjian (2005) on the basis of her experience in Sri Lanka, feature a culturally congruent psychological component. In particular, volunteer psychotherapists endeavor to provide empathy and reduce the virtually universal sense of survivor guilt. Individual, group, and art therapy are used to that end and were supplemented by desensitization and breathing exercises. Unanswerable "why" questions tend to give way to asking "What can we do now?," as coping replaces helplessness.

Converging data from a variety of sources strongly suggest that traditional healing techniques are beneficial in their respective cultural milieus (see chapters 6, 9, and 11 in this volume). If so, what accounts for their effectiveness? Altered states of consciousness may make persons more open to change in behavior and ideation, especially when they are experiencing suffering and distress (Prince, 1980). An encounter with a person outside of the usual network of conventional relationships may be helpful (Draguns, 1975). The ambiguous status of healers in some cultures may enable them to question rigid practices and perceptions, thereby unblocking adaptation and growth (Finkler, 2004; Krippner, 2002). Torrey (1972) claimed that there are no substantive differences between the operations of indigenous healers, and that modern psychiatry should be re-examined in light of the great many active and specific ingredients of psychotherapy which have been uncovered by researchers in the last three decades (e.g., Grawe, 2004); it remains to be seen if they are discernable in both healers' and psychotherapists' interventions.

Culturally Distinct Therapy in Modern Settings: Morita, Naikan, and Zen Therapies in Japan

In Japan, the gamut of psychotherapeutic services originating in Europe or the United States coexist with several local therapies of which Morita and Naikan are the best known. Their respective originators, Shoma Morita (1874–1938) and Ishin Yoshimoto (1916–1988), were modern mental-health professionals conversant with international developments in psychotherapy. As described by Reynolds (1980) and Tanaka-Matsumi (2004), both of these therapies aim at restoring social fit and harmony between the client and her or his family and community. Based as they are on Buddhist values, practices, and theories, they emphasize reflection and are highly structured and directive.

Morita therapy involves a four-stage sequence that starts with isolation and inactivity and is followed by experiences of ever higher activity levels that eventually approximate those of everyday life. Communication between client and therapist proceeds in accordance with a pre-established protocol. The client is directed to shift attention from his or her anxiety or fright to the concrete tasks of daily living. The expected end result is the disappearance of disruptive anxiety symptoms. Radford (2005) has pointed out that individual treatment appears to receive more emphasis nowadays than it did historically. Moreover, the role of nurses has been given greater importance, harking back to the early stages of Morita therapy in which Mrs. Morita played a crucial, though largely overlooked, role.

Naikan therapy aims to re-establish interdependence by intensive self-observation and meditation. Emphasis is placed on re-experiencing wrongs committed against other persons, especially one's mother, and contrasting them with the benevolence received from her. The resulting contrast provokes guilt that is relieved through atonement. Both of these therapies are particularly effective in counteracting the manifestations of uniquely Japanese syndromes, especially those marked by agitation and restlessness, social anxiety, and extreme shyness or alleged self-centeredness.

Zen-based therapies are also practiced in Japan (Radford, 2005; Reynolds, 1980). Regulated discipline, removal from one's hectic environment, and reflection appear to be some of the active components of anxiety reduction experienced in these settings. A specially designed Zen

chair is used to facilitate abdominal breathing exercises. Hayashi and
Mizamae (2004) have documented the beneficial psychological and physiological effects of this procedure.

Are these procedures applicable outside of Japan? Tseng, Lee, and Lu
(2005) report that Morita therapy has acquired considerable popularity in
mainland China. The German psychologist, Ingeborg Wendt (1973) proposed inaugurating a Morita clinic in Europe; it is not known whether
this proposal has been implemented. Reynolds (1980) blended a key
Morita feature, the annotated diary, into his therapeutic interventions
with U.S. clients, with positive results on the case level.

Other Potential Interventions Based on Major Religious Traditions

Al-Issa and Al-Subaie (2004) have described Islamic therapy procedures
that combine prayer and ritual with psychological interventions based
on Frankl's concept of will to meaning. Hinduistic conceptions of health
as balance, and meditation techniques designed to restore a homeostatic
equilibrium have served as foundations for a variety of therapeutic
approaches in India (Jaipal, 2004; Kapur, 2001). Indian meditation exercises were incorporated into a stress reduction program for the New Delhi
police that was found effective in light of both internal and external criteria (Kumar, 2000). Hindu traditions of introspection and of concentration
on subjective experience are a rich fund of culture-fitting techniques, some
of which have already been applied in therapy settings (Kapur, 2001;
Kumar 2000). Rubin (2004) identified both similarities and differences
between the Buddhist path of seeking enlightenment and the psychoanalytic quest for insight. He concluded that "Buddhism points toward possibilities for self-awareness, freedom, wisdom, and compassion that Western
psychology in general and psychoanalysis in particular has never mapped"
(p. 268).

EXPECTATIONS, PREFERENCES, AND STYLES: CULTURAL CHARACTERISTICS AND DIFFERENCES

Psychotherapy in action has rarely been compared across cultures.
Experienced clinicians, however, have amassed observations on the characteristic, preferred, and tolerated modalities of therapeutic interaction in
various sociocultural settings (see chapters 9 and 11 in this volume). Tseng,
Lu, and Yin (1995) cautioned therapists against interpreting unconscious,

and especially psychosexual, material to their Chinese clients too quickly even if it is expressed and communicated in therapy, lest clients feel threatened and their sense of propriety is offended. Leung and Lee (1996) found that Chinese counselees are less prepared than their U.S. counterparts to tolerate ambiguity and are more receptive to directive and authoritative suggestions, and Waxer (1989) reported that Chinese clients prefer directive rational-emotive therapy to client-centered therapy. Hsu (1995) pointed out that the paradoxical approach (i.e., suggesting a course of action that the therapist expects the family to reject) with Chinese families might provoke threat and bafflement. Tseng et al. (2005) attempt to dispel the misconception that Chinese patients are inherently low in psychological mindedness and locked into somatization, both in experience and communication. Rather, there is a culturally mediated reticence to put these cognitive and affective communications into words, unless the right conditions for it have been established, a challenge for the therapist's social, cultural, and personal sensitivity.

According to Ilechukwu (1991) and Peltzer (1995), African group orientation poses an obstacle to focusing on individual problems, and preoccupation with somatic symptoms makes it difficult to deal with affect. As Peltzer (2001) put it, "credibility, trust, 'giving gifts,' for the client (or that something is taken home from the therapeutic encounter) is important from the client's perspective" (p. 253). Therapists tend to be perceived as authority figures and are expected to be problem solvers rather than facilitators. Setting specific goals and using improvisation and flexibility in implementing them can overcome these challenges. In India, Varma (1988) also advocated brief goal-oriented and directive therapy, with mutually agreed upon therapy objectives. Laungani (2004) identified two assumptions that are deeply engrained in Western psychotherapy, but are alien to Indian and other South Asian clients, egalitarianism and individualism. He appended two admonitions that are worth heeding in all cross-cultural counseling or psychotherapy encounters: "Always expect the unexpected and expect to be taken by surprise" (p. 225), and, "wisdom lies in recognizing the culturally relevant beliefs and practices of one's clients" (p. 226). (These sentiments are elaborated on in chapters 9–11 in this volume.)

DISCOVERY OF KEY CONCEPTS AND THEMES: A BY-PRODUCT OF PSYCHOTHERAPY IN CULTURE

Psychotherapy has sometimes led to serendipitous discoveries of key emic, or culturally unique, yet implicit concepts. Bin Kimura (1995) in Japan analyzed phenomenologically the terms used by his clients in describing their subjective states and central concerns. One of such word is *ki*, which defies an exact translation, but can be approximately rendered as "cohumanity" or a state of being inextricably bound to other human beings. To many Japanese, *ki* is central to their sense of being, and their self is not internalized but rather expressed through multiple bonds to other humans. Japanese clients who seek psychotherapy suffer from the disruption and disharmony in their "interpersonality," which is another way of approximating *ki*. Re-establishing *ki* becomes an important therapy goal.

The concept of *amae* refers to a cultural dynamic, discovered by the Japanese psychoanalyst, L. Takeo Doi (1973; see chapter 5, this volume, for a more detailed analysis of this East Asian construct). It represents the frequently frustrated wish to be taken care of by others by presuming upon their benevolence. As a psychoanalyst, Doi noted expressions of *amae* in his clients' fantasies, dreams, symptoms, and patterns of behavior. As an observer of his culture, he encountered direct and camouflaged manifestations of *amae* in various domains of living. Doi concluded that *amae* is probably a universal human dynamic that is, however, more salient in Japan than elsewhere.

FROM THEMES TO DIMENSIONS: TOWARD GLOBAL STUDY OF PSYCHOTHERAPY

Despite decades of speculation, research on psychotherapy across national cultures remains in its infancy. Yet, the understanding of the interplay of helping services with the setting in which they are applied is crucially dependent on the initiation and pursuit of this endeavor. In a worldwide multivariate investigation of work-related attitudes, Hofstede (2001) identified four fundamental dimensions along which cultures vary. A fifth dimension was later added on the basis of a different methodology. Briefly described, these five dimensions are as follows:

1. Individualism–collectivism, or the degree to which a person experiences herself or himself as autonomous and separate from other human beings and groups, or as a member of his or her family, community, or nation.
2. Power distance, or the extent to which a person feels close to or remote from holders of power in his or her society.
3. Uncertainty avoidance, or the degree to which persons in a society seek or avoid contact with whatever is new, unpredictable, or uncertain.

4. Masculinity–femininity, marked by the extent of gender differences in a society and also by the extent to which caring for other people is subordinated to productivity and performance, or vice versa.
5. Short-term versus long-term time perspective, which describes cultural differences in ability to pursue long-term goals as opposed to seeking immediate rewards, and which also has to do with self-subordination as a characteristic of long-term and self-enhancement as reflective of short-term time.

Draguns (2004) hypothetically extended these five axes to psychotherapy and predicted that:

1. Individualistic cultures would promote self-actualization and collectivistic ones, social harmony as the paramount therapy goal.
2. High power distance would foster an emphasis on a therapist's expertise and authority whereas low power distance would emphasize personal sensitivity and nondirectiveness.
3. Uncertainty avoidance would be positively correlated with scientific, often biomedical, explanations and with explicit techniques and that it would be negatively associated with the coexistence of a multiplicity of therapy approaches and the preponderance of tentative or speculative psychological and philosophical explanations.
4. Masculinity–femininity would be expressed through enhancement of personal competence in masculine cultures and of expressiveness and creativity in feminine cultures.
5. Long-term orientation would be associated with somatic and short-term orientation with psychological interventions.

Thus far, only the predictions pertaining to individualism–collectivism have been systematically tested by Snider (2003) in Australia, who was able to confirm Draguns' hypothesis relative to expectations of individualistic Australian and U.S. students (i.e., individualistic) and their collectivistic Chinese counterparts (i.e. collectivistic).

Apart from research on global dimensions, a variety of piecemeal projects can be envisaged. They range from quantified case studies, both descriptive and hypothesis testing, of novel culturally oriented therapies or of their application in a different cultural environment through bicultural comparisons of therapy practices, to meta-analyses of psychotherapy in several countries with the international dimension explicitly incorporated. In particular, opportunities for quasi-experimental research in which therapists and/or clients differ in culture, but share a location, as do, for example, French and English speakers in Montréal, Canada, and French and German speakers in Fribourg, Switzerland, have not yet been utilized (Draguns, 2004).

A recent major international research project (Orlinsky & Ronnestad, 2005) has investigated the professional development of psychotherapists in 12 countries. Orlinsky and Ronnestad extracted three second-order factors labeled healing involvement, stressful involvement, and controlling involvement, respectively. These second-order factors have been found to vary across years of experience, theoretical orientation, and a number of social and situational parameters, including national culture.

PSYCHOTHERAPY AND POLITICS: THE IMPACT OF IDEOLOGY AND SUDDEN POLITICAL CHANGE

Psychotherapy in Post-Communist Russia

What happens to the practice and orientation of psychotherapy when a political system collapses and an ideologically explicit, totalitarian regime is replaced by a chaotic, unregulated pluralism? Such a change occurred in Russia in 1991, and reverberations of this abrupt transformation continue to affect psychotherapy to this day. For a variety of ideological reasons, some theoretical systems (e.g., psychoanalysis) were proscribed in the Soviet Union and others (e.g., Pavlovian theory) were elevated to the status of an official doctrine (Balachova, Levy, Isurina, & Wasserman, 2001; Korolenko & Dmitriyeva, 1999; Lauterbach, 1984). Soviet policy toward psychotherapy was ambivalent and complex; it received very limited funding, and provisions for training and supervision were miniscule. A somatopsychic orientation, positing biomedical causes for psychological disorders, held sway. Little was done to provide help with problems of living to persons not psychiatrically diagnosed. Such problems were regarded as remnants from the precommunist era that were expected to disappear (Korolenko & Dimitrieva, 1999). Within these constraints, the scope of psychotherapy was narrow. Psychotherapists in Leningrad (now, once again, St. Petersburg) carved out a somewhat wider zone of freedom than their colleagues in Moscow, and two schools of psychotherapy that originated in Leningrad continue to be practiced. Miasishchev's (1960) pathogenetic school of psychotherapy combines a rational explanation of the patient's neurosis with the recognition of the conflict between his or her wishes and environmental constraints, although the role of the unconscious is not explicitly acknowledged. The cornerstone of imago therapy (Volpert, 1968) is the enactment of roles preselected from works of literature for relevance to the person's current situation and issues. Therapy proceeds through an elaborate succession of stages and aims to integrate the roles enacted into the patient's behavioral repertoire, in a manner reminiscent of George Kelly's (1955) fixed role therapy. Both of these therapies have survived the demise of the Soviet Union and continue to be practiced. Another original school of therapy was developed late in the Soviet era by Karvasarsky (1985), who emphasized reconstruction of the person's formative experiences and expression of personality in the course of psychotherapy.

In the 1970s, Western currents of thought and practice started trickling through Poland and Lithuania, and visits by prominent psychotherapists such as Carl Rogers and Virginia Satir followed (Cote, 1998; Korolenko & Dmitriyeva, 1999). Rogers' presentations sparked an explosive growth of humanistic psychology, which the Russian public found particularly congenial during the cataclysmic political, economic, and social changes that swept through the country in the 1990s. After the demise of the Soviet system, freedom of choice and innovation blossomed, but a lot of suffering was brought about by the abrupt dismantling of the command economy and the brutal and often mismanaged transition to a market-driven system (Balachova et al., 2001). Psychoanalysis was reintroduced (Etkind, 1997). Behavioral and cognitive behavioral methods, dismissed in the Soviet era as mechanistic despite their partially Pavlovian origins, became an important part of the available mental-health services. Endemic psychosocial problems have emerged in Russia: alcoholism and drug abuse, widespread despair and high suicide rates, and economic and social dislocations with deleterious and far-reaching consequences for adjustment (Balachova et al., 2001). In Novosibirsk in Siberia, Korolenko and Dmitriyeva (1999) have developed a comprehensive sociodynamic approach to psychotherapy. It rests on traditionally psychoanalytic and neo-Freudian foundations and includes innovative techniques for dealing with current and unanticipated human problems. Korolenko and Dmitiyeva have found that somatization and neurasthenia, prevalent in the Soviet era, have been replaced by the states of free-floating anxiety and confused helplessness in the face of new and unanticipated circumstances.

Social Transition in China: Fragmentary Information

China has gone through an unprecedented economic transformation although its political system has remained intact. Hsieh-Shih (1995) has traced the tortuous progression of mental-health services in mainland China through the Cultural Revolution, during which psychotherapy, along with all teaching and application of psychology, was prohibited. Psychotherapy

gradually re-emerged in the 1980s and has continued to develop in the ensuing years. Before the Cultural Revolution, a specific form of communist psychotherapy was practiced (Leung & Lee, 1996). It emphasized equality
between patients and therapists, yet exercised a strong pressure toward con-
formity in an atmosphere of therapeutic optimism that considered changes
in attitude and behavior easy to accomplish. With the increasing diversity
of modern China and greater openness to outside influences, these interventions have virtually disappeared. Pluralism has replaced dogmatism.
Euroamerican therapies, from psychoanalysis to behavior therapy, are again
practiced. Yet, traditional Chinese orientation exercises a strong influence
over the conduct of psychotherapy. Yang (2004) identified three of its: direc-
tiveness, holism, and harmony with nature. A distinctly Chinese system, the
cognitive apprehension theory, has come into being. It encourages spontaneous self-expression and aims at the development of insight and awareness
of the unconscious (Zhong, as cited in Yang, 2004). Chinese psychologists
are evaluating the effectiveness and relevance of traditional Chinese therapies in order to blend and combine them with Western approaches (Yang,
2004). Thus, psychotherapy in mainland China is buffeted by the challenges
of modernization and traditionalism. Unique potential opportunities exist
for comparing psychotherapy in mainland China with Hong Kong, Macao,
and Taiwan, thereby holding Chinese culture constant despite varying economic and/or political systems. Parenthetically, a similar situation is open to
retrospective, historical study in Germany, where, prior to reunification, psychotherapy in the former German Democratic Republic and in the Federal
Republic of Germany was developing along very different paths.

CONCLUSIONS

The following conclusions appear to be justified in light of the previous,
brief and cursory review:

1. Psychotherapy is a global enterprise embedded in a variety of cul-
    tures around the world. Innovations in psychotherapy have origi-
    nated at diverse sites, and they continue to do so. Psychotherapists
    in North America stand to benefit from the advances of their
    colleagues in the rest of the world, just as the enterprise of psy-
    chotherapy in other countries has been enriched by the develop-
    ments in the United States for more than a century.
2. Research in the United States and abroad has conclusively
    demonstrated the effectiveness of psychotherapy in the relief of

distress and removal of disability. Since that question has been essentially answered, research on psychotherapy has shifted to more specific and circumscribed concerns. In this endeavor, investigators from all regions of the world are co-equal contributors and participants.

3. The relationship of psychotherapy to its sociocultural and political context is better understood now than it was even 2 or 3 decades ago. Yet, a host of unanswered questions remain, which can only be tackled productively and conclusively through interdisciplinary and international collaboration on a variety of approaches (see chapter 1 in this volume). National cultures and political structures may well be important sources of variance in psychotherapeutic transactions, but there is as yet no conclusive information on the extent and nature of their influence.

4. Language barriers remain an important impediment to the global diffusion of information about psychotherapy around the world. The notion that everything worthwhile about psychotherapy is published in English is a self-serving fallacy (Draguns, 2001). English continues to be the principal international medium of scientific communication, and its role is likely to increase. However, a noteworthy, though unknown, proportion of research on psychotherapy is published for domestic consumption, and a significant professional literature on psychotherapy may exist in 15 or more languages. It is imperative that an inclusive international repository of clinical and research writings on psychotherapy be instituted. In its absence, the writing of this chapter was made possible by a network of personal contacts with psychologists in several countries who have greatly contributed to its international coverage. In their review of psychotherapy research, Orlinsky, Ronnestad, and Willutzki (2004) systematically scanned relevant contributions from German-speaking countries and from Northern Europe; this praiseworthy practice should be extended to all regions of the world.

5. Despite the diversity of orientations and methodologies, the worldwide trend in psychotherapy is toward unification rather than fragmentation (this trend is also evident in various other domains of contemporary psychology, as discussed in chapter 6 in this volume). This development dovetails the potent integrative movement across schools and theories of psychotherapy. It may be emblematic that one of its first harbingers of this trend was a symposium in Montréal, in which both Anglophone and Francophone

psychotherapy researchers from North America participated
(Lecomte & Castonguay, 1987), and that some of the early stir-
rings toward psychotherapy integration also appeared in
Czechoslovakia (Knobloch, 2003), Germany (Grawe, 1994), Italy
(Alberti, 1997), and Spain (Feixas & Miró, 1993).

6. What does the worldwide accumulation of information reviewed
    in this chapter have to offer therapy practitioners? First, it suggests
    the need for flexibility; therapeutic objectives are attained by very
    different means. Second, it highlights openness to information of
    diverse provenance; relevant and useful leads may come from
    remote and unexpected sources. Third, the results point to the
    subtle intertwining of personal experience and cultural milieu. As
    researchers and theoreticians continue trying to unravel this nexus
    generically, psychotherapists face the challenge of helping unique
    clients optimize their functioning within the constraints and
    opportunities of their specific sociocultural environment.

RECOMMENDED READINGS

Fish, J. M. (1996). *Culture and therapy: An integrative approach.* Northvale, NJ: Jason
    Aronson.
Gielen, U. P., & Comunian, A. L. (Eds.). (1999). *International approaches to the family
    and family therapy.* Padua, Italy: UNIPRESS.
Gielen, U. P., Fish, J., & Draguns, J. G. (Eds.). (2004). *Handbook of culture, therapy,
    and healing.* Mahwah, NJ: Lawrence Erlbaum Associates.
Jilek, W. G. (1982). *Indian healing: Shamanic ceremonialism in the Pacific Northwest
    today.* Surrey, BC: Hancock House.
Ng, K. S. (2003). *Global perspectives in family therapy.* New York: Brunner-Routledge.
Orlinsky, D. E., & Ronnestad, M. H. (2005). *Therapeutic work and professional
    development: The psychotherapist's perspective.* Washington, DC: American
    Psychological Association Books.
Peltzer, K. ((1993). *Psychology and health in African cultures: Examples of ethnopsycho-
    therapeutic practice.* Frankfurt: IKO—Verlag für Interkulturelle Kommunikation.
Peltzer, K., & Ebigbo, P. O. (Eds.). (1989). *Clinical psychology in Africa.* Frankfurt:
    IKO—Verlag für Interkulturelle Kommunikation.
Tseng, W.-S. (2001). *Handbook of cultural psychiatry.* San Diego, CA: Academic Press.
Tseng, W.-S. (2003). *Clinician's guide to cultural psychiatry.* San Diego, CA: Academic
    Press.

ACKNOLWEDGMENTS

The following colleagues have greatly helped the author by enabling him to
include sources from several countries and in several languages: Aidis Putiņš
(Australia), Fanny Cheung and Wen-Shing Tseng (China); Daniel Regli

(France and French-speaking countries); Martin Grosse Holtforth (Germany and Switzerland); Jun Sasaki, M. H. B. Radford, and Junko Tanaka-Matsumi (Japan); Tatiana Balachova, Lucy Mikaelian, and Cesar Korolenko (Russia); and Maria Teresa Miró (Spain). They merit more than the usual courtesy acknowledgement. The worldwide information circuit often fails to transcend the language barrier, and without the help of these informed and expert individuals it would have been impossible to include a great many international contributions. For helping to overcome this obstruction in international scientific exchange, all of the persons listed deserve not only the author's, but also the editors' and readers' sincere gratitude.

REFERENCES

Alberti, G. G. (1997). Il futuro delle psicoterapie como processo integrativo [The future of psychotherapy as an integrative process]. *Revista Sperimentale di Freniatria, 121*, 456–477.

Al-Issa, I., & Al-Subaie, A. (2004). Native healing in Arab-Islamic societies. In U. P. Gielen, J. M. Fish, & J. G. Draguns (Eds.), *Handbook of culture, therapy, and healing* (pp. 343–366). Mahwah, NJ: Lawrence Erlbaum Associates.

Balachova, T., Levy, S., Isurina, G. I., & Wasserman, L. I. (2001). Medical psychology in Russia. *Journal of Clinical Psychology in Medical Settings, 8*, 61–68.

Ball, J., Mitchell, P., Malhi, G., Skillcorn, A., & Smith, M. (2003). Schema-focused cognitive therapy for bipolar disorder: Reducing vulnerability to relapse through attitudinal change. *Australian and New Zealand Journal of Psychiatry, 37*, 41–48.

Banninger-Huber, E., Peham, D., & Juen, B. (2002). Mikroanalytische Untersuchung der Affektregulierung in der therapeutischen Interaktion mittels Videoaufnahmen [Microanalytic investigation of affect regulation in therapeutic interaction by means of video tapes]. *Psychologische Medizin, 13*, 11–16.

Bernardi, R., Defey, D., Elizalde, J. H., Fiorini, H., Fonagy, P., Gril, S., Jimenez, J. P., Kaechele, H., Kernberg, O., Montado, G., Rivera, J., & Sandell, R. (2001). *Psicoanálisis, focos y aperturas* [Psychoanalysis, foci, and openings]. Montevideo, Uruguay: Psicolibros.

Bleger, J. (1967). *Simbiosis y ambiguedad.* [Symbiosis and ambiguity]. Buenos Aires, Argentina: Paidos.

Blomberg, J., Lazar, A., & Sandell, R. (2001). Long-term outcome of long-term psychoanalytically oriented therapies: First findings of the Stockholm Outcome of Psychotherapy and Psychoanalysis Study. *Psychotherapy Research, 11*, 368–382.

Boss, M. (1977). *"I dreamt last night ..." A new approach to the revelations of dreaming and its uses in psychotherapy.* New York: Gardner.

Butollo, W., Rosner, R., & Wentzel, A. (1999). *Integrative Psychotherapie bei Angststörungen* [Integrative psychotherapy in anxiety disorders]. Göttingen, Germany: Verlag Hans Huber.

Caspar, F. (1989). *Beziehungen und Probleme verstehen. Eine Einführung in die Praxis der psychotherapeutischen Plananalyse* [Understanding relationships and problems: An introduction to the practice of psychotherapeutic analysis of plans]. Göttingen, Germany: Verlag Hans Huber.

Caspar, F., Grossmann, C., Unmussig, C., & Schramm, E. (2005). Complementary therapeutic relationship: Therapist behavior, interpersonal patterns, and therapeutic effects. *Psychotherapy Research*, *15*, 91–102.

Claver, B. G. (1976). Problèmes de guérissage en Côte d'Ivoire [Healing problems in Côte d'Ivoire]. *Annales Médico-Psychologiques*, *31*, 23–30.

Cote, M. (1998). *Russian psychology in transition: Interviews with Moscow psychologists.* Commack, NY: Nova Science Publishers.

Dahl, H., Kachele, H., & Thoma, H. (Eds.). (1988). *Psychoanalytic process research strategies.* Berlin: Springer-Verlag.

Davies-Osterkamp, S., Strauss, B. M., & Schmitz, N. (1996). Interpersonal problems as predictors of symptom-related treatment outcome in long-term psychotherapy. *Psychotherapy Research*, *6*, 164–177.

Doi, L. T. (1973). *Anatomy of dependence.* Tokyo: Kodansha International.

Draguns, J. G. (1975). Resocialization into culture: The complexities of taking a worldwide view of psychotherapy. In R. W. Brislin, S. Bochner, & W. J. Lonner (Eds.), *Cross-cultural perspectives on learning* (pp. 3–27). Beverly Hills, CA: Sage.

Draguns, J. (2001). Toward a truly international psychology: Beyond English only. *American Psychologist*, *56*, 1019–1030.

Draguns, J. G. (2004). From speculation through description toward investigation: A prospective glimpse of cultural research in psychotherapy. In U. P. Gielen, J. F. Fish, & J. G. Draguns (Eds.), *Handbook of culture, therapy, and healing* (pp. 369–387). Mahwah, NJ: Lawrence Erlbaum Associates.

Draguns, J. G., Gielen, U. P., & Fish, J. M. (2004). Approaches to culture, healing, and psychotherapy. In U. P. Gielen, J. M. Fish, & J. G. Draguns (Eds.), *Handbook of culture, healing, and psychotherapy* (pp. 1–11). Mahwah, NJ: Lawrence Erlbaum Associates.

Ehlers, W. (2004). Clinical evaluation of structure and process of defense mechanisms before and during psychoanalytic treatment. In U. Hentschel, G. Smith, J. G. Draguns, & W. Ehlers (Eds.), *Defense mechanisms: Theoretical, research, and clinical perspectives* (pp. 353–392). Amsterdam: Elsevier.

Ehlers, A., & Clark, D. M. (2000). A cognitive model of posttraumatic stress disorder. *Behaviour Research and Therapy*, *38*, 319–345.

Emmelkamp, P. M. G. (1994). Behavior therapy with adults. In A. E. Bergin & S. L. Garfield (Eds.), *Handbook of psychotherapy and behavior change* (4th ed., pp. 379–427). New York: Wiley.

Etkind, A. E. (1997). There are no naked thoughts: Psychoanalysis, psychotherapy, and medical psychology in Russia. In E. Grigorenko, P. Ruzgis, & R. J. Sternberg (Eds.), *Psychology of Russia: Past, present, future* (pp. 59–82). Commack, NY: Nova Science Publishers.

Eysenck, H. J. (1952). The effects of psychotherapy: An evaluation. *Journal of Consulting Psychology*, *16*, 319–324.

Eysenck, H. J. (1959). Learning theory and behavioral therapy. *Journal of Mental Science*, *105*, 61–75.

Feixas, G., & Miró, M. T. (1993). *Aproximaciones a la psicoterapia* [Psychotherapy approximated]. Madrid: Paidos.

Finkler, K. (2004). Traditional healers in Mexico: The effectiveness of spiritual practices. In U. P. Gielen, J. M. Fish, & J. G. Draguns (Eds.), *Handbook of culture, therapy, and healing* (pp. 161–175). Mahwah, NJ: Lawrence Erlbaum Associates.

Fivaz-Depeursinge, E., de Roten, Y., Corboz-Warnery, A., Metraux, J.-C., & Ciola, A. (1994). A pilot study of gaze interactions between therapist and couple. *Psychotherapy Research, 1*, 107–114.

Frankl, V. E. (1960). Paradoxical intention: A logotherapeutic technique. *American Journal of Psychotherapy, 14*, 520–535.

Frankl, V. E. (1981). *The will to meaning: Foundations and applications of logotherapy.* New York: New American Library.

Garma, A. (1969). *Psicoanálisis de los ulcerosos* [Psychoanalysis of ulcer patients]. Buenos Aires: Paidos.

Gau, S.-F., & Chen, C.-C. (1998). Structured family therapeutic interviewing for Chinese psychiatric cases. In U. P. Gielen & A. L. Comunian (Eds.), *The family and family therapy in international perspective* (pp. 186–201). Trieste, Italy: Lint.

Gielen, U. P., & Comunian, A. L. (Eds.). (1999). *International approaches to the family and family therapy.* Padua, Italy: Unipress.

Gillespie, K., Duffy, M., Hackman, A., & Clark, D. M. (2002). Community-based cognitive therapy in the treatment of post-traumatic stress disorder following the Omagh bomb. *Behaviour Research and Therapy, 40*, 345–357.

Gilliéron, E. (1997). *Manuel de psychothérapies brèves* [Manual of brief psychotherapies]. Paris: Dunod.

Grawe, K. (1994). Psychotherapie ohne Grenzen—Von den Therapieschulen zur allgemeinen Psychotherapie [Psychotherapy without boundaries: From schools of therapy to general psychotherapy]. *Verhaltenstherapie und Psychosoziale Praxis, 26*, 357–370.

Grawe, K. (2004). *Neuropsychotherapie* [Neuropsychotherapy]. Göttingen, Germany: Hogrefe.

Grawe, K., Donati, R., & Bernauer, F. (1994). *Psychotherapie im Wandel—Von der Konfession zur Profession* [Psychotherapy in transition: From confession to profession]. Göttingen, Germany: Hogrefe.

Groupe d'Experts. (2004). *Psychothérapie, trois approaches évalues. La synthése* [Psychotherapy: Three approaches evaluated. Synthesis]. Paris: Editions INSERM.

Guidano, V. F. (1987). *Complexity of the self.* New York: Guilford.

Haby, M. M., Donelly, M., Corry, J., & Voss, T. (2006). Cognitive behavioural therapy for depression, panic disorder, and generalized anxiety disorder: A meta-regression of factors that may predict outcome. *Australian and New Zealand Journal of Psychiatry, 40*, 9–19.

Hartmann, H., Kris, E., & Loewenstein, R. M. (1946). Comments on the formation of psychic structure. *Psychoanalytic Study of the Child, 2*, 11–38.

Hayashi, Y., & Mizamae, S. (2004). Group home in Zen temple. *Japanese Bulletin of Social Psychiatry, 13*, 307.

Hentschel, U., & Bijlefeld, C. C. J. H. (1995). It takes two to do therapy: On differential aspects of the formation of therapeutic alliance. *Psychotherapy Research, 5*, 22–32.

Hentschel, U., Kiessling, M., Heck, B., & Willoweit, I. (1992). Therapeutic alliance: What can be learned from case studies? *Psychotherapy Research, 2*, 204–223.

Hill, P. H. F. (2002). *Using Lacanian clinical techniques: An introduction.* London: Press for Habilitation of Psychoanalysis.

Hofstede, G. (2001). *Culture's consequences: Comparing values, behaviors, institutions, and organizations across nations* (2nd ed.). Thousand Oaks, CA: Sage.

Holtforth, M. G., & Castonguay, L. G. (2005). Relationship and techniques in cognitive behavioral therapy: A motivational approach. *Psychotherapy, Theory, Research, Practice, Training, 42*, 443–455.

Holtforth, M. G., & Grawe, K. (2002). Bern Inventory of Treatment Goals: First application of a taxonomy of treatment goal themes. *Psychotherapy Research, 12,* 79–99.

Hölzer, M., Pokorny, D., Kächele, H., & Luborsky, L. (1997). The verbalizations of emotions in the therapeutic dialogue: A correlate of therapeutic outcome? *Psychotherapy Research, 7,* 261–273.

Hsieh-Shi, C. (1995). Development of mental health systems of care in China from the 1940s to 1980s. In T.-Y. Lin, W.-S. Tseng, & E.-K. Yeh (Eds.), *Chinese societies and mental health* (pp. 314–325). Hong Kong: Oxford University Press.

Hsu, J. (1995). Family therapy for the Chinese: Problems and strategies. In T.-Y. Lin, W.-S. Tseng, & E.-K. Yeh (Eds.), *Chinese societies and mental health* (pp. 295–314). Hong Kong: Oxford University Press.

Ilechukwu, S. P. C. (1991). Psychiatry in Africa: Special problems and unique features. *Transcultural Psychiatric Research Review, 28,* 167–218.

Ionescu, S. (1998). La psychoanalyse et l'évaluation de ses résultants [Psychoanalysis and the evaluation of its results]. In T. Nathan (Ed.), *Psychothérapies* (pp. 170–220). Paris: Odile Jacob.

Jaipal, R. (2004). Indian conceptions of mental health, healing, and the individual. In U. P. Gielen, J. M. Fish, & J. G. Draguns (Eds.), *Handbook of culture, therapy, and healing* (pp. 293–308). Mahwah, NJ: Lawrence Erlbaum Associates.

Jilek, W. G. (1971). From crazy witchdoctor to auxiliary therapist: The changing image of the medicine man. *Confina Psychiatrica, 4,* 200–220.

Jilek, W. G. (1982). *Indian healing: Shamanic ceremonialism in the Pacific Northwest today.* Toronto: Hancock House.

Jilek, W. G. (2004). The therapeutic aspects of Salish spirit dance ceremonials. In U. P. Gielen, J. M. Fish, & J. G. Draguns (Eds.), *Handbook of culture, therapy, and healing* (pp. 151–160). Mahwah, NJ: Lawrence Erlbaum Associates.

Juen, B., & Bänninger-Huber, E. (2002). Therapeut–Klient Interaktionen versus Mutter–Kind Interaktionen: Ein Vergleich [Therapist–client versus mother–child interactions: A comparison]. *Psychologische Medizin, 13,* 17–21.

Kaechele, H. (1992). Narration and observation in psychotherapy research: Reporting on a 20-year-long journey from qualitative case study reports to quantitative studies on the psychoanalytic process. *Psychotherapy Research, 2,* 1–15.

Kaechele, H., & Kordy, H. (1992). Psychotherapieforschung und therapeutische Versorgung [Research on psychotherapy and therapeutic services]. *Der Nervenarzt, 63,* 517–526.

Kalayjian, A. (2005). *Sri Lanka: Post tsunami mental health outreach program lessons learned.* Retrieved September 1, 2005, from http://www.meaningfulworld.com/projects.html

Kapur, M. (2001). Mental health, illness, and therapy. In J. Pandey (Ed.), *Psychology in India revisited* (pp. 412–473). New Delhi: Sage.

Karvasarsky, B. D. (1985). *Psikhoterapiya* [Psychotherapy]. Leningrad: Meditsina.

Kelly, G. (1955). *Psychology of personal constructs.* New York: Norton.

Kimura, B. (1995). *Zwischen Mensch und Mensch* [Between one human being and another]. Darmstadt, Germany: Akademische Verlagsanstalt.

Knobloch, F. (2003). A heuristic path to psychotherapy integration: One early European development. *Journal of Psychotherapy Integration, 13,* 107–129.

Kociunas, R. (2003). *Psikhologicheskoye konsul'tirovaniye i grupovaia terapiya.* [Psychological consultation and group therapy]. Moscow: Academic Project.

Kordy, H. (1995). Does psychotherapy research answer the questions of practitioners and should it? *Psychotherapy Research, 5*, 128–130.

Korolenko, C. P., & Dmitriyeva, N. V. (1999). *Sotsiodinamicheskaya psikhiatriya* [Sociodynamic psychiatry]. Novosibirsk, Russia: NGPU Publishers.

Krippner, R. (2002). Conflicting perspectives on shamans and shamanism: Points and counterpoints. *American Psychologist, 57*, 962–978.

Kumar, S. (2000). Tension-ridden job causes mental health problems for police in New Delhi. *The Lancet, 355*, 1082.

Lacan, J. (1966). *Écrits* [Writings]. Paris: Édition du Seuil.

Lacan, J. (1977). *Écrits: A selection* (A. Sheridan, Trans.). London: Tavistock.

Ladouceur, R. (2002). *Understanding and treating the pathological gambler.* Chichester, UK: Wiley.

Lamb, W. K. (2005a). *A meta-analysis of outcome studies in long-term psychodynamic psychotherapy and psychoanalysis.* Unpublished Doctoral Dissertation, University of California at Berkeley (UMI Microform 3165451).

Lamb, W. (2005b). *The effectiveness of psychoanalysis: A meta-analysis of outcomes studies from twelve countries.* Paper presented at the meeting of the American Psychological Association, Washington, DC.

Lambo, T. A. (1964). Patterns of psychiatric care in developing African countries. In A. Kiev (Ed.), *Magic, faith, and healing* (pp. 443–453). New York: Free Press.

Laungani, P. (2004). *Asian perspectives in counseling and psychotherapy.* Hove, UK: Brunner-Routledge.

Lauterbach, W. (1984). *Soviet psychotherapy.* Oxford, UK: Pergamon.

Lauterbach, W. (1996). The measurement of personal conflict. *Psychotherapy Research, 6*, 213–225.

Lecomte, C., & Castonguay, L. G. (1987). *Rapprochement et intégration en psychothérapie. Psychoanalyse, behaviorisme et humanisme* [Rapprochement and integration in psychotherapy: Psychoanalysis, behaviorism, and humanism]. Chicoutimi, Quebec: Gaetan Morin.

Leung, P. W. L., & Lee, P. W. H. (1996). Psychotherapy with the Chinese. In M. H. Bond (Ed.), *Handbook of Chinese psychology* (pp. 440–456). Hong Kong: Oxford University Press.

Liberman, D. (1970). *Linguistica, interaccion comunicativa y proceso psicoanalítico.* [Linguistics, communicative interaction, and psychoanalytic process]. Buenos Aires: Nueva Vision.

Liotti, G. (1981). Un modello cognitivo-comportomantale dell'agorafobia [A cognitive-behavioral model of agoraphobia]. In V. F. Guidano & M. A. Reda (Eds.), *Cognitivismo e psicoterapia* (pp. 149–170). Milan: Franco Agneli.

Liotti, G. (2004). Trauma, dissociation, and disorganized attachment: Three strands of a single braid. *Psychotherapy: Theory, Research, Practice, Training, 41*, 472–485.

Luthe, W. (1969). *Autogenic therapy.* New York: Grune and Stratton.

Maldavsky, D. (2004). *La investigación psicoanalítica del lenguaje: Algoritmo David Liberman* [Psychoanalytic research on language: David Liberman algorithm]. Buenos Aires: Editorial Lugar.

Matt, G. E. (1993). Comparing classes of psychotherapeutic intervention: A review and reanalysis of English-language and German-language meta-analyses. *Journal of Cross-Cultural Psychology, 24*, 5–25.

May, R. (1958). *Existence.* New York: Basic Books.

Miasishchev, V. N. (1960). *Lichnost' i nevrozy* [Personality and neuroses]. Leningrad, Leningrad State University.

Miró, M. T. (2000). El probléma del otro en el postracionalismo [The problem of the other in post-rationalism]. *Revista de Psicoterapia, 11*, 115–127.

Monsen, J. T., Odland, T., Faugli, A., Daae, E., & Eilertsen, D. E. (1995). Personality disorders: Changes and stability after intensive psychotherapy focusing on affect consciousness. *Psychotherapy Research, 5*, 33–48.

Mosconi, A., Gonzo, M., Sorgato, R., Tirelli, M., & Tomas, M. (1999). From counterparadox and the Milan model to therapeutic conversation and the Milan systemic approach: Origin and development of the Milan Center for Family Therapy. In U. P. Gielen & A. L. Comunian (Eds.), *International approaches to the family and family therapy* (pp. 9–42). Padua, Italy: Unipress.

Nathan, T. (1994). *L'influence qui guérit* [The healing influence]. Paris: Odile Jacob.

Nathan, T., & Hounkpatin, L. (1996). *La guérison yoruba* [Yoruba healing]. Paris: Odile Jacob.

Ng, K. S. (2003). *Global perspectives in family therapy.* New York: Brunner-Routledge.

Orlinsky, D. E., & Ronnestad, M. H. (2005). *Therapeutic work and professional development: The psychotherapist's perspective.* Washington, DC: American Psychological Association Books.

Orlinsky, D. E., Ronnestad, M. H., & Willutzki, U. (2004). Fifty years of psychotherapy process-outcome research: Continuity and change. In M. J. Lambert (Ed.), *Bergin and Garfield's handbook of psychotherapy and behavior change* (5th ed., pp. 307–391). New York: Wiley.

Öst, L. G. (1989). One session treatment of specific phobias. *Behavior Research and Therapy, 27*, 1–7.

Pavlov, I. P. (1941). *Lectures on conditioned reflexes: Vol. 2. Conditioned reflexes and psychiatry.* New York: International Publishers.

Peham, D., Ganzer, V., Bänninger-Huber, E., & Juen, B. (2002). Schuldgefühlspezifische Regulierungsprozesse in Mutter–Tochter Interaktionen und Psychotherapeut–Klient Beziehungen: Ein Vergleich [Regulation processes of guilt feelings in mother–daughter interactions compared to psychotherapist–client relationships]. *Psychologische Medizin, 13*, 22–27.

Peltzer, K. (1995). *Psychology and health in African cultures: Examples of ethnopsychotherapeutic practice.* Frankfurt-am-Main: IKO-Verlag für Interkulturelle Kommunikation.

Peltzer, K. (2001). An integrative model for ethnocultural counseling and psychotherapy of victims of organized violence. *Journal of Psychotherapy Integration, 11*, 241–262.

Pichon Rivière, E. (1971). *El processo grupal: Del psicoanalísis a la psicología social* [Group process: From psychoanalysis to social psychology]. Buenos Aires: Galerna.

Plotkin, M. (2001). *Freud in the Pampas: The formation of a psychoanalytical culture in Argentina.* Palo Alto, CA: Stanford University Press.

Prince, R. H. (1980). Variations in psychotherapeutic procedures. In H. C. Triandis & J. G. Draguns (Eds.), *Handbook of cross-cultural psychology: Vol. 6. Psychopathology* (pp. 291–350) Boston: Allyn and Bacon.

Rachman, S. (1969). *The effects of psychotherapy.* London: Pergamon Press.

Radford, M. H. B. (2005). *Some thoughts on the current state of psychotherapy in Japan.* Unpublished manuscript.

Rastogi, M., & Wampler, K. S. (1998). Couples and family therapy and Indian families: Some structural and intergenerational considerations. In U. P. Gielen & A. L. Comunian (Eds.), *The family and family therapy in international perspective* (pp. 257–273). Trieste, Italy: Edizioni Lint Trieste.

Regli, D., Bieber, K., Mathier, F., & Grawe, K. (2001). Realization of therapeutic bond and activation of resources in initial therapy sessions. *Verhaltenstherapie und Verhaltensmedizin, 22,* 399–420.

Rennie, D. L. (2004). Anglo-North American qualitative counseling and psychotherapy research. *Psychotherapy Research, 14,* 37–55.

Reynolds, D. L. (1980). *The quiet therapies.* Honolulu: University Press of Hawaii.

Rubin, J. B. (2004). Psychoanalysis and Buddhism. In U. P. Gielen, J. M. Fish, & J. G. Draguns (Eds.), *Handbook of culture, psychotherapy, and healing* (pp. 253–276). Mahwah, NJ: Lawrence Erlbaum Associates.

Sachse, R. (1998). The effects of intervention phrasing on therapist–client communication. *Psychotherapy Research, 12,* 275–283.

Sachse, R. (2002). *Klärungsorientierte Psychotherapie* [Psychotherapy oriented toward clarification]. Göttingen, Germany: Hogrefe.

Salkovskis, P. M. (1996). The cognitive approach to anxiety: Threat beliefs, safety-seeking behavior, and the special case of health anxiety and obsessions. In P. M. Salkovskis (Ed.), *Frontiers of cognitive psychotherapy* (pp. 48–74). New York: Guilford.

Salkovskis, P. M. (2006, June). *Cognitive behavioral approaches to understanding and treating anxiety disorders.* Keynote Address, VII International Baltic Psychology Conference, Riga, Latvia.

Scharfetter, C. (1985). Schamane: Zeuge alter Kultur—wieder belebbar? [Shaman as a witness to ancient culture: Can he be resuscitated?]. *Schweizerische Zeitschrift für Neurologie, Neurochirurgie und Psychiatrie, 136,* 81–95.

Schechtman, Z., & Tsegahun, H. (2004). Psychotherapy to enhance self-disclosure and client–therapist alliance in an intake interview with Ethiopian immigrants to Israel. *Psychotherapy Research, 14,* 367–377.

Selvini Palazzoli, M., Cirillo, S., Selvini, M., & Sorrentino, A. M. (1989). *Family games: General models of psychotic processes in the family* (V. Kleiber, Trans.). New York: Norton.

Semerari, A. (Ed.). (1999). *Psicoterapia cognitive del paziente grave: Metacognizione e relazione terapeutica* [Cognitive psychotherapy of severe patients. Metacognition and therapeutic relationship]. Milan: Raffaello Cortina.

Smith, M. L., Glass, G. V., & Miller, T. I. (1980). *The benefits of psychotherapy.* Baltimore: Johns Hopkins University Press.

Snider, P. D. (2003). *Exploring the relationship between individualism–collectivism and attitudes toward counseling among ethnic Chinese, Australian, and American university students.* Unpublished doctoral dissertation, Murdoch University, Perth, Western Australia.

Strauss, B. M., & Kaechele, H. (1998). The writing on the wall: Comments on the current discussion about empirically validated treatments in Germany. *Psychotherapy Research, 8,* 158–170.

Strupp, H. H. (1996). The tripartite model and the *Consumer Reports* study. *American Psychologist, 51,* 1017–1024.

Tanaka-Matsumi, J. (2004). Japanese forms of psychotherapy: Naikan therapy and Morita therapy. In U. P. Gielen, J. M. Fish, & J. G. Draguns (Eds.), *Handbook of culture, therapy, and healing* (pp. 277–291). Mahwah, NJ: Lawrence Erlbaum Associates.

Tanaka-Matsumi, J., Higginbotham, N. H., & Chang, R. (2002). Cognitive-behavioral approaches to cross-cultural counseling: A functional analytic approach for clinical application. In P. B. Pedersen, J. G. Draguns, W. J. Lonner, & J. E. Trimble (Eds.), *Counseling across cultures* (5th ed., pp., 337–354). Thousand Oaks, CA: Sage.

Torrey, E. F. (1972). *The mind game: Witchdoctors and psychiatrists*. New York: Emerson Hall.

Toyokawa, T., & Nedate, K. (1996). Application of cognitive behavior therapy to interpersonal problems: A case study of a Japanese female client. *Cognitive and Behavioral Practice, 3*, 289–302.

Tseng, W.-S. (2001). *Handbook of cultural psychiatry*. San Diego: Academic Press.

Tseng, W.-S., & Lee, S., & Lu, Q. (2005). The historical trends of psychotherapy in China: Cultural review. In W.-S. Tseng (Ed.), *Asian culture and psychotherapy: Implications for East and West* (pp. 249–264). Honolulu: University of Hawaii Press.

Tseng, W.-S., Lu, Q.-Y., & Yin, P. Y. (1995). Psychotherapy for the Chinese: Cultural considerations. In T.-Y. Lin, W.-S. Tseng, & E.-K. Yeh (Eds.), *Chinese societies and mental health* (pp. 281–294). Hong Kong: Oxford University Press.

Turkle, S. (1992). *Psychoanalytic politics: Jacques Lacan and Freud's French revolution*. New York: Guilford.

Varma, V. K. (1988). Culture, personality, and psychotherapy. *International Journal of Social Psychiatry, 34*, 142–149.

Volpert, I. E. (1968). Vosproizvedeniye obraza kak metod psikhoterapii [Recreation of the image as a method of psychotherapy]. *Zhurnal Nevropatologii I Psikhiatrii, 68*, 902–906.

Waxer, P. H. (1989). Cantonese versus Canadian evaluation of directive versus nondirective therapy. *Canadian Journal of Counseling, 23*, 263–272.

Wendt, I. (1973). Eine japanische Zen-Klinik im Westen? [A Japanese Zen clinic in the West?] *Schweizerische Zeitschrift für Psychologie und ihre Anwendungen, 24*, 366–370.

Wessells, M. G., & Monteiro, C. (2004). Healing the wounds following protracted conflict in Angola: A community-based approach to assisting war-affected children. In U. P. Gielen, J. M. Fish, & J. G. Draguns (Eds.), *Handbook of culture, psychotherapy, and healing* (pp. 321–332). Mahwah, NJ: Lawrence Erlbaum Associates.

Wittmann, W. W., & Matt, G. E. (1986). Meta-Analyse als Integration von Forschungsergebnissen am Beispiel deutschsprachiger Arbeiten zur Effektivität von Psychotherapie [Meta-analysis as integration of research results, as exemplified by studies on the effectiveness of psychotherapy] *Psychologische Rundschau, 37*, 20–40.

Wolpe, J. (1958). *Psychotherapy by reciprocal inhibition*. Stanford, CA: Stanford University Press.

Yang, Y. (2004). Advances in psychology in China. In M. J. Stevens & D. Wedding (Eds.), *Handbook of international psychology* (pp. 179–192). New York: Brunner-Routledge.

Yates, A. J. (1970). *Behavior Therapy*. Oxford, UK: Wiley.

9

Macro-Level Interventions: Psychology, Social Policy, and Societal Influence Processes

Michael G. Wessells
Christian Children's Fund

Andrew Dawes
Human Sciences Research Council

INTRODUCTION

As a discipline, psychology has focused primarily on individuals, families, and small groups. This micro-level focus, although productive, sits at odds with the aspirations of many psychologists to make a positive difference in regard to the greatest contemporary problems facing humankind. These problems, which include armed conflict, racism, sexism, poverty, and the HIV/AIDS pandemic, among many others, occur at macro-social levels involving large numbers of people from local communities, nations, ethnically diverse regions, and even the world. Since the challenges affect significant numbers of people, interventions need to occur to scale if any significant impact is to be felt, and scale is normally achieved only through macro-level policy implementation or large-scale programatic intervention carried out with the support of policymakers and other major stakeholders.

Our task in this chapter is to show how psychology has the potential to address these challenges at the macro level, not through the sorts of individual and small-group interventions that are traditional in the discipline, but through macro-level approaches associated with social policies and societal influence processes. The chapter is divided into three parts. The first lays the conceptual foundation and provides a critical lens for thinking about how psychology can inform our approach to macro-level problems. Next, we examine social policy work and mass-scale psychosocial interventions as two kinds of macro-level intervention. For both categories, we provide examples of psychologically informed interventions, and discuss their role, impact, and challenges.

CONCEPTUAL FOUNDATIONS

The logic of macro-level interventions stands on a systems-analytic framework that views each level of a social system as having emergent properties and as dynamically interacting with other levels. A country, for example, is usefully conceptualized as an organized, layered system consisting of diverse subgroups, subsystems, institutions, agencies, norms, and people. The dynamism of the system is visible in the rich interactions within levels and also between levels, such as grassroots, community groups, district or provincial-level groups or associations, and national groups and agencies, including official government bodies. Within the system, diverse levers for change exist. Although power is vested officially in top government leaders, extensive power is wielded also by the media, religious leaders, and leaders of popular movements. Macro-social interventions, which aim to have an influence at broad levels such as the national and international levels, frequently target actors and institutions at several levels and exploit the linkages between them.

Change Strategies

Psychologists who seek to achieve macro-level change may use a mixture of top–down, bottom–up, and middle–out strategies (Lederach, 1997). They are not mutually exclusive, as we will explain later. Top–down strategies attempt to influence subnational, national, regional, or international authorities, urging them to implement psychologically informed policies and programs. An example would be to argue for extended support for comprehensive early childhood-development programs for children in poor communities using evidence of their effectiveness in improving a range of psychosocial outcomes for children over the long term (Young, 2002; Zigler, 1994). If the provision of such programs were mandated by policy, then the national government would be obligated to oversee their development and implementation. This is a top–down approach in that the programs originate at the top level of national government, which then guides implementation at lower levels.

Bottom–up strategies attempt to influence significant numbers of people using psychologically informed methods to achieve desired intervention outcomes. An example would be community-based initiatives informed by psychological theory and evidence that seek to promote condom use in order to reduce the prevalence of HIV/AIDS (Ajzen, 1991; Campbell, 2003; Eaton, Flisher, & Aaro, 2003; Shisana & Simbayi, 2002). For such an approach to be optimally effective, the support of local authorities is needed. Bottom–up strategies frequently build on grassroots initiatives for social change, such as women's empowerment movements that do not have a specific psychological focus, but rather can be enriched through the addition of psychological elements or dimensions.

Middle–out strategies attempt to influence mid-level leaders, who in turn influence both leaders above them and their public constituencies. For example, efforts to reform education by reducing the frequency of corporal punishment often move forward by training not the highest level leaders of a nation, but by working with Ministry of Education leaders in different provinces or states. These mid-level leaders influence higher-level leaders and also mobilize public opinion in their areas of jurisdiction, creating an environment favorable for social change.

An important part of the successful application of macro-social intervention is to use different strategies in complementary ways by, for example, combining the use of top–down and bottom–up strategies. After all, new government policies are more likely to be implemented if there is a sufficient base of popular support for the new measures. Conversely, strong popular sentiments frequently induce leaders to make policy changes.

The effective use of these strategies is most likely to occur through collaborative, multidisciplinary efforts. Indeed it is most unlikely that complex social problems can be addressed solely from a psychological point of departure. Psychologists tend not to be trained in the range of skills needed for policy-oriented work. Skills such as policy analysis and advocacy are seldom parts of the graduate curriculum in psychology (see chapter 11 for details on how to prepare psychologists to meet contemporary global challenges). In contrast, they are regular components of training in disciplines such as political science, economics, sociology, and social work. It is far more common for graduates in these fields to have experience in macro-social interventions. Therefore, psychologists who wish to address macro-social issues should, wherever possible and appropriate, take a multidisciplinary team-based approach to the problem (see chapter 1 in this volume). Multidisciplinary collaboration is rarely easy. Different professional languages, bodies of knowledge, approaches to knowledge production, and disciplinary rivalry must be bridged if projects are to be successful. In addition, psychologists who wish to address macro-level issues face the twin pitfalls of reductionism and universalism (these pitfalls are also addressed in chapters 1, 5, 6, 7, 10, and 11 in this volume).

Reductionism

Reductionism occurs in two main ways, the first of which is an emphasis on the relative importance of psychological causes. In examining the causes of war, for example, it is natural for psychologists to showcase the importance of psychological processes such as social identity, existential fear, enemy images, obedience to authority, moral exclusion, dehumanization, de-individuation, and projection, among others. However, psychological processes alone cannot provide a comprehensive account of war, which has complex historical, political, social, and cultural roots (Christie, Wagner, & Winter, 2001). A significant problem arises when psychologists privilege psychology over other disciplines by examining psychological processes in isolation or implying that psychological processes carry the main explanatory burden in regard to war. The resulting decontextualized analyses cannot do justice to the complexity of the phenomena of war.

Fortunately, this problem may be overcome through a mixture of humility and positioning of psychological analysis within a wider multidisciplinary framework that reflects the rich interplay of psychological, political, economic, and other processes influencing war. Typically, proponents of this approach, such as Kelman (1965), acknowledge that psychology accounts for a rather small portion of the total variance of the phenomena to be explained. This acknowledgement is valuable both in recognizing the complexity of macro-social phenomena and in defining the limits of psychological analyses.

Reductionism also occurs through the uncritical application of concepts and processes identified at one social level to higher social levels. For example, it is not uncommon to hear assertions that racism could be abolished through the reduction of individual prejudice. If every person's prejudice could be eliminated, so the argument goes, there would be no more racism. This view conflates prejudice, an individual phenomenon, with racism, a macro-social institutional phenomenon grounded in abuses of power by groups having vested interests. Although the "end racism by ending prejudice" approach has considerable moral appeal, it fails analytically to come to terms with the fact that racism is more than the sum of the prejudice held by individuals in a system. To understand racism in contexts such as the caste system in India, the segregation era in the U.S., or the Apartheid system in South Africa, one needs to examine the legitimization and codification of racism in laws, the power of government elites who protect the system over its victims, the economics of privilege, the history leading to exploitative intergroup relations, and a host of other factors beyond the individual level.

Similarly, in analyses of problems such as nuclear proliferation, it is not uncommon to see statements, such as a particular state feared its neighbor, thereby leading it to develop or acquire additional weapons. Whatever shorthand value such references have is outweighed by the problematic implication that states are like individuals. Aside from the ontological question as to whether a state entity has emotions (which are individual properties), the view that a state feared its neighbor raises many questions about who in fact felt the fear and what differences existed among people within the state. A state is composed of diverse groups and institutions, which typically have separate subinterests and spheres of influence, such as education, health, security, and judicial matters. Not only are states reservoirs of enormous diversity and contesting polities, but also their actions reflect decisions and actions at many different levels. Typically, decisions are made not by one person, but rather by a variety of agencies and actors in a system containing checks and balances. Even in totalitarian states, in which the leader makes the key decisions, diverse agencies and actors implement the decisions, often with guidance from their own agendas or understanding of the leader's wishes.

Both examples indicate the existence of an epistemological trap in which theories derived from an individual, micro-level of analysis are applied wholesale to a larger, macro-level of analysis (Kelman, 1965). In keeping with the Gestalt axiom "the whole is greater than the sum of its parts," higher social levels, such as the state, have emergent properties not visible in lower levels, such as individuals and families. Different social levels require different levels of explanation. For psychologists whose theories derive primarily from the analysis of individuals and small groups, this insight recommends critical self-scrutiny and a spirit of learning to develop contextually appropriate explanations at the macro-social level.

Universalism

Like all sciences, psychology aspires to universal laws, principles, theories, and tools. The vast majority of psychological research, however, is conducted in highly industrialized countries in Australia, Europe, and the United States. These areas feature high material standards of living, relatively high levels of political and economic stability, and cultures that largely reflect Western values and a scientific worldview. In contrast, the majority of the world's people live in developing countries with low material standards of living, higher levels of political and economic instability, and cultures that in certain respects diverge sharply from those of Western societies (see chapter 4 for a more detailed description of psychology in the majority world).

As cultural psychologists, such as Shweder (1990), have suggested, mainstream psychology is best viewed as a cultural product that embodies the values and cultural dimensions of highly industrialized and wealthy Western countries. This is particularly evident in those disciplinary domains that deal with personhood, spirituality, interpersonal and social relations, and mental health. Although the principles and methods of the discipline have considerable utility in many contexts, one cannot assume that they apply to all cultures and contexts (see chapters 6 and 7 on the normative origins of psychological theories and methods). Indeed, it is appropriate to ask: What would psychology have looked like had it been invented in China or the Central African Republic (see chapter 5 for more on the indigenization movement in psychology, particularly in East Asia)?

The hegemony of Western formulations of mind, the person, and mental health creates significant opportunities for cultural bias and abuses of power. The commonly made assumption by psychologists that people everywhere are more similar than different is contradicted by observations that cultures differ in their concepts of childhood (Boyden, 1997), family structure and function (Kağitçibaşi, 1996; Roopnarine & Gielen, 2005), mental health and mental illness (Lee & Sue, 2001; Lopez & Guarnaccia, 2000), self (Triandis, 2001), spirituality (Honwana, 1997), and social power (Anderson, 1996; Osman, 1985). This is not to deny the cross-cultural validity of many Western concepts. Neither should we descend into cultural essentialism when appreciating cultural difference. Nor should we gainsay the fact that, as a result of processes associated with globalization, many people, particularly the young in developing regions, are taking on modern practices and identities. Rather, it is to caution against the practice of assuming that constructs of selfhood, emotion, and sociality that have been developed in the West are transportable unchanged to other parts of the world. Similarly, one cannot assume that a theory, which has underpinned a successful intervention in, say, New York, will have sufficient external validity when transported to Abidjan.

Universalism is challenged also due to the enormous situational differences separating Western societies from developing countries (Dawes & Donald, 1994), in which the fabric of society has been ravaged by colonial exploitation, armed conflict, political instability, HIV/AIDS, chronic poverty, and natural disasters, such as the 2004 tsunami. Can one say with any confidence, for example, that children who grow up in a village in which HIV/AIDS has killed all adults will pass through Eriksonian life stages (Erikson, 1963) in the manner of children who grow up in Western societies? Populations ravaged by poverty, armed conflict, and HIV/AIDS have made normal and adaptive certain forms of behavior that would seem maladaptive by Western standards. For example, Western psychologists tend to view children who live and work on the streets as potentially pathological and as products of failed families. Research on "street children," however, indicates that in Latin American and African countries, male street children function better and are less prone to pathology than many boys who elect to stay with their families, particularly where these families are seriously troubled. The boys on the streets often come from caring families that have been wracked by enormous economic and social stresses (Aptekar, 2004).

The quest for universal principles also sometimes obscures local knowledge and practice, thereby marginalizing indigenous psychology. In countries such as Mozambique and Sierra Leone, for example, local people view child soldiers who have killed or who have survived rape as needing not Western therapy or counseling, but a purification ritual that cleans them of spiritual impurities picked up during the war (Honwana, 1997; Kostelny, 2004). Most Western psychologists who enter war zones such as Angola, however, show little interest in local rituals and culture, and eagerly apply their theories of trauma, many of which attract significant funding from Western donors, but few of which have been validated in non-Western societies. This imposition of outsider ideas finds support among local people who, desperate for money and outside support, silence their own culture and learn to talk the language of post-traumatic stress disorder (PTSD; see Marsella, Bornemann, Ekblad, & Orley, 1994).

Ironically, little correlation exists in Angola between scores on PTSD scales and social dysfunction (Eyber & Ager, 2004).

When imposition occurs, psychology becomes an instrument of cultural imperialism and a means of dominating local people (Dawes & Cairns, 1998; Wessells, 1999). Not infrequently, the actions of local psychologists aggravate the problem. Wanting the imprimatur of Western science, psychologists from developing countries may adopt Western standards and practices with a zeal going well beyond that exhibited by Western psychologists themselves. This problem is not corrected automatically by the use of national paraprofessional staff from the affected areas. Being university educated, many national paraprofessionals represent the elite in their own society and are eager to supplant local cultural practices, which they frequently regard as atavistic and embarrassing, with Western scientific approaches.

As is evident from the discussion thus far, macro-social interventions face daunting challenges of culture and power extending well beyond traditional discussions of the need for cultural sensitivity. Before conceptualizing or launching an intervention, it is wise to reflect critically on the relationship between epistemology, power, and ethics.

Regardless of whether it is intentional or not, abuse of power through the imposition of Western psychology and its values violates the "Do no harm" principle (see chapter 10 on issues related to ethical practice in an increasingly globalized world). Although this problem accompanies all psychological interventions, it is of particular concern in regard to macro-level interventions, which could cause harm on a large scale. Ethical reflection and a self-critical attitude are essential ingredients of any macro-social intervention. A critical stance is needed not only in the conduct of the intervention, but also in the planning, when one needs to ask whether the research or the intervention is really needed, who benefits from the project, and whether the potential benefits of the project outweigh its risks. We cannot escape the fact that there is enormous pressure for academics to secure research grants in a highly competitive market. Considerable prestige is attached to securing the "big ones," particularly in such fields as HIV/AIDS (e.g., grants from the U.S. National Institute of Health, the U.S. Agency for International Development, and the Global Fund). There is little doubt that, while these are very significant opportunities for applied social science that can inform macro-level interventions, they can also distort the process of knowledge production. And, it is vulnerable populations who will be the victims of insensitive practices where these occur.

POLICY CHANGE

Psychologists contribute to policy development and social change through diverse practices, including policy-relevant research, expert testimony, dialogues and workshops with leaders whose agencies oversee particular policies, advocacy, and the development of policy standards. We will illustrate these through case studies from the United States, Southern Africa, and the United Nations.

School Desegregation in the United States

A common error is for discussions of macro-level problems and interventions to focus exclusively on poor, developing societies. This not only stigmatizes developing countries, but also implies that relatively developed countries have evolved to the point where they are no longer subject to basic problems, such as racism. The fallacy of this view is evident in the case of school desegregation in the United States. Also, this case is important because it shows poignantly both the role of psychologists as shapers of valuable national policy changes and the limits of national policy change as an instrument for achieving macro-social change.

On entry into the 20th century, racial segregation was a societal norm in the United States, enforced through Jim Crow laws and the omnipresent threat of violence. Using the infamous formula "separate but equal," the Supreme Court ruling on *Plessy v. Ferguson* (1896) had legalized the segregation of schools. Legalized segregation, however, sat poorly with a constitution guaranteeing the equality of all, and the enormous burdens of black oppression weighed heavily on the conscience of many whites. It also flew in the face of U.S. experience in World War II, in which the U.S. military had taken significant strides toward desegregation, thereby extending to Black soldiers greater equality than they had enjoyed in civilian society. Also, many psychologists across the country worked to oppose segregation in all its forms. If it was inevitable that the system would change, school desegregation was a likely target because segregated schools embodied racism and taught children early in life the stereotypes and modes of behavior that provided the psychological infrastructure of racism.

By the 1940s, research by social scientists, including psychologists, had documented the glaring inequality between Black and White schools and also the psychological damage inflicted on all parties by school desegregation (Clark, Chein, & Cook, 1952/2004; Deutsch & Chein, 1948).

Perhaps the best-known research was the Clark and Clark (1947) study showing how segregation created in Black children a sense of inferiority, as illustrated by their preferences for White dolls. Based on this study and many others, a group of distinguished psychologists wrote an influential brief that served as expert testimony in the case of *Brown v. Board of Education* (1954), in which the Supreme Court prohibited separate schools and mandated the desegregation of education.

This policy change enshrined in the *Brown* ruling led to the restructuring of the U.S. system of education and lifted hopes that sweeping social change was at hand, not only in education, but also in the wider society. In fact, the ruling has had significant impact on the educational system. A recent review of research (Pettigrew, 2004) pointed out that compared with Black children from segregated schools, those in desegregated schools are more likely to earn degrees from predominantly White colleges, work alongside White colleagues and have better jobs, live in racially mixed neighborhoods, and have more positive attitudes toward Whites. Also, Whites from desegregated schools have more positive attitudes toward Blacks than do Whites from segregated schools.

Unfortunately, the years following the initial *Brown* decision have witnessed not the end of racism, but the rise of barriers, backsliding, and retrenchment toward a norm of de facto segregation and inequality. In 1955, the Supreme Court opened the door for foot-dragging by issuing a vague order to implement the 1954 ruling with all deliberate speed (Pettigrew, 2004). In the absence of strong implementation guidelines and benchmarks, Southern federal district courts were free to stall, obfuscate, and evade the law, which they did. Also, lower court rulings and public sentiments reduced what had been a grand vision of social transformation into narrow, technical concerns about "squeezing bodies into buildings, buses, and classrooms" (Fine, 2004, p. 503). Relatively wealthy Whites evaded the policy by sending their children to private schools and living in areas that used a variety of subterranean methods to keep Blacks out. Many cities became embroiled in controversy over forced busing and the burdens imposed on children by long rides to and from school each day. As pointed out by elder psychologists, whose work on desegregation spans many decades, the fundamental problem was that White elites were unwilling to relinquish their privileged position (Fine, 2004). At present, White students enjoy higher graduation rates from high school and college than Black, Latino, and American Indian students (Kao & Thompson, 2003).

This ongoing case indicates that the establishment of psychologically informed policy changes is important, but is at best only one part of the foundation for social change. When progressive policies outstrip public attitudes, norms, and practices, they are at risk of becoming achievements on paper only. To enable effective implementation, policy changes should be coupled with efforts to mobilize mass opinion, win the support of local leaders, and change behavior at grassroots levels. The promise of the civil rights movement in the United States has not been broken, as significant improvements in race relations have occurred and continue to occur. But, neither has it fulfilled the dream of Martin Luther King, Jr. and millions of U.S. citizens. Large-scale change often comes slowly and may occur over time periods measured in decades and centuries.

Institutionalization of Orphans

The value of policy change as a means of effecting macro-social change is also visible in sub-Saharan Africa, where the twin ravages of armed conflict and HIV/AIDS have created large numbers of orphans. Worldwide, some 40 million children who have lost one or both parents are at risk of child soldiering, dangerous child labor, and other high-risk activities (Hunter & Williamson, 2002).

In Angola, a multi-decade war had orphaned large numbers of children, and the numbers of orphans soared as a result of intense fighting between 1992 and 1994. Wanting to protect the orphans, the Angolan government followed the path of many governments worldwide by placing the children in institutions, the conditions of which were shocking. Fifty or more children were jammed into a sleeping room, providing ideal conditions for the spread of disease. Two or three seldom-paid staff struggled to oversee hundreds of children, including many infants who had little food, stimulation, or contact with the outside world. Extensive psychological research has shown that such institutional environments rob children of the care, stimulation, and protection needed for healthy development (Bowlby, 1979; Grossman, Grossman, & Waters, 2005). In Angola, as in most societies having strong traditions of extended family, orphans fare better through carefully selected and monitored placements in homes of extended family members or foster families (Tolfree, 2003).

To address this problem, numerous nongovernmental organizations (NGOs), such as the Christian Children's Fund (CCF) and Save the Children/UK, conducted a focused advocacy campaign in which they lobbied key members of the Angolan government, including those who oversaw the policy on institutionalizing orphans. The strategy was to express respect for the government's good intentions, but to argue that institutionalization was not in the children's best interests as set forth in the *Convention on the Rights of the Child* adopted by the United Nations General Assembly in 1989. Also, the institutionalization policy contradicted psychological research and was an inferior alternative by comparison to other available low-cost options. As a result of this multi-agency effort, the Angolan government wisely changed its national policy of leaving orphans in institutions and invested more in processes of tracing and uniting these children with extended family members. Although institutionalization of orphans continues, partly as a residue of socialist thinking, thousands of children benefited from this policy change.

Development of Standards

Psychologists have also had a macro-level influence by using their distinctive expertise to develop policy standards regarding mental health and psychosocial assistance. For example, the international humanitarian community had constructed in the late 1990s the *Standards for Intervention in Humanitarian Emergencies* (The Sphere Project, 1997), which outlined the minimum global standards for emergency assistance in sectors such as health, water and sanitation, and shelter construction. The conspicuous absence of standards for psychosocial support reflected the tendency of most humanitarian agencies to regard psychosocial support as a second-tier concern. However, psychologists had long argued that, in crises associated with armed conflict and natural disasters, the impact of psychological and social wounds is enormous and may be as great as that of physical wounds. Building on the expanding, though nascent, base of field research and practice on psychosocial assistance in complex emergencies, psychologists developed a set of standards for psychosocial assistance, which are included in the recently revised standards associated with The Sphere Project. This constitutes a significant milestone in the professionalization of psychosocial assistance in emergency situations (see chapter 10 for more on the need to professionalize standards for macro-level interventions).

The value of developing standards is visible also in psychologists' increased involvement with the United Nations (see chapter 12 for more on the role of psychology at the U.N.). For example, psychologists played an important role in drafting and reviewing the guidelines for the *Psychosocial Care and Protection of Tsunami-Affected Children* (Interagency Working Group on Separated and Unaccompanied Children, 2004), which helped to guide practice in the aftermath of the 2004 tsunami. Also, several psychologists currently serve as informal advisors to former President Clinton in his role as U.N. Special Envoy for Tsunami Recovery. Similarly, psychologists consulted extensively with the team that authored the 1996 United Nations General Assembly report on the *Impact of Armed Conflict on Children*. The report, and its four-year follow-up, broke new ground by creating a much more holistic framework for conceptualizing how children have been affected by armed conflict and by calling attention to the psychosocial impact of armed conflict.

Psychologists also contributed to the drafting of the *Earth Charter* (Earth Charter Commission, 2000), which outlines a vision and a set of collective responsibilities for the protection of our ecological heritage. Psychologists have also contributed to the work of the NGO Committee on Human Rights and through other NGO initiatives that are important satellite activities at the United Nations. In light of the increasing maturation of global psychology and the increased U.N. engagement of global psychology organizations, such as the International Union of Psychological Science, it is reasonable to expect that the influence of psychology on U.N. policies and activities will only increase in the future.

MACRO-LEVEL INFLUENCE PROCESSES

Outside the arena of policy change, psychologists conduct macro-level interventions in a multitude of ways that, for purposes of convenience, may be grouped under the heading "macro-level influence processes." Typically, these interventions make changes in civil society on a scale extending beyond one or a handful of villages. Since it is beyond the scope of this chapter to catalogue these interventions, we will illustrate the strategies and approaches that address issues of war and peace and HIV/AIDS.

South Africa's Truth and Reconciliation Commission

The decision to hold a Truth and Reconciliation Commission (TRC) in South Africa was taken during negotiations for a post-Apartheid political dispensation between 1990 and late 1993. The TRC was the product of intense struggle between the negotiators. Many, particularly those who had suffered the violence of the Apartheid state, felt that perpetrators of human-rights abuses should be put on trial in the manner of Nuremberg, Germany. The Apartheid government made it clear they would not accept this approach. They could not afford to take a position in which they and their security forces, many of whom had perpetrated human-rights crimes, would be subject to prosecution. They also made it clear that their supporters and those on the far right of the political spectrum would force them to break from the negotiation process. A realistic concern was that sections of the White population would take up arms, as occurred for a brief period in 1994. Hence, there was need for a process that could hold the parties together, rather than risk further division and a civil war. Senior members of the liberation movements took heed of these warnings and worked toward a compromise. Their agreement to a reconciliatory interim South African constitution in 1993 was to be the mechanism. It laid the principles for the foundation of the TRC, which was established by an act of Parliament two years later (Parliament of the Republic of South Africa, 1995). The full record of the TRC's proceedings is available at http://www.doj.gov.za/trc.

The interim constitution and its final version are most unusual among such instruments in recognizing the history of division and pain that preceded its enactment, as well as the need to build a new nation on the basis of a process of reconciliation. Vengeance and retaliation were rejected. The constitution provided for the establishment of the TRC as a mechanism for the promotion of national unity and reconciliation. As part of the process, provision was also made for granting amnesty to those who had committed gross violations of human rights, whether these be acts of commission or omission, while pursuing their political objectives. This approach was promoted by Nelson Mandela in particular, and strongly supported by church leaders, including Archbishop Emeritus Desmond Tutu.

There is no record of psychologists having offered or been asked for input at this stage or later when formulating the statute that determined the terms of the TRC. Nonetheless, those who formulated the TRC unwittingly included features of Lederach's (1997) change strategies, to which we alluded at the outset. First, we see a major policy initiative driven in a top–down manner. Those who negotiated the TRC saw it as an instrument of reconciliation and nation building, and they went ahead with it despite resistance from the right and the left of the political spectrum. It also has elements of a bottom–up strategy, as will be discussed later, in the use of public hearings that contained scenes of confession, apology, and reconciliation. Finally, as will also become evident, middle–out strategies emerged once psychologists became involved and were able to influence the TRC as an institution and process.

The TRC had four key provisions, which though drafted by lawyers, have profound psychological significance. First, the central mandate of the TRC was to rewrite history and come to an understanding of how the system of Apartheid and the perpetration of human-rights violations occurred. In the words of the Promotion of National Unity and Reconciliation Act (Parliament of the Republic of South Africa, 1995), the TRC sought to gain:

> as complete a picture as possible of the causes, nature and extent of the gross violations of human rights which were committed during the period 1 March 1960 to the cut-off date (10 May 1994), including the antecedents, circumstances and context of such violations ... as well as the perspectives of those responsible for commissions of violations. (Section 3[1a])

The TRC enabled an uncovering of the "truth" about the past, a peeling back of the layers of individual and collective consciousness that had covered up painful memories. The revelation of falsehoods and distortions perpetrated by those on all sides of the conflict enabled a re-writing of history and a re-casting of memory. The fact that many and different stories were told, even about the same event, enabled observers from different sides of the political spectrum to appreciate, if they were prepared to, the situations in which their enemies had positioned themselves.

Second, as part of this process, the TRC afforded victims an opportunity to express the human-rights violations they endured. On a quasi-therapeutic level, this opportunity functioned as a process of unburdening for survivors and perpetrators alike.

Third, the TRC granted reparations, as well as the rehabilitation and restoration of human and civil dignity, to those whose human rights had been violated. The provision of reparatory compensation for suffering, albeit small, enabled people to feel that their reality had been acknowledged and had not been in vain.

Fourth, amnesty was offered to perpetrators of gross human-rights violations on both sides if they fully disclosed the relevant facts about such acts committed in the course of pursuing political objectives during the period of conflict. From the point of view of the need to reconcile and heal the nation, the amnesty provision was, perhaps, the most important. Those who came before the amnesty hearings and revealed all to the satisfaction of the judge received amnesty, provided their acts were deemed to fall within the parameters of the Promotion of National Unity and Reconciliation Act. Thus, those who committed murder and torture received amnesty as long as such action was in pursuance of an objective associated with the political conflict of the day and the perpetrator was judged to have disclosed fully. An apology was not a necessary condition for amnesty.

The Promotion of National Unity and Reconciliation Act did not lay down the details of how the TRC process would play out. However, once it had been established, it was inevitable that both religious and psychological discourse and practices would become evident in the proceedings. For example, the Chair, Desmond Tutu, was an Anglican Archbishop and his deputy, Alex Boraine, had once been a Methodist minister. Both were anti-Apartheid veterans and champions of reconciliation.

Following a middle–out strategy, psychologists sought to shape the TRC process in a manner that would achieve its objectives while being as psychologically effective as possible within the constraints of the Promotion of National Unity and Reconciliation Act. Psychologists and social workers were among the commissioners and played an important role in the design of sensitive procedures for the hearings. The TRC staff, many of whom were trained lay counselors, prepared victims for the hearings, supported them during their testimony, and debriefed them afterwards. The TRC did not have a budget for therapeutic follow-up of survivors, which became a major concern during the hearings when the extent of their re-traumatization became apparent. The service gap was filled by a small band of volunteer mental-health workers from several professions, NGOs, and religious institutions. However, the services provided were hopelessly inadequate to the task of supporting those who came before the TRC. More than 25,000 people applied for classification as victims of gross human-rights violations and about half actually appeared before the TRC. The lesson for future endeavors of this kind is that mental-health services must be provided from the outset and a budget set aside for this purpose.

The involvement of psychologists in the TRC is not at first glance a macro-intervention and the activities described previously are not macro-level. Psychologists did, however, play a role in more macro-level processes. One example is in the reparations process. A psychologist commissioner was appointed to head the Reparations Committee. The mandate of that body was to design an appropriate reparation policy and determine the form and level of compensation to be awarded to those classified as victims of gross human-rights violations under the Promotion of National Unity and Reconciliation Act. Many challenges needed to be addressed. The standard actuarial approach used in claims for compensation could not be relied on, as very limited funds were available. There was concern about an individualized approach to compensation that would be seen to benefit a few, rather than contribute to the spirit of nation building that was integral to the TRC. Also, the definition of a gross violation of human rights was quite narrow; it covered torture, killing, and associated acts of violence. The vast majority of the population had suffered under the everyday banality of Apartheid. All had suffered the indignity of statutory race classification. Millions had been forced out of their homes and dumped in the *veldt*. They had no recourse to the TRC. Finally, it was known that many victims did not come forward to testify and could not therefore access the reparations.

The Reparations Committee wisely endorsed a multi-level approach to reparations that mirrored elements found in public-health interventions. It was decided that rebuilding communities should form a key component of reparation wherever possible, with the notion that reparation should benefit communities as much as possible. Thus, in areas that had suffered severely (e.g., where many had been killed), a memorial would be built or a new clinic or school erected, often named in memory of those who had given their lives. This approach recognized the many in the community who had suffered but might not be eligible for personal compensation. At an individual level, financial compensation was equalized to the extent possible across those who qualified, although the long delay caused much anger and pain for claimants.

Another psychologically important element of the TRC was that it sought to establish the fate or whereabouts of the victims, as mandated by the Promotion of National Unity and Reconciliation Act. Many loved ones had "disappeared" during the anti-Apartheid struggle. It was unknown whether they were dead or alive. The TRC provided an opportunity for survivors to reach closure and even to face those responsible for these disappearances. The reparation process made provisions for the proper burial of loved ones, whose remains were discovered following disclosures made by those seeking amnesty, and for other forms of compensation, such as contribution to the education of children whose parents or guardians had died.

The TRC generated a veritable research industry as both local and international scholars descended on the process and the material it generated, leading some skeptics to call it an academic "feeding frenzy." South African psychologists contributed to the TRC Report, and a few continue to play an important role in unraveling some of the most important questions raised by the TRC. For example, what psychological factors, at both an individual and group level, make politically oppressive and racist systems like Apartheid possible? Particularly important work has brought a psychological lens to bear on the processes that underlie individual and collective perpetration of gross human-rights violations (Foster, 2000a, 2000b; Foster, Haupt, & de Beer, 2005). Inquiries such as these seek to provide "as complete a picture as possible of the causes, nature and extent of the gross violations of human rights ... including the antecedents, circumstances and context of such violations ... as well as the perspectives of those responsible for commissions of violations" (Promotion of National Unity and Reconciliation Act, Section 3[1a]).

The conclusions of these scholars, based on their inspection of the TRC records and interviews with perpetrators, reveals the politically and socially embedded nature of the heinous acts that were committed. Although it is obviously necessary to understand the individual psychological make-up and history of the perpetrator, this is not enough. There is little evidence that most perpetrators suffered from psychopathology. Foster (2000a) argues that the role of politics and political identity in justifying violence is crucial to appreciate. Political leaders and their parties played a key role in constructing enemies, which in the case of South Africa were those fighting for democracy or justifying power inequalities, such as Apartheid. When normalized through the ideological messages perpetuated by the school system and the church, as they were in South Africa (Dawes & Finchilescu, 2002), and coupled with polarized group identities, the stage is set for the dehumanization of "the Other" and acceptance of the necessity for the assertion of power, including, if need be, murder in order to protect society.

The South African TRC has inspired others around the world (e.g., Chile, Rwanda). From a psychological perspective, perhaps its greatest value has been the opportunity to deepen our understanding of the psychology of evil and the fact that we have to bring several disciplinary lenses to bear on this phenomenon. Whether the TRC had a positive outcome for South African society as a means of addressing conflict and forging reconciliation is difficult to determine. Obviously, it is difficult to separate the influence of the TRC from the many statutory processes enacted after 1994 that were designed to bring social justice to the country. These are too numerous to mention, but include a strong rights-based constitution, a constitutional court, and mechanisms for land restitution for the dispossessed. Recent work by political scientists (e.g., Gibson, 2004) suggests that, overall, the TRC has been a vehicle of reconciliation.

Interactive Problem Solving

An excellent example of the middle–out strategy for achieving macro-social impact comes from the pioneering work of Herbert Kelman (1972, 1996, 1997, 2004) on interactive problem solving in the Israeli–Palestinian conflict. Kelman has shown how that conflict is animated by existential fear, historic grievances on both sides, and a deepening social divide that cannot be overcome through formal peace agreements alone. In fact, he argues that, since this is a conflict between two societies, the members of which demonize and avoid each other, it is highly unlikely that, without the aid of specific interventions, the parties will be able to achieve either formal agreements or a willingness of their respective societies to stop fighting. Further, official diplomacy has limited ability to resolve internal conflicts since external political pressures on both sides constrain negotiation. Top leaders are frequently unwilling to meet with the other side out of fear of tacitly legitimating them. If they do meet, they may feel highly constrained in what they can say and consider without evoking backlash from external constituencies. What is needed is a method of unofficial diplomacy that sets the stage for official diplomacy and improves relations between the warring societies before, during, and following formal negotiations and mediations.

Building on the work of Australian diplomat John Burton and others (Fisher, 1997), Kelman has convened and facilitated over 25 years a significant number of workshops, most of which have brought together three to six Israelis with an equal number of Palestinians for two-and-a-half days of private, off-the-record dialogue. The participants are well-respected influentials, who hold no official positions, exhibit moderateness and openness, have the freedom from outside pressures to explore various options, and are likely to assume official political leadership positions. The meetings are conducted in a neutral country, typically in an academic setting, which is conducive to reflection and open discussion. Consistent with the emphasis on building positive relationships, the participants live in the same place and interact informally over meals and during free time.

The structured meetings engage the participants in careful analytic, problem-solving discussions conducted under rules, such as no blaming or ad hominem comments. Since a key task is to build empathy, the process often begins with each side explaining how they understand the conflict, its history, and its key issues. As one side tells its story, the other side listens and is subsequently asked to play it back, with corrections given for any errors that occur. The corrections lead to a revised playback, creating a cycle that continues until the telling side agrees that the listening side has understood their views well. Next, the process is repeated, with the former listeners and tellers reversing roles. This process of listening not only builds empathy, but also helps each side to see that the others are willing to work hard to achieve a more complete understanding and to accept corrections. This in itself is highly valuable in breaking stereotypes of "the Other" as disinterested in peace and unwilling to work together toward a common goal.

Next, the participants examine the main issues at stake in the conflict, explore their concerns and fears, and identify possible solutions and steps that might help to overcome the psychological and political barriers on both sides. The group process centers not on a clash of ideas, but rather a cooperative analysis of particular problems and the identification of options that meet the needs of both sides. The participants are encouraged to ask "what if" questions and to explore options not under discussion publicly. In a variation of the method, the participants become part of a series of ongoing workshops that examine particular issues such as refugees' right of return. Conducted privately, these workshops, too, have enabled the participants to generate and analyze carefully bold options for reducing the conflict.

A significant part of the methodology is that, following the workshops, the participants return to their respective communities and share the fruits of their learning. The workshop participants embody the well-tested social psychological principle that, in regard to attitude change, the communication source is often as significant as the message itself (Hovland, Janis, & Kelley, 1953). Because the workshop participants are highly respected, they are in a good position to influence peers and members of the community, who may be more willing to listen to someone they trust and respect than to others whom they do not know. As rising leaders, they are also well positioned to share their experiences and ideas with leaders who occupy high positions in their respective societies. In this manner, their communication and influence extends both downward and upward as well as horizontally.

To date, the workshops have been instrumental in establishing positive communication and empathy, altering dehumanizing stereotypes of "the Other," and stimulating constructive dialogue across conflict lines in highly segregated societies. They have also helped set the stage for official negotiations and for official back-channel secret meetings, such as those which led to the Oslo Accords. Peace-building methods have faced a much more difficult context following the eruption of Intifada II in September 2000 and the bitter fighting on both sides since then. Nevertheless, the workshops have been useful in planting seeds that may germinate when conditions improve.

Community Empowerment and Capacity Building

Macro-level interventions also consist of community-based programs implemented on a large scale in a manner that contributes to peace and social justice. Because the majority world remains torn by armed conflicts that take a heavy toll on civilians, this section focuses on armed conflicts, examining psychologically informed programs constructed by and with communities living in the midst of war or struggling to convert a fragile ceasefire into a durable peace.

In the Democratic Republic of Congo (DRC), a protracted war that has killed over three million people and has engaged armies from numerous surrounding countries has had a profound impact on children, many of whom are recruited by force into armed groups (Coalition to Stop the Use of Child Soldiers, 2004). In DRC, girl soldiers are abused sexually on a wide scale, as occurs in many other conflicts (McKay & Mazurana, 2004). In addition to being a blatant violation of children's rights, the exploitation of children as soldiers is a mechanism for extending armed conflicts (Singer, 2005; Wessells, 2002). In fact, troop-hungry commanders frequently replenish their depleted armies through forced recruitment of children. Although the fighting continues in DRC, a high priority is to get children out of armed groups and to enable them to transition into civilian life.

To address this situation, Save the Children/UK has implemented a large-scale program in partnership with local communities (Verhey, 2003). On escape or release from armed groups, former child soldiers are taken to interim care centers, where they receive basic health care, protection, and psychosocial support through peer dialogues and participation in expressive activities, cooperative games, and nonformal education. The expressive activities and other aspects of the centers are selected and developed through a process of consultation and dialogue between the center staff, most of whom were from DRC, and local people. This collaboration with local people is vital for winning support of the local villagers, many of whom initially fear that child soldiers pose a danger to their families, insuring that the center's activities are culturally appropriate, and engaging local help in tracing the location of the former child soldiers' families. For former child soldiers, family tracing and reunification are potent forms of psychosocial support, ones that African families are eager to implement.

Because the risks of child recruitment and re-recruitment were high, Save the Children worked in partnership with local villages to construct Community Child Protection Networks (CCPN), in which local people organized themselves to discuss all forms of abuse against children and steps that can be taken to prevent abuse. Using a strategy of tapping into existing grassroots networks, a typical CCPN consisted of 25 to 40 people and included women, health workers, teachers, religious leaders, and local authorities. Following a capacity-building approach, CCPN members received training on how to prevent and report various abuses to children, and they developed projects aimed at getting children out of armed groups and reintegrating former child soldiers into civilian life. In numerous cases, CCPN members negotiated directly with local commanders to secure the release of child soldiers. In others, they helped to construct village schools and create job opportunities of the kind that enable former child soldiers to acquire needed life skills, earn a living, and enter civilian social roles. Often, effective psychosocial support for the reintegration process occurs not through counseling, but through steps that enable young people to find a place in their communities and to function well in culturally constructed roles. Although it is too early to discern the wider impact of such programs, the protection offered to children is significant, and there is hope that CCPNs will enable communities to build peace at a grassroots level.

Psychosocial support for former child soldiers is also a key part of post-conflict peace building since, following the signing of a ceasefire, there remain large numbers of former child soldiers who have no jobs, vocational skills, or education. Lacking support, many youth turn to crime and banditry and, in regions such as West Africa, many become mercenaries in neighboring countries (Human Rights Watch, 2005). In this respect, the reintegration of former child soldiers on a national scale is a vital element in the wider task of rebuilding society for peace.

To address this task in Angola, which by 1996 had suffered decades of internal war, CCF/Angola developed a four-province program through a consultative process between local villages and CCF's all-Angolan staff. Initially, the villages were reluctant to discuss child soldiers since most of the people under 18 years of age who were in armed groups were 14 to 17 years old. In rural Angola, as in many parts of sub-Saharan Africa, people in this age range are regarded as adults since they have completed the culturally defined rites of passage into adulthood and perform adult roles. Rather than imposing on local villages the human rights and international legal standards that define childhood as ending at 18 years, CCF staff took an approach based on dialogue and negotiation. Since local people agreed that 14- to 17-year-olds should not be part of armed groups, but should be engaged in positive tasks, such as starting families and caring for land and animals, they decided that it would be useful to develop community-reintegration supports for people who under international law were regarded as former child soldiers. An agreement was also reached to speak not of child soldiers, but of "underage soldiers."

This demonstration of respect for local cultural norms was part of a wider process of working with local cultural leaders and resources in designing and developing the program. Before the program had been designed, CCF staff had learned through a related program that some child soldiers regarded spiritual stresses as one of their greatest challenges. One former child soldier who had problems sleeping and concentrating, and who exhibited many symptoms of PTSD said he could not sleep because he was visited at night by the spirit of a man he had killed. The spirit asked, "Why did you do this to me?" According to local views, the boy was spiritually polluted, that is, contaminated by an angry spirit. Interestingly, both the boy and the members of his village viewed this not as an individual problem, but as a collective problem in which the spiritual pollution had caused a breach in the contract between the living community and ancestors, whose protection and support is necessary for well-being. Bringing an angry spirit into the village was believed to bring misfortune, in forms such as crop failures and bad health, not only on the boy, but also on his family and members of the community. Aside from the veracity of these beliefs, there was little question that they posed a significant obstacle to reintegration.

Interviews with local healers, elders, and underage soldiers indicated that the conduct of traditional purification rituals could purge the angry spirits, restore harmony between the living community and ancestors, and open the door for the reintegration of former soldiers. Typically, the rituals include demarcation of a safe space by burning special herbs, ritual washings and inhalation of vapors believed to purge bad spirits, offering a sacrifice to the angry spirit, and asking forgiveness (Wessells & Monteiro, 2004). At the end of the ceremony, as the former soldier steps across the threshold of the space where the ceremony was conducted and, as the community looks on, the healer announces, "this boy's life as a soldier has ended, and he now rejoins our people and community."

Preliminary research, which indicated no unethical aspects of the rituals and discernible benefits in terms of enabling both the soldier and community members to feel it was now safe to interact because the spiritual pollution had ended, led to a decision to make traditional healing part of the reintegration program. This decision valorized local cultural traditions, which, though radically different from Western supports, such as counseling, offer psychosocial support by reinforcing a sense of continuity and safety following overwhelming experience. Also, local people said that the support of an international organization for traditional healing boosted their confidence in their own culture, which they had learned to regard as inferior through hundreds of years of colonial domination, and elevated hopes that they could solve their problems.

In addition to traditional healing, the project empowered local communities to receive returning child soldiers and to support their reintegration. At the heart of the empowerment process were *activistas*, local activists for social justice who were widely respected for their previous work with children. The *activistas* received training on how children have been affected by their war experiences and how to implement various project elements, such as community sensitization, family tracing and reintegration, collaboration with traditional healers, and small income-generating projects. Following training, the *activistas* worked with local leaders and communities to weaken stereotypes regarding former child soldiers and to create a welcoming environment. They also facilitated the tracing and family reunification process for over 2,000 former child soldiers, many of whom participated in welcoming ceremonies and cleansing rituals on their return home. Ongoing psychosocial support was provided through peer-group discussions and participation in normalizing activities, such as soccer games. Because the returning soldiers indicated that one of their greatest needs was to be able to earn a living, the *activistas* organized skills training through local artisans and provided small loans for launching small businesses, such as bakeries. Although this work was interrupted by another wave of war in late 1998, it illustrates that psychosocial support on a large scale need not involve outside Western approaches alone, but can blend local and imported tools and approaches. In fact, large-scale programs for psychosocial support are most likely to succeed when they build on local strengths. This lesson serves as a poignant reminder to psychologists about the importance of taking an anthropological approach aimed at learning about and making use of local cultural resources, rather than imposing programs developed elsewhere.

Addressing HIV/AIDS

An urgent question is how to address the HIV/AIDS pandemic worldwide. The enormity of this question is highly evident in Africa, where approximately 12.3 million children have become orphans due to HIV/AIDS (UNICEF, 2004). In some villages in areas hit hardest by HIV/AIDS, all the people over 20 years of age have died, leaving many children to live in child-headed households. The world has only begun to discern the psychological and social burdens imposed on children by the combination of losses, watching parents and loved ones die, being infected themselves by HIV/AIDS, and struggling to survive in an environment saturated with poverty and offering few opportunities (see chapter 1, this volume, on the link between poverty and disease).

Although HIV/AIDS has been recognized as a profound health issue and a significant development issue, it is also an important peace issue (Price-Smith & Daly, 2004). As economic hardships increase due to increased health burdens, worker illness, and deaths of productive workers, local people may experience a mixture of hopelessness and disaffection that heightens their susceptibility to political manipulation through promises of better times. As death thins the ranks of police, business people, and civilian agencies, local communities become less able to resist the rise of armed groups and organized crime.

To address this issue, psychologists have contributed to the development of macro-level programs designed to support orphans and prevent the spread of HIV/AIDS. A case in point is the COPE program implemented by Save the Children/U.S. in Malawi, where the HIV/AIDS epidemic had nearly single-handedly decreased the average life expectancy from 52 years in 1990 to 37 years in 1999 (Mann, 2002). Before the program began in the late 1990s, the impact on children was staggering. Nearly 46% of new infections in Malawi occurred among young people between the ages of 15 and 24 years. To cope with their difficult economic situations, many orphans had dropped out of school in order to work. Most orphans faced very difficult conditions due to stigmatization, lack of access to basic resources, and a lack of social and emotional support. Desperate to survive, many girls engaged in commercial sex work, which helped to spread the disease.

To support orphans and prevent the spread of HIV/AIDS, the COPE program used a mixture of bottom–up and top–down processes aimed at creating a multi-level safety net. The bottom–up process entailed community-sensitization dialogues among village members, who then established committees at the village level. The top–down component consisted of the establishment of structures at the district and community levels that the government and UNICEF had established to deal with the crisis (Mann, 2002). The program trained committee members on the effects of HIV/AIDS, holistic support for affected children, children's rights, appropriate living arrangements for orphans (Tolfree, 2003), and strategies for raising awareness about HIV/AIDS and its prevention. At the grassroots levels, village committees organized community-based child-care centers, supervised recreational activities, and organized community gardens to provide a steady supply of food to affected households, home visits for terminally ill people, and peer counseling for youth. They also organized health screening, income-generating activities, and prevention activities by youth, such as the performance of dramas about and HIV/AIDS and ways to promote life skills that aid psychosocial adjustment.

After the village committees had been activated and had become reasonably effective, the staff turned its attention increasingly to building the capacity of the community and district committees. A key task of the community committees was to monitor the situation of orphans, insuring that those who lived with members of their extended family or had been placed in foster care did not suffer discrimination and abuse. The community committees also raised awareness of the causes of the epidemic and means of preventing it, arguing against myths such as the belief of some older men that having sex with a virgin would cure them of AIDS. At the district level, committees networked with wider initiatives and linked with government agencies in order to institutionalize the system and ensure the responsiveness of the government to the issues.

In its first six years, the program assisted over 10,000 orphans and over 2,500 home-care patients. Community members demonstrated greater awareness of the causes of the epidemic, the problems orphans face, and appropriate means of supporting orphans. Having taken steps to de-stigmatize the issue, communities had become much more open in discussing how to prevent HIV/AIDS. Orphans had achieved a greater voice and participation in decisions that affected them and said they felt more hopeful about the future. Youth, too, said they had learned the value of prevention and felt more positively toward the future as a result of the program. Although the program faces challenges, such as burnout associated with working with large numbers of HIV/AIDS affected people, it offers one model of how to address the problem on a large scale.

Improving Child Outcomes in Poverty Environments

The HIV/AIDS epidemic and the massive insults to child development caused by poverty in developing regions of the world provide a strong impetus both for scaling up psychosocial interventions and for evaluating outcomes carefully.

In a seminal paper published at the start of the new millennium, Lerner, Fisher, and Weinberg (2000) noted growing interest in what they term applied developmental science (ADS), which seeks "to advance the integration of developmental knowledge with actions—policies and programs—that promote development and/or enhance the life chances of vulnerable children and families. Through this integration, ADS may become a major means to foster a science for and of the people (and) may contribute to social justice" (p. 11). The emergence of ADS as an approach to doing scientifically rigorous research in the interests of social transformation is very timely. Appropriately, it stresses that attempts to address the situation of children and families at risk must be underpinned by the best evidence, theory, and methods that are available in collaboration across disciplines, policy-making entities, and communities so as to ask the right questions and find effective solutions.

As we have noted, psychosocial programs are commonly thought of as individualized and directly psychological in nature. If we are to go to scale with interventions designed to produce positive psychosocial outcomes for children in the context of challenges such as the AIDS pandemic and the major threats to child development posed by deep and enduring poverty, we often must proceed via indirect routes.

We conclude this section of the chapter with reference to a highly promising ongoing macro intervention that is evidence-based, rigorously evaluated, and designed to support families in poverty and improve child outcomes. Although its primary objective is poverty reduction, it seeks to achieve human-capital development as a parallel outcome. An exemplar of ADS, it takes its evidence base from the field of early childhood development (Young, 2002; Zigler, 1994).

The intervention is known as *Opitunidades* (formerly known as *Progresa*). The program has its roots in Mexico, where it has been running since 1997. *Opitunidades* was evaluated in a study conducted by the World Bank in 500 communities that were randomly assigned to an experimental group that received a set of conditional grants and a control condition that received conventional social assistance. The study demonstrated that considerable gains in child health and education can be achieved through the provision of conditional cash transfers and nutritional supplements to caregivers who agree to participate in a series of activities that improve child survival and promote child development while also benefiting from poverty relief (Gertler, 2000; Schultz, 2000a, 2000b). For example, in the Mexican case, caregivers are provided with conditional grants if they attend antenatal clinics and parenting classes. Additional grants are available to those who ensure that their children are immunized, attend school, and participate in health-promotion activities. Apart from significant reductions in child mortality, outcomes have improved dramatically in targeted areas, such as school attendance. This type of systematic outcome research, which weds science and practice, is greatly needed to expand the base of proven, psychologically informed macro-level interventions.

CONCLUSION

A central assumption behind this chapter is that, if we are to tackle the serious problems before us, we have to think in terms of the large-scale, rather than small, individualized projects that have characterized the discipline of psychology for decades. As noted at several points in this chapter, we must also take a multidisciplinary approach.

Psychologists stand to contribute much through their engagement in macro-social interventions, and one can reasonably expect this to be an area of considerable interest and growth in the decades ahead. If pursued with ethical and cultural sensitivity and with an eye toward the collective good, these macro-social interventions offer psychologists unusual opportunities to address real-world issues, engage in political- and social-change processes, and most importantly, make a positive difference in the world. Perhaps, it is time to not only "give psychology away," as George Miller had suggested, but also to give it away on a large scale and in ways that address the pressing issues of our time.

RECOMMENDED READINGS

Christie, D., Wagner, R., & Winter, D. (Eds.). (2001). *Peace, conflict, and violence: Peace psychology for the 21st century.* Upper Saddle River, NJ: Prentice-Hall.
Foster, D., Haupt, P., & de Beer, M. (2006). *The theater of violence.* Cape Town: Human Services Research Council Press.
Gertler, P. (2000). *Final report: The impact of progress on health.* Washington, DC: International Food Policy Research Institute.

Gielen, U. P., Fish, J., & Draguns, J. G. (Eds.). (2004). *Handbook of culture, therapy, and healing.* Mahwah, NJ: Lawrence Erlbaum Associates.

Machel, G. (2001). *The impact of war on children.* Cape Town: David Philip.

Miller, K., & Rasco, L. (Eds.). (2004). *From clinic to community: Ecological approaches to refugee mental health.* Upper Saddle River, NJ: Prentice-Hall.

Young, M. (2002). *From early child development to human development: Investing in our children's future.* Washington, DC: World Bank.

Zigler, E. (1994). Reshaping early childhood intervention to be a more effective weapon against poverty. *American Journal of Community Psychology, 22,* 37–47.

REFERENCES

Ajzen, I. (1991). The theory of planned behavior. *Organizational Behavior and Human Decision Processes, 50,* 179–211.

Anderson, B. (1996). *Mythology and the tolerance of the Javanese* (2nd ed.). Ithaca, NY: Cornell Modern Indonesia Project.

Aptekar, L. (2004). The changing developmental dynamics of children in particularly difficult circumstances: Examples of street and war-traumatized children. In U. P. Gielen & J. Roopnarine (Eds.), *Childhood and adolescence: Cross-cultural perspectives and applications* (pp. 377–410). Westport, CA: Praeger.

Bowlby, J. (1979). *The making and breaking of affectional bonds.* London: Tavistock.

Boyden, J. (1997). Childhood and the policy makers: A comparative perspective on the globalization of childhood. In A. James & A. Prout (Eds.), *Constructing and reconstructing childhood: Contemporary issues in the sociological study of childhood* (pp. 184–215). London: Falmer.

Brown v. Board of Education, 347 U.S. 483 (1954).

Campbell, C. (2003). *Letting them die: Why HIV/AIDS prevention programs fail.* Oxford, UK: James Currey.

Christie, D., Wagner, R., & Winter, D. (Eds.). (2001). *Peace, conflict, and violence: Peace psychology for the 21st century.* Upper Saddle River, NJ: Prentice-Hall.

Clark, K., Chein, I., & Cook, S. (2004). The effects of segregation and the consequences of desegregation: A (September 1952) social science statement in the *Brown v. Board of Education of Topeka* Supreme Court case. *American Psychologist, 59,* 495–501. (Original work published 1952)

Clark, K., & Clark, M. (1947). Racial identification and preferences in Negro children. In T. Newcomb & E. Hartley (Eds.), *Readings in social psychology* (pp. 169–178). New York: Holt.

Coalition to Stop the Use of Child Soldiers. (2004). *Child soldiers global report 2004.* London: Author.

Dawes, A., & Cairns, E. (1998). The Machel Study: Dilemmas of cultural sensitivity and universal rights of children. *Peace and Conflict: Journal of Peace Psychology, 4,* 335–348.

Dawes, A., & Donald, D. (1994). *Childhood and adversity: Psychological perspectives from South African research.* Cape Town: David Philip.

Dawes, A., & Finchilescu, G. (2002). What's changed? South African adolescents' racial attitudes between 1992 and 1996. *Childhood: A Global Journal of Child Research, 9*, 147–165.

Deutsch, M., & Chein, I. (1948). The psychological effects of enforced segregation: A survey of social science opinion. *Journal of Psychology, 26*, 286–287.

Earth Charter Commission. (2000). *Earth charter.* Retrieved July 1, 2005, from http://www..earthcharter.org

Eaton, L., Flisher, A. J., & Aaro, L. E. (2003). Unsafe sexual behavior in South African youth. *Social Science and Medicine, 56*, 149–165.

Erikson, E. (1963). *Childhood and society.* New York: Norton.

Eyber, C., & Ager, A. (2004). Researching young people's experiences of war: Participatory methods and the trauma discourse in Angola. In J. Boyden & J. de Berry (Eds.), *Children and youth on the front line: Ethnography, armed conflict and displacement* (pp. 189–208). New York: Berghahn.

Fine, M. (2004). The power of the *Brown v. Board of Education* decision: Theorizing threats to sustainability. *American Psychologist, 59*, 502–510.

Fisher, R. (1997). *Interactive conflict resolution.* Syracuse, NY: Syracuse University Press.

Foster, D. (2000a). The Truth and Reconciliation Commission and understanding perpetrators. *South African Journal of Psychology, 30*, 2–9.

Foster, D. (2000b). Entitlement as explanation for perpetrators' actions. *South African Journal of Psychology, 30*, 10–13.

Foster, D., Haupt, P., & de Beer, M. (2005). *The theater of violence.* Cape Town: Human Services Research Council Press.

Gertler, P. (2000). *Final report: The impact of progress on health.* Washington, DC: International Food Policy Research Institute.

Gibson, J. L. (2004). *Overcoming Apartheid.* Cape Town: Human Services Research Council Press.

Grossman, K., Grossmann, K., & Waters, E. (2005). *Attachment from infancy to adulthood.* New York: Guilford.

Honwana, A. (1997). Healing for peace: Traditional healers and post-war reconstruction in Southern Mozambique. *Peace and Conflict: Journal of Peace Psychology, 3*, 293–305.

Hovland, C., Janis, I., & Kelley, H. (1953). *Communication and persuasion.* New Haven, CT: Yale University Press.

Human Rights Watch. (2005). *Youth, poverty and blood: The lethal legacy of West Africa's regional warriors.* New York: Author.

Hunter, S., & Williamson, J. (2002). *Children on the brink: Strategies to support children isolated by HIV/AIDS.* Washington, DC: U.S. Aid for International Development.

Interagency Working Group on Separated and Unaccompanied Children. (2004). *Psychosocial care and protection of tsunami-affected children.* Retrieved July 1, 2005, from http://www.iicrd.org/cap/node/view/383

Kağitçibaşi, Ç. (1996). *Family and human development across cultures: A view from the other side.* Hillsdale, NJ: Lawrence Erlbaum Associates.

Kao, G., & Thompson, J. (2003). Racial and ethnic stratification in educational achievement and attainment. *Annual Review of Sociology, 29*, 417–442.

Kelman, H. C. (Ed.). (1965). *International behavior: A social-psychological analysis.* New York: Holt, Rinehart & Winston.

Kelman, H. C. (1972). The problem-solving workshop in conflict resolution. In R. L. Merritt (Ed.), *Communication in international politics* (pp. 168–204). Urbana: University of Illinois Press.

Kelman, H. C. (1996). The interactive problem-solving approach. In C. Crocker, F. Hampson, & P. Aall (Eds.), *Managing global chaos* (pp. 501–520). Washington, DC: U.S. Institute of Peace.

Kelman, H. C. (1997). Group processes in the resolution of international conflicts: Experiences from the Israeli-Palestinian case. *American Psychologist, 52,* 212–220.

Kelman, H. C. (2004). The nature of international conflict: A social-psychological perspective. In H. Langholtz & C. Stout (Eds.), *The psychology of diplomacy* (pp. 59–77). Westport, CT: Praeger.

Kostelny, K. (2004). What about the girls? *Cornell International Law Journal, 37,* 505–512.

Lederach, J. (1997). *Building peace: Sustainable reconciliation in divided societies.* Washington, DC: U.S. Institute of Peace.

Lee, J., & Sue, S. (2001). Clinical psychology and culture. In D. Matsumoto (Ed.), *The handbook of culture and psychology* (pp. 287–305). New York: Oxford University Press.

Lerner, R. M., Fisher C. B., & Weinberg, R. A. (2000). Toward a science for and of the people. Promoting society through the application of developmental science. *Child Development, 71,* 11–20.

Lopez, S., & Guarnaccia, P. (2000). Cultural psychopathology: Uncovering the social world of mental illness. *Annual Review of Psychology, 51,* 571–598.

Mann, G. (2002). *Family matters: The care and protection of children affected by HIV/AIDS in Malawi.* Washington, DC: Save the Children Federation.

Marsella, A., Bornemann, T., Ekblad, S., & Orley, J. (Eds.). (1994). *Amidst peril and pain: The mental health and well-being of the world's refugees.* Washington, DC: American Psychological Association.

McKay, S., & Mazurana, D. (2004). *Where are the girls? Girls in fighting forces in Northern Uganda, Sierra Leone, and Mozambique: Their lives during and after war.* Montréal: International Center for Human Rights and Democratic Development.

Osman, T. (1985). The traditional Malay socio-political worldview. In T. Osman (Ed.), *Malaysian world view* (pp. 46–75). Singapore: Institute of Southeast Asian Studies.

Parliament of the Republic of South Africa. (1995). *Promotion of National Unity and Reconciliation Act* (No. 34). Retrieved July 29, 2005, from http://www.doj.gov.za/trc/legal/act9534.htm

Pettigrew, T. (2004). Justice deferred: A half century after *Brown v. Board of Education. American Psychologist, 59,* 521–529.

Plessy v. Ferguson, 163 U.S. (1896).

Price-Smith, A., & Daly, J. (2004). *Downward spiral: HIV/AIDS, state capacity, and political conflict in Zimbabwe. Peaceworks No. 53.* Washington, DC: U.S. Institute of Peace.

Roopnarine, J., & Gielen, U. P. (Eds.). (2005). *Families in global perspective.* Boston: Allyn & Bacon.

Schultz, T. P. (2000a). *Impact of PROGRESA on school attendance rates in the sampled population*. Washington, DC: International Food Policy Research Institute.

Schultz, T. P. (2000b). *School subsidies for the poor: Evaluating a Mexican strategy for reducing poverty*. Washington, DC: International Food Policy Research Institute.

Shisana O., & Simbayi, L. (2002). *Nelson Mandela/HSRC study of HIV/AIDS: South African national HIV prevalence, behavioral risks and mass media household survey*. Cape Town: Human Sciences Research Council Press.

Shweder, R. (1990). Cultural psychology: What is it? In J. Stigler, R. Shweder, & G. Herdt (Eds.), *Cultural psychology: Essays on comparative human development* (pp. 1–43). New York: Cambridge University Press.

Singer, P. (2005). *Children at war*. New York: Pantheon.

The Sphere Project. (1997). *Standards for intervention in humanitarian emergencies*. Retrieved October 1, 2004, from http://www.sphereproject.org

Tolfree, D. (2003). *Community based care for separated children*. Stockholm: Save the Children Sweden.

Triandis, H. (2001). Individualism and collectivism: Past, present, and future. In D. Matsumoto (Ed.), *The handbook of culture and psychology* (pp. 35–50). New York: Oxford University Press.

UNICEF. (2004). *Children on the brink 2004: A joint report of new orphan estimates and a framework for action*. New York: Author.

United Nations General Assembly. (1989). *Convention on the Rights of the Child* [GA resolution 44/25].

United Nations General Assembly. (1996). *Impact of armed conflict on children* [GA document A/51/306 and Add. 1].

Verhey, B. (2003). *Going home: Demobilizing and reintegrating child soldiers in the Democratic Republic of Congo*. London: Save the Children/UK.

Wessells, M. G. (1999). Culture, power, and community: Intercultural approaches to psychosocial assistance and healing. In K. Nader, N. Dubrow, & B. Stamm (Eds.), *Honoring differences: Cultural issues in the treatment of trauma and loss* (pp. 267–282). New York: Taylor and Francis.

Wessells, M. (2002). Recruitment of children as soldiers in sub-Saharan Africa: An ecological analysis. In L. Mjoset & S. Van Holde (Eds.), *The comparative study of conscription in the armed forces: Vol. 20 (Comparative Social Research)* (pp. 237–254). Amsterdam: Elsevier.

Wessells, M. G., & Monteiro, C. (2004). Healing the wounds following protracted conflict in Angola: A community-based approach to assisting war-affected children. In U. P. Gielen, J. Fish, & J. G. Draguns (Eds.), *Handbook of culture, therapy, and healing* (pp. 321–341). Mahwah, NJ: Lawrence Erlbaum Associates.

Young, M. (2002). *From early child development to human development: Investing in our children's future*. Washington, DC: World Bank.

Zigler, E. (1994). Reshaping early childhood intervention to be a more effective weapon against poverty. *American Journal of Community Psychology, 22*, 37–47.

10

Toward a Global Professionalization of Psychology

Jean L. Pettifor
University of Calgary

INTRODUCTION

When my parents immigrated to western Canada at the beginning of the last century, it was unlikely that they would ever see their families of origin again. When I was a child my world consisted of the family farm, the local town (population 500), the grain elevators, and the railway station. I could see the railway tracks vanishing on the horizon, and I knew that these tracks must lead to some unknown world beyond. When I became a teacher and a psychologist, my world broadened, but still was contained within close geographical boundaries. Today, the revolution in transportation and communication provides worldwide access to information in ways that are almost beyond belief. It has affected every aspect of our lives, hopefully for the better, but still with many challenges.

In accepting the challenge to write this chapter, I was initially overwhelmed by the amount of information to which I have access and my limited capacity to absorb, experience, and integrate it all. Valuable as scholarly publications are in understanding the movement toward a global professionalization of psychology, they do not give a picture of the lived experience of psychologists and those with whom they interact. Ideally, dialogue with professional psychologists worldwide would be a foundation for this chapter.

Global means worldwide. International means across nations. International, therefore, can mean cooperation and communication between two countries, or among several countries, but this is not necessarily worldwide. However, as collaboration spans more and more nations, we move closer to a global professionalization of psychology.

Professional psychology, for the purposes of this chapter, means psychologists serving primarily the needs of individuals, families, groups, and communities. This is in contrast to psychologists who are primarily involved in addressing societal and political issues or who are primarily involved in conducting research. Although professional psychologists may be concerned about social problems and may conduct research and publish to some extent, overall, they are much less likely to do so because these activities are not supported in their place of work.

This chapter on the global professionalization of psychology focuses on two major aspects of standards that are sometimes complementary and sometimes not, namely the *legislated regulation* of the profession and the *development of guidelines for ethical practice*. The development of each is seen as an indicator of progress toward the globalization of the profession. A globalized world for professional psychology must encompass respect for cultural diversity while maintaining a foundation in psychological theory, research, and application. The backdrop for this discussion on the global professionalization of psychology is the observation that the Western world, the English-speaking world, and especially the United States (Draguns, 2001; Stevens & Wedding, 2004) have dominated the psychology agenda and ignored developments in non-Western countries. Fortunately such ethnocentrism is being recognized and is giving way, step by step, to mutual collaboration and understanding.

In the chapter, I discuss:

1. What professional psychologists do.
2. The nature of international professional psychology.
3. The regulation and mobility of professional psychologists.
4. Professional ethics across national boundaries.
5. What we can learn from the international codes of ethics of allied professions.
6. How globalized the world may become for professional psychology.

WHAT DO PSYCHOLOGISTS DO?

A dictionary definition may define psychology as a science dealing with the mind and with mental and emotional responses, or as a science whose purpose is to understand, predict, and change human behavior. The practice of psychology, as described in professional legislation, may include a modification of such statements as "the observation, description, evaluation, interpretation, and/or modification of human behavior by the application of psychological principles, methods, or procedures for the purpose of preventing or eliminating symptomatic, maladaptive, or undesired behavior and of enhancing interpersonal relationships, work and life adjustment, personal effectiveness, behavioral health and mental health" (Association of State and Provincial Psychology Boards, 2001, p. 2). The traditional branches of professional psychology include clinical/counseling, school/educational, and industrial/organizational (work) psychology, with new specialty emphases in such domains as applied gerontology and psychoneuroimmunology. These categories are not mutually exclusive in terms of the professional activities that they subsume. Practice in each of these branches may involve assessment and diagnosis, interventions, consultation, supervision, teaching, and research. Clients may include individuals, couples, families, groups, communities, and organizations. A review of the reported work settings in different countries (Stevens & Wedding, 2004) includes hospitals, clinics, mental health centers, and schools. Military or police settings employ psychologists in substantial numbers in Colombia, Singapore, and Turkey. Psychological testing, counseling, and psychotherapy appear to be common activities worldwide.

Beyond traditional areas of practice others appear, such as (a) political engagement to eradicate female genital mutilation in Kenya (Koinange, 2004); (b) transportation and traffic psychology in Germany (Plath & Eckensberger, 2004) and Turkey (Boratav, 2004); (c) peace building in the areas of conflict resolution, crisis management, mediation, and lobbying in Kenya (Koinange, 2004) and the Philippines (Montiel & Teh, 2004); (d) assisting survivors of political detention, torture, war-rape, and other forms of military atrocities (Montiel & Teh, 2004); (e) establishing joint Israeli–Palestinian projects to defuse ethnic conflict in Israel (Kelman, 1997); (f) counseling clients with HIV/AIDS in Africa and South Asia (Stead, 2004); and (g) working with Mothers of the May Square and other human rights organizations to assist victims of the 1976–1983 military dictatorship in Argentina (Klappenbach, 2004). Psychologists chafe under the dominance and supervision of physicians and psychiatrists in countries such as Argentina, Indonesia, Iran, the Philippines, and Thailand, where psychology is not recognized as an independent profession. With the exceptions of some Arab countries (e.g., Egypt), Japan, and Nigeria, more women than men are training and practicing in psychology. Women are more likely to have applied positions and men to have managerial, administrative, and research ones (Stevens & Wedding, 2004). A review of the gender of those serving in official capacities in international organizations also shows a preponderance of males.

The demands of people in the developing world for psychological interventions to address the multi-faceted contextual realities of their existence (see chapter 8, this volume for a detailed presentation on psychotherapy and related interventions around the globe) are scarcely recognized in the systems established to define the scope of professional practice. Regulatory systems that are established to protect the public appear to reflect two assumptions of Western societies' strong emphasis on individualism: (a) that identified clients have individual problems that need to be diagnosed and treated in order to change client behavior, and (b) psychologists are totally responsible for their own actions and are expected to comply with the rules, independent of the contextual circumstances in which they and their clients find themselves. In both instances the interdependent relationships of individuals with others and the importance of social context appear to be minimized or ignored. For example, in a collectivist culture it may not be possible or desirable to insist on individual consent and individual confidentiality; also, in a climate of poverty and limited resources, it may not be possible to provide the best care for individual clients.

What is the public image of professional psychology in different parts of the world? A clear picture does not emerge from the literature. In North American and European countries, and others such as South Africa and Australia that are generally considered industrialized, relatively well resourced, and politically stable, professional psychology is well established and positively viewed. In most African countries that are impoverished and underdeveloped, professional psychology may be seen as an irrelevant Western import that cannot replace native spiritual healers. Psychologists in a number of countries, which appear to fall between the rich and the poor or to be recovering from political and economic turmoil, may see a need for greatly increased psychological services provided that such services are relevant to addressing local problems and cultural beliefs. The implication is that the public image will depend on how well these needs are met.

INTERNATIONALIZATION OF PSYCHOLOGY:
FACT, FICTION, OR TRANSITION?

Professional psychology may be considered international in the sense that it is growing in all parts of the world and that there is increasing collaboration across national boundaries. Professional psychology may be progressing toward a worldwide status. It also can be argued that scientific psychology is primarily a Western phenomenon. Adair, Coelho, and Luna (2002) report that U.S. psychology has a greater scholarly presence than any other country, including all of the European countries combined when PsycLIT entries, participation in international congresses, and membership in international associations are considered (however, other formulae noted later indicate that there are more professional psychologists in Europe than in the United States). Adair and colleagues reported that psychology has a significant presence in nearly 50 countries, but minimal to none in 82 others, the latter consisting of most developing nations. Draguns (2001) contends that the development of a truly international psychology is obstructed by the massive disregard of contributions that are published in languages other than English. An increasing number of Western psychologists are advocating openness to cooperation and learning from international colleagues. The American Psychological Association (APA) established the Division of International Psychology in 1997 for the purpose of understanding the multidimensional nature of a changing world. The APA lists 94 countries in its Directory of National Psychological Associations. In addition, the APA *Monitor on Psychology* frequently publishes material with international perspectives.

Moghaddam (1987) identified three worlds on the basis of power, resources, and political systems as relevant to the establishment of psychology in a given country. The first world is the United States where resources support a flourishing psychology that is exported to other worlds. The second world comprises other industrialized nations that attempt to compete for attention on the world stage. The third world, which consists of developing countries with meager resources, has imported psychology from the first and second worlds. Moghaddam (1987) and Paranjpe, Ho, and Rieber (1988) saw the third world beginning to challenge the first and second worlds on the global relevancy of their psychologies and to develop relevant third-world indigenous psychologies.

The dilemma for some Western professionals is the fear that cultural adaptation will result in losing the scientific grounding of the discipline in favor of folklore traditions and, in doing so, will lose the identity of the discipline (Bickle, 2004; Okasha, 2000). Another fear is that if psychologists accept cultural beliefs that result in extreme harm or death, they will violate their own professional ethic to serve the well being of others. The internationalization of psychology appears to be in process, neither completely absent nor fully developed, and the internationalization process leads to globalization.

INTERNATIONAL ORGANIZATIONS OF PSYCHOLOGY

Many international psychology organizations promote the exchange of information and ideas among psychologists across different countries especially in areas of academic training and research (Pawlik & d'Ydewalle, 1996; Stevens & Wedding, 2004). Such organizations generally hold regular international congresses, invite scientific papers, publish journals and newsletters, and organize working committees and regional associations (see chapters 2, 3, and 12, this volume, for more details on international psychology organizations).

The International Association of Applied Psychology was established in 1920 to promote the science and practice of applied psychology around the world. It has some 1,500 individual members from more than 80 countries. Most of its work is done through standing committees. The International Union of Psychological Science (IUPsyS) was established in 1951 to exchange ideas and scientific information among psychologists from different countries and, in particular, to organize international congresses and other meetings on subjects of general or special interest in psychology. Membership consists of representatives of psychology organizations. It maintains a large number of initiatives and affiliations to promote the internationalization of scientific and professional psychology.

The International Council of Psychologists was established in 1959 by restructuring the International Council of Women Psychologists that was established in 1941 under the name of the National Council of Women Psychologists for the purpose of promoting women's services for the war effort. The International Council of Psychologists' members are individual psychologists, and the purpose of the organization today is to provide opportunities to share ideas worldwide.

The International Association of Cross-Cultural Psychology was founded in 1972 to facilitate communication among persons interested in a diverse range of issues that involve the intersection of culture and psychology. It has a membership of about 800 from over 85 countries.

Although there is no shortage of international organizations for psychologists, the majority of professional psychologists may either be unaware of them or do not see them as relevant to their practice. Congress programs tend to emphasize scientific presentations on theory and research, and therefore vary in their appeal to professional psychologists. The financial cost of attending international congresses is another deterrent.

Many international associations of interest to professional psychologists also have formed around special practice interests, as may be seen from any list of upcoming conferences, such as cognitive therapy, family therapy, hypnosis, rehabilitation, victims of torture, and the prevention of family violence. Members of such organizations often include psychologists as well as other allied professionals.

REGIONAL ASSOCIATIONS OF PSYCHOLOGY

Regional psychology organizations play an important role in the internationalization of psychology (see chapter 3, this volume). The regional focus provides a greater commonality of interest and availability to larger numbers of participants, but is also open to presentations from worldwide participants.

The European Federation of Psychologists' Associations (EFPA) undertakes many activities on an ongoing basis to promote high standards of practice across European countries, including common standards for professional training and for ethical practice. The Interamerican Society of Psychology (Spanish- and Portuguese-speaking Central and South America) works for the advancement of psychology in Latin American countries. The Association of State and Provincial Psychology Boards (largely Canada and the U.S.) promotes common standards in the regulation of professional psychology. The newly formed Asia–Oceania regional association has the objective of sharing common concerns regarding regulation, advocacy, standards, and ethics. The Middle Eastern Psychologists Network (Sabourin & Knowles, 2004) held their initial meeting in 2003 for psychologists interested in this unique cultural, geographical, and religious region who are also interested in coordinating efforts for continuing education, certification, and skills enhancement through collaboration with international and local experts.

REGULATION AND MOBILITY OF PROFESSIONAL PSYCHOLOGISTS

General

The legislated regulation of professional psychologists, which involves establishing standards that protect the public from harm, is considered the hallmark of a mature profession. Regulation enhances public credibility inasmuch as the criteria for competent and ethical practice are defined and the identity of the profession is established. Functions of the regulatory body normally include establishing academic and experience criteria for entrance to the profession, granting a license or permit to practice, establishing a code of ethics and other practice guidelines, setting continuing competence requirements, implementing disciplinary procedures for investigating and hearing complaints, and sanctioning members who are guilty of professional misconduct. For many years, there have been concerns that barriers exist for psychologists wanting to move from one jurisdiction to another because each jurisdiction sets its own rules. Step by step, this is beginning to change.

Worldwide variations exist on how regulation is undertaken. The United States led the way with the first legislative act to regulate the practice of psychology in North America in Connecticut in 1945. Legislated regulation now exists in all North American jurisdictions and in an increasing number of jurisdictions in Europe and other parts of the world. Some psychology organizations are fully regulated; others have most aspects in place but lack the legislated authority to enforce; and still others remain unregulated. The regulation of psychology in the United States is governed by state legislation, in Canada by provincial or territorial legislation, and in Europe by national legislation. Some regulatory boards are appointed by government, some are elected by their members; in others regulation is administered as a function of government, such as Mexico and the Northwest Territories in Canada. In some countries, regulation may apply only to a specialty area in psychology, such as clinical, but not to other areas of practice. Some regulatory boards apply only to psychology whereas others may govern a group of allied professions.

Association of State and Provincial Psychology Boards

The Association of State and Provincial Psychology Boards (ASPPB), established in 1961, has been a powerful force in the development of common standards and structures for the regulation of professional psychology in Canada and the United States. Today, with a total membership of 62 jurisdictions, the U.S. members outnumber the Canadians by a ratio of approximately 5:1. Although it does not have legal authority over its member jurisdictions, the ASPPB has provided a means for establishing common standards. It has undertaken a wide range of projects, including the establishment of standards for entrance to the profession, the promotion of mobility for practitioners, and standards for the management of disciplinary actions. The prescriptive nature of its standards has promoted a high level of commonality in Canadian and U.S. regulatory practices, but may not be conducive to meeting the needs of people living in other cultures and less developed countries.

The doctoral level of training for professional psychologists has been broadly endorsed in North America and strongly supported by the ASPPB as the entry-level degree, particularly in such fields as clinical and counseling psychology. The Boulder Conference in the United States in 1949 established the doctorate and the scientist-practitioner model for the training of professional psychologists. Although there is not 100% compliance in Canadian and U.S. jurisdictions, the doctoral degree based on a scientist-practitioner model becomes a major issue when considering the possible globalization of psychology. Controversy continues on the appropriateness of the doctoral degree based on a scientist-practitioner model for the training of professional psychologists. There are other models for professional training in which a Diploma or a Master's degree is considered the appropriate level of training for professional practice, whereas the doctoral degree is deemed appropriate for academic and research activities. It is a challenge to North American credentialing committees to evaluate the equivalence of other model training models program to determine if the required knowledge and skills for competent practice have been addressed.

A major achievement of the ASPPB was the creation of the Examination for Professional Practice in Psychology (EPPP) in 1965, which is now a requirement for registration in almost every Canadian and U.S. jurisdiction. In 2001, the EPPP was computerized. A French-Canadian version has been developed. It is mandatory for jurisdictions to be members of the ASPPB if they wish to use the examination as a criterion to enter the profession. Although this examination has not escaped criticism, it is probably the only identical standard for entrance to the profession in North America. It has been considered an indicator of competency; however, it is more realistic to consider it a measure of foundational knowledge relevant to the practice of psychology. European countries do not use a written examination as part of their criteria for entrance to the profession and have not adopted the U.S. model.

The ASPPB has established two mechanisms to promote the mobility of psychologists from one jurisdiction to another. One is a system of reciprocity agreements between adjoining jurisdictions, including Canadian and U.S., to recognize each other's entrance requirements for eligibility to practice. The other is a system established in 1998 whereby individual psychologists bank their credentials with the ASPPB and are issued a Certificate of Professional Qualification if they meet the required standards. If a psychologist wishes to practice in another jurisdiction than where the psychologist was originally registered, the new jurisdiction will accept the certificate as an indication that all entrance requirements have been met. Nearly three fourths of the 62 member jurisdictions have voted to accept the certificate, although some of them are still waiting for necessary legislative changes. The requirements for these two mobility routes include a recognized doctoral degree in psychology, the EPPP, supervised practice, and an absence of disciplinary actions. In this respect the ASPPB controls the standards for using these mechanisms, and it is difficult for jurisdictions to deviate.

In Canada and the United States these mechanisms work to some extent in reducing geographical barriers to mobility. However, these standards may not be relevant outside of North America because of differences in professional training, the relative lack of regulatory mechanisms, philosophical differences on the purpose of regulation, the requirement of a doctoral degree, and the EPPP.

Under ASPPB auspices, and in view of the historical development of professional psychology in North America, Canadian and U.S. jurisdictions appear committed to the established regulatory structures, whereas those outside of North America, generally more advanced in their regulatory mechanisms, may have more choices. Cross-jurisdictional or regional mechanisms for mutual recognition of credentials could be developed in internationally relevant ways. The ASPPB has sponsored or co-sponsored three International Congresses on Licensure, Certification and Credentialing (New Orleans, U.S. in 1996; Oslo, Norway in 2000; and Montreal, Canada in 2004). These congresses have enabled psychologists world-wide to share information and opinions about the regulation of practice, evaluate different approaches to regulation, and foster a sense of international community among psychologists. The ASPPB also maintains liaisons with a large number of associations related to education, regulation, and practice of psychology, although the only formal liaison outside of North America is the EFPA.

Canada

Canadian psychology's provincial and territorial jurisdictions signed a Mutual Recognition Agreement (2001) that allows easier mobility for psychologists moving from one province or territory in Canada to another. The agreement is a consequence of the Federal and Provincial Governments' Agreement on Internal Trade, which is intended to remove inter-provincial barriers to the movement of goods and services. Although many of the criteria for entrance to the profession are unchanged and similar to those in the United States, the emphasis is now on evaluating competencies. Canadian governments require that restrictions on admission to the profession must relate only to competency to practice, (i.e., protection of the public) and not on criteria unrelated to competency, such as residency, language, religion, and country of origin.

The Master's-Doctoral controversy is only partially resolved by allowing psychologists who are registered in a jurisdiction with a Master's degree as an entry requirement to use a subordinate title, such as "psychological associate," if they move to a jurisdiction where the doctoral degree is required. When a jurisdiction registers psychologists for independent practice, whether it is based on Master's or Doctoral academic training, those psychologists neither increase nor decrease their competence by moving to another jurisdiction. Mutual recognition is of the originating jurisdiction's decision to grant a "license to practice" and not of the title. Thus, jurisdictions that have the doctorate as the entry level maintain a distinction between doctoral and nondoctoral psychologists.

Agreement on mutually acceptable ways of evaluating competencies is still a work-in-progress. Special recognition is given to psychologists who graduated from programs that were accredited by the American or Canadian Psychological Associations or who are listed in the U.S. National Register of Health Service Providers in Psychology or the Canadian Register of Health Service Providers in Psychology.

There is increased interest in Canada in developing a PsyD (Doctor of Psychology) degree that will place less emphasis on research and appeal to Master's-level psychologists who wish to upgrade their training. The province of Quebec in Canada is already establishing such programs. There is a belief that the elimination of Master's-level entrance to the profession would result in a higher level of basic education and a greater compliance with the educational standard elsewhere in North America.

Europe

European professional psychology presents a different picture. Regulation is a more recent development, with 25 of 31 member countries of the EFPA either having professional legislation or pending legislation. Even without legislated authority to regulate the profession, the British Psychological Society, for example, has well developed standards, and it charters qualified psychologists who choose to belong on a voluntary basis.

Over a period of six years the EFPA developed, and in 2001 approved, the European Diploma in Psychology that will require psychologists to have the equivalent of a Master's-level university education of six years duration, including one year of supervised practice (Lunt, 2002, 2005). The approval in June 2005 by the Council of Europe and the European Parliament brings the project a step closer to becoming the common standard for training of professional psychologists for member countries of the European Union. It will ensure and promote the mobility and quality of psychologists in Europe and will establish psychology as a profession in Europe in a permanent, irreversible manner (Tikkanen, 2004).

Today, EFPA represents 200,000 professional psychologists via its member associations, although the number of persons with training in psychology in the 31 EFPA nations (excluding Russia) is estimated to be as high as 293,000. By 2010, the number of European psychologists is expected to top 371,000 (Tikkanen, 2005). The present ratio of psychologist to inhabitants is 1:1,850, and is expected to become 1:1,500 by 2010. Some countries, such as, Belgium, Croatia, Denmark, Iceland, and Netherlands already have a ratio better than 1:1,000. In comparison, as of 2004 membership in the APA was approximately 155,000, including 82,190 members and fellows, 51,896 student affiliates, and 3,878 foreign affiliates. It should be noted that the European figures are based on the number of psychologists within the EFPA member associations and the membership in the APA is based on voluntary individual memberships. Although the statistics are not entirely comparable, they suggest that the number of psychologists in the United States may be well below that in Europe and that psychologists in the United States do not anticipate a level of growth similar to that in Europe.

Africa

It is beyond the scope of this chapter to address the many countries in the African continent. Psychology is well established in South Africa.

However, most African countries could be placed in Moghaddam's (1987) Third-World category that is characterized by poverty, lack of resources, little education, and minimal access to the outside world. Sub-Saharan Africa with its cultural beliefs in witchcraft, the authority of elders, and connections with the spirit world, is seen as especially incompatible with a scientific approach to healing and problem solving, although there are clear psychosocial underpinnings to these traditions and practices. In this context psychology and psychiatry are not well established (Olatawura, 2000) and training local persons abroad to bring back Western practices may be poorly received, irrelevant, and potentially harmful (Mpofu, Zindi, Oakland, &, Peresuh, 1997).

Middle Eastern States

Psychology in the Arab states requires special attention when considering psychology worldwide, partly because psychologists in the Western world know so little about it, publications in English are rare, and there is meager Western understanding of the range of Islamic beliefs. Ahmed and Gielen (1998), Soueif and Ahmed (2001), and Ahmed (2004) describe the long history of Arab scholarship and the short history, largely at universities, of scientific psychology imported from the West. They report that the public's perception of the status and role of psychologists is weak in most Arab states and the profession is generally seen as irrelevant. Okasha (2000) describes the Western-trained mental health professional's frustration in accommodating decision making by the large family unit over that of the individual and the belief that anything that happens is the will of God. Although psychology is established more strongly in Egypt than in other Arab states, Ahmed (2004) reports a growing need for psychology to address the cultural and social realities of the Arab world. In Iran, Birashk (2004) describes psychology as being in a stage of transition in which it must integrate religious beliefs with Western and international understandings and apply psychological knowledge to meet the needs of Iranian society.

Other Countries

The details of the advances and the challenges in developing professional psychology in South America, Asia, and the Pacific Rim countries are beyond the scope of this chapter (see chapters 3 and 4, this volume, for more on current trends in psychology worldwide and psychology in the developing world, respectively). Examples of countries that do not have legislation for the regulation of the profession include India, Iran, Japan, Kenya, Nigeria, Pakistan, the Philppines, Poland, Russia, Singapore, Thailand, Turkey, and the United Kingdom. In several of these countries, psychologists are working to obtain licensing legislation. In some countries that do not have professional legislation, psychologists have developed ethical standards of practice for the guidance of their members in the same manner as would be required under legislation.

The story of Sri Lanka (de Zoysa & Ismail, 2002) is interesting, because as a very small country with a very small number of psychologists, it has established the legal regulation of clinical psychologists and has achieved the status of a profession independent from medicine. It has shown that it does not require size and a long history in order to enact professional legislation.

Western scientific psychology, without cultural adaptation or indigenization, is not seen as relevant in many countries (Gergen, Gulerce, Lock, & Misra, 1996). The following countries described in the *Handbook of International Psychology* (Stevens & Wedding, 2004) either have developed or perceive the need to develop an indigenous of psychology that is relevant for them: the Arab states, China, Colombia, India, Indonesia, Japan, Nigeria, Pakistan, Singapore, South Africa, and Turkey (see chapter 5, this volume, on the emergence of the indigenization movement in psychology). At the same time many of these countries have adopted codes of ethics on the model of the APA that do not appear to reflect their own needs or cultural beliefs.

With some exceptions, the existence of professional regulation reflects the level of development of professional psychology in that country. A profession needs to establish an identity and credibility before there is something to be regulated. However, there is a downside to regulation if the standards that are intended to protect the public limit the flexibility of psychologists to use professional judgment in accommodating cultural differences, and in attempting to think globally. Regulation by its nature establishes specific rules that make it easier to assess compliance, but make it more difficult to consider the context of circumstances and relationships, a major aspect of which is cultural.

Jurisdictions are legally defined geographical boundaries, and psychologists are permitted to practice within the boundaries within which they are registered. Yet, in times of major disasters, such as earthquakes, floods, tornados, or acts of terrorism, psychologists may join humanitarian relief efforts to support the recovery of persons and communities outside of the jurisdictions in which they are licensed to practice and outside the culture with which they are familiar. The tsunami relief effort is an example of coping with such a major catastrophe. Providing services over the Internet also defies geographical boundaries. The means by which professional psychology is regulated is based on the geographical jurisdictions that today act as a deterrent to practicing across borders.

This chapter does not cover in detail the differences in cultural, economic, historical, political, and religious forces that are the contexts in which professional psychology has thrived, made tentative beginnings, or precluded engagement. More detail on the development of psychology in some 27 countries representing all continents is available in the *Handbook of International Psychology* (Stevens & Wedding, 2004).

POLITICAL DETERMINANTS

Professional psychology appears to be growing rapidly and unevenly worldwide. In contrast to much of the developing world, Western countries became industrialized, rich in resources, secular, and democratic, with science replacing religion as the major source of perceived "truth." The rights of the individual were emphasized over those of family, community, and nation. Economic, political, and social conditions have influenced the nature and the rate of development of psychology worldwide and disproved the myth of a value-free discipline.

In the United States several factors enhanced the development of professional psychology, such as the public's recognition of psychology's contribution to the World War II effort, generous government funding for professional training, and the need for psychological services in Veterans' Hospitals. Today, in the United States managed-care programs are changing the face of independent practice in ways that reduce the scope of clinical judgment of psychologists, and are intended to control accountability and costs. The current movement to obtain privileges for psychologists to prescribe psychotropic medications will change the nature of professional practice in the United States.

Many political circumstances that had been deterrents to the development of international psychology have changed over time. The founding of the Turkish Republic in 1923 under the leadership of Kemal Ataturk opened doors to Western ideas and learning (Boratav, 2004). The end of China's Cultural Revolution (1966–1978) resulted in psychology being rehabilitated as a scientific practice and discipline (Yang, 2004). When the repression of psychology under Soviet rule and its social and political isolation ended, Russian psychology was renewed (Balachova, Isurina,

Levy, Tsvetkova, & Wasserman, 2004). Psychology also was renewed in Spain after the repression of the Spanish Civil War (1936–1939) and the Franco regime (1939–1975; Prieto & Garcia-Rodriguez, 2004). The end of Argentina's bloody dictatorship in 1955 allowed a resurgence of scientific and professional psychology (Klappenbach, 2004). Today, destabilization resulting from war remains a deterrent to the internationalization of psychology.

Psychology often has accommodated the political ideology of the day (see chapters 2 and 8, this volume, on the role of politics in psychology and psychotherapy, respectively). For example, before and during World War II, German psychology shifted to support Nazi racism and militarism (Plath & Eckensberger, 2004). South African psychology, until the government became democratically elected in 1994, supported racial segregation and condoned Apartheid (Stead, 2004). Psychology in Soviet and Soviet-occupied countries was used to support totalitarian ideologies (Kreegipuu & Maartis, 2002). Psychology in the United States appears to endorse an ideology of a competitive market economy in which a significant proportion of psychologists practice independently, whereas in many countries a higher proportion of psychologists are salaried employees in such work settings as hospitals, schools, community agencies, and residential institutions (Stevens & Wedding, 2004).

It is clear that political circumstances influence the nature of psychological practice in a given country and that political systems that support openness in communication are more conducive to the internationalization of psychology than those that are isolationist. The challenge today in moving toward a globalization of professional psychology is dependent on the successful application of psychological knowledge to resolving the issues, individual and collective, that are of concern in different parts of the world (see chapter 1, this volume, for a review of applications of psychology to various regional and global concerns).

Professional regulation provides a structure in which standards of practice can be clearly defined and made public. One challenge is the development of indigenous psychologies that retain, rather than lose the identity and foundational knowledge of psychology. Another is the development of regulatory structures that are flexible enough to accommodate differences, rather than impose a restrictive Canadian–U.S. model. Small steps have been taken to increase the ability of professional psychologists to have their credentials recognized across different jurisdictions, but these steps fall far short of world legislation, world mobility, or world consensus on the requirements for psychologists to practice competently and ethically. For the foreseeable future, out of respect for diversity, that lack of consensus probably will and should remain.

GUIDELINES FOR ETHICAL PRACTICE

General

All societies have beliefs about what is good and evil and what is right and wrong. An important feature of both regulatory and collegial professional associations is the development of ethical principles and codes of ethics. Sinclair, Poizner, Gilmour-Barrett, and Randall (1987) summarized the purposes of ethics codes as described in the interdisciplinary and international literature as (a) helping to establish a group as a profession, (b) acting as a support and guide to individual professionals, (c) helping to meet the responsibilities of being a profession, and (d) providing a statement of moral principle that helps individual professionals resolve ethical dilemmas.

Psychology's professional codes of ethics have two major historical roots: (a) the aspirational one, which articulates the overarching philosophical ethical principles used to evaluate "right" versus "wrong" behavior, and (b) the more recent prescriptive one, which defines "enforceable" acceptable behaviors to protect the public from harm. It appears there is greater consensus worldwide on statements of moral principles than on prescriptive behaviors. Sinclair (2003/2004, 2005) found similarity in the ethical or moral principles put forward for physicians over the centuries and across Eastern and Western cultures. Ethics may be described in terms of the nature and quality of relationships between the psychologist and others, and also by obligations to observe certain standards of behavior.

Psychology has a much longer history than the codification of ethics to regulate the behavior of psychologists. The post-World War II revulsion against the human abuses in Nazi Germany and the concurrent rapid growth of professional psychology, were strong incentives to develop ethics codes that would prevent harm from being done to others. In the 1950s, the APA led the way in developing a code of ethics, the last revision of which is *Ethical Principles for Psychologists and Code of Conduct* (American Psychological Association, 2002). The U.S. code has been a model for psychology associations in both Eastern and the Western countries, partly as the result of students from developing countries studying in the United States.

The *Canadian Code of Ethics for Psychologists* (Canadian Psychological Association, 1986, 1991, 2000) has been referenced in recent revisions of psychology codes in the EFPA, New Zealand, Mexico, and South Africa. Two of the outstanding features of the Canadian code are the linkage of all the standards to clearly articulated and overarching ethical principles, and the inclusion of ethical decision-making steps to aid in resolving dilemmas when principles are in conflict (Canadian Psychological Association, 2000).

Psychologists in countries such as Iran, Japan, Poland, Singapore, and the United Kingdom have developed codes of ethics even though they do not yet have legislated regulation.

Inuit *Qaujimanituqangit*

The newly created territory of Nunavut in northern Canada in 1999 presents a unique example of an aboriginal culture holding power and privilege in the formation of government and in using Inuit traditional values as guiding principles for all activities of government, including the licensing of psychologists. This is in sharp contrast to psychology associations modeling their codes of ethics on those in the Western world. Nunavut has a largely aboriginal population of about 29,000 in a territory covering two million square kilometers stretching to the North Pole. The *Qaujimanituqangit Principles* include the following four core values: (a) *Pijitsirniq*, or the concept of serving, (b) *Aajiiqatigiingniq*, or the concept of consensus decision making, (c) *Pilimmaksarniq*, or the concept of skills and knowledge acquisition, and (d) *Piliriquatigiingniq*, or the concept of collaborative relationships.

Wihak (2004), interested in whether there was a potential conflict in values between the those of the Nunavut licensing body and those of the rest of Canada, compared the Inuit *Qaujimanituqangit Principles* with those of the third edition of the *Canadian Code of Ethics for Psychologists* (Canadian Psychological Association, 2000). She found a high level of compatibility between the two sets of principles on "what is good" and suggested that the differences on the relative importance of individual well being over that of the community may be resolved when one considers that the well being of the individual is interdependent with the well being of the community. She also found potential conflict between Western science as the source of truth and the "felt" and "revealed" truth of traditional Inuit knowledge. Otherwise she found a high level of compatibility between Inuit values and ethical principles espoused and the *Canadian Code of Ethics for Psychologists*.

Empirical Studies

Some recent studies have compared ethical perspectives across national boundaries. Leach and Harbin (1997) analyzed the percentage of the standards in the APA's *Ethical Principles of Psychologists and Code of Conduct* (American Psychological Association, 2002) that appear in other countries' codes and the percentage of countries that include each standard in their respective codes. There was a high percentage of agreement with the standards of the U.S. code.

In 1995, a small group of psychologists from different countries agreed to replicate the Pope and Vetter (1992) study, which asked psychologists to describe an ethically troubling incident that they had encountered during the past year. Countries in which such studies were conducted included the United Kingdom (Lindsay & Colley, 1995), Norway (Odland & Nielsen, 1996), Sweden (Colnerud, 1997), Finland (Colnerud, Hansson, Salling, & Tikkanen, 1996), South Africa (Slack & Wassenaar, 1999), Colombia (Sinclair & Pettifor, 1996), New Zealand (Davis, Seymour, & Read, 1997), Canada (Sinclair & Pettifor, 1996), and Mexico (Hernández-Guzmán & Ritchie, 2001). There was a high level of agreement on the types of ethical dilemmas that were encountered, with confidentiality being the most common. Country-specific differences seemed related to different types of work settings for psychologists, population characteristics, and the nature of payment for psychological services rather than to differences in cultural beliefs (Pettifor & Sawchuk, 2006). However, non-Western countries were not represented.

In comparing ethics codes for psychologists across countries and across disciplines, Gauthier (2003, 2005) identified five moral principles that are common across the codes of ethics of psychologists in many countries: (a) respect for the dignity and rights of persons, (b) caring for others and concerns for their welfare, (c) competence, (d) integrity, and (e) professional, scientific, and social responsibility.

GOING INTERNATIONAL

General

The interest in an international declaration of ethical principles is not new. The IUPsyS approved the *Statement of the IUPS* that requested each member-society to enact a code of ethics and to take action against any member guilty of abuses against rights of human beings (International Union of

Psychological Science, 1976). However, concerns continued over the
alleged use of psychology for the mistreatment of political dissidents by
authoritarian regimes (Holtzman, 1979). Nuttin (1979) from Belgium
explored the question of whether it is possible to have universal professional standards that apply to psychologists in all countries. He was looking for mechanisms to enforce sanctions against psychologists who were
involved in acts causing serious harm, but at the same time he believed
that universal ethical standards must be general and few in number in
order for interpretations to be culture-specific within each country or
region. Tomaszewski (1979) from Poland was concerned about the abuses
of psychological knowledge that seriously harm individuals, races, and
nations and urged psychologists not only to oppose abuses, but to demonstrate how psychology can be used for the welfare of humanity. He saw
some of the principles of the *Universal Declaration of Human Rights*
(United Nations, 1948) as relevant.

European Federation of Psychologists' Associations (EFPA)

The work of the Standing Committee on Ethics of the EFPA is an example of how a regional association of psychologists with members from different countries is able to promote a commonality of high standards for
ethical practice. The EFPA (1995) adopted the *Meta-Code of Ethics* as the
ethical frame of reference to guide the content of the ethics codes of its
member associations and to provide assistance in the evaluation of their
members' conduct. Since then, national associations have revised codes of
ethics to be consistent with the meta-code. In 1999 EFPA approved
Recommendations for Teaching Ethics for Psychologists. Lindsay (2005)
reported on the Standing Committee's recent activities. Minimal changes
have been made to update the meta-code (European Federation of
Psychologists Associations, 2005). Also in 2005, the EFPA approved the
document, "Recommendations on Evaluative Procedures and Corrective
Actions in Cases of Complaints about Unethical Conduct." This document consists of two parts, namely (a) guidance to national associations
based on principles, similar to the approach used in the meta-code, and
(b) an example of how procedures may be created in practice. Future plans
for the work of the EFPA Standing Committee on Ethics include the
development of a guidebook on the revised meta-code, development of
guidelines on the use of mediation in cases of minor complaints, and

support to member associations in the development of their own ethics codes and systems for dealing with complaints about members.

Nordic Countries

Psychology jurisdictions that adopt common ethical guidelines demonstrate a movement toward internationalization. The five Nordic countries (Denmark, Finland, Iceland, Norway, and Sweden) adopted the same code of ethics in 1988 (Aanonson, 2003). In 1998, they revised their code to be consistent with the EFPA meta-code.

New Zealand

The *Code of Ethics for Psychologists Working in Aotearoa/New Zealand* (New Zealand Psychological Society, 2002; Seymour, 2003) is modeled on the *Canadian Code of Ethics for Psychologists* (Canadian Psychological Association, 1991), but it has features that bridge Western and aboriginal values about respect for the dignity of peoples as well as individuals. It also accepts the need for equality and social justice as promised to the Maori people in the 1840 *Treaty of Waitangi*, signed between Queen Victoria and the Maori Chiefs (New Zealand–Treaty of Waitangi, 1840). Yet, the code does not incorporate the concept of identity, as described by Love (2000), a Maori psychologist, in which there is connectedness between past and future generations, between self and family, community and nation, and between the person and the natural world.

Islamic Ethics

Reference to the *Islamic Code of Medical Ethics* (n.d.) is included briefly here because there is minimal information in English on professional ethics in Islamic countries, and this code appears to apply across countries rather than a single jurisdiction. The *Islamic Code of Medical Ethics* is consistent with the Hippocratic Oath although it places a stronger emphasis on the role of the physician as an instrument of God's mercy. Siddiqi (2001), in addressing the Interfaith Council of Westminster in California, emphasized the values that are common across the world's major religions, namely the dignity and basic equality of all human beings, universal human rights, and fundamental freedom of thought, conscience, and belief. The Web site, www.crescentlife.com, has many articles in English describing the Islamic faith.

A Universal Declaration of Ethical Principles for Psychologists

Twenty-six years after the IUPsyS (1976) urged member nations to develop codes of ethics that prohibited psychologists from abusing human rights, the IUPsyS, in conjunction with the International Association of Applied Psychology, appointed Janel Gauthier to chair an ad hoc Joint Committee, representing major regions and cultures, to draft a Universal Declaration of Ethical Principles for Psychologists. At the time of this writing, this work is still in progress. When Gauthier (2002, 2003) compared the principles of codes of ethics worldwide, he found considerable similarity among them as well as with the ethical principles expressed in the *Universal Declaration of Human Rights* (United Nations, 1948). Two points should be noted here: (a) the focus for a universal declaration of ethical principles for psychologists is on moral/ethical principles rather than on prescribed behaviors, and (b) although the U.N. *Universal Declaration of Human Rights* commits signatory nations to treat people fairly and to prohibit abuse, in some countries that are alleged to violate human rights, these criticisms are seen as serving political rather than humanitarian agendas (Evers, 2002).

ETHICAL GUIDELINES OF ALLIED INTERNATIONAL ASSOCIATIONS

International associations that have adopted ethical guidelines for the practice of their members worldwide include the World Medical Association (1994), International School Psychology Association (Oakland, Goldman, & Bischoff, 1997), International Council of Nurses (2000), World Psychiatric Association (2002), International Association of Marriage and Family Counselors (2002), and the International Federation of Social Workers (2004).

The International Federation of Social Workers (2004) approved a revision of their *Ethics in Social Work Statement of Principles*. It has only two overarching ethical principles: (a) human rights and human dignity and (b) social justice. The purpose of the statement is to promote ethical debate and reflection in member associations and among the providers of social work in member countries. It gives general guidelines for member associations to develop and regularly update their codes of ethics specifically to meet their own needs.

The *Ethical Standards* of the International Association of Marriage and Family Counselors (2002) state that members do not impose personal values on the families with whom they work, that they become multiculturally competent, and that they use indigenous healing practices when appropriate. The International School Psychology Association (Oakland et al., 1997) expects its members to respect the cultural environments within which they work and to provide appropriate ways to serve diverse populations.

The World Psychiatric Association adopted the *Declaration of Madrid* in 1996 (World Psychiatric Association, 2002). In addition to covering the topics of informed consent, confidentiality, competency, and quality of care, the declaration prohibits euthanasia, torture, the death penalty, and the selection of children on the basis of their sex. Statements were added in 1999 on ethnic discrimination, genetic counseling, and the use of mass media. Sartorius (1999) sees these social and political issues as closely aligned with the U.N. *Universal Declaration of Human Rights* (United Nations, 1948).

Okasha, Arboleda-Florez, and Sartorius (2000) describe the cultural challenges worldwide for psychiatrists attempting to practice according to the standards of the *Declaration of Madrid*. Challenges exist in different cultures around the themes of individualism and collectivism (i.e., of family, tribe, and state), democratic and authoritarian regimes, secular and theocratic societies, and science and folklore approaches to healing. Okasha (2000) raises crucial questions for Western professionals in addressing the apparent conflict between universality of ethical principles and respect for diversity. He questions how, in adhering to our ethical guidelines, we can necessarily respect local values and norms, or in respecting local values and norms, we can always avoid harming our clients.

What we learn is that international associations want to respect diversity; provide quality research, teaching, and practice; avoid harming or condoning harm done to others; and stop violations of human rights. However, ethical guidelines, approved by international associations, often appear to be written for Western professionals working with non-Western persons, and to address such issues as respect for individuals, informed consent, confidentiality, privacy, and conflict of interest, all of which are subject to cultural interpretations. They provide little guidance on how to recognize and address non-Western cultural beliefs and practices. They give little guidance for situations in which Western values are irrelevant or inconsistent with the local cultures or when one must consider what is meant by indigenization. International students training to become counselors and psychologists feel racial discrimination when the literature and courses on diversity always place the minority person as the client and the white mainstream person as the professional.

I wonder sometimes if international codes of ethics express good intentions, but unintentionally ignore values and beliefs upheld in non-Western cultures. A universal declaration of ethical principles may help to unify the profession and raise standards of practice worldwide, but it should not in fact or in appearance impose Western worldviews on the rest of the world. The model found in the approaches of the International Federation of Social Workers, the recently established committee to develop a universal declaration of ethical principles for psychologists, and the EFPA, is to provide a template of overarching principles to guide the development of culture-specific and jurisdiction-specific ethical standards and codes. This approach holds promise for a universal declaration of ethical principles, whereas the prescription of standard behaviors does not.

Social Justice

Although psychologists in many countries, such as Egypt, India, Indonesia, Iran, Pakistan, South Africa, and Turkey, say that psychology is needed to address such social problems as addictions, crime, ethnic strife, HIV/AIDS, the marginalization of women, poverty, and racism, international guidelines and professional codes of ethics generally fall short on issues of social justice, responsibility to society, and collective well-being. The *Seminar on Ethics in Science and Technology* (Chinese Association for Science and Technology, 2002) emphasized the social responsibility of scientists to benefit society and to minimize negative social impacts caused by the misuse of scientific results. Stevens and Wedding (2004) describe international psychology as a specialty area of psychology that addresses international problems, such as terrorism, global warming, human trafficking, threats to the natural environment, intergroup conflict, and disempowered groups (see chapter 1, this volume), but these aspects of psychological practice are scarcely reflected in international professional codes of ethics. The International Federation of Social Workers' (2004) and the New Zealand Psychological Society's (2002) codes of ethics are exceptions in their strong emphasis on the obligation to promote social justice.

By definition international psychology incorporates a commitment to social justice about which professional psychology seems reticent. Problems that are defined as inadequacies of individuals will be treated with individual interventions whereas problems that are defined as social problems will require different interventions (O'Neill, 2005). The rules for the regulation of psychology and the ethical guidelines for the practice of psychology seem to define "protection of the public" only in the context of identified clients rather than in the context of large-scale social interventions to change the conditions that bring about individual "inadequacies." Arguments can be made that psychologists are not trained to be agents of social change and that there is insufficient empirical evidence to support actions that are socially and politically controversial. The concern of governments in legislating the regulation of professions is to protect the public from professionals doing harm rather than supporting social change that reduces harm. Yet, those who treat suffering individuals cannot avoid being concerned about the societal causes of human suffering. It is beyond the scope of this chapter to describe initiatives calling for psychologists to commit themselves to social change (see chapter 9, this volume, on macro-social interventions that meld psychology and social policy). However, it seems clear that a global profession must address global issues rather than remain encapsulated in a culture that regulates the practice of individual professionals only in the context of their practice with individual clients.

Global Ethics

If we expand our attention beyond psychology and its allied professions, we find a growing concern for an ethic of world citizenship and a belief in the existence of universal values. The *Declaration of a Global Ethic* (Center for Global Ethics, 1993) was produced at the Council of World Religions as a commitment to: (a) a culture of non-violence and respect for life, (b) solidarity and just economic order, (c) tolerance and a life of truthfulness, and (d) equal rights and partnership between men and women. In 1997, the United Nation Education, Scientific and Cultural Organization (UNESCO, n.d.) established the *Universal Ethics Project* to identify basic ethical principles for an emerging global society and to forge new understandings of universality in the context of cultural diversity. UNESCO (2001) adopted the *Universal Declaration on Cultural Diversity*. The InterAction Council (1997), founded by a former prime minister of Japan, began its search for universal ethical standards in 1987 and in 1997 proposed a *Universal Declaration of Human Responsibilities* that was modeled on the *Declaration of a Global Ethic*. It was submitted to, but not adopted by the U.N. The High Level Expert Group that developed the *Declaration* included spiritual and political leaders (mostly former heads of state). Work is currently underway by UNESCO to develop a *Universal Declaration on Bioethics and Human Rights* (UNESCO, 2005).

OBSERVATIONS ON WHERE TO GO FROM HERE

Concerns for developing international ethical guidelines derive from at least two sources: (a) a deep concern for preventing serious abuse and the exploitation of human beings, and (b) a need to define professional guidelines for respecting the diversity of human lives. Scientific psychology has been imported from the West to other countries and, today, many psychologists see the need to amend, revise, and integrate Western psychology in keeping with the local culture in order to attend to local human needs. More information is needed on how the indigenization of psychology is accomplished. In dramatic contrast to the indigenization of Western psychology is the experience of psychologists in the newly established Canadian territory of Nunavut where the government is articulating traditional Inuit values in order to guide all government activities. There appears to be more global consensus on moral/ethical principles than on how principles are expressed in specific behavioral rules.

Codes of ethics inevitably reflect the values, politics, and beliefs of the cultural contexts in which they are created. The extent to which professionals can think globally will be reflected in the ethical guidelines that are formulated. In seeking a moral higher ground, it is important to recognize Bersoff's (1999) caution to minimize those conditions that may jeopardize the moral integrity of codes of ethics. He suggests that codes tend to be anachronistic, conservative, ethnocentric, and the product of political compromise. However, in my opinion this applies more to the specific, legally defensible standards and rules that are established by regulatory bodies than to the moral principles that guide aspirational dimensions of ethical guidelines. Rigid enforcement of rules may disallow cultural sensitivity to context. However, whether state-directed or individually implemented, prohibitions of abusive acts are universally appropriate.

Some of the alleged barriers to a global ethic for professionals seem easier to address than others. Individualism and collectivism may be consciously bridged, except in extreme forms, because they overlap.

Psychologists are committed to the well being of both individuals and the societies in which they live. Authoritarian regimes are generally not compatible with professional ethics, but will vary from one setting to another; or some aspects, such as psychological testing, may be more acceptable than individual psychotherapy or lobbying for social change. The disintegration of a society through warfare and internal strife is not conducive to the practice of psychology, although the need for psychological services may be great. The need for food, shelter, and safety may be greater. The accommodation of science to what scientists may perceive as folklore and witchcraft is more difficult; however, an indigenization process of blending cross-cultural interventions is being developed in several countries (see chapters 8 and 9, this volume). Combining science and the freedom of secular societies with the restrictions of fundamentalist religious states is perhaps more difficult because authority that is interpreted as divine is often not subject to questioning or critical thinking. However, neither theocratic nor secular states can remain isolated from the rest of the world and, therefore, cannot escape considering how to integrate religion, science, materialism, and the needs of their own people.

Worldwide psychology is enhanced when psychologists think globally and are open to global dialogue and new developments. They need to think about what is good and beneficial within the cultural contexts in which people live and how psychological knowledge and skills can be used sensitively and effectively. Professional psychologists have the potential to collaborate in changing unfortunate aspects of society without being fettered by narrow definitions of scope of practice. Psychologists in all countries, especially in those countries and cultures that have dominated the discipline, hopefully can break the blinders of ethnocentrism in order to listen, hear, dialogue, and collaborate internationally and globally. Today, professional psychology is international, but not yet global.

What Can Be Done to Facilitate a Globalization of Professional Psychology?

To facilitate a more global profession, I suggest:

1. International organizations should devote more time at international congresses and in international journals to regulatory and ethical issues. This not only enhances the sharing of information

and search for answers to common concerns, but also provides a moral framework for planning strategies to enhance the well being of people worldwide. Discussions need to be collaborative in terms of meeting the needs of people, rather than simply exporting and importing psychological knowledge.

2. Psychology organizations at all levels should consider the practical implications for their members of the various international declarations and documents that are intended to serve the well being of people and prevent harm.

3. Psychology organizations at all levels should learn about and contribute to the development of a universal declaration of ethical principles for psychologists.

4. University training programs should increase their attention to cultural beliefs, including spiritual ones, with a view to mutual understanding and international exchange programs for students, teachers, and practitioners (see chapter 11, this volume, on guidelines for education and training in a globalized world).

5. University training programs should address the process of indigenization in order to nurture the cultural relevancy of psychological services and also maintain the scientific foundations of professional psychology.

6. Regulatory bodies and the government departments to whom they are accountable, in the interests of evaluating competence of international applicants, should work toward a realistic evaluation of the equivalence of their training programs and supervisory experiences.

7. Psychology as a profession should conduct an extensive review of regulatory mechanisms to determine how they can be used to promote quality of care internationally and worldwide rather than act as a deterrent. Such a review will need to look beyond formal credentials to address ways of identifying and evaluating the knowledge and skills required to conduct psychological activities in nontraditional ways and settings.

8. Psychology as a profession should consider how professional psychology designed to serve identified persons can be integrated with international and global initiatives to address social problems and issues of social justice.

Hopes for professional psychology's contribution to a better world require the promotion of aspirational ethical principles and flexibility or reform in regulatory requirements. There is the promise of worldwide benefit for psychologists, and those whom they serve, in expanding psychologists' international horizons and, thereby lengthening the pathway between themselves and the vanishing point of their visions. May the vanishing point vanish as a new vision encompasses the globe.

RECOMMENDED READINGS

Gauthier, J. (2005). Toward a universal declaration of ethical principles for psychologists: A progress report. In M. J. Stevens & D. Wedding (Eds.), *Psychology: IUPsyS global resource* [CD-ROM] (6th ed.). Hove, UK: Psychology Press.

Leach, M., & Harbin, J. (1997). Psychological ethics codes: A comparison of 24 countries. *International Journal of Psychology, 32*, 181–192.

Okasha, A., Arboleda-Florez, J., & Sartorious, N. (Eds.). (2000). *Ethics, culture, and psychiatry: International perspectives.* Washington, DC: American Psychiatric Press.

Sinclair, C. (2003, 2004). A brief history of ethical principles in professional codes of ethics. In J. B. Overmier & J. A. Overmier (Eds.), *Psychology: IUPsyS global resource* [CD-ROM] (4th and 5th eds.). Hove, UK: Psychology Press.

Sinclair, C. (2005). The Eastern roots of ethical principles and values in current codes of ethics. In M. J. Stevens & D. Wedding (Eds.), *Psychology: IUPsyS global resource* [CD-ROM] (6th ed.). Hove, UK: Psychology Press.

Stevens, M. J., & Wedding, D. (Eds.). (2004). *Handbook of international psychology.* New York: Brunner-Routledge.

REFERENCES

Aanonsen, A. (2003). EFPA Metacode on ethics and the Nordic Code. In J. B. Overmier & J. A. Overmier (Eds.), *Psychology: IUPsyS global resource* [CD-ROM] (4th ed.). Hove, UK: Psychology Press.

Adair, J. G., Coelho, E. L. C., & Luna, J. R. (2002). How international is psychology? *International Journal of Psychology, 37*, 160–170.

Ahmed, R. (2004). Psychology in Egypt. In M. J. Stevens & D. Wedding (Eds.), *Handbook of international psychology* (pp. 387–403). New York: Brunner-Routlege.

Ahmed, R. A., & Gielen, U. P. (1998). Introduction. In R. A. Ahmed & U. P. Gielen (Eds.), *Psychology in the Arab countries* (pp. 3–48). Menoufia, Egypt: Menoufia University Press.

American Psychological Association. (2002). *Ethical principles of psychologists and code of conduct.* Washington, DC: Author.

Association of State and Provincial Psychology Boards. (2001). *Model act for licensure of psychologists.* Birmingham, AL: Author.

Balachova, T., Isurina, G., Levy, S., Tsvetkova, L., & Wasserman, L. I. (2004). Psychology in Russia. In M. J. Stevens & D. Wedding (Eds.), *Handbook of international psychology* (pp. 293–209). New York: Brunner-Routledge.

Bersoff, D. (1999). *Ethical conflicts in psychology* (2nd ed.). Washington, DC: American Psychological Association.

Bickle, G. (2004). Professional ethics needs a theoretical background. *European Psychologist, 9*, 273–277.

Birashk, B. (2004). Psychology in Iran. In M. J. Stevens & D. Wedding (Eds.), *Handbook of international psychology* (pp. 405–418). New York: Brunner-Routledge.

Boratav, H. B. (2004). Psychology at the cross-roads: The view from Turkey. In M. J. Stevens & D. Wedding (Eds.), *Handbook of international psychology* (pp. 387–403). New York: Brunner-Routlege.

Canadian Psychological Association. (1986, 1991, 2000). *Canadian code of ethics for psychologists*. Ottawa: Author.

Center for Global Ethics. (1993). *Toward a universal declaration of a global ethic*. Retrieved December 8, 2003, from http://astro.temple,edu/~dialogue/geth.htm

Chinese Association for Science and Technology. (2002). *Seminar on ethics in science and technology and its impact on society proceedings*. Beijing: Author.

Colnerud, G. (1997). Ethical dilemmas of psychologists: A Swedish example in an international perspective. *European Psychologist, 2*, 164–170.

Colnerud, G., Hansson, B., Salling, O., & Tikkanen, T. (1996). Ethical dilemmas of psychologists: Finland and Sweden [Abstract]. *International Journal of Psychology, 31*, 476.

Davis, G., Seymour, F., & Reid, J. (1997). Ethical dilemmas encountered by New Zealand registered psychologists: A national survey. *The Bulletin, 91*, 7–14.

de Zoysa, P., & Ismail, C. (2002). Psychology in an Asian country: A report from Sri Lanka. *International Journal of Psychology, 37*, 110–111.

Draguns, J. (2001). Toward a truly international psychology: Beyond English only. *American Psychologist, 56*, 1019–1030.

European Federation of Psychologists' Associations. (1995). *Meta-code of ethics*. Brussels: Author.

European Federation of Psychologists' Associations. (2005). *Revised meta-code of ethics*. Brussels: Author.

Evers, K. (2002). Ethics in science: A socio-political challenge. In Chinese Association for Science and Technology (Ed.), *Seminar on ethics in science and technology and its impact on society proceedings* (pp. 114–121). Beijing: Author.

Gauthier, J. (2002, July). *Ethics and human rights: Toward a universal declaration of ethical principles for psychologists*. Paper presented at the International Congress of Psychology, Singapore.

Gauthier, J. (2003). Toward a universal declaration of ethical principles for psychologists. In J. B. Overmier & J. A. Overmier (Eds.), *Psychology: IUPsyS global resource* [CD-ROM] (4th ed.). Hove, UK: Psychology Press.

Gauthier, J. (2005). Toward a universal declaration of ethical principles for psychologists: A progress report. In M. J. Stevens & D. Wedding (Eds.), *Psychology: IUPsyS global resource* [CD-ROM] (6th ed.). Hove, UK: Psychology Press.

Gergen, K., Gulerce, A., Lock, A., & Misra, G. (1996). Psychological science in cultural context. *American Psychologist, 51*, 496–503.

Hernández-Guzmán, L., & Ritchie, P. L.-J. (2001). Hacia la transformación y actualización empíricas del códigoetico de los psicologos mexicanos [Toward the transformation and updating of the Ethics code for Mexican psychologists]. *Revista Mexicana de Psicología, 18*, 347–357.

Holtzman, W. (1979). The IUPS project on professional ethics and conduct. *International Journal of Psychology, 14*, 107–109.

InterAction Council. (1997). *A universal declaration of human responsibilities.* Retrieved February 24, 2005, from http://www.interactionscouncil.org

International Association of Marriage and Family Counselors. (2002). *Ethical standards.* Retrieved May 29, 2005, from http://www.iamfc.com/ethical_codes.html

International Council of Nurses. (2000). *The ICN code of ethics for nurses.* Retrieved February 1, 2004, from http://www.icn.ch/ethics.htm

International Federation of Social Workers. (2004). *Second draft document: Ethics in social work statement of principles.* Retrieved May 30, 2005, from http://www.ifsw.org/GM-Ethics-2draf.html

International Union of Psychological Science. (1976). *Statement by the International Union of Psychological Science.* Retrieved May 25, 2005, from http://web.amnesty.org/pages/health-ethics6–eng

Islamic Code of Medical Ethics. (n.d.). Retrieved May 13, 2005, from http://www.islam-set.com/ethics/code/oath.html

Kelman, H. C. (1997). Group processes in the resolution of international conflicts: Experiences from the Israeli-Palestinian case. *American Psychologist, 52,* 212–220.

Klappenbach, H. (2004). Psychology in Argentina. In M. J. Stevens & D. Wedding (Eds.), *Handbook of international psychology* (pp. 129–150). New York: Brunner-Routledge.

Koinange, J. (2004). Psychology in Kenya. In M. J. Stevens & D. Wedding (Eds.), *Handbook of international psychology* (pp. 25–41). New York: Brunner-Routledge.

Kreegipuu, M., & Maartis, I. (2002, July). *Historical and political constraints to the development of ethical codes for psychologists.* Paper presented at the European Congress of Psychology, London.

Leach, M., & Harbin, J. (1997). Psychological ethics codes: A comparison of 24 countries. *International Journal of Psychology, 32,* 181–192.

Lindsay, G., & Colley, A. (1995). Ethical dilemmas of members of the Society. *The Psychologist, 8,* 448–453.

Lindsay, G. (2005, July). *Report of the EFPA Standing Committee on Ethics to the General Assembly.* Report presented at the European Congress of Psychology, Granada, Spain.

Love, C. (2000). Cultural origins, sharing, and appropriation: A Maori reflection. In G. Bedford & J. Hudson (Eds.), *Family group conferencing: New directions in community-centered child and family practice* (pp. 15–30). New York: Aldine de Gruyter.

Lunt, I. (2002). A common framework for the training of psychologists in Europe. *European Psychologist, 7,* 180–191.

Lunt, I. (2005). The implications of the "Bologna Process" for the development of a European qualification in psychology. *European Psychologist, 10,* 86–92.

Moghaddam, F. M. (1987). Psychology in the three worlds: As reflected by the crisis in social psychology and the move toward indigenous third-world psychology. *American Psychologist, 42,* 912–920.

Montiel, C., & Teh, L. (2004). Psychology in the Philippines. In M. J. Stevens & D. Wedding (Eds.), *Handbook of international psychology* (pp. 467–480). New York: Brunner-Routledge.

Mpofu, E., Zindi, F., Oakland, T., & Peresuh, M. (1997). School psychological practices in East and Southern Africa. *Journal of Special Education, 31,* 387–402.

Mutual Recognition Agreement. (2001). Retrieved June 3, 2005, from http://www.cpa.ca/MRApdf

New Zealand Psychological Society. (2002). *Code of ethics for psychologists working in Aotearoa/New Zealand*. Auckland: Author

New Zealand—*Treaty of Waitangi*. (1840). Retrieved May 29, 2005, from http://treatyofwaitangi.govt.nz/

Nuttin, J. (1979). Are there universal standards that apply to psychologists in all countries? *International Journal of Psychology, 14*, 111–114.

Oakland, T., Goldman, S., & Bischoff, H. (1997). Code of the International School Psychology Association. *School Psychology International, 18*, 291–298.

Odland, T., & Nielsen, S. (1996). Ethical dilemmas of psychologists: Norway [Abstract]. *International Journal of Psychology, 31*, 476.

Okasha, A. (2000). The impact of Arab culture on psychiatric ethics. In A. Okasha, J. Arboleda-Florez, & N. Sartorius (Eds.), *Ethics, culture, and psychiatry: International perspectives* (pp. 15–28). Washington, DC: American Psychiatric Press.

Okasha, A., Arboleda-Florez, J., & Sartorius, N. (Eds.). (2000). *Ethics, culture, and psychiatry: International perspectives*. Washington, DC: American Psychiatric Press.

Olatawrura, M. (2000). Ethics in sub-Saharan Africa. In A. Okasha, J. Arboleda-Florez, & N. Sartorius (Eds.), *Ethics, culture, and psychiatry: International perspectives* (pp. 103–108). Washington, DC: American Psychiatric Press.

O'Neill, P. (2005). The ethics of problem definition. *Canadian Psychology, 45*, 13–20.

Paranjpe, A., Ho, D. Y. F., & Rieber, R. W. (1988). *Asian contributions to psychology*. London: Praeger.

Pawlik, K., & d'Ydewalle, G. (1996). Psychology and the global commons: Perspectives of international psychology. *American Psychologist, 51*, 488–495.

Pettifor, J. L., & Sawchuk, T. (2006). Psychologists' perceptions of ethically troubling incidents across international borders. *International Journal of Psychology 41*, 216–225.

Plath, I., & Eckensberger, L. (2004). Psychology in Germany. In M. J. Stevens & D. Wedding (Eds.), *Handbook of international psychology* (pp. 331–349). New York: Brunner-Routledge.

Pope, K., & Vetter, V. (1992). Ethical dilemmas encountered by members of the American Psychological Association: A national survey. *American Psychologist, 47*, 397–411.

Prieto, J. M., & García-Rodríguez, Y. (2004). Strengthening psychology in Spain. In M. J. Stevens & D. Wedding (Eds.), *Handbook of international psychology* (pp. 351–369). New York: Brunner-Routledge.

Sabourin, M., & Knowles, M. (2004). Middle East and North Africa regional conference of psychology, Dubai, United Arab Emirates. *International Journal of Psychology, 39*, 145–152.

Sartorius, N. (1999). The declaration of Madrid and current psychiatric practice: Users' and advocates' views. Introduction. *Current Opinion in Psychiatry, 12*, 1–2.

Seymour, F. (2003). Other considerations in the New Zealand revised code of ethics. In J. B. Overmier & J. A. Overmier (Eds.). *Psychology: IUPsyS global resource* [CD-ROM] (4th ed.). Hove, UK: Psychology Press.

Siddiqi, M. (2001). *Unity and diversity: Islamic perspective*. Retrieved May 13, 2005, from http://www.crestlife.com/spirituality/unity_and_diversity_islamic_perspective.htm

Sinclair, C. (2003, 2004). A brief history of ethical principles in professional codes of ethics. In J. B. Overmier & J. A. Overmier (Eds.), *Psychology: IUPsyS global resource* [CD-ROM] (4th and 5th eds.). Hove, UK: Psychology Press.

Sinclair, C. (2005). The Eastern roots of ethical principles and values in current codes of ethics. In M. J. Stevens & D. Wedding (Eds.), *Psychology: IUPsyS global resource* [CD-ROM] (6th ed.). Hove, UK: Psychology Press.

Sinclair, C., & Pettifor, J. (1996). Ethical dilemmas of psychologists: Canada [Abstract]. *International Journal of Psychology, 31*, 476.

Sinclair, C., Poizner, S., Gilmour-Barrett, K., & Randall, D. (1987). The development of a code of ethics for Canadian psychologists. *Canadian Psychology, 28*, 1–8.

Slack, C., & Wassenaar, D. (1999). Ethical dilemmas of South African clinical psychologists: International comparisons. *European Psychologist, 4*, 179–186.

Soueif, M. I., & Ahmed, R. A. (2001). Psychology in the Arab world: Past, present, and future. *International Journal of Group Tensions, 30*, 211–240.

Stead, G. (2004). Psychology in South Africa. In M. J. Stevens & D. Wedding (Eds.), *Handbook of international psychology* (pp. 59–73). New York: Brunner-Routledge.

Stevens, M. J., & Wedding, D. (Eds.). (2004). *Handbook of international psychology.* New York: Brunner-Routledge.

Tikkanen, T. (2004, April). *The European diploma in psychology and the future of the profession in Europe.* Paper presented at the International Congress on Licensure, Certification and Credentialing of Psychologists, Montréal, Canada.

Tikkanen, T. (2005, July). *The present status and future prospects of the profession of psychologists in Europe.* Retrieved July 5, 2005, from http://www.efpa.be/news.php?ID=12

Tomaszewski, T. (1979). Ethical issues from an international perspective. *International Journal of Psychology, 14*, 131–135.

United Nations. (1948). *Universal declaration of human rights.* New York: Author.

United Nations Educational, Scientific, and Cultural Organization. (2001). *The UNESCO universal declaration on cultural diversity.* Retrieved May 29, 2005, from http://portal.unesco.org/cultural

United Nations Educational, Scientific, and Cultural Organization. (2005). *Preliminary draft declaration on universal norms on bioethics.* Retrieved May 12, 2005, from http://portal.unesco.org/shs/en/ev.php-URL_ID=7359&URL_do+Do-TOPIC&URL_SECTION=201.html

United Nations Educational, Scientific, and Cultural Organization. (n.d.) *The universal ethics project at a glance.* Retrieved May 29, 2005, from http://www.unesco.org/opi2/philosophyandethics/intro.htm

Wihak, C. (2004). Psychologists in Nunavut: A comparison of the principles underlying Inuit Qaujimanituqangit and the Canadian Psychological Association code of ethics. *Pimatisiwin: A Journal of Aboriginal and Indigenous Community Health, 2*, 29–40.

World Medical Association. (1994). *International code of medical ethics.* Retrieved December 8, 2003, from http://www.wma.net/e/policy/c8.htm

World Psychiatric Association. (2002). *Madrid declaration on ethical standards for psychiatric practice.* Retrieved December 8, 2003, from http://www.wpanet.org/generalinfo/ethicl.html

Yang, Y. (2004). Advances in psychology in China. In M. J. Stevens & D. Wedding (Eds.), *Handbook of international psychology* (pp. 387–403). New York: Brunner-Routledge.

11

Education and Training for a Global Psychology: Foundations, Issues, and Actions

Anthony J. Marsella
University of Hawaii

INTRODUCTION: THE GLOBAL CONTEXT OF OUR LIVES

As we enter the 21st century, human survival and well being have become enmeshed in a complex web of political, economic, social, and environmental events and forces, many of which are local or regional in origin but have global consequences and implications (e.g., terrorism). The scale, complexity, and impact of these events and forces are new, and they constitute a formidable challenge for psychology as a science and profession. At the core of this challenge is the need for psychology to rethink its assumptions, methods, and interventions and to redefine its role in describing, understanding, and resolving the global problems posed by these events and forces. What is at stake is not only the resolution of the global challenges posed by these events and forces, but the very definition, identity, and viability of psychology as a science and a profession.

The challenges of today's world require a "new" psychology—a global psychology—that recognizes and acknowledges the major global forces and events that are shaping the context of our daily lives, and that acknowledges and prizes the cultural variations in psychologies across the world. The forces and events shaping our world today, including globalization, poverty, migration, environmental degradation, terrorism, wars, and civil conflicts, are having an undeniable impact on individual and societal health and well-being (Marsella, 1998; see chap. 1, this volume for details on how these events and forces are being conceptualized, studied, and addressed).

Tables 11.1 and 11.2 list some of the global forces and events shaping our world today. These events and forces are both causes and effects of others because of their interactive relations (e.g., war-refugees-disease-migration-poverty). Although it may appear that many of these events and forces are distant in place, time, and consequence for the United States, the fact of the matter is that they do have a profound impact on our individual and collective health and well-being. These events and forces find their way into all of our lives via political, economic, and social uncertainties, confusion, and tensions that generate a sense of fear, danger, and insecurity. They constitute the daily milieu in which all of our lives are lived. They press upon us with urgent and immediate demands that are uncontrollable, leaving us feeling that we are hapless victims in a storm. Yet, even amidst the turmoil and turbulence, there are emerging resources that hold much promise for a better world. Psychology needs to increase its awareness and consciousness of these events and forces. It must respond with a new vision of responsibility. In reconfiguring itself to address the global challenges of the 21st century, psychology must acknowledge and incorporate human diversity as the foundation for a paradigm shift in the education and training of psychologists.

PSYCHOSOCIAL IMPACT OF GLOBAL CHANGE

A number of writers have pointed out that the changes we are experiencing have profound psychological consequences. They are creating tensions and fears that we are having difficulty negotiating. Some claim that they are shaping a new character for our age. For example, more than a decade ago, Jay Lifton (1993) noted the emergence of a *protean self*:

> We are becoming fluid and many sided. Without quite realizing it, we have been evolving a sense of self appropriate to the restlessness and flux of our times. This mode of being differs radically from that of the past, and enables us

TABLE 11.1
Major Global Challenges

1.	*Hegemonic Globalization.*	The process and product of increased global interdependency fostered by telecommunications, transportation, and the transnational movement of financial capital and wealth. Control and benefits of globalization have been confined to Western power sources, although Japan and, more recently, China and India are benefiting from the shift of economic and political power from the West to the East.
2.	*Transportation.*	Rapid transportation technology (e.g., airlines, automobiles, bullet trains).
3.	*Telecommunications and Media.*	Rapid communication technology (e.g., e-mail, television, fax) and emerging global cyberspace subcultures.
4.	*Global and Transnational Corporations.*	Corporations and commercial enterprises of global proportion that have no national allegiance or identity thus constituting a powerful new economic, political, and social force.
5.	*Population.*	Rapid and massive world population growth (i.e., 6.5 billion in 2006, projected to exceed 9 billion by 2050 or earlier). Changes in demographic distributions in many countries: population growth will occur mainly in developing countries and reductions in birth rates within developed countries except among minority populations.
6.	*Poverty.*	Twenty percent of the world's population living in absolute poverty (i.e., no adequate food, housing, or water). The poorest 20% of the world's population have 1.4% of the global income. Access to clean, safe, and sufficient water is emerging as a serious problem in both developing and developed nations.
7.	*Inequitable Wealth Distribution.*	Increasing gap in the distribution of wealth between rich and poor. Largest wealth gap among industrialized nations is now in the United States.
8.	*Migration and Refugees.*	Existence of 40 million refugees and internally displaced persons, most from developing nations. Massive legal and illegal migration waves from south to north, east to west.

(Continued)

TABLE 11.1 (Continued)
Major Global Challenges

9.	Urbanization.	More than 50% of the world's population live in cities that are unprepared to deal with the problems of urban blight and decay, especially in developing countries. Slums continue to develop and to become sources of violence and discontent. Homelessness and street children are major problems.
10.	Environment.	Environmental problems with air, water, and land pollution, degradation, and desertification. Problems with ocean-fish depletion, rain forest loss, reduction in biodiversity, global climatic changes, and species extinction.
11.	Raw Materials.	The increasing competition for raw materials and natural resources worldwide (e.g., oil).
12.	Global Warming.	Increases in global temperatures as a result of abuses in fossil-fuel use and use of other products resulting in rising ocean-water levels and the potential disappearance of island nations and cultures.
13.	War.	Existence of more than 30 low-intensity wars (e.g., Afghanistan, Congo, Kashmir, Israel–Palestine, Russia, Sri Lanka, Sudan). Governmental repression of autonomy movements (e.g., Tibet, Kurds in Turkey, Chechnya). Continuation of a major war in Iraq.
14.	Crime and Violence.	International problems in crime and violence including organized criminal syndicates controlling illegal drugs, prostitution (e.g., Natasha Circle), gambling, illegal arms sales.
15.	Terrorism.	Increase in worldwide terrorism. Growing risk of massive biological, chemical, and nuclear terrorism (i.e., weapons of mass destruction).
16.	Health and Disease.	Major advances in medical knowledge, technology, and services that are extending life spans and producing new ethical and moral challenges (e.g., genetic cloning, stem cell research, medicalization of social problems). Emergence of major international diseases (e.g., AIDS, Avian flu, plague) and health risks (e.g., illegal drugs, tobacco addiction, and alcoholism).

TABLE 11.1 (*Continued*)
Major Global Challenges

17.	*Well-Being and Mental Health.*	Massive problems in mental health, psychosocial well being, and social deviancy as rapid social changes, often in the form of hegemonic Western cultural penetration, result in cultural disintegration, collapse, and loss of traditional life styles and decline in indigenous populations.
18.	*Human Rights Violations.*	Widespread violations of human rights in countries throughout the world. Documented use of torture and rendition by the United States, thus reducing its moral authority and legitimacy.
19.	*Labor Exploitation of Children, Women, and Certain Occupations.*	Increased reliance on cheap labor by using children and women for mass production products in developing countries and as illegal labor in developed countries. Certain occupations such as miners in China and South Africa are at increased risk of death and illness because of poor working conditions.
20.	*The Isms.*	Racism, ageism, sexism, and related prejudices and hate-filled biases challenge peace and understanding and encourage categorical responses that limit human relations.
21.	*Theocratic Movements.*	Rise of religion-dominated political forces that advocate theocratic governments in developing (e.g., Iran) and developed nations (e.g, Israel, the United States). Use of religion to justify violence and political dominance.

to engage in continuous exploration and personal experiment. I have named it the "protean self" after Proteus, the Greek sea god of many forms. The protean self emerges from confusion, from widespread feeling that we are losing our psychological moorings. We feel ourselves buffeted by unmanageable historical forces and social uncertainties … Enduring moral convictions, clear principles of action and behavior: we believe these must exist, but where? Whether dealing with world problems or child rearing, our behavior tends to be *ad hoc*, more or less decided upon as we go along. We are beset by a contradiction. Schooled in the virtues of constancy and stability—whether as individuals, groups, or nations—our world and our lives seem inconstant and utterly unpredictable. We readily come to view ourselves as unsteady, neurotic, or worse. (p. 1)

TABLE 11.2
Major Global Resources

1.	*The World is Flat.*	Thomas Friedman (2005), the *New York Times* columnist, recently argued that the massive informational and economic changes occurring in the world today are producing a "flat world" or equal playing field, in which Western hegemonic dominance, with all of its implications for power asymmetries and cultural abuses, is being compelled to accommodate to others. This growing "equality" is a wonderful advancement in which the talents and abilities of an entire world can be called upon to address global challenges rather than keeping control within the narrow limits of the West.
2.	*Equal Access to Knowledge.*	Through the Internet, every individual and organization, even in the most isolated and distant village, has access to the world's knowledge. For example, every work in The Library of Congress is accessible to a village youth in Northern India. The only barrier is any political system that denies access. This equalizes access to knowledge.
3.	*Advances in Sciences and Humanities.*	Continued progress in advancing knowledge about our universe in astronomy, astrophysics, and space sciences, knowledge about our world in oceanography and earth sciences, knowledge about human history in archaeology and historical studies, and knowledge about human nature in the social and behavioral sciences and the humanities is accumulating and opening new vistas of understanding.
4.	*Advances in Medical Knowledge.*	Increasing advances in medical knowledge and practice are saving lives and improving the quality of life for the many people burdened by illness. Continued work on the human genome and the development of new medications and surgical procedures hold much promise for all.
5.	*Global Conscience and Consciousness.*	Although there are many reasons to believe the opposite, progress is occurring in world peace and justice. Increasingly, people are protesting war and violence and speaking out against commercial and government corruption, human rights and environmental abuses, and the continuation of inequities in wealth, health, and security. The global response to the recent South Asian tsunam represents yet another example of conscience and consciousness.

TABLE 11.2 *(Continued)*
Major Global Resources

6. *Improvements in Human Rights.*	Although human rights abuses remain extensive in number and enormous in their individual and societal consequences, progress is occurring in reducing these abuses and in restoring justice.
7. *Increase in Non-Government Organizations.*	It is impossible to determine the number of NGOs in the world today. But, what is clear is that the number is growing and their positive impact upon key issues (e.g., human rights, honest government, poverty, peace) is increasing.
8. *Citizen Activism.*	Throughout the world, citizens from different nations are choosing to participate actively in their society. Through mass protests in favor of democracy to more quiet local actions, citizens are speaking out and acting in favor of necessary changes.
9. *Spirituality.*	Even as radical religious fundamentalism continues to assert its destructive head among the Abrahamitic religions and their related subgroups, sects, and cults, it is clear that growing numbers of people are turning from the allure and promises of these dogmatic views in favor of more spiritual beliefs and views. Spirituality embodies a sense of connection, relationship, and interdependency with humanity and the cosmos without a blind adherence to dogma, ritual, and unassailable beliefs. Inherent within the spiritual view is a commitment to humanity and to humanitarian efforts.
10. *Growth of Psychology.*	Around the world, psychology as a profession and science is growing in leaps and bounds. Even as interest in psychology continues to increase in Europe and the United States, it is noteworthy that the growth is faster in Asia and that the number of psychologists in this region may out number those in the United States. This is a resource for the world if psychology chooses to expand its vistas, methods, and special skills.

Within the mental health field, numerous disorders related to the stress of our times are emerging, including specific syndromes of distress and disorder associated with this problem, such as future shock, culture shock, alienation/anomie, acculturation stress, meaninglessness, rootlessness, paranoid states, and identity confusion (see chapters 1 and 8, this volume). Also emerging are societal and group disorders such as cultural disintegration, cultural dislocation, ethnic cleansing, social disillusionment, social fragmentation, urban blight and decay, and endemic crime and violence (Marsella, 2000a; see chapters 1 and 9, this volume).

Schneider (1975), Gergen (1991), Sandel (1996), and Sloan (1996), have all written about the psychological and psychiatric consequences of living in our demanding, confusing, and uncertain times. For Sandel, this situation calls for a new citizen who can "abide the ambiguity associated with divided sovereignty" and "who can think and act as multiply situated selves" (p. 74). According to Sandel, the new world will require multiple loyalties. The requirement of multiple loyalties, multiple identities, multiple citizenships relating to cities, nations, regions, and ultimately the world, all promise to challenge the current ways of thinking about psychology as a science and profession. A new psychology is needed that is relevant to the present situation.

With these thoughts in mind, it is clear that we must train new generations of psychologists to be culturally, ethnically, and racially sensitive, and to be increasingly alert to the ethnocentricity and racial biases inherent in psychology because of its Western origins. We must prepare students to value and honor the diversity in our world and to help preserve it, since diversity rather than uniformity is what offers us choices to see and experience the world in different ways. We must also teach social justice across the curriculum, pointing out the abuses to human dignity that have characterized our history and continue to exist today.

These are some of the reasons that we need to educate for a global psychology. Psychology must be responsive to the global challenges of our age by virtue of knowledge, methods, and practices that are valid and relevant to our times. Psychology must simultaneously attend to the pressing concerns of the human spirit for identity, purpose, and meaning by advocating justice, equality, and peace.

At present, psychology as a science and profession is inadequately prepared by virtue of its educational assumptions, methods, and practices. Psychology's continued commitment to the anachronistic assumptions of logical positivism remains a reactionary source of influence and control over its future. Specifically, the tendency of logical positivism to dismantle and decontextualize psychosocial and sociocultural phenomena robs the discipline and profession of an opportunity to understand more fully and respond more effectively to global needs and challenges. There is an urgent need for a reconsideration of psychology's entire educational content and process. From assumptions to training sites, from the classroom to field experiences, new and imaginative approaches are needed. The simple fact of the matter is that psychology, as presently defined and conceived, is inadequately prepared to address the challenges of our global age (Marsella, 1998). Tod Sloan (1996b), a leading figure in the liberation and critical psychology movements challenging the hegemony of Western psychology, writes:

> ... the major problem lies less in the theoretical limits of Western psychology, although these are serious, than in the social functions of Western psychology. As scientific psychology entrenches itself further in industrial nations, its function as a sociopolitical stabilizing mechanism has gradually become more obvious ... psychological theory and practice embody Western cultural assumptions to such an extent that they primarily perform an ideological function. That is, they serve to reproduce and sustain societal status quo characterized by economic inequality and other forms of oppression such as sexism and racism. The core operative assumptions that produce this ideological effect both in theory and practice are individualism and scientism. (p. 39)

MEETING THE CHALLENGES

In the 1990s, the convergence of a number of events of global proportion and consequence—ethnopolitical wars in the Balkans, Africa, and Asia, increases in the frequency and scale of domestic and international terrorism, and a growing awareness of the consequences of hegemonic globalization— fostered a new consciousness and conscience among some sectors of Western psychology. For some psychologists, especially those within the critical psychology and cultural psychology sectors (e.g., Fox & Prilleltensky, 1997; Hoshmand, 1994; Martín-Baró, 1994; Sampson, 1989; Sloan, 1996b), these events signaled a new awareness of the need for psychology to reposition itself on the international stage (see chapter, 2, this volume, for psychology's international roots and uprooting). There was a sense that psychology could do much more to address global challenges, but not within the context of its existing assumptions, methods, and power distribution. Graduate courses and research methods rooted in Western culture and the positivistic tradition were doing little to advance the field. There was a particular concern for acknowledging psychology's need to pursue social justice and to refrain from supporting institutions and societal values that maintained the status quo. Fox and Prilleltensky (1997) wrote:

> ... we believe that psychology's traditional practices and norms hinder social justice, to the detriment of individuals and communities in general and of

oppressed groups in particular ... as you will discover throughout this book, mainstream psychology is also inherently value-laden. It seeks to maintain things essentially as they are, supporting societal institutions that reinforce unjust and unsatisfying conditions. Psychology is not, and cannot be, a neutral endeavour conducted by scientists and practitioners detached from social and political circumstances. It is a human and social endeavour. Psychologists live in specific social contexts. They are influenced by differing interests and complex power dynamics. Mainstream psychologists too often shy away from the resulting moral, social, and political implications. (p. 1)

Efforts were emerging that challenged the consequences of the Western psychology's historical culture with its emphasis on individualism, materialism, competition, reductionism, patriarchy, and empiricism. Implicit to the nature and meaning of psychology, these assumptions were generating a fundamental question: "Is this type of psychology useful, valid, and meaningful for understanding life in a global age?" The answer was a resounding "No!" Consciousness and conscience in psychology were coming together to forge new directions for psychology at a number of different levels.

During this period, a number of groups, including the American Psychological Association (APA) and the International Union of Psychological Science (Overmier & Overmier, 2000) published commentaries and resource materials that documented scientific and professional psychology's rapidly growing popularity around the world and the challenges and opportunities this presented (see Fowler, 1996; Overmier & Overmier, 2000). Building on the earlier work of Sexton and Hogan (1992), Stevens and Wedding (2004) began work on the *Handbook of International Psychology*, an edited volume that summarized the current status of psychology in 27 countries, highlighting both the origins, growth, approaches, and current challenges to scientific and professional psychology, including the education and training of psychologists. This landmark book offered contemporary psychology a foundation for building new educational programs for global psychology.[1]

However, it was in the persuasive articulation of the need for a different psychology—one fitted to the demands of a global age—that the impetus for change found its focus. This occurred via the publication of a

---

[1]International psychology and global psychology are often used interchangeably. However, the former implies the idea of nations as defining the boundaries for discussion, whereas the latter tends to be more inclusive of groups, cultures, societies, and other collectives. See chaptet 1, this volume, for more on the issues related to the use of these terms.

series of articles in *American Psychologist* (e.g., Gergen, Gulerce, Lock, & Misra, 1996; Lunt & Poortinga, 1996; Marsella, 1998; Mays, Rubin, Sabouriun, & Walker, 1996; Moghaddam, 1987; Pawlik & d'Ydewalle, 1996a; Prilleltensky, 1997); other journals (e.g., Sloan, 1990); and some liberating books (e.g., Carr & Schumaker, 1996; Fox & Prilleltensky, 1997; Kim & Berry, 1993; Martín-Baró, 1994; Mustakova-Possardt, 2003; Sloan, 1996a). These publications articulated the vision, definition, and conscience of the field of global psychology. Pawlik and d'Ydewalle (1996) openly stated that "Future challenges from society will require behavioral-science based approaches to meet new global conditions of life" (p. 488). The impact of these publications was augmented by the efforts of the APA's Committee on International Relations to promote the internationalization of the psychology curriculum (Marsella, 2000b; Marsella & Pedersen, 2004) and the emergence of the APA's Division of International Psychology as a major proponent of global psychology.

A growing number of non-Western and ethnic minority psychologists are noting that psychology with its emphases on the individual, objectivity, quantification, narrow disciplinary specialization, and universal "truths," may be irrelevant and meaningless for non-Western peoples and their life contexts (chapters 4 and 5, this volume, speak to the limitations of Western psychology when applied to the majority world and indigenous cultures, respectively). They argue that international organizations, training programs, research activities, and publications remain rooted within Western psychology and, thus, cannot serve as the foundation for a psychology that is responsive to our present global context. Western psychology, they contend, can at best offer only a limited perspective that reflects its present position of power and privilege. For example, Misra, an Asian Indian psychologist, wrote:

> The current Western thinking of the science of psychology in its prototypical form, despite being local and indigenous, assumes a global relevance and is treated as a universal mode of generating knowledge. Its dominant voice subscribes to a decontextualized vision with an extraordinary emphasis on individualism, mechanism, and objectivity. This peculiarly Western mode of thinking is fabricated, projected, and institutionalized through representation technologies and scientific rituals and transported on a large scale to the non-Western societies under political-economic domination. As a result, Western psychology tends to maintain an independent stance at the cost of ignoring other substantive possibilities from disparate cultural traditions. Mapping reality through Western constructs has offered a pseudo-understanding of the people of alien cultures and has had debilitating effects in terms of misconstruing the special realities of other people and exoticizing or disregarding

psychologies that are non-Western. Consequently, when people from other cultures are exposed to Western psychology, they find their identities placed in question and their conceptual repertoires rendered obsolete. (Gergen et al., 1996, pp. 497–498)

Moghaddam (1997) concluded that Third-World psychologists may require a different type and content of education and training. He suggests Third-World psychologists should be trained in their own countries with materials and research methods that are culturally appropriate, including despecialization. He states:

> The training of Third-World psychologists should take place with culture at its core with the goal of achieving skills in the understanding and assessment of normative systems that are prescriptive and able to inform people as to what is correct behavior in a given context and the skills that people acquire through socialization, to identify and to use normative systems as a guide for *how to behave*, and as a basis for ascribing meaning to behavior. (p. 56)

Thus, the arguments are numerous and clear. There is a need for a "new" psychology that is responsive to the global challenges we face today and critical of the biases and limitations inherent in Western psychology as presently positioned and sustained within academia. Thankfully, there appears to be movement in such countries as Brazil and China. Even in the conservative Arab world there is movement toward a more responsive and responsible psychology that is better suited to meet local needs as defined by global events and forces (Stevens & Wedding, 2004).

GLOBAL PSYCHOLOGY

The emerging concern for a psychology capable of meeting the challenges of a global age has led to a number of changes in assumptions, values, and methods in psychology (see chapters, 6, 7, and 9, this volume, for additional information on alternative conceptualizations, research approaches, and large-scale interventions, respectively). In my opinion, these changes included the following:

1. *Interest in Global Problems*. Psychology must show interest in addressing and helping to resolve major global challenges (e.g., war and violence, poverty, famine, urban decay, refugees and displaced persons, international migration, terrorism).
2. *Acknowledgement of Socio-Political Forces in Psychology*. As a science and profession, psychology involves the distribution of power assigned

to different institutional sectors, knowledge bases and priorities, and leading figures. It is not value free, nor is it objective. It is a political enterprise controlled and operated by those who have access to power. This determines the content, procedures, and consequences of education and training in psychology by emphasizing a particular canon to the exclusion of others. Both academic departments and professional organizations play a part in this process.

3. *Commitment to the Importance of Culture*. The field must include cultural and ethnic minority psychologies in coursework and acknowledge the risks of ethnocentricity and bias. Within psychology itself, there are numerous new specialties emphasizing cultural determinants of behavior (e.g., cultural psychology, cross-cultural psychology, ethnic minority psychology, multicultural psychology, indigenous psychologies, international psychology, transcultural mental health); yet, these specialties are often marginalized or isolated as electives rather than being considered essential requirements for a global age. International understanding is predicated on respect for cultural diversity and the choices and options this offers for understanding reality.

4. *Multidisciplinary, Multisectoral, and Multinational Connections*. Psychology must show interest in multidisciplinary studies (e.g., environmental conservation, illness prevention), multisectoral competences (e.g., working with judicial, educational, medical, commercial, and religious sectors), and multinational issues and organizations (e.g., the U.N., International Red Cross, World Health Organization, Doctors Without Borders).

5. *Emphasis on New Approaches and Values*. The revolution in thought and practice that has emerged in the last few decades has introduced new conceptual models (e.g., chaos theory, complexity theory, postmodernism, social constructionism, feminist theory), assumptions (e.g., subjectivity, context determination, historical determination), research methodologies (e.g., participant observation, qualitative methods, action research), values and priorities (e.g., diversity promotion, cultural sensitivity and competence, social justice, activism), and disciplinary subspecialties (e.g., peace and conflict resolution, disaster management, public policy).

6. *Concern for Peace, Justice, and Nonviolence*. It is customary in many academic disciplines for education and training to ignore any reference to certain values that may guide the program, other

than the usual generalities about promoting human welfare and
responding in an ethical manner. These are, of course, valuable
signposts to follow, but it is also clear that in our global age, in
which local and national events have consequences for the global
community, certain values must be given some priority in guiding
the education and training enterprise. In my opinion, three values
are essential: peace, justice, and nonviolence. In coursework,
extracurricular activities, and other aspects of education and training, these must be clearly articulated and supported.

These six dimensions of change in psychology, in my opinion, constitute the foundations for a global psychology and, as such, require both
curricular and institutional adjustments and changes that are consonant
with them and with the complex dynamics of our global age. In my opinion, the adjustments and changes must occur at multiple levels including
the APA, universities and colleges, and the curricular and extracurricular
activities offered by psychology departments.

What is needed are new approaches to education in psychology as a
science and profession that can train psychologists motivated and capable of meeting the challenges of life in a global age. We need approaches
that endorse and support research and applied knowledge and skills that
are multidisciplinary, multisectoral, multilevel, and multicultural. The
approaches to education will also require teaching new conceptual
models and analytical methodologies that move beyond conventional knowledge based on Western scientific assumptions and quantitative methods, and their associated ideological foundations. Further, it will
require a concern for the moral dimension of one's work, especially with
regard to justice and equality (e.g., Marsella, in press).

Indeed, our current knowledge and training not only neglects to
prepare psychologists for meeting the challenges of a global age, but may
actually interfere with progress by insisting on dated, biased, and unwar-
ranted course content. This does not mean a turning away from or
moving against traditional psychology, but rather a careful review of what
is known through Western psychological theories, methods, and interventions that can be accommodated with new demands.

EDUCATION AND TRAINING IN GLOBAL PSYCHOLOGY

In considering the education and training content and processes for global
psychology, I chose to emphasize three components: *person*, *philosophy*, and

process and content. Each of these points must be considered at departmental levels if educating and training for global psychology is to be more than just an elective course in an existing array of professional and scientific options. This is an expansive position and, because of this, may not sit well given existing limitations in staff and funding. Yet, imagine the possibilities of construing global psychology as a distinct specialty area in psychology that integrates existing professional and scientific skills with a philosophy commensurate with the challenges we face in a global age and the training content and processes that are geared to these challenges. Thus, I am arguing here for more than a course in global psychology, admirable and necessary as that may be (see Appendix B for a sample course syllabus and contact information for those who have developed and/or taught such courses). I am arguing for a new and imaginative field that combines existing courses and training activities with new courses and activities.

Person

Not everyone can be an effective global psychologist. Much as there are variations in the personal styles, talents, and abilities among psychologists who choose different specialties (e.g., physiological psychology, quantitative methods, clinical psychology), the decision to pursue a career in global psychology should be guided by similar considerations. Although temperament may not be critical, personal style, values, and commitments are important. The global psychologist, in my opinion, must have a profound commitment to improving the human condition through social activism and the pursuit of justice and equality. He or she cannot be indifferent to the challenges we are facing nor apathetic in his or her willingness to improve the situation. Such a psychologist must have interpersonal skills that include, but are not limited to, empathy, compassion, and communication sensitivities. The challenges we face in this global age will test all our skills, talents, and values as psychologists and as human beings.

At the core of any education and training in global psychology is the issue of human values and character. Global psychology is not simply an occupation, career, or profession; it is a way of life that requires a commitment to the enduring human values of peace, justice, honor, charity, and human rights. Unlike some occupations in which the separation of work and person is inconsequential, global psychology requires an intentional fusion of person and profession. This is because the demands of addressing global challenges vis-à-vis psychology are both numerous and arduous. In many ways, the work of the global psychologist is revolutionary in the full sense of this term since intervention and prevention activities will likely involve the encouragement and promotion of massive social changes in existing social structures and institutions. Within this context, character is not incidental, but rather a requirement that brings added strength and resources to one's work, including determination, empathy, and resilience. The work impacts one's character, enhancing one's intellectual and spiritual dimensions, and in return, one's character impacts one's work. This reciprocity is essential.

The global challenges we face will test all of our skills, talents, and abilities as both psychologists and human beings. Joining our personal and professional lives is a necessity. In this regard, Franklin (1998) called for "full capacity global citizens," writing:

> For me [there] … are heartwarming examples of people stepping into the role of what I call "full capacity global citizens"—people willing to take on the twin challenge of deepening their personal capacities (intuitive, spiritual, intellectual) as well as assuming responsibility for the planet and the whole of humanity. These examples, and those from countless other groups and individuals demonstrate that we are capable of a societal vision that transcends unbridled individualism and materialism—one that is more sustainable, equitable, and multifaceted, and includes spiritual and psychological, as well as economic growth. … The shift in consciousness that seems to be required includes an accommodation of our interdependence and our need to find a basis for shared meaning and purpose. (p. 3)

Consistent with the ethical principle and moral value of social responsibility that is captured by an evolving universal code of ethics (Gauthier, 2005), I call upon psychologists to express their respect for and duty to humankind by determining how best to measure the qualities of a full capacity global citizen and devising curricula and pedagogies that nurture and sustain these qualities.

Philosophy

In this global age, global psychologists must live their profession, and their profession must be an integral part of their life, an extension of what they value and are willing to commit themselves to in order to find purpose, meaning, and fulfillment (see chapter 10, this volume, on professional psychology in a globalized world). Anything less is insufficient for the global challenges we face. However, to achieve this union will

require that universities and colleges, as the societal sectors most responsible for sharing the accumulated wisdom of generations and for generating new knowledge to promote human welfare and well being, reconsider
many of their current assumptions, objectives, and practices. In the
author's opinion, the academy—that glorious and noble institution that
traces it roots to the streets and forums of ancient Greece—is failing in
its mission to impart both the knowledge and the wisdom necessary for
survival and success in a global age. It is failing because it is not teaching
that at the heart of a meaningful education is the issue of character and
the values so desperately needed to bring peace and social justice to our
world today (e.g., Prilleltensky, 1997).

If global psychology is to address and resolve the myriad of complex
challenges enumerated in Table 11.1 and to make use of the resources
listed in Table 11.2, then the motivation must stem from a substantive
personal and collective discontent and intolerance of the massive injustices and insecurities that abound in our world. Yet, this is too often
ignored in the educational process. Although some may consider it
unethical, or even dangerous, for the educational process to intrude into
the "characterological" aspects of a student's life, it is clear to me that
quite the opposite is true—not challenging the students to think about
the sources and consequences of their character is the greater risk.
Indeed, leaving the hapless human psyche open to the questionable
machinations of government, business, military, and religion is a far
greater risk to a society's survival. We may give out degrees and diplomas,
but we cannot claim we educate our students. We need to encourage
students to grasp the sources and consequences of their actions—the
critical role of culture in constructing their realities. We need to encourage students to evaluate their own society, including its unpleasant and
unsavory history. We need, as professors and mentors, to model these
behaviors.

The APA's Task Force on Undergraduate Psychology Major Competencies (2002) was formed in part to prepare psychology students to
understand behavior and experience that transcend geographic boundaries and cultures. Among other educational outcomes is the acquisition
of critical thinking skills, values, and sociocultural and global awareness.
The Task Force also recommended pedagogical strategies for achieving
these outcomes, including adopting an attitude of open-mindedness and
skeptical inquiry; evaluating the level of fulfillment of one's civic, social,
and global duties; and examining how privilege, power, and oppression
may affect prejudice, discrimination, and inequity. These efforts continue

through the APA Working Group to Internationalize the Psychology Curriculum.

Mustakova-Possardt (2003), in her brilliant and articulate discussion of critical consciousness in our global age, writes:

> Young people need to understand that in the current stage of historical unfolding of the collective human consciousness the greatest battle is for global justice and peace. As part of their educational development, they need to ask themselves what will be their individual roles in this grand historical process of learning to establish justice and peace on the planet ... The ultimate testimony of their successful education would be the evolving of a world-embracing vision, an understanding of the historical processes convulsing different parts of the world, and a choice to commit to a specific field of human endeavor as a conscious localized contribution to the peaceful and sustainable globalization of the planet. (p. 163)

Lastly, no discussion of the philosophical foundations for education and training in global psychology would be complete without pointing out the importance of cultural diversity and why it is important to preserve it. It is clear that cultural diversity gives us choices and alternatives when faced with challenges. Different cultures offer different views of reality and with them different opportunities to see the world in a different way and to choose a different path. Homogenization of the world's cultures limits and constrains our options. Mikhail Gorbachev (1995), former President of the former Soviet Union, has written eloquently on the importance of preserving diversity. In an article on developing a new civilization for the 21st century, he wrote:

> The philosophy of the twenty-first century must be grounded in a philosophy of diversity. If life, as such, is the highest value, then even more precious is the singular identity of every nation and every race as a unique creation of nature and human history. ... The beauty and uniqueness of life lies in the unity of diversity. Self-identification—of every individual and of every of the many different nations, ethnic groups, and nationalities—is the crucial condition for preserving life on Earth. Struggles and conflicts burn out diversity of life, leaving a social wasteland in their wake. Honoring diversity and honoring the Earth create the basis for genuine unity. (p. 13)

Process and Content

Efforts to internationalize the educational experience are not new (see chapter 12, this volume). From the Fulbright Program that provides student and faculty exchanges to formal institutions (e.g., The Institute of International Education, United Nations University), educators have long understood the need to increase global awareness and sensitivity in and through education. Occasionally, there is even a bright spot in our government such as the U.S. Institute for Peace's peace essay contest for high school students and provision of post-conflict curricular materials. However, in all candor, this Institute maintains such a low and inconsequential profile in the U.S. government that many do not even know of its existence, and it certainly is not a visible voice questioning international governmental policies and actions.

Internationalizing (Globalizing) the Curriculum

I have published a series of papers and offered presentations on internationalizing the curriculum in psychology (e.g., Marsella, 1998, 2000a, 2000b, 2000c, in press; Marsella & Pedersen, 2004). In these efforts, I have acknowledged that internationalizing the psychology curriculum would be no easy matter because traditional psychology is rooted within a psychology curriculum that both reflects and supports the personal values, epistemologies, praxiologies, and training cultures of the power elite of the discipline. I have pointed out that we need to proceed toward the development of new Western psychologies, indigenous psychologies, and syncretic psychologies that resist the hegemonic imposition or privileged positioning of any one psychology because of its powerful economic, political, or cultural context (Marsella, 1998, 2000a, 2000b, 2000c). I see internationalizing or globalizing the psychology curriculum as a potent first step toward resolving the challenges facing the world because so many of these are rooted within political ideologies and economic systems that are culturally and nationally contextualized and generated.

Other writers have also been concerned with the process and content of international and global psychology at both a general level and with respect to specific challenges. For example, Spariosu (2004) has written an engaging volume entitled *Global Intelligence and Human Development: Toward an Ecology of Global Learning*, which advocates an optimistic pathway for addressing global challenges through an education that emphasizes values, content, and processes rooted within an increased awareness of the global context of our lives, and the possibilities this presents for a peaceful, just, and harmonious future. He cites the need for a broadening of content as well as conceptual and research strategies to include chaos theory, catastrophe theory, cybernetics, systems theory, and ecological approaches. Like others, he encourages more multidisciplinary and multicultural approaches in education. Mustakova-Possardt (2003) goes beyond curricular concerns to advocate the necessity of including moral and spiritual knowledge, and of giving greater attention to issues of conscience as well as political and social abuses in our educational approaches. She writes:

> The challenge we are facing is, above all, a spiritual challenge. We need a fundamental change in consciousness, a movement away from reductionistic materialism as a dominant philosophy, as well as from its forms of social and political expression. (p. 189)

Both of these writers point to the need to move beyond Western psychology, which they see as a cultural creation rooted within Western historical events and concerns. They join critical psychologists in pointing out an apparent reluctance among many psychologists and psychology departments to accept a very basic "truth"—that Western psychology is rooted in an ideology of individualism, rationality, and empiricism that needs to be reconsidered within the global age in which we are living. Spariosu's discussion of Asian philosophy and its implications for behavior is very enlightening. In fairness, it can be said that some of the criticisms and suggestions Spariosu and others have advocated are themselves Western in origin. Moreover, some offshoots of the indigenous movement in psychology embrace the creative and productive application of traditional scientific methods to the study of local culture (see chapter 5, this volume, for examples within East Asian psychology).

In addition to general approaches to internationalizing the curriculum, different groups have also offered course curricula for the specific topics, such as the study of ethnopolitical warfare (e.g., American Psychological Association and Canadian Psychological Association Task Forces, 2001). This report was prepared under the auspices of the Psychologists for Social Responsibility (http://www.psysr.com), an organization, in the author's opinion, that best typifies the values and recommendations of the present chapter. What is especially admirable about this report is its delineation of much-needed competencies, knowledge, skills, attitudes, and values.

In proposing to internationalize or globalize the psychology curriculum, I believe we should begin with a recognition of the competencies that are needed by psychologists to function successfully (validly) in today's world. As psychologists, we do many things, including teaching, conceptualizing, researching, consulting, assessing, evaluating, mediating,

TABLE 11.3
Knowledge–Attitude–Practice Education and Training Paradigm

Knowledge	Attitude	Practice
Cultural variations in:	Openness to alternative views	Empathy
Values	Diversity	Process > Product
Behavior	Interdependency	Assessment skills
Morality	Social interest	Evaluation skills
Communication	Peace and justice	Rapport building
Social Structure	Equality	Mediation skills
Language	Globalism	Communication
Cultural construction of reality	Participation	Civility/Politeness
History	Humility	Activism
Impact of social changes	Awareness of ethnocentrism	Peace building
International/Regional studies	Activism	Nation building
Peace/Conflict resolution		Public speaking
Disasters/Terrorism/War		
Foreign languages		
Multidisciplinary training in:		
Urban planning		
Global public health		
Ethnography		
Ethics		
Nation building		

intervening, and preventing. Obviously, we need to be aware of cultural differences, share knowledge of these differences, consult across cultures, and/or actively participate in bringing about cultural changes. Each step in this progression requires greater cultural and global competency and, perhaps, even formal certification. The interesting fact is that, even as we speak of educating our students, it will also be necessary to educate our faculty. Table 11.3 lists some competencies according to the popular knowledge–attitude–practice paradigm (see American Psychological Association and Canadian Psychological Association Task Forces, 2001; Marsella, 2000a, 2000b, 2000c).

Teaching About Cultures. The concept of culture and its variations is at the heart of the present chapter. Definitions of culture have proved to be difficult and are subject to much controversy; however, there is some value in offering a definition at this time because of global psychology's emphasis on understanding the many different ethnocultural traditions in the world and the numerous subcultures that also require understanding. I define culture as:

> Culture is shared learned behavior and meanings that are socially transferred in various life-activity settings for purposes of individual and collective adjustment and adaptation. Cultures can be (1) transitory (i.e., situational, even existing for only a few minutes), (2) enduring (e.g., ethnocultural life styles), and in all instances are (3) dynamic (i.e., constantly subject to change and modification. Cultures are represented (4) internally (i.e., values, beliefs, attitudes, axioms, orientations, epistemologies, consciousness levels, perceptions, expectations, personhood) and (5) externally (i.e., artifacts, roles, institutions, social structures). Cultures also (6) develop within subgroup settings such as those that exist in hospitals, academic departments, gangs, the military, and the Internet. Cultures (7) shape and construct our realities (i.e., they contribute to our world views, perceptions, orientations) and with this, our concepts of normality, morality, aesthetics, and other dimensions.

Awareness and understanding of subgroup cultures (as mentioned previously) is also important for education and training in global psychology. The breakdown in the viability of national governments and borders and the emergence of pan-national and global-cultural subgroup loyalties and affiliations requires attention. For example, consider the impact that Internet computer technology has had on our lives. With a stroke of the finger, we can enter a "cyber society" that stretches across the globe, ignoring national and natural borders. The new rules, symbols, and activities constitute a new subculture that has powerful socializing influences— it constructs a new identity in structured space (e.g., Jones, 1997; Kraut et al., 1998).

Because of its widespread use, the Internet could be used to raise global consciousness about common challenges regarding sustainable economies, environmental preservation, and world peace. But, at the same time, it becomes a new subculture replete with its own psychology and behavioral consequences. For example, consider the impact that Internet computer technology has had on our lives (e.g., Kraut et al., 1998). This raises issues about the preferred behavioral characteristics of people around the globe. Are there certain values, behavioral patterns, and lifestyles that can optimize our local and global quality of life? Are there certain values we can and should share even as we promote cultural diversity? Consider, for example, justice, civility, interdependency, social interest (*gemeinschaftsgefühl*), diversity, and human rights.

Other global subcultures are also generating psychologies unique to their homogenized cultural premises and practices. For example, universities throughout the world have many similarities; so do corporations, hospitals, military forces, and major urban settings. One wonders if these global subcultures may generate identities specific to them, transcending the normal national boundaries we associate with certain groups or nations. And, if this occurs, what are the consequences? The spread of global subcultures also raises issues about preferred common behavioral characteristics of people around the globe. Cultural awareness training as well as formal academic coursework will be a critical part of continuing education. I recommend Paul Pedersen's (2004) recent book on multicultural learning, which offers scores of culture-learning exercises for teaching students about their own culture and the culture of others. Culture learning is an essential part of education and training for global psychology.

Academic Coursework.   How should we train students for global psychology (see chapter 12, which contains pedagogic resources and suggestions for instructors and students)? In my opinion, a training program should include courses in such areas as cross-cultural psychology, cultural psychology, indigenous psychologies, international relations, cultural anthropology, urban sociology/urban planning, community psychology, public health, international business, peace studies, future studies, and macroeconomics. It can include coursework in systems, chaos, and complexity theory. The training must involve education in multicultural, multidisciplinary, and multisectoral premises, methods, and interventions. This will ultimately promote intercultural, interdisciplinary, and intersectoral thinking. The training will require more distance learning, field research and service activities, global modeling analyses, and international activities. New technologies, such as global modeling, can assist in introducing "global-community psychologists" to the dynamic and interdependent spectrum of global forces acting upon human behavior.

It is possible to offer both specialized seminars in various topics related to global psychology (e.g., disaster psychology, conflict resolution and mediation, psychology of war and peace) or to integrate these topics into existing courses in community, clinical, and/or applied social psychology. For example, Psychologists for Social Responsibility (2001) has published on the World Wide Web *A Graduate-level Curriculum for Trauma Intervention and Conflict Resolution in Ethnopolitical Warfare* that includes extensive references and ideas for the design of courses on this contemporary topic (http://www.psysr.org). The awarding of certificates for completion of work in specialized areas is also an option. For example, the University of Hawaii (http://www.hawaii.edu/psychology) offers a graduate specialization in Community and Culture leading to the doctorate. The importance of multidisciplinary education is recognized and, hence, the core curriculum is combined with offerings from other academic departments. The specialization includes certificate options in Planning Studies, Disaster Management and Humanitarian Assistance, and Conflict Resolution, all of which are grounded in an empirical orientation to professional activity in social and cultural contexts and settings that is geared toward the prevention of human problems and enhancement of social competence. Students complete graduate coursework in disaster management, terrorism, war, peace, migration, and area studies, along with a supervised field practicum. The University of South Dakota (http://www.usd.edu/dmhi/academics.cfm) offers a graduate certificate in Disaster Mental Health to students in master's level counseling, psychiatric nursing, and marriage and family therapy programs, to doctoral students in clinical and counseling psychology, and to psychiatric residents. The certificate is also available to already licensed mental health professionals. Required coursework includes crisis intervention, disaster mental health, international disaster psychology, posttraumatic stress disorder, and serving the diverse community in disaster.

Imagine supervised practica and internships in new settings (e.g., refugee camps, international organizations) for both scholars and practitioners. These would offer opportunities to merge academic and applied knowledge. Imagine also the consequences of increasing foreign language fluency and use among psychologists (see Stevens & Wedding, 2004). Heretofore, English has been the primary language for international communication, but consider the possibilities if North American psychologists are encouraged to learn Bahasa Indonesian, Chinese, Hindi, Japanese, and the languages of indigenous people. With language fluency there would be an increased access to understanding the psychologies of non-Western cultures, and with this, a sense of respect and regard for diversity.

Readings.   There are scores of new journals that could become part of the global-community psychology training and education, including *International Journal of Psychology; The European Psychologist; Revista Interamericana de Psicología; Psychology and Developing Societies; Indian Journal of Psychology; International Journal of Asian Social Psychology; The Journal of Psychology in Africa; Culture and Psychology; Transcultural Psychiatry; International Journal of Social Psychiatry; Culture, Medicine, and Psychiatry; Medical Anthropology; Identities; Journal of International Affairs;*

South Pacific Journal of Psychology; *International Journal of Politics, Culture, and Society*; *International Negotiation: A Journal of Theory and Practice*; *Global Governance*; *Peace and Conflict: Journal of Peace Psychology*; and *Global Public Health*. The names themselves hint at the intellectual treat that lies ahead for psychology and the potential for psychologists to make new contributions.

Research.   In recent years, some progress has been made in introducing and legitimizing qualitative research methods in psychology. Qualitative research has introduced a new dimension into psychology's findings because of its emphasis on the subjective. There are numerous emerging research orientations and paradigms that support qualitative research methods including, action research, constructionism, feminist theory, hermeneuetics, indigenous psychologies, symbolic interactionism, postmodernism, and naturalistic research. Examples of qualitative research include active interviewing, case studies, content analysis, ethnography, focus-group discussions, narrative analysis, and oral histories. The virtues of qualitative research for global psychology are numerous including the following facts:

1. It preserves the real-life or naturalistic context of events being studied.
2. It seeks meanings, interpretation, symbols, and other indices of subjective experience.
3. It values the opinions, interpretations, and perceptions of both the researchers and the subject.
4. It acknowledges the social and cultural construction of reality.
5. It adjusts methods to the topic and situation under study (see Carr, Marsella, & Purcell, 2002 for a detailed discussion of the virtues of qualitative research as well as chapter 7 in this volume).

CLOSING THOUGHTS

In discussing education and training for global psychology, I have tried to contextualize my remarks within a larger discussion of the challenges and promise of our global age. In doing so, I am hopeful that the suggestions and recommendations that I have offered regarding person, philosophy, and process and content in global psychology will assume a global perspective that involves not only a recognition of the challenges we face, but also our personal and collective responsibilities for responding to these challenges as full-capacity global citizens. Good intentions are not enough! What is required is participation and activism.

Global psychology is committed to more than the resolution of the many challenges facing our world today. Its fundamental calling is to pursue, support, and promote peace and justice. The very word "global" in its identity means that the process and content are oriented toward the world—not toward the group, the state, the nation. Humanity, in its totality, is its focus and concern. The welfare and well being of each person, though admittedly impossible to attain, is nevertheless the goal. Though reality may constantly diminish this vision, it is nevertheless the horizon toward which the global psychologist proceeds. Every act we perform as psychologists is a moral act and has moral implications. The topics we choose to study, the research methods we use to understand our topic, the data analyses we choose to explain and summarize our data, the interpretations of our results, the conclusions we reach are all moral acts. In our world today, we cannot pretend that somehow what we do and how we do it escapes the moral imperative to be aware and responsive to our actions. This concern for morality is, in my opinion, at the heart of what we do as global psychologists, and the moral arbiter we choose is the welfare and well being of humanity through peace and social justice.

There is so much for the global psychologist to do. Global psychologists can help change behaviors associated with problems (e.g., sustainable agriculture, environmental management, urban design, conflict resolution, healthy lifestyles, population control, humanitarian aid, a civil society). They can assist in envisioning, negotiating, designing, and evaluating a humane social order and a meaningful world peace. They can help clarify, reconcile, or better negotiate the divisive dialectical tensions between the rational and the intuitive, the secular and the sacred, the individual and the group, and the sciences and arts. Who, after all, is better positioned to do this? Imagine a new psychology with an expanded vision and horizon— a psychology respectful of differences in ideas, methods, and practices—a psychology tolerant of change, excited by challenge, and open to opportunity and responsibility. That is global psychology!

RECOMMENDED READINGS

Carr, S., & Schumaker, J. (Eds.). (1996). *Psychology and the developing world*. New York: Praeger.
Eysenck, M. W. (2004). *Psychology: An international perspective*. Hove, UK: Psychology Press.

Gielen, U. P., & Adler, L. L. (Eds.). (2002). *Cross-cultural topics in psychology.* Westport, CT: Praeger.

Leong, F. T. L., Pedersen, P. B., & Marsella, A. J. (2005). *Internationalizing psychology: Meeting the challenges of our changing global community.* Manuscript in preparation.

Marsella, A. J. (1998). Toward a global-community psychology: Meeting the needs of a changing world. *American Psychologist, 53,* 1282–1291.

Marsella, A. J., & Pedersen, P. (2004). Internationalizing the curriculum in counseling psychology. *Counselling Psychology Quarterly, 17,* 413–424.

Pedersen, P. (2004). *110 Experiences for multicultural learning.* Washington, DC: American Psychological Association.

Price, W. F., & Crapo, R. H. (2005). *Cross-cultural perspectives in introductory psychology* (5th ed.). Pacific Grove, CA: Wadsworth.

Spariosu, M. (2004). *Global intelligence and human development: Toward an ecology of global learning.* Cambridge, MA: MIT Press.

Task Force on Undergraduate Psychology Major Competencies. (2002). *Undergraduate psychology major learning goals and outcomes: A report.* Washington, DC: American Psychological Association, Board of Educational Affairs.

REFERENCES

American Psychological Association and Canadian Psychological Association Task Forces. (2001). *A graduate level curriculum for trauma intervention and conflict resolution in ethnopolitical warfare.* Washington, DC: Psychologists for Social Responsibility.

Carr, S., Marsella, A. J., & Purcell, I. (2002). Researching intercultural relations: Toward a middle-way? *Asian Psychologist, 3,* 58–64.

Carr, S., & Schumaker, J. (Eds.). (1996). *Psychology and the developing world.* New York: Praeger.

Fowler, R. (1996). APA's role in global psychology. *APA Monitor, 27,* 3.

Fox, D., & Prilleltensky, I. (Eds.). (1997). *Critical psychology: An introduction.* London: Sage.

Franklin, W. (1998). Vision and values. *Noetic Sciences Review, 44,* 2–3.

Friedman, T. (2005). *The world is flat: A brief history of the twenty-first century.* New York: Farrar, Strauss, & Giroux.

Gauthier, J. (2005). Toward a universal declaration of ethical principles for psychologists: A progress report. In M. J. Stevens & D. Wedding (Eds.), *Psychology: IUPsyS global resource* [CD-ROM] (6th ed.). Hove, UK: Psychology Press.

Gergen, K. (1991). *The saturated self.* New York: Basic Books.

Gergen, K., Gulerce, A., Lock, A., & Misra, G. (1996). Psychological science in cultural context. *American Psychologist, 51,* 496–503.

Gorbachev, M. S. (1995). *The search for a new beginning: Developing a new civilization* (P. Palazchenko, Trans.). San Francisco: Harper.

Hoshmand, L. (1994). *Orientation to inquiry in a reflective professional psychology.* Albany: State University of New York Press.

Jones, S. (1997). *Virtual culture: Identity and communication in cybersociety.* Thousand Oaks, CA: Sage.

Kim, U., & Berry, J. (1993). *Indigenous psychologies: Research and experience in cultural context*. Newbury Park, CA: Sage.

Kraut, R., Patterson, M., Lundmark, V., Kiesler, S., Mukopadhyay, T., & Scherlis, W. (1998). Internet paradox: A social technology that reduces social involvement and psychological well-being. *American Psychologist, 53*, 1017–1031.

Lifton, R. (1993). *The protean self: Human resilience in an age of fragmentation*. New York: Basic Books.

Lunt, I., & Poortinga, Y. H. (1996). Internationalizing psychology: The case of Europe. *American Psychologist, 51*, 504–508.

Marsella, A. J. (1998). Toward a global-community psychology: Meeting the needs of a changing world. *American Psychologist, 53*, 1282–1291.

Marsella, A. J. (2000a, August). *Internationalizing the psychology curriculum*. Paper presented at the meeting of the American Psychological Association, Washington, DC.

Marsella, A. J. (2000b). Internationalizing the psychology curriculum: Toward new competencies and directions. *International Psychology Reporter, 4*(3), 6–8.

Marsella, A. J. (2000c). The new APA Committee on International Relations in Psychology. *Psychology International, 11*, 2–3.

Marsella, A. J. (in press). Justice in a global age: Becoming counselors to the world. *Counselling Psychology Quarterly*.

Marsella, A. J., & Pedersen, P. (2004). Internationalizing the curriculum in counseling psychology. *Counselling Psychology Quarterly, 17*, 413–424.

Martín-Baró, I. (1994). *Writings for a liberation psychology*. Cambridge, MA: Harvard University Press.

Mays, V., Rubin, J., Sabourin, M., & Walker, L. (1996). Moving toward a global psychology: Changing theories and practice to meet the needs of changing world. *American Psychologist, 51*, 485–487.

Moghaddam, F. (1987). Psychology in the three worlds: As reflected by the crisis in social psychology and the move towards indigenous third world psychology. *American Psychologist, 42*, 912–920.

Moghaddam, F. (1996). Training for developing world psychologists: Can it be better than psychology? In S. Carr & J. Schumaker (Eds.), *Psychology and the developing world* (pp. 49–59). Westport, CT: Prager.

Mustakova-Possardt, E. (2003). *Critical consciousness: A study of morality in global, historical context*. Westport, CT: Praeger/Greenwood.

Overmier, B., & Overmier J. (Eds.). (2000). *Psychology: IUPsyS Global Resource* [CD-ROM] (2nd ed.). Hove, UK: Psychology Press.

Pawlik, K., & d'Ydewalle, G. (1996). Psychology and the global commons: Perspectives of international psychology. *American Psychologist, 51*, 488–495.

Pedersen, P. (2004). *110 Experiences for multicultural learning*. Washington, DC: American Psychological Association.

Prilleltensky, I. (1997). Values, assumptions, and practices: Assessing the moral implications of psychological discourse and action. *American Psychologist, 52*, 517–535.

Psychologists for Social Responsibility. (2001, May). *A graduate-level curriculum for trauma intervention and conflict resolution in ethnopolitical warfare*. Retrieved August 1, 2005, from http://www.psysr.org

Sampson, E. (1989). The challenge of social change for psychology: Globalization and psychology's theory of the person. *American Psychologist, 44,* 914–921.

Sandel, M. (1996, March). The source of discontent: America's search for a new public philosophy. *Atlantic Monthly, 277,* 57–74.

Schneider, M. (1975). *Neurosis and civilization: A Marxist-Freudian synthesis.* New York: Seabury Press.

Sexton, V. S., & Hogan, J. D. (Eds.). (1992). *International psychology: Views from around the world.* Lincoln: University of Nebraska.

Sloan, T. (1990). Psychology for the Third-World. *Journal of Social Issues, 46,* 1–20.

Sloan, T. (1996a). *Damaged life: The crisis of the modern psyche.* New York: Routledge

Sloan, T. (1996b). Psychological research methods in developing countries. In S. Carr & J. Schumaker (Eds.), *Psychology and the developing world* (pp. 38–45). New York: Praeger.

Spariosu, M. (2004). *Global intelligence and human development: Toward an ecology of global learning.* Cambridge, MA: MIT Press.

Stevens, M. J., & Wedding, D. (Eds.). (2004). *Handbook of international psychology.* New York: Brunner-Routledge.

Task Force on Undergraduate Psychology Major Competencies. (2002). *Undergraduate psychology major learning goals and outcomes: A report.* Washington, DC: American Psychological Association, Board of Educational Affairs.

IV

CHALLENGES AND PROSPECTS FOR A GLOBAL PSYCHOLOGY

Part IV of *Toward a Global Psychology: Theory, Research, Intervention, and Pedagogy* contains one chapter: "Getting Involved in Global Psychology" by Harold Takooshian and Leyla Faw Stambaugh. Bringing this volume to a close, chapter 12 provides detailed information for readers who are interested in acquiring the competencies needed to engage meaningfully as psychologists in the world today, and identifies a host of diverse avenues for such participation.

Psychologists and psychology students who do not have the benefit of a sophisticated orientation to contemporary global issues will be severely handicapped in their careers. Hence, the focus of chapter 12, in which Takooshian and Stambaugh describe how psychology instructors, researchers, practitioners, and students can become more involved in the rapidly expanding field of global psychology. Following a brief historical background on global psychology, which complements chapter 2, the authors review useful resources for those in the United States and other nations, including international psychology organizations (also presented in chapter 3), publications in various formats related to global psychology, governmental and private sources of grant funding, and recommendation for teachers and students who seek to bring global psychology into the curriculum. The latter material adds to the emphasis in chapter 11 on the challenges to the education and training of psychologists posed by the global forces and events that are shaping the context of our daily lives. Takooshian and Stambaugh provide rich and varied information and set of Internet links and readings, that will assist psychologists and psychology students to face the rapidly changing, increasingly interconnected, and culturally diverse world of the 21st century with sensitivity, knowledge, and skill.

12

Becoming Involved In Global Psychology

Harold Takooshian
Fordham University

Leyla Faw Stambaugh
Duke University Medical Center

INTRODUCTION

Is psychology a global field? Naturally. From its very origins in 1879, it is remarkable how our modern "science of behavior and mental processes" energetically fanned out with Wilhelm Wundt's students within 10 years to all corners of the globe, from the U.S. to Australia, Chile, and Japan (Fernberger, 1933; Lamberti, 1995; Misiak & Sexton, 1966). Yet, for much of the 20th century, just one nation, the U.S., has contained over half of all the world's psychologists (Rosenzweig, 1984). This balance tipped in the 1990s, as our fast-growing field now grows even faster across Europe and other regions making psychology more global than ever before (see chapters 2 and 3).[1]

How can one become more involved in this global psychology? This simple question is becoming more important for many among us, whether

---

[1]In 1958, the first edition of the IUPsyS *International Directory of Psychologists Outside the U.S.* listed only 7,000 names. This figure increased to 8,000 in 1966, then 17,000 in 1980. The latest edition in 1985, funded by UNESCO, is a 1,181-page tome listing 32,000 psychologists in 48 nations (Pawlik, 1985). By comparison, the APA *Biographical Directory* listed 63,000 North American psychologists in 1981, 68,300 in 1989, and 84,300 in 2001.

we are students, teachers, researchers or practitioners. From a decade of experience as the Executive Officer of the American Psychological Association (APA) from 1989–2003, Raymond Fowler warned students that, "new psychologists who do not have the benefit of a sophisticated orientation to international issues will be severely handicapped in their career options" (2000, p. 12). Similarly, many U.S. teachers seek to integrate more non-U.S. theory, research, and practice into their courses, and researchers seek to incorporate non-U.S. findings into their scientific investigations. Yet sadly, for many students and professionals alike, the resources to become more involved in global psychology clearly "are scattered and difficult to locate" (Stevens, 2002, p. 12).

This chapter pulls together useful resources for those in the U.S. and other nations who wish to become more involved in global psychology.[2] After a brief review of the curvilinear history of what we now call global/international psychology,[3] this review describes current psychology organizations, sources of information about global psychology, and some helpful suggestions for teachers and students.

HISTORY

The international history of psychology is long and somewhat curvilinear, stretching far back before the origins of scientific psychology in 1879 (David & Buchanan, 2003), yet not gaining traction in the U.S. until the 1990s. This can be seen in Table 1, which summarizes the interplay of developments between international organizations, the APA, and major publications.[4]

---

[2]The authors thank editors Michael Stevens and Uwe Gielen for several helpful resources noted in this chapter. The authors welcome comments and inquiries from readers at takoosh@aol.com or at leyla.stambaugh@gmail.com.

[3]"Global/international psychology" is defined here simply as "organized psychology across nations," a bit different from several related terms (Takooshian, Velayo, Draguns, Merenda, & Rayburn, 2003), cross-cultural psychology (Triandis & Berry, 1980), cultural psychology (Cole, 1996), indigenous psychology (see chapter 5), multicultural psychology (Ponterotto et al., 2001), or the psychology of diversity (Trimble et al., 2004). Chapter 1 of this volume examines the definition of the field and related specialties in depth.

[4]In addition to the international history of psychology that appears elsewhere in the volume (see chap. 2), there are several fine histories in print on international psychology organizations, which vary in their depth and, interestingly, do not cite one another. John Davis (2000) focuses on the four largest international psychology organizations, while Wade Pickren and Raymond Fowler (2003) expand this to a few dozen major regional and specialty associations. Ernest Hilgard (1987, pp. 731–771), Peter Merenda (1995), and others (Gielen, Adler, & Milgram, 1992; Rosenzweig, 1992; Rosenzweig, Holtzman, Sabourin, & Bélanger, 2000) also offer detailed overviews of psychology worldwide. Henry David and Joan Buchanan (2003) trace 2,500 years of global trends in psychology, while John Hogan (Hogan, 1995; Hogan & Sussner, 2001) focuses on its more recent past and likely future.

TABLE 12.1
Timeline of Key International Events in Psychology
Organizations (o), Publications (p), and the APA (a)

1889 o	First International Congress of Psychology (ICP) in Paris under Jean Charcot.
1920 p	Wundt publishes *Folk Psychology*, 10 volumes on psychology of culture.
1920 o	The International Association of Applied Psychology (IAAP) is formed.
1929 a	The APA hosts the first ICP in the U.S. at Yale University.
1941 o	The International Council of Psychologists (ICP) is established.
1944 a	The APA launches its Committee on International Relations in Psychology (CIRP).
1951 o	The International Union of Psychological Science (IUPsyS) is inaugurated.
1958 p	The IUPsyS publishes its first *International Directory of Psychologists*.
1961 a	The APA's CIRP forms an International Affairs Office, reporting to the President.
1966 p	Debut of the IUPsyS' *International Journal of Psychology*.
1972 o	The International Association for Cross-Cultural Psychology (IACCP) is formed.
1976 p	The first book on international psychology appears (Sexton & Misiak, 1976).
1980 p	The *Handbook of Cross-Cultural Psychology* is published (Triandis & Berry, 1980).
1984 p	The IUPsyS publishes its *International Directory of Psychologists*.
1993 p	The first cross-cultural introductory textbook appears (Allen & Santrock, 1993).
1996 a	The APA's *American Psychologist* commits to promoting international research.
1997 a	The APA charters its new Division of International Psychology (D52).
1997 p	The *Handbook of Cross-Cultural Psychology* (2nd ed.) is published (Berry et al., 1997).
1999 a	At the meeting of the APA, Psi Chi proposes an international student group.
1999 p	*Psychology: IUPsyS Global Resource* CD-ROM debuts (Overmier & Overmier, 1999).
2000 o	The International Psychology Student Organization (IPSO) is formed.
2000 a	The APA is admitted by the U.N. as a NGO.
2004 p	First international introductory psychology textbook is published (Eysenck, 2004).

Organizations

As the science of psychology suddenly leapt from Leipzig to the remotest corners of the globe within a mere 10 years, the International Congress of Psychology debuted in 1889 in Paris under Jean Charcot, and has become a regular event since then, currently meeting every four years. This global expansion of psychology has now segued into well over 100 cross-national psychology associations and annual conferences representing different specialties or regions of the globe.

The American Psychological Association

The APA hosted its first International Congress in 1929 at Yale University, "the most impressive gathering of psychologists in the history of the field," drawing together such luminaries as Ivan Pavlov, James McKeen Cattell, Jean Piaget, and Kurt Lewin (Takooshian & Salovey, 2004, p. 11). The APA formed its Committee on International Relations in Psychology (CIRP) in 1944, and its International Affairs Office in 1961, which promoted the APA's worldwide activities during the 1960s (Hollander, 2005). Yet, it was not until the term of its CEO Raymond Fowler (1989–2003) that the APA's global activities accelerated in the 1990s. This included the "internationalization" of the *American Psychologist* on its 50th anniversary in 1996 (Fowler, 1996), the long-awaited recognition of a new Division of International Psychology (Division 52) on February 21, 1997, a proposal for an international student organization in 1999 (Van Rossen, McCaslin-Rodrigo, & Owusu-Banahene, 2002), and the APA's entry as a nongovernmental organization (NGO) with the U.N. in 2000. A 2002 survey of the 53 divisions of the APA found that all favored the concept of internationalizing psychology, and nearly half of these specialties are already working toward this objective (Takooshian, 2003).

Publications

With the exception of Wundt's (1916) prescient 10–volume culture-based treatise on *Folk Psychology* (1920), psychology developed as a "universalist" science that largely ignored cultural differences in behavior. In 1976, the tome, *Psychology Around the World*, edited by Misiak and Sexton, became the first of eight volumes to describe how psychology varies across nations. Similarly, in 1980, the long-awaited six-volume *Handbook of Cross-Cultural Psychology* (Triandis & Berry, 1980) marked the coming-of-age of this growing specialty, emphasizing the importance of cross-national theory and research. In his book, *Even the Rat was White*, Guthrie (1998) described an era when laboratory researchers based their entire science of behavior squarely on small, unrepresentative samples of white U.S. male college students, a by-gone practice with today's growth of cross-cultural and global/international psychology.

Challenges

The challenges to a truly global psychology are clear: the familiar challenges of distance, time, money, cultural differences, and language. About language, for example, observers like Draguns (2001) noted how the emergence of English as a universal language both aids the global transmission of psychological science while at the same time limits its full diversity. Psychology is surely not exempt from our human tendency toward ethnocentrism, that is, to feel more comfortable focusing on the familiar than on the unfamiliar.

A humorous, if stark, example of ethnocentricity in psychology was documented in the Soviet Union in 1988 (Takooshian, 1992). A content analysis of major Soviet psychology textbooks found that all 10 of the 10 most-cited researchers were themselves Soviets, in this order of frequency: Alexei Leontyev, Sergei Rubinstein, Boris Ananyev, Lev Vygotsky, Alexander Luria, Alexander Kovalev, Ivan Sechenov, Boris Teplov, Alexander Zaparozhets, and Dmitri Uznadze. When this list was used to construct a 10–point match game, asking Soviet and U.S. psychologists to pair these 10 names with their major contributions, 75 Soviets had a mean score of 9.0 correct in recognizing their own leaders, whereas 125 U.S. psychologists scored a mean of 0.9 correct, just a bit below chance at one-in-ten. Most U.S. respondents readily admitted they were seeing most of these 10 names for the very first time. As each nation has a tendency to study and teach its indigenous psychology, it takes intentional effort to go beyond this. Such ethnocentricity in psychology may be even more accentuated in the U.S., considering the dominance of its psychology and use of English as the *lingua franca* of psychology (Draguns, 2001).

Value

Yet, the value of a genuinely global science of psychology is also clear. Every world traveler knows the immense impact that culture has on human behavior and mental processes, an impact that should be studied rather than ignored. Like several other APA presidential addresses, the address by APA President Donald Campbell (1975) stressed this point, that a science of psychology is incomplete if it ignores cultural differences, rather than try to integrate these into our work (Fish, 2000; see chapters 5 through 8 for related material on the importance of culture to contemporary scientific psychology). Indeed, since the formation of CIRP in 1944, the APA has worked alongside other international groups to develop innovative programs to overcome this ethnocentricity, an effort which gained traction in the 1990s with the demographic shift "from Americanization to internationalization" (David & Buchanan, 2003, p. 515), and the advent of a global Internet (Velayo, 2004). For much of the 20th century, over half of the world's psychologists were concentrated in one nation, the U.S. (Rosenzweig, 1984), but this is no longer the case, as world psychology grows even faster than psychology in the U.S. and, since the 1990s, over half of the world's psychologists now live outside North America (Stevens & Wedding, 2004, pp. 2, 482).

How does one become more involved in global psychology? The remainder of this chapter focuses on international organizations, informational resources, and suggestions for teachers and students.

ORGANIZATIONS

Today, one who knows where to look will find an abundance of roughly 200 cross-national psychology organizations, which fall into four major categories: national, regional, specialty, and students (see chapters 2 and 3 for additional information on international psychology organizations of significance). Although these 200 groups are largely independent of one another, they all share a mission to globalize psychology in distinct ways.

1. National. About 75 nations have a national psychology association. Like the U.S., about 20 of these nations have more than one association to represent separately scientific or professional psychology. The APA website (www.apa.org/international) maintains a current roster of contacts for these national groups.

2. Regional. There are about 20 regional groups, such as the Interamerican Society of Psychology (SIP, formed in 1951) or the European Federation of Psychologists' Associations (EFPA, formed 1981) (Pickren & Fowler, 2003).

3. Specialty. About 100 international societies focus on a specialty topics in psychology, such as the International Society for the Study of Behavioral Development (ISSBD, formed in 1969), International

Society of Political Psychology (ISPP, formed in 1978), International Test Commission (ITC, formed in 1974), International School Psychology Association (ISPA, formed in 1982), Society for the Psychological Study of Social Issues (SPSSI, formed in 1936), and the Society for Research in Child Development (SRCD, formed in 1933).

4. Students. About 10 groups serve psychology students, such as the American Psychological Association of Graduate Students (APAGS, formed in 1983), Psi Chi Honor Society (formed in 1929), Psi Beta Honor Society (formed in 1981), European Federation of Psychology Student Associations (EFPSA, formed in 1987), and International Psychology Student Organization (IPSO, formed in 1999). The EFPSA is a federation of student associations in 23 nations (not individual members), while the IPSO has 400 individual members in 70 nations.

A list of electronic links to these four types of groups is maintained on the websites of the International Union of Psychological Science (www.am. org/iupsys/links.html) and the APA (www.apa.org/international).

Among these 200 organizations, 7 stand out and warrant further scrutiny here based on their large size and broad ken to advance global psychology.

1. International Association for Applied Psychology (IAAP, formed in 1920) numbers about 1,600 members worldwide, offers a quarterly journal, *Applied Psychology: An International Review*, and a quadrennial congress (www.iaapsy.org).

2. International Council of Psychologists (ICP, formed in 1941) numbers 500 members worldwide, offers a quarterly newsletter, the *International Psychologist*, and an annual convention coordinated with the APA or IAAP meeting locations (www.icppsych.tripod. com) (Cautley, 1992; Sapir & Smith, 1992). For three years (1995–1997), the ICP published a quarterly journal, *World Psychology*. (For past issues, see www.iiccp.freeservers – refer to e-books.)

3. International Union of Psychological Science (IUPsyS, formed in 1951) is a union of 70 member nations (no individual members) comprised of representatives of national psychology organizations across all continents, publishes the bimonthly *International Journal of Psychology*, hosts a quadrennial Congress of Psychology and, since

1999, publishes annually a cumulative reference tool as a CD-ROM, *Psychology: IUPsyS Global Resource* (www.iupsys.org).

4. International Association of Cross-Cultural Psychology (IACCP, formed in 1972) numbers about 800 members, offers a bimonthly *Journal of Cross-Cultural Psychology*, and hosts a biennial meeting (www.iaccp.org).

5. Office of International Affairs of the APA (OIA, formed in 1961) works with the APA's CIRP to publish a quarterly newsletter, *Psychology International*, and provides a website and other services for globally oriented psychologists (www.apa.org/international).

6. Division of International Psychology (Division 52) of the APA (formed in 1997) numbers 1,000 members in 40 nations, publishes a quarterly *International Psychology Bulletin*, plans an international book series, posts announcements on its monthly listserv and web site, and meets semiannually at the meetings of the APA and other regional organizations in the U.S. Division 52 is separate from the approximately 3,900 "international affiliates" who belong to the APA, but are not necessarily members of its specialty international division (www.internationalpsychology.net).

7. International Psychology Student Organization (IPSO, founded in 1999) is an emerging group operated by and for students, which provides an opportunity for electronic networking (www.psychologystudents.org).

INFORMATIONAL RESOURCES

Since the 1990s, there is a clear and healthy trend to include more information on global psychology in virtually all resources: introductory textbooks, databases, and major encyclopedias like Freedheim and Weiner's (2003) 12–volume *Handbook of Psychology* and Spielberger's (2004) three-volume *Encyclopedia of Applied Psychology*.

Publications

For those interested in a profile of the field of psychology in different nations, there is a series of eight tomes, each offering a timeless snapshot that is not superseded by later volumes. The first is *Psychology Around the World*, the pioneering collection of chapters on 28 nations, edited by Virginia Sexton and Henryk Misiak (1976). The follow-up volume,

International Psychology: Views from Around the World (Sexton & Hogan, 1992), expanded to 55 contributors describing 45 nations. In 1987, Arthur and Carol Gilgen edited their *International Handbook of Psychology*, with 30 chapters covering 30 regions. In 1992, Mark Rosenzweig's volume, *International Psychological Science*, pulled scattered information into one volume. In 2000, the *International Handbook of Psychological Science*, edited by Kurt Pawlik and Mark Rosenzweig for the IUPsyS, provided cross-national reviews of specialty areas within psychology. In 1999, Bruce and Judith Overmier published *Psychology: IUPsyS Global Resource*, the first CD-ROM to compile extensive lists of international psychology programs, organizations, meetings, key documents, reference works, and national profiles, which are updated annually (Stevens & Wedding, 2005b). In 2004, Michael Stevens and Danny Wedding published their *Handbook of International Psychology*, with chapters on psychology in 27 countries in nine geographic regions. In 2004, Michael Eysenck published his unique introductory psychology textbook, *Psychology: An International Perspective*, which can double as an encyclopedia replete with global research and sources. Between them, these eight reference works by different authors and publishers offer a panoramic view of psychology world-wide that has been hard to find in more traditional sources. In addition the *International Journal of Psychology* publishes occasional collections of articles on psychology in specific regions, such as the special issues on scientific psychology (December, 2001) and psychological specialties in China (October, 2003).

Funding

In view of the inherent challenges to globalizing psychology, one common question is where to find funding for our cross-national research, teaching, or service projects. The three traditional sources of funding are government, private corporations, and nonprofit foundations (Takooshian, Velayo, & Prohaska, 2002).

Government funding typically involves highly formalized procedures through dozens of national programs, such as those in the United Kingdom (www.rdinfo.org.uk), or in the U.S. for the National Science Foundation, National Institutes of Health, and others listed in the *Catalog of Federal Domestic Assistance* (General Services Administraion, n.d.). For international programs, two outstanding sources are the Fulbright program (www.cies.org), which has offered an ever-growing number of teaching and research grants since 1946, and the International Research and

Exchanges Board (www.irex.org), which has an ever-changing array of priority areas.

At the other extreme, private corporations also offer extensive funding for global work in psychology, but through highly varied and informal procedures, basing decisions on a project's value to the corporation. Since there is no central listing, one must contact the appropriate office in each corporation—public relations in some, or corporate giving in others—to ask for any specific funding guidelines.

Nonprofit foundations are the preferred source of grant funding for many psychologists because their information is so highly accessible through the Foundations Center and its network of libraries. For foundation funding, the two primary reference volumes for international projects are both published by the Foundation Center: (a) *Grants for Foreign and International Programs* (Foundation Center, 2004a), which lists 10,530 existing grants totaling $2.2 billion, and is cross-indexed by subject, geographic region, and recipient; and (b) *Guide to Funding for International and Foreign Programs* (Foundation Center, 2004b), which contains 9,500 funding sources, also cross-indexed by geographic region, topic, and type of project. The Foundation Center resources are available on-line at www.fdncenter.org, some with unlimited access and others limited to "associates" in an institution that pays a subscription fee.

Based on Foundation Center (2004a) data, foundation funding for international projects rose by 34% between 1990 and 1994, from $508 million to $679 million. Between 1998 and 2001, international funding further rose 131%, accounting for 15% of all foundation-grant dollars. This increase is partly due to U.S. foundations, which are "going global," up from 47% in 1994 to 63% in 2001. The fastest growth is in health programs, which quadrupled from 1998 to 2001, totaling $715 million. Of all funding for international programs in 2001, the three largest areas were health (29%), education (17%), and economic development (12%).

For funding or other support for international programs, some sources naturally stand out among the tens of thousands that are available. For graduate and professional teaching and research abroad, the U.S. Fulbright program (www.cies.org) has greatly expanded the types of grants to scholars and students since the 1950s, as has the International Research and Exchanges Board (www.irex.org) and Rotary Club grants (www.rotary.org). The massive Gates Foundation (www.gatesfoundation.org) emphasizes global health and education projects, while the Soros Foundation and Open Society Institute (www.soros.org) offer a wealth of travel and other opportunities, as do the Ford (www.fordfound.org), Rockefeller (www.rockfound.org), and Spencer

Foundations (www.spencer.org). Programs for scholars include the American Association for the Advancement of Science (www.aaas.org), American Council of Learned Societies (www.acls.org), American Philosophical Society (www.amphilosoc.org), Guggenheim Foundation (www.hfg.org), Social Science Research Council (www.ssrc.org), and Woodrow Wilson International Center (www.wilsoncenter.org). Then, there are the federal research and action programs, such as the National Science Foundation (www.nsf.gov), National Institutes of Health (www.nih.gov), National Institute of Drug Abuse (www.nida.gov), Department of Education (www.education.gov), and U.S. Peace Institute (www.usip.org). Students seeking international scholarships can browse some university websites, like the one at Fordham University's Office of Prestigious Fellowships (www.fordham.edu/fellowships), as well as many competitive programs, like the Rhodes Scholarships (www.rhodesscholar.org). Student researchers might peruse a list of over 100 international and other funding sources available through the Psi Chi website, www.psichi.org (Takooshian et al., 2002). Students and others interested in work or study abroad can easily find helpful resources for volunteering, such as www.studyabroad.org, www.teachabroad.org, www. peacecorps.org, www.ciee.org, www.internationalstudent.com, www.daad.de/portrait/404.html, and www.iie.org for study programs. Although www. internabroad.org compiles attractive internship opportunities overseas, Arbolino (2003) cautions psychology students to proceed carefully since accreditation by the Association of Psychology Postdoctoral and Internship Centers (www.appic.org) is useful if the internship is to count toward future licensing or career goals. The U.N. website at www.un.org is the portal to hundreds of resources, including its many affiliate world organizations for health (WHO), children (UNICEF), education and science (UNESCO), and non-governmental civil societies (www.ngocongo.org).

Training and Credentialing

There are naturally huge variations in psychology credentialing among the U.N.'s 191 member nations, from very formal rules for doctoral training and state licensure in the U.S., to virtually no credentialing of psychologists in many developing nations, who function with a baccalaureate only (Stevens & Wedding, 2004, 2006). At the same time, the status of credentialing in psychology is in flux, with a clear worldwide trend toward increased mobility of psychological training and credentialing across territorial and national borders (Levant, 2005). Two points are notable:

Training.   Cross-national exchanges are on the increase worldwide, with Europe leading the way. In 1987, the European Commission initiated its Erasmus Program (http://europa.eu.int/comm/education/programmes/socrates/erasmus/erasmus_en.html) to promote mobility in higher education. Named for the well-traveled scholar Erasmus of Rotterdam (1465–1536), the now massive Erasmus Program offers government subsidies to encourage cross-national European student exchanges, faculty exchanges, and collaborative programs. Since its formation in 1987 with 3,000 students in 11 European nations, the Erasmus Program has expanded as of 2005 to 31 nations that have exchanged 1.2 million students and 14,400 faculty. Other well-established exchange programs in Europe include Fondation Simone et Cino del Duca in France (http://www.andes.asso.fr/GUIDE/chapitreV/node37.php) and the German Academic Exchange Service (http://www.daad.org/).

Credentialing.   As in other fields like law and medicine, credentialing in psychology is evolving. Although psychologists trained in one nation often do not meet the qualifying standards of another nation, there is a worldwide trend toward greater mobility of credentials (see chaps. 3 and 10 for additional details on this global trend). Just 16 years after the state of Connecticut in the U.S. mandated licensure for psychologists, the Association of State and Provincial Psychology Boards (ASPPB) was formed in 1961 to develop sound credentialing standards which today, in most of the 50 U.S. states, entails a doctorate in psychology, supervised work experience, and a passing score on the ASPPB's Examination for Professional Practice in Psychology (EPPP). The ASPPB developed its first French-language EPPP in 1995 for use in Canada and is now considering a Spanish EPPP. To mark the 50th anniversary of governmental licensure in 1995, the ASPPB also hosted its first International Congress on Licensure, Certification, and Credentialing of Psychologists, with an eye toward increased cross-national mobility. Based on its success, the ASPPB convened a second conference in Oslo, Norway in 2000. Considering the clear differences separating indigenous psychologies in even the most developed nations (Stevens & Wedding, 2004), credentialing has far to go before cross-national mobility becomes the norm. Until then, individuals who are contemplating global careers must consider the matter of licensure well ahead when planning their education and training (see Stevens & Wedding [2006] for licensing requirements in other nations).

Adjusting to Relocation

How much must a psychologist or psychology student adapt when working for a short or long stay far from home? Such adjustment naturally involves both logistical and psychological challenges. With regard to logistics, expatriates are often surprised to find how nations can have such different rules or customs for dealing with everyday issues. For example, many European banks require a letter of reference from a bank in the home country in order to establish a new account. Since opening a bank account is typically one of the first tasks on an expatriate's list, this kind of news can come as an unwelcome surprise.

Fortunately, many resources exist for expatriates to prepare for these challenges. The web magazine, *Transitions Abroad*, provides guidance on living and working abroad, and includes an extensive list of expatriate websites from around the world (e.g., www.transitionsabroad.com). These websites include forums where one can connect with the local expatriate community and acquire valuable local information. Career centers at universities also provide help to both students and alumni in navigating the red tape of visas, work permits, etc. Several fine books are available to advise those planning to work abroad, which address both the logistical and the psychological side of adjusting to a new culture (e.g., Hess & Linderman, 2002; Kohls, 2001; Tsang-Feign, 1993).

The psychological challenge of adjustment to a stay abroad can be as overwhelming for some as it is not for others. The stages of acculturation are applicable to anyone who relocates to a new culture, whether he or she plans to stay for months or years. For example, after the initial "honeymoon stage," in which everything seems new and exciting, many expatriates enter a stage of "culture shock," in which feelings of anxiety, irritability, and homesickness may emerge. Recognizing that this is normal is the first step in coping with these issues.

The second step in responding to the challenge of adjustment is to be proactive in seeking out helpful resources. Joining a local expatriate club can provide reassurance and social support. In addition, most university alumni clubs have branches in cities across the globe. This can be an excellent way to make both friends and connections. For those who are not yet alumni, any university study-abroad office will usually have a wealth of information on adjusting to a new culture as well as adjusting to the return home. Likewise, the local university in the host country will likely have resources for foreign faculty and students.

TEACHING AND THE PSYCHOLOGY CURRICULUM

How can teachers incorporate more global information into their introductory and other psychology courses? Consider this: A 2002 content analysis of 50,000 publications in the U.S.-based PsycLIT found that 22,000 of these (45%) are by non-U.S. authors, and that this trend "has steadily increased over time" (Adair, Coêlho, & Luna, 2002, p. 168). However, such a trend is not mirrored in U.S. psychology textbooks. A sedulous content analysis of 30 major U.S. psychology textbooks by Linda Woolf's team at Webster University found that the percentage of non-U.S. citations varied from 0.2% to 4.6% (Woolf, Hulsizer, & McCarthy, 2002a). Another content analysis of 12 U.S. psychology textbooks further found that about half of the minuscule percentage of non-U.S. references were from Western Europe, leaving the remaining half from the four non-Western continents of Africa, Latin America, Asia, and Australia (Denmark, Marquez, & Velayo, 2004).

In 2004, an APA Task Force on diversity in teaching published an informative 32–page guide for teachers, "Towards an Inclusive Psychology: Infusing the Introductory Psychology Textbook with Diversity Content" (Trimble, Stevenson, & Worrell, 2004). Interestingly, international was not included among its five diversities: Aging, Culture, Disability, Gender, and Sexuality. The APA's CIRP has long discussed a globally oriented curriculum: a few former CIRP members are now seeking to develop such curricula (Leong, Pedersen, & Marsella, 2005). As of 2005, a new APA Working Group to Internationalize the Psychology Curriculum is crafting a five-point plan to approach this goal (Velayo, 2005).

The psychology classroom of the future has become increasingly global in a few ways. "A total of 586,323 international students [were] studying in the U.S. in 2003" (Poyrazli, 2005, p. 18), about 10% of these in the social sciences or psychology. More students at U.S. universities are opting to study abroad. Furthermore, like some U.S. schools, "the University of Maryland University College (UMUC) alone has 51,000 students on campuses abroad" (Murray, 2005, p. 20). Even at the high-school level, there is an invisible, yet extensive network of 900 U.S. international schools overseas, where U.S. and indigenous students study psychology using an International Baccalaureate or Advanced Placement curriculum (Beaman, 2002). These international schools, and their position vacancies for teachers, are listed on the websites of the International Schools Services (www.iss.edu), Search Associates (www.search-associates. com), University of Northern Iowa (www.uni.edu/placement/overseas/), and the International Educator (www.tieonline.com).

Teachers who seek global information to enrich their current courses or to create new ones might consider the following 10 resources:

1. There are eight volumes with a global focus, previously described, that limn psychology across nations, beginning with *Psychology Around the World* (Sexton & Misiak, 1976). One of these eight warrants special mention, the fact-saturated *Psychology: IUPsyS Global Resource CD-ROM* (Stevens & Wedding, 2006) which, among other things, contains brief descriptions and country-specific information on the discipline and profession of psychology in 86 countries (e.g., history, basic and applied research foci, requirements and regulation of training including that in ethics, journals).

2. The Office of Teaching Resources in Psychology (OTRP) is a website affiliated with the APA's Society for the Teaching of Psychology (www.lemoyne.edu/OTRP), and offers invaluable cross-cultural activities and teaching materials compiled by master teachers G. William Hill (1998a, 1998b) and Linda Woolf (2002a, 2002b).

3. The website of the APA's Office of International Affairs (www. apa.org/international) also offers a wealth of up-to-date material on international organizations, programs, resources, and people.

4. The new website of the APA's Division of International Psychology (www.internationalpsychology.net), launched in 2004, offers cutting-edge information, including links to various scholarly resources and websites.

5. Those who use the PsycLIT database can specify in the search fields LA (language) or PL (population location) to find published research on specific groups. For example, entering "Polish" in LA yields 3,517 entries appearing in that language, while entering "Poland" in PL calls up 1,462 entries from Poland.

6. A few journals stand out for their global content: *International Journal of Psychology, Applied Psychology: An International Journal, Journal of Cross-Cultural Psychology, International Journal of Behavioral Development, International Journal of Intercultural Relations, Social Science and Medicine, Asian Journal of Social Psychology, European Psychologist, European Journal of Social Psychology*, and *Psychololgia* (published in Japan).

7. The quadrennial International Congress of Psychology now offers its program on the Internet as a valuable 400–page resource for perusal (www.icp2004.psych.ac.cn/proceedings.htm).

8. The rising use of Blackboard and other distance-learning technologies is opening new avenues for global materials (Takooshian & Velayo, 2004; Velayo, 2004). Such innovations are often described in the *International Psychology Bulletin*, the publication of the APA's Division of International Psychology. For example, Chia and Poe (2004) described how they used an Internet-based Tandberg 880 synchronous video projector to hold a class between Soochow University in China and East Carolina State University in the U.S.

9. Some innovative books (e.g., Border & Chism, 1992; Pedersen, 2005) offer classroom exercises to increase diversity and global content. Other books are appearing as cross-cultural supplements to more traditional textbooks, such as Price and Crapo's (2005) reader, *Cross-Cultural Perspectives in Introductory Psychology*, which offers 32 cross-cultural readings on 16 standard topics that appear in traditional textbooks. In addition, there are already a growing number of textbooks and readers on cross-cultural psychology (e.g., Adler & Gielen, 2002; Berry, Poortinga, & Segall, 2002; Lonner, Dinnell, Hayes, & Sattler, 2003; Matsumoto & Juang, 2004; Ponterotto, Casas, Suzuki, & Alexander, 2001; Segall, Dasen, Berry, & Poortinga, 1999; Shiraev & Levy, 2003; Thomas, 2004; Van de Vijver & Leung, 1997). The authoritative *Handbook of Cross-Cultural Psychology* has been edited by an international team of experts (Berry et al., 1997). Other books review in considerable detail studies conducted in major countries situated around the world. Typical examples include Pandey (2000, 2001, 2004) for India, Bond (1996) for China and Chinese societies, Gielen and Bredenkamp (1997/2004) for the German-speaking countries, and Ahmed and Gielen (1998) and Gregg (2005), respectively, for the Arab countries and the Middle East. Finally we can point to an extensive literature that covers specific research areas and topics across cultures. Many of these books contain chapters by international authors. Representative efforts include: For developmental processes, Gardiner and Kosmitzki (2005), Gielen and Roopnarine (2004), Kağitçibaşi (1996); for adolescence, Arnett (2006), Brown, Larson, and Saraswathi (2002); for family studies, Roopnarine and Gielen (2005); for gender roles, Adler (1993); for counseling, therapy and healing, Gielen, Fish, and Draguns (2004), Laungani (2004), and Pedersen, Draguns, Lonner, and Trimble (2002); for social psychology, Moghaddam (1997) and Smith and Bond (1998); for migration, Adler and Gielen (2003).

10. Until recently, a full-fledged course in global/international psychology did not exist at any university, but now a few pioneers in the U.S. and abroad are developing model syllabi for such a course, including John Davis at Texas State University, Gloria Grunwald at Webster University, Sondra Leftoff at the John Jay College of Criminal Justice, Anthony Marsella at University of Hawaii (Marsella, 2000), Kurt Pawlik at the University of Hamburg, Rainer Silbereisen at the University of Jena, and Michael Stevens at Illinois State University (see Appendix B).

STUDENT INVOLVEMENT

How can forward-looking psychology students heed Fowler's (2000) advice to become more involved in global psychology? There is certainly an increasing push for this within universities around the world, as evidenced by the sharp increase in international students noted above (Murray, 2005; Poyrazli, 2005). Students might consider 10 ways to add a global component into their college or other studies (adapted from Russo & Takooshian, 2002).

1. Co-curricular. Over 1,100 U.S. colleges have a Psi Chi chapter, a Psi Beta chapter, or a psychology club with local funds to plan co-curricular activities that complement classroom learning. It is usually easy to work with these local clubs to arrange global topics and speakers.
2. Local connection. With more than a half-million international students in the U.S., most colleges have an international student office or an English as a Second Language (ESL) program where students can easily connect to make global contacts.
3. Professors. In many schools, a student can find a professor involved in global work, and try to complete a course or independent study with that professor (Adler, 1994; Takooshian & Stevens, 2001), perhaps involving a research report suitable for presentation or publication. For example, one college student who volunteered for one week of service at the U.N. described how she found herself completing a research course and internship at the U.N., which will likely be of value for her long-term goal of a career in international law (Bonet, 2005).
4. Network. Students should not wait until graduation to network with professionals. Students are encouraged to join at least one

professional association as a student affiliate at a reduced rate in order to enter the pipeline early for valuable professional information and opportunities.[5]

5. Conferences. Students should try to attend at least one of the dozens of international meetings each year, to meet colleagues and potential mentors from overseas, as well as local persons interested in global issues.

6. Web. There are a multitude of global websites, such as the U.N. (www.un.ngo), that disseminate news and opportunities in various fields of psychology.

7. Language. Though universities normally require one language, learning a second language can open additional doors for careers and future work. For instance, there is typically a shortage of paid translators in U.S. schools, clinics, and courtrooms. Practice for greater fluency may be readily available in a school's local ESL program.

8. Study abroad. Most schools offer opportunities for study abroad for a year, semester, or summer, though students too often fail to take advantage of these opportunities. In addition, there are growing opportunities through the web to engage in a variety of time-limited international educational experiences (www.study abroad.com).

9. Work abroad. Students also overlook the benefits of working or teaching English abroad (www.teachabroad.com). In addition to people world wide who seek to learn English, Bronwyn Murray (2005) noted there are U.S. expatriate communities around the world, and one can arrange work overseas for valuable cross-cultural experience through the website above or www. internationalstudent.com/jobsearch/index.html.

10. Travel. An ambitious student might use personal or family travel to conduct cross-national field experiments or surveys (Adler, 1994; Takooshian & Stevens, 2001). About survey research, for example, a student already scheduled to travel to her family in Israel for a week was able to collect over 100 surveys on feminism during two days, and present her cross-national findings on feminism

---

[5]For example, since its formation in 1997, the APA's Division of International Psychology has intentionally maintained a low student fee of $10, which includes the Division's quarterly newsletter (*International Psychology Bulletin*), monthly listserv, and news of the annual meetings at the APA each summer.

in Israel at a professional conference (Katz, 2005). About field experiments, students of Professor Robert Levine were able to test systematically "the kindness of strangers" during their personal travels, thus contributing to a remarkable cross-national report of findings in 36 U.S. cities and 23 nations, which was completed with no external funding (Levine, 2003).

CONCLUSION

While our millennium is still new, futurists already liken it to the time of Columbus in the 1490s, with a new world order underway. In *The World is Flat: A Brief History of the 21st Century*, futurist Thomas Friedman (2005) described the current mega-trend of globalization that is reducing the economic, political, and cultural differences that have always separated nations. Imagine how the same e-mail that was a novelty 10 years earlier has become a necessity today. Similarly, within psychology, the trend is clear that it is the wise student, teacher, and professional who prepares today for tomorrow's inevitable changes. The growing, but scattered resources culled in this chapter should be useful for those who seek to become more involved in this mega-trend. We can hope that our science of behavior and mental processes will somehow retain its distinctive differences in each region, while also coalescing into a common core that all psychologists will recognize and share.

RECOMMENDED READINGS

Adler, L. L., & Gielen, U. P. (Eds.). (2002). *Cross-cultural topics in psychology* (2nd ed.). Westport, CT: Praeger. [A many-sided overview offered by several experts in cross-cultural psychology.]

Draguns, J. G. (2001). Toward a truly international psychology: Beyond English only. *American Psychologist, 56,* 1019–1030. [The 2001 APA International Psychology Award winner presents a cogent analysis.]

Eysenck, M. W. (2004). *Psychology: An international perspective.* Hove, UK: Psychology Press. [A landmark 934-page compendium of cross-national research.]

Fowler, R. D. (2000, Spring). Internationalizing the curriculum. *International Psychology Reporter, 4,* 10–12. [The former CEO of the APA presents his far-reaching outlook.]

Gielen, U. P. (Ed.). (in press). *Conversations with international psychologists.* Greenwich, CT: Information Age Publishing. [Extensive interviews with leading psychologists around the world.]

Russo, N. F., & Takooshian, H. (2002, Spring). Student involvement in international psychology: Why and how. *Eye on Psi Chi, 6,* 14–15. [One of a series of international columns for students at www.psi.chi.com.]

Sexton, V. S., & Misiak, H. (1984). American psychologists and psychology abroad. *American Psychologist, 39*, 1026–1031. [The print version of Sexton's prescient 1984 EPA presidential address, "Is American Psychology Xenophobic?"]

Stevens, M. J., & Wedding, D. (Eds.). (2004). *Handbook of international psychology.* New York: Brunner-Routledge. [An authoritative 536–page overview of international psychology today.]

Stevens, M. J., & Wedding, D. (Eds.). (2006). *Psychology: IUPsyS global resource* [CD-ROM] (7th ed.). Hove, UK: Psychology Press. [An outstanding resource for details on global psychology today.]

REFERENCES

Adair, J. G., Coêlho, A. E. L., & Luna, J. R. (2002). How international is psychology? *International Journal of Psychology, 37*, 160–170.

Adler, L. L. (1993). *International handbook on gender roles.* Westport, CT: Greenwood.

Adler, L. L. (1994, August). Collaborating with researchers across countries and cultures. *International Psychologist*, 8–19.

Adler, L. L., & Gielen, U. P. (Eds.). (2002). *Cross-cultural topics in psychology* (2nd ed.). Westport, CT: Praeger.

Adler, L. L., & Gielen, U. P. (Eds.). (2003). *Migration: Immigration and emigration in international perspective.* Westport, CT: Praeger.

Ahmed, R. A., & Gielen, U. P. (Eds.). (1998). *Psychology in the Arab countries.* Menoufia, Egypt: Menoufia, University Press.

Allen, L., & Santrock, J. W. (1993). *Psychology: The contexts of behavior.* Dubuque, IA: Brown and Benchmark.

Arbolino, L. (2003, Summer). Internships abroad: How we can facilitate new sites. *International Psychology Reporter, 7*, 15.

Arnett, J. J. (Ed.). (2007). *International encyclopedia of adolescence.* New York: Routledge.

Beaman, A. L. (2002, Fall). The hidden world of international education. *International Psychology Reporter, 6*, 11–12.

Berry, J. W., Poortinga, Y. H., Pandey, J., Dasen, P. R., Saraswathi, T. S., Segall, M. H., & Kağitçibaşi, Ç. (Eds.). (1997). *Handbook of cross-cultural psychology* (2nd ed.). Needham Heights, MA: Allyn and Bacon.

Berry, J. W., Poortinga, Y. H., & Segall, M. H. (Eds.). (2002). *Cross-cultural psychology: Research and applications* (2nd ed.). Cambridge, MA: Harvard University Press.

Bond, M. H. (Ed.). (1996). *The handbook of Chinese psychology.* Hong Kong: Oxford University Press.

Bonet, C. (2005, Summer). A student intern at the United Nations: Working with a living legend at the U.N. *International Psychology Reporter, 9*, 25.

Border, L. L. B., & Chism, N. V. N. (Eds.). (1992). *Teaching for diversity.* San Francisco: Jossey-Bass.

Brown, B. B., Larson, R. W., & Saraswathi, T. S. (Eds.). (2002). *The world's youth: Adolescence in eight regions of the world.* Cambridge, UK: Cambridge University Press.

Campbell, D. T. (1975). On the conflicts between biological and social evolution and between psychology and moral tradition. *American Psychologist, 30*, 1103–1126.

Cautley, P. W. (1992). Fifty years of the International Council of Psychologists. In U. P. Gielen, L. L. Adler, & N. A. Milgram (Eds.), *Psychology in international perspective* (pp. 3–18). Amsterdam: Swets and Zeitlinger.

Chia, R., & Poe, E. (2004, Spring). Innovations in international education. *International Psychology Reporter, 8*, 7–8.

Cole, M. (1996). *Cultural psychology: A once and future discipline.* Cambridge, MA: Harvard University Press.

David, H. P., & Buchanan, J. (2003). International psychology. In D. K. Freedheim (Ed.), *Handbook of psychology: History of psychology* (Vol. 1, pp. 509–533). New York: Wiley.

Davis, J. M. (2000, Spring). Four international organizations in psychology: An overview. *Eye on Psi Chi, 4*, 33–37.

Denmark, F. L., Marquez, M. M., & Velayo, R. S. (2004, April). *Where is international psychology in psychology textbooks?* Paper presented at the meeting of the Eastern Psychological Association, Washington, DC.

Draguns, J. G. (2001). Toward a truly international psychology: Beyond English only. *American Psychologist, 56*, 1019–1030.

Eysenck, M. W. (2004). *Psychology: An international perspective.* Hove, UK: Psychology Press.

Fernberger, S. W. (1933). Wundt's doctorate students. *Psychological Bulletin, 30*, 80–83.

Fish, J. M. (2000, September). What psychology can learn from anthropology. *American Anthropologist, 102*, 552–563.

Foundation Center. (2004a). *Grants for foreign and international programs.* New York: Author.

Foundation Center. (2004b). *Guide to funding for international and foreign programs* (7th ed.). New York: Author.

Fowler, R. D. (1996). Editorial: 50th anniversary of the *American Psychologist. American Psychologist, 51*, 5–7.

Fowler, R. D. (2000, Spring). Internationalizing the curriculum. *International Psychology Reporter, 4*, 10–12.

Freedheim, D. K., & Weiner, I. (Eds.). (2003). *Handbook of psychology.* New York: Wiley.

Friedman, T. L. (2005). *The world is flat: A brief history of the twenty-first century.* New York: Farrar, Straus and Giroux.

Gardiner, H. W., & Kosmitzki, C. (Eds.). (2005). *Lives across cultures: Cross-cultural human development* (3rd ed.). Boston: Allyn and Bacon.

General Services Administration. (n.d.). *Catalog of federal domestic assistance.* Retrieved July 31, 2005, from http://www.cfda.gov

Gielen, U. P., Adler, L. L., & Milgram, N. A. (Eds.). (1992). *Psychology in international perspective: 50 years of the International Council of Psychologists.* Amsterdam: Swets and Zeitlinger.

Gielen, U. P., & Bredenkamp, J. (Eds.). (1997/2004). *World psychology: Special issue. Psychology in the German-speaking countries.* Online at http://www.iiccp.freeservers.com

Gielen, U. P., Fish, J. M., & Draguns, J. G. (Eds.). (2004). *Handbook of culture, therapy, and healing.* Mahwah, NJ: Lawrence Erlbaum Associates.

Gielen, U. P., & Roopnarine, J. (Eds.). (2004). *Childhood and adolescence: Cross-cultural perspectives and applications.* Westport, CT: Praeger.

Gilgen, A. R., & Gilgen, C. K. (Eds.). (1987). *International handbook of psychology.* Westport, CT: Greenwood.

Gregg, G. S. (2005). *The Middle East: A cultural psychology.* New York: Oxford University Press.

Guthrie, R. V. (1998). *Even the rat was white: A historical view of psychology* (2nd ed.). Boston: Allyn & Bacon.

Hess, M.B., & Linderman, P. (2002). *The expert expatriate: Your guide to successful relocation abroad - moving, living, thriving.* Yarmouth, ME: Nicholas Brealey Publishing/Intercultural Press.

Hilgard, E. R. (1987). *Psychology in America.* Orlando, FL: Harcourt Brace Jovanovich.

Hill, G. W. (1998a). *Activities and videos for teaching cross-cultural issues in psychology.* Retrieved June 27, 2005, from http://www.lemoyne.edu/DTRP

Hill, G. W. (1998b). *Informational resources for teaching cross-cultural issues in psychology.* Retrieved June 27, 2005, from www.lemoyne.edu/OTRP

Hogan, J. D. (1995). International psychology in the next century: Comment and speculation from a U.S. perspective. *World Psychology, 1,* 9–25.

Hogan, J. D., & Sussner, B. D. (2001). Cross-cultural psychology in historical perspective. In L. L. Adler & U. P. Gielen (Eds.), *Cross-cultural topics in psychology* (2nd ed., pp. 15–28). Westport, CT: Praeger.

Hollander, E. P. (2005, Summer). APA international activities at the U.N. in the early 1960s. *International Psychology Reporter, 9,* 22–23.

Kağitçibaşi, Ç. (1996). *Family and human development across cultures: A view from the other side.* Hillsdale, NJ: Lawrence Erlbaum Associates.

Katz, T. (2005, April). *Feminism among Israeli women.* Paper presented at the 33rd Hunter College Psychology Conference, New York.

Kohls, R. L. (2001). *Survival kit for overseas living: For Americans planning to live and work abroad.* Yarmouth, ME: Nicholas Brealey Publishing/Intercultural Press.

Lamberti, G. (1995). *Wilhelm Maximillian Wundt (1832–1920). Leben, Werk und Persöenlichkeit in Bildern und Texten* [Wilhelm Maximilian Wundt (1832–1920): Life, work and personality in the form of pictures and texts]. Bonn: Deutscher Psychologen Verlag.

Laungani, P. (2004). *Asian perspectives in counseling and psychotherapy.* Hove, UK: Brunner-Routledge.

Leong, F. T. L., Pedersen, P. B., & Marsella, A. J. (2005). *Internationalizing psychology: Meeting the challenges of our changing global community.* Manuscript in preparation.

Levant, R. F. (2005, June). President's Column: Licensure mobility and prescriptive authority. *Monitor on Psychology, 36,* 5.

Levine, R. V. (2003). The kindness of strangers. *American Scientist, 91,* 226–233.

Lonner, W. J., Dinnel, D. L., Hayes, S. A., & Sattler, D. N. (Eds.). (2003). *On-line readings in culture and psychology.* Bellingham, WA: Western Washington University, Center for Cross-Cultural Research.

Marsella, A. J. (2000, Spring). Internationalizing the psychology curriculum: Toward new competencies and directions. *International Psychology Reporter, 4,* 21–22.

Marsella, A.J., & Pedersen, P. (in press). Internationalizing the counseling psychology curriculum: Toward new values, competencies, and directions. *Counselling Psychology Quarterly.*

Matsumoto, D., & Juang, L. (2004). *Culture and psychology* (3rd ed.). Belmont, CA: Wadsworth.

Merenda, P. F. (1995). International movements in psychology: Major international associations of psychology. *World Psychology, 1,* 27–48.

Misiak, H., & Sexton, V. S. (1966). *History of psychology: An overview.* New York: Grune and Stratton.

Moghaddam, F. M. (1997). *Social psychology: Exploring universals across cultures.* New York: W. H. Freeman.

Murray, B. (2005, Spring). U.S. students abroad. *Eye on Psi Chi, 9,* 20–21.

Overmier, J. B., & Overmier, J. A. (1999). *Psychology: IUPsyS global resource* [CD-ROM]. Hove, UK: Psychology Press.

Pandey, J. (Ed.). (2000). *Psychology in India revisited – Developments in the discipline: Vol. 1. Psychological foundation and human cognition.* Delhi, India: Sage.

Pandey, J. (Ed.). (2001). *Psychology in India revisited – Developments in the discipline: Vol. 2. Personality and health psychology.* Delhi, India: Sage.

Pandey, J. (Ed.). (2004). *Psychology in India revisited – Developments in the discipline: Vol. 3. Applied social and organizational psychology.* Delhi, India: Sage.

Pawlik, K. (Ed.). (1985). *International directory of psychologists, exclusive of the U.S.A.* (4th ed.). Amsterdam: Elsevier.

Pawlik, K., & Rosenzweig, M. R. (Eds.). (2000). *International handbook of psychology.* Thousand Oaks, CA: Sage.

Pedersen, P. B. (2005). *110 experiences for multicultural learning.* Washington, DC: American Psychological Association.

Pedersen, P. B., Draguns, J. G., Lonner, W. J., & Trimble J. E. (2002). *Counseling across cultures: Counseling and psychotherapy in focus* (5th ed.). Thousand Oaks, CA: Sage.

Pickren, W. E., & Fowler, R. D. (2003). Professional organizations. In D. K. Freedheim & I. Weiner (Eds.), *Handbook of psychology: History of psychology* (Vol. 1, pp. 535–544). New York: Wiley.

Ponterotto, J., Casas, J. M., Suzuki, L., & Alexander, C. (Eds.). (2001). *Handbook of multicultural counseling* (2nd ed.). Thousand Oaks, CA: Sage.

Poyrazli, S. (2005, Winter). International students at U.S. universities: Overcoming the challenges. *Eye on Psi Chi, 9,* 18–19.

Price, W. F., & Crapo, R. H. (2005). *Cross-cultural perspectives in introductory psychology* (5th ed.). Pacific Grove, CA: Wadsworth.

Roopnarine, J., & Gielen, U. P. (Eds.). (2005). *Families in global perspective.* Boston: Allyn & Bacon.

Rosenzweig, M. R. (1984). U.S. psychology and world psychology. *American Psychologist, 39,* 877–884.

Rosenzweig, M. R. (Ed) (1992). *International psychological science: Progress, problems, and prospects.* Washington, DC: American Psychological Association.

Rosenzweig, M. R., Holtzman, W. H., Sabourin, M., & Bélanger, D. (Eds.). (2000). *History of the International Union of Psychological Science, IUPsyS.* Hove, UK: Psychology Press.

Russo, N. F., & Takooshian, H. (2002, Spring). Student involvement in international psychology: Why and how. *Eye on Psi Chi, 6,* 14–15.

Sapir, S. G., & Smith, K. M. (1992). The International Council of Psychologists and the United Nations. In U. P. Gielen, L. L. Adler, & N. A. Milgram (Eds.), *Psychology in international perspective* (pp. 19–29). Amsterdam: Swets and Zeitlinger.

Segall, M., Dasen, P., Berry, J., & Poortinga, Y. (1999). *Human behavior in global perspective: An introduction to cross-cultural psychology*. Boston: Allyn & Bacon.

Sexton, V. S., & Hogan, J. D. (Eds.). (1992). *International psychology: Views from around the world*. Lincoln, NE: University of Nebraska.

Sexton, V. S., & Misiak, H. (Eds.). (1976). *Psychology around the world*. Monterey, CA: Brooks/Cole.

Shiraev, E., & Levy, D. (2003). *Cross-cultural psychology: Critical thinking and contemporary applications* (2nd ed.). Boston: Allyn and Bacon.

Smith, P. B., & Bond, M. H. (1998). *Social psychology across cultures*. Boston: Allyn & Bacon.

Spielberger, C. D. (Ed.). (2004). *Encyclopedia of applied psychology*. Amsterdam: Elsevier.

Stevens, M. J. (2002, Fall). Getting more involved in international psychology. *Eye on Psi Chi, 7,* 12–13.

Stevens, M. J., & Wedding, D. (Eds.). (2004). *Handbook of international psychology*. New York: Brunner-Routledge.

Stevens, M. J., & Wedding, D. (Eds.). (2006). *Psychology: IUPsyS global resource* [CD-ROM] (7th ed.). Hove, UK: Psychology Press.

Takooshian, H. (1992). Increasing communication between Soviet and U.S. psychologists. *International Journal of Psychology, 27,* 533.

Takooshian, H. (2003). Counseling psychology's wide new horizons. *Counseling Psychologist, 31,* 420–426.

Takooshian, H., & Salovey, P. (2004, November). Psign of the times. *APS Observer, 17,* 11–12.

Takooshian, H., & Stevens, M. J. (2001, Fall). Collaborating in cross-national survey research: Why and how. *International Psychology Reporter, 5,* 13–15.

Takooshian, H., & Velayo, R. S. (2004). Internationalizing our psychology curriculum. *Newsletter of the Society for Teaching of Psychology,* Spring, 8–9.

Takooshian, H., Velayo, R. S., Draguns, J. G., Merenda, P. F., & Rayburn, C. A. (2003, March). Multiple diversities within psychology: Multicultural, cross-cultural, international, gender. *Proceedings of the meeting of the Eastern Psychological Association, 74,* 77–78.

Takooshian, H., Velayo, R. S., & Prohaska, V. (2002, Spring). Funding undergraduate research. *Eye on Psi Chi, 6,* 34–35.

Thomas, A. (Ed.). (2004). *Kulturvergleichende Psychologie: Eine Einfuehrung* [Culture-comparative psychology: An introduction] (2nd ed.). Göttingen, Germany: Hogrefe Verlag.

Triandis, H. C., & Berry, J. W. (1980). *Handbook of cross-cultural psychology*. Boston: Allyn and Bacon.

Trimble, J. E., Stevenson, M. R., & Worell, J. P. (2004). *Toward an inclusive psychology: Infusing the introductory psychology textbook with diversity content*. Washington, DC: American Psychological Association.

Tsang-Feign, C. (1993). *Self-help for foreigners: How to keep your life, family and career intact while living abroad*. Hong Kong: Asia 2000.

Van de Vijver, F., & Leung, K. (1997). *Methods and data analysis for cross-cultural research*. Thousand Oaks, CA: Sage.

Van Rossen, E., McCaslin-Rodrigo, S., & Owusu-Banahene, N. O. (2002, Fall). The International Student Psychology Organization (IPSO). *International Psychology Reporter, 6,* 15–16.

Velayo, R. S. (2004, April). *Strategies in using distance learning to internationalize the psychology curriculum.* Paper presented at the meeting of the Eastern Psychological Association, Washington, DC.

Velayo, R. S. (2005, Spring/Summer). Internationalizing the undergraduate psychology curriculum: An APA update. *International Psychology Reporter, 9,* 2.

Woolf, L. M., Hulsizer, M. R., & McCarthy, T. (2002a). *International psychology: A compendium of textbooks for selected courses evaluated for international content.* Retrieved June 27, 2005, from www.lemoyne.edu/OTRP

Woolf, L. M., Hulsizer, M. R., & McCarthy, T. (2002b). *International psychology: Annotated bibliography, relevant organizations, and course suggestions.* Retrieved June 27, 2005, from www.lemoyne.edu/OTRP

Wundt, W. (1916). *Elements of folk psychology: Outlines of a psychological history of the development of mankind* (E. L. Schaub, Trans.). London: Allan and Unwin.

Epilogue: Some Questions for the Future

Michael J. Stevens
Illinois State University

Uwe P. Gielen
St. Francis College

The contributing authors to *Toward a Global Psychology: Theory, Research, Intervention, and Pedagogy* have introduced and described the parameters of a relatively new, but increasingly important specialty within the discipline of psychology. They have delineated the mission and foci of global psychology; its origins, development, and current status in the industrialized and postmodern world and in the less familiar majority world; its emerging conceptual models, research methods, psychotherapeutic and macro-level practices, ethical and legal regulatory mechanisms, and educational and training needs; and avenues for becoming more competent and engaged as globally oriented psychologists and psychology students.

Toward a Global Psychology offers rich and varied evidence for the globalizing of psychology. In part, the globalizing of psychology seems to be an outgrowth of a more general process of globalization. The economic, political, social, and technological developments that are accelerating in the early 21st century represent macro-level forces, which are moving psychology toward a science and profession without borders vis-à-vis understanding, dialogue, and integration of knowledge across countries and cultures. A number of significant paradigm shifts are underway that attest to the transformation of psychology into a less insular discipline. Examples include the rise and acceptance of cross-cultural psychology and multiculturalism, the growing interest in cultural and indigenous psychologies, and the challenge posed by normative alternatives to mainstream "universalist" perspectives in psychology that emphasize the situated and relational nature of human action and experience. Concrete evidence for the globalizing of psychology can be found in ongoing efforts to formulate a universal code of ethics for psychologists, the proliferation of exchange programs and sources of funding that support transnational goals and activities in psychology, more urgent calls for the revision of the existing psychology curriculum to meet the needs of a rapidly changing world, and the growing commitment by international psychology organizations to diversify their membership by including psychologists in the majority world, to capacity-build scientific psychology in the majority world, and to establish ties with policy-making entities to improve the quality of life in the majority world.

At the same time, many areas of psychology, at least as understood and taught in the U.S., remain relatively untouched by these developments. For example, the history of psychology is frequently conceptualized in a thoroughly parochial manner, such that the contributions of most non-U.S. authors to post-World War II developments in psychology are ignored (e.g., Schultz & Schulz, 2004). Textbooks delineating theories of personality remain wedded to individualistic models that ignore extensive research on more collectivistic modes of personality functioning. Handbooks of social psychology implicitly present "Americanized" models of social functioning as if they can account for social behavior everywhere. Considerable work must be done in order to break free from these ethnocentric versions of psychology.

THE GLOBAL EXPANSION OF PSYCHOLOGY

During the last 30–40 years, the presence of psychology has grown in many Western and non-Western countries. European psychology, for example, has not only regained the vitality that it partially lost in the 1930s–1950s, but it also has expanded rapidly in recent decades. In this context, Tikkanen (2005) estimates that the number of individuals trained in psychology in the 31 countries comprising the European Federation of Psychologists' Associations (excluding Russia, Ukraine, and some other nations) is 293,000, and that the number of professional psychologists in Europe will likely surpass 371,000 by 2010. By way of comparison, the U.S. Census Bureau (2003) reports a total of 277,000 employed psychologists in the U.S. for the year 2002.

Large numbers of psychologists have also been reported for some Latin-American countries, such as Brazil and Argentina. Hutz, McCarthy, and

Gomes (2004) state that at present over 140,000 licensed psychologists practice in Brazil alone, although only about 900 of them hold doctoral degrees. And, what is the world's capital of psychology as measured by the number of licensed psychologists? It is Buenos Aires, where, according to Klappenbach (2004), 32,976 predominantly psychoanalytically oriented psychologists practice. However, "research is not a principal activity in Argentine psychology" (Klappenbach, 2004, p. 143), and the same may be said for psychology in many other countries in the majority world, including Brazil, Indonesia, and Nigeria. One consequence of this state of affairs is that psychologists from these countries have exerted little influence on mainstream academic psychology in Europe and the U.S., although Argentine psychologists have played a significant role in the global landscape of psychoanalysis.

The rapid worldwide expansion of psychology has never been fully analyzed. Consequently, a number of questions can be raised that only future studies and events can fully answer. Here are some of those questions:

- At present, U.S. psychology occupies a central place in psychology worldwide. Will European psychology gradually assume a similar position in the near future given evidence that the number of European psychologists has surpassed the number of psychologists in the U.S.?
- English has become the language of global psychology thanks to the cultural, economic, military, and scientific dominance of the U.S. Will this trend continue or will other languages, such as Chinese and Spanish, become more important over time? What effects might this have on global psychology? Will international congresses of psychology become more linguistically diverse? Will some regional psychology associations become dominated by languages other than English?
- Some majority-world countries report more psychological activity and accomplishments of a certain kind than others, for example, research productivity (e.g., China vs. Indonesia). What are the sources of variation in the specific activities of psychologists in different parts of the majority world? Under what circumstances do applied psychological issues become so prominent that a culture of basic research can emerge only with great difficulty in a given country or region?
- Similarly, economic and political factors have most often been cited as mediating the state of psychology in countries of the majority

world. To what extent do cultural variables, such as individualism, ethnicity, language, and religion contribute to the acceptance of psychology, the length of time it has existed in a particular country, and its future prospects?

THEORY, RESEARCH, INTERVENTION, AND PEDAGOGY

Notwithstanding the panoply of viewpoints within *Toward a Global Psychology*, there are several key themes that run through the book, which deserve mention. These include the criticism of mainstream, reductionistic psychology as being parochial and inadequate to tasks of making sense of, studying, and intervening in psychological phenomena-in-context; advocacy for multidisciplinary, multilevel approaches to studying and responding to global issues and problems that have psychological dimensions; the importance of transnational collaboration both regionally and worldwide; concern about pressing global challenges, including intergroup conflict, degradation of the natural environment, threats to physical and mental health, the status of at-risk populations (e.g., women, children and adolescents, migrants and refugees); and the need for greater contextual sensitivity, knowledge, skill, and an ethic of social responsibility among psychologists already involved in global psychology as well as among psychology students.

Toward a Global Psychology has succeeded in laying out the history and contemporary standing of the specialty, which do not bear repeating here. However, it is reasonable to examine where global psychology has left off and where it may be headed. That is, given its origins and development, is it possible to discern the direction that global psychology is likely to take in the next decade or so? In contemplating the future of global psychology, we chose to identify a number of unanswered questions raised by our contributing authors that we believe must be addressed if the conceptual models, investigative strategies, practical applications, and professional training in global psychology are to advance to a more mature stage. Although many more unanswered questions could be raised that might clarify the future course of the field, the ones listed below address matters of a more general and urgent nature. While the answers to these question are as yet unknown, they will become evident, as will the way in which the field will move ahead, as globally oriented psychologists focus their talents and energy on them.

Theory

- What are the respective merits of reductionistic, normative, and mixed conceptual models as applied to psychological phenomena-in-context?
- To what extent do normative and mixed models meet the formal criteria of theory, and should they be subjected to such an evaluation, which is itself culture-bound?
- Under what circumstances is each approach—reductionistic, normative, and mixed—most promising in facilitating an understanding of global phenomena and providing direction for research and practice?
- One question that deserves special attention pertains to normative paradigms, whose popularity is gaining momentum among social scientists across many disciplines. Clearly, there is a host of different normative systems throughout the world. If the aim of global psychology is to incorporate these systems, might not an epistemological nightmare emerge in which global psychology becomes a highly fragmented Tower of Babel of countless different psychologies? How can global psychologists forge a more global psychology out of these multiple normative systems, one that is characterized by the distillation of genuine universals, or at least a more complete understanding of the social practices that give meaning to human action and experience?
- The indigenous analysis of academic achievement in East Asia, as reported in chapter 5, provides an in-depth illustration of a phenomenon-in-context. Are there other examples of how indigenous theories, methods, and practices "fit" different phenomena-in-context or are there limits to what indigenous approaches can explain even within the same cultural context?
- In a related vein, what are the benefits and drawbacks of different forms of indigenous psychologies, for example, those which reject entirely any contribution to theory, research, intervention, and pedagogy that is not grassroots in origin as opposed to the adaptation of psychological tools born in a different culture to the realities of psychological phenomena-in-context in the host culture?

Research

- To what extent are qualitative research methods sensitive to and capable of capturing human action and experience in diverse societies and cultures? Can they be matched in a systematic fashion to specific sociocultural contexts so as to maximize the validity and utility of their findings?

- How can qualitative research methods be used to study problems associated with the majority world, such as mounting population pressures, epidemics, human rights violations, poverty, urban life, and violent conflict?
- How can qualitative research methods be applied to support indigenous psychologies (i.e., a psychology developed within a culture) and indigenization (i.e., the adaptation of psychological tools imported from another culture)?
- Like the distinct theoretical approaches noted above, there are quantitative, qualitative, and mixed-method approaches. Under what circumstances does each appear to be most promising?
- How can we facilitate the integration of research findings from non-English speaking countries and from majority-world countries into the global mainstream of psychology?

Intervention

- What does global psychology mean in terms of practice within the cultural, economic, historical, political, religious, and social fabric of a given country or region?
- How does global psychology address such dimensions as individualism-collectivism, science-folklore, secular-theocratic, and democratic-authoritarian when it comes to applied practice, particularly in times of rapid sociocultural change during which the relevance of these dimensions within a particular context may be in flux?
- To what extent are macro-level interventions conceptually driven, whether by a system-analytic perspective or some other formulation that purports to be sensitive to culture, ethics, and power?
- What guidelines are available to accommodate clashing cultural values in the planning and implementation of macro-level interventions?
- Are preventive macro-level efforts feasible regionally and worldwide, just as they are with at-risk individuals within a single locale or society?
- What are the methodologies available for appropriately evaluating the outcomes of macro-level interventions, especially when implemented in unfamiliar cultural settings?
- Most existing ethical and legal mechanisms for regulating the practice of psychology rest on assumptions of individualism and fail to account for prevailing conditions that foster individual dysfunction. What

ethical guidelines and legal mandates should be developed that address toxic contextual conditions and that guide grassroots and larger-scale interventions to emancipate people from such conditions?

- How can a universal code of ethics be truly applicable across diverse cultural contexts whose values and traditions rest on differing assumptions of what constitutes morality and the good life? Is there a set of basic humans values to guide the development of universally ethical practice in psychology?

- Do preliminary guidelines for universally ethical practice need to be more concise with respect to the growing number of psychologists who teach, conduct research, and practice transnationally?

Pedagogy

- How can existing theories, research findings, and practices from cross-cultural psychology be more fully integrated into undergraduate and graduate textbooks and curricula so that globally oriented discussions of cultural influences on human action and experience become important ingredients of mainstream psychology?

- Beyond the call for more relevant education and training, what should constitute a core curriculum, professional coursework, and supervised experience in the field of global psychology? In particular, what is the curriculum needed to create a full capacity global citizen, one who embodies a value-based fusion of the individual and the discipline?

- How are psychologists and psychology students to acquire the knowledge, skill, and dedication to social responsibility to function effectively in the globalized world of the 21st century?

- How can psychologists and psychology students be trained to work in different sociocultural contexts and in research and applied settings around the world?

- How can pedagogical outcomes relevant to a global psychology be validly assessed if they are to be improved?

CONCLUSION

As we noted, these are but a few pointed questions that globally oriented psychologists are posing and for which they are beginning to pursue answers. Those answers, and other developments in theory, research, intervention, and pedagogy, will certainly advance the field of global psychology greatly over the next few years. While it is an exciting period for psychologists and psychology students who are interested in global psychology, it is also a challenging one. There are myriad forces and events that could influence the direction of the specialty, some of which can be dimly envisaged (e.g., the expected course of globalization) and others which cannot be anticipated. The future course of global psychology also rests on the awareness and commitment of psychologists to communicate and collaborate in a horizontal and multidisciplinary fashion on various levels in an effort to understand and address the shared concerns and issues that face humankind.

Perhaps, the most telling question that remains to be answered concerns the foundation and identity of the discipline of psychology as we know it. As the process of globalizing psychology ensues, how will its science and practice be transformed from the form in which it is currently constituted? Psychology will continue to evolve as it has in the past. Although this inevitable evolution can be forecast with limited accuracy, it would seem that the beliefs and customs of other cultures will be incorporated more extensively into the fabric of scientific and professional psychology in the future. Conversely, as psychology becomes more globally integrated, the history of psychology will be reconceptualized as transnational and multilingual, rather than as Western and English-dominated. New books that deconstruct the history of psychology (e.g., Brock, 2007) will play a significant role in how psychologists and psychology students construe the discipline of psychology and their own identity within it.

REFERENCES

Brock, A. (Ed.). (2007). *Internationalizing the history of psychology*. New York: New York University Press.

Hutz, C. S., McCarthy, S., & Gomes, W. (2004). Psychology in Brazil: The road behind and the road ahead. In M. J. Stevens & D. Wedding (Eds.), *Handbook of international psychology* (pp. 151–168). New York: Brunner-Routledge.

Klappenbach, H. (2004). Psychology in Argentina. In M. J. Stevens & D. Wedding (Eds.), *Handbook of international psychology* (pp. 129–150). New York: Brunner-Routledge.

Schultz, D. P., & Schultz, S. E. (2004). *A history of modern psychology* (8th ed.). Belmont, CA: Wadsworth/Thomson Learning.

Tikkanen, T. (2005). *The present status and future prospects of the profession of psychologists in Europe*. Paper presented to the European Congress of Psychology, Grenada, Spain. Paper retrieved August 25, 2005, from http://www.efpa.be/news.php? ID=12

U.S. Census Bureau. (2003). *Statistical abstract of the United States: 2003. Section 12: Labor force, employment, and earnings* (pp. 381–432). Retrieved September 9, 2005, from http://www.census.gov/prod/2004pubs/03statab/labor.pdf

Appendix A

Rubén Ardila, Ph.D.

Rubén Ardila received his baccalaureate in psychology from the National University of Colombia in Bogotá and his doctorate at the University of Nebraska-Lincoln in experimental psychology. His research areas are the experimental analysis of behavior, psychobiology, and history of psychology. He has been Chair of the Psychology Department of the National University of Colombia, Chair of the Psychology Department at the University of the Andes, and Director of the Psychology Graduate Program at the University of St. Thomas. Dr. Ardila has written 27 books and more than 250 scientific papers published in several countries and languages. He has been visiting professor in Argentina, Germany, Puerto Rico, Spain, and the U.S. He is also a member of the Executive Committee of the International Union of Psychological Science and the International Council of Psychologists, and was President of the Interamerican Society of Psychology. He is founder and editor of the *Latin American Journal of Psychology*.

Andrew Dawes, Ph.D.

Andrew Dawes is a clinical and developmental psychologist. He is currently a Research Director in the Child, Youth, and Family Development research program at the Human Sciences Research Council of South Africa. He is also an Emeritus Professor at the University of Cape Town and an Associate Member of the Department of Social Policy and Social Work at the University of Oxford. For many years he has been committed to conducting applied research with relevance to social policy. During the Apartheid period, Dr. Dawes played an active role in the anti-Apartheid movement, including activities to promote human rights and clinical services to adults and children affected by political oppression, imprisonment, and torture. His current research is mainly policy-oriented and embraces several areas, including child rights and well-being monitoring systems, HIV/AIDS, juvenile justice, mental health, sexual abuse, and violence. In addition to four books, Dr. Dawes has produced a number of journal articles, book chapters, and conference papers.

Juris G. Draguns, Ph.D., DHC

Juris G. Draguns was born in Riga, Latvia, where he completed his primary schooling. Displaced in WWII, he graduated from high school in Germany and, upon immigrating to the U.S., obtained his B.A. with a major in psychology at Utica College of Syracuse University and his Ph.D. in clinical psychology from the University of Rochester. After working as a clinical psychologist at the Rochester, NY and Worcester, MA State Hospitals, Dr. Draguns accepted a faculty appointment at The Pennsylvania State University in University Park, from which he retired as Professor Emeritus in 1997. He has taught and lectured at Clark University in Worcester, MA, Johannes Gutenberg University in Mainz, Germany, the East-West Center in Honolulu, Hawaii, Flinders University of South Australia, National Taiwan University in Taipei, University of Latvia in Riga, and Universidad de las Americas/Puebla in Cholula in Mexico. He is a recipient of the American Psychological Association's (APA) Award for Distinguished Contributions to the International Advancement of Psychology and holds an honorary doctoral degree from the University of Latvia. He is President of the Society for Cross-Cultural Research for 2006–2007.

Christina E. Erneling, Ph.D.

Christina E. Erneling is Associate Professor and Chair at the Institute of Communication, Lund University, Helsingborg Campus, where she teaches cognition and communication. She has also taught psychology and philosophy at Umeå University, Sweden, and at York University, Canada. Her book, *Understanding Language Acquisition: The Framework of Learning* (1993), develops a language acquisition model that emphasizes the social nature of learning. She is the co-editor of two books on the future of psychology and the nature of the mind: *The Future of the Cognitive Revolution* (1997) and *The Mind as a Scientific Object: Between Brain and Culture* (2005). She is chair of the Swedish History of Psychology Association. Her current research is focused on educational technology and on the pedagogical and psychological thinking of Jean Piaget.

Uwe P. Gielen, Ph.D.

Uwe P. Gielen received his Ph.D. in social psychology from Harvard University. His work has centered on cross-cultural and international psychology, moral development, and Tibetan studies. A professor, former chair of the Psychology Department, and executive director of the Institute for International and Cross-Cultural Psychology at St. Francis College, he is the editor, co-editor, and co-author of 17 books on cross-cultural and international psychology. In addition, he has served as editor of the *International Journal of Group Tensions* and *World Psychology*. He is former president of the International Council of Psychologists and the Society for Cross-Cultural Research, has done fieldwork in the Himalayas, conducted research in North America, the Caribbean, Europe, Asia and the Arab world, and lectured in 31 countries. His most recent books include *Handbook of Culture, Therapy, and Healing* and *Childhood and Adolescence: Cross-cultural Perspectives and Applications*.

John D. Hogan, Ph.D.

John D. Hogan received his Ph.D. degree from Ohio State University in 1970 in developmental psychology. A professor at St. John's University, his major areas of research interest include the history of psychology, international psychology, and developmental psychology. He has published more than 150 articles, book reviews and chapters, and has co-edited two books: *International Psychology: Views From Around the World* (1992), with Virginia S. Sexton, and *A History of Developmental Psychology in Autobiography* (1997), with Dennis N. Thompson. He has held offices in several professional organizations including Division 52 (International Psychology) of the APA, the Eastern Psychological Association, the New York State Psychological Association, and the New York Academy of Sciences. His most recent publications include chapters on G. Stanley Hall, Anne Anastasi, and June Downey.

Uichol Kim, Ph.D.

Uichol Kim is professor of psychology at Inha University, Incheon, Korea. He has also taught at the University of Hawaii at Manoa, U.S. and the University of Tokyo, Japan. He has published over 100 articles and 12 books including *Indigenous Psychologies* (Sage, 1993), *Individualism* and *Collectivism* (Sage, 1994), *Progress in Asian Social Psychology* (John Wiley & Sons, 1997), *Democracy, Human Rights and Islam in Modern Iran* (Fagbokforlaget, 2003), and *Indigenous and Cultural Psychology* (Springer, 2006). He has conducted research in the area of family and parent-child relationships, education attainment and school violence, organizational culture and change, health and subjective well being, and democracy, human rights, and political culture. He has provided consulting services for governmental agencies and multinational companies in Asia, Europe, and North America. He is the founding editor of *Asian Journal of Social Psychology* and currently the president of the Division of Psychology and National Development, International Association of Applied Psychology.

Naomi Lee, B.S.

Naomi Lee is a graduate student at Georgetown University in the doctoral program in Human Development and Public Policy.

Anthony J. Marsella, Ph.D, DHC

Anthony J. Marsella is Emeritus Professor of Psychology at the University of Hawaii where he was a member of the faculty for 35 years. Prior to his retirement, he served as Director of the World Health Organization Field Psychiatric Research Center in Honolulu and Director of the Disaster Management and Humanitarian Assistance Program. He has published 13 books and 160 book chapters, journal articles, and technical reports, and was awarded numerous research and training grants in the areas of culture, psychopathology, and global challenges. His most recent book, *Understanding Terrorism: Psychosocial Roots, Consequences, and Interventions*, co-edited with Fathali M. Moghaddam, was selected as a 2004 "Outstanding Academic Title" by CHOICE (Current Reviews for Academic Libraries) of the American Library Association. Dr. Marsella has served as a visiting professor and lecturer at universities, hospitals, and institutes around the world. He has received numerous national and international awards for his teaching, research, and service, including the Medal of Highest Honor from Soka University in Japan (1994), an honorary doctorate from the University of Copenhagen (1999), and the APA's award for Distinguished Contributions to the International Advancement of Psychology (1996) and International Psychologist of the Year (2004).

Maritza Montero, Ph.D.

Maritza Montero is Professor in the Department of Social Psychology of Universidad Central de Venezuela. She is author of *Ideología, Alienación e Identidad Nacional* (*Ideology, Alienation and National Identity*) (1985), editor of two volumes on political psychology (1986, 1991), and co-editor of another two books, one of them on Latin America (1995) and the other on France, Spain, and Latin America (1993). Her primary work includes analyses of ideology and alternative modes of action, published in journals throughout the Americas and Europe.

Fathali M. Moghaddam, Ph.D.

Fathali M. Moghaddam is Professor of Psychology at Georgetown University, having previously worked for the U.N. and McGill University in Canada. He received his graduate training, including the doctorate from the University of Surrey in the UK. His most recent books related to global psychology are *Social Psychology: Exploring Universals Across Cultures* (1998), *The Individual and Society: A Cultural Integration* (2002), *The Self and Others* with Rom Harré (2004), and *Great Ideas in Psychology: A Cultural and Historical Introduction* (2005). His current research is directed to make theoretical and empirical contributions toward psychology as a normative science.

Elizabeth Nair, Ph.D.

Elizabeth Nair received her Ph.D. from the University of Nottingham, U.K., for her research on "Stress Inoculation in Relation to War." Executive Board Member (2000–2008) of the International Union of Psychological Science, she is the Psychology Capacity-Building Chair, and Chief Liaison for the Psychological Study of Peace. She was Organizing Chair and Scientific Program Co-Chair for the 2002 International Congress of Applied Psychology in Singapore. A Board Member (1998–2006) of the International Association of Applied Psychology (IAAP), she is also the *IAAP Newsletter* Editor (2002–2006). From Chief Psychologist at the Singapore Ministry of Defense, she moved to academia at the National University of Singapore in 1989. At present, she is Principal Consultant Psychologist with Work & Health Psychologists in Singapore. Dr. Nair's awards include the Efficiency Medal in 1984 from the Singapore Civil

Service, Distinguished International Psychologist Award in 2001 from the APA Division of International Psychology, and the 2003 Inaugural Award for Outstanding Service to Psychology in Singapore.

Young-Shin Park, Ph.D.

Young-Shin Park is a professor of educational and counseling psychology at the Department of Education, Inha University, Incheon, South Korea. She has published over 80 articles and 10 books on the topics of parent-child relationships, academic achievement, self-efficacy, delinquent behavior, school violence, trust, quality of life, and indigenous and cultural psychology. Her publications include *Parent-child Relationship in Korea: Indigenous Psychological Analysis of Self-concept and Family Role* (2004, Kyoyook Kwahaksa) and *Adolescent Culture and Parent-child Relationship in Korea: Indigenous Psychological Analysis* (2004, Kyoyook Kwahaksa). She is currently the editor-in-chief of the *Korean Journal of Psychological and Social Issues* and the consulting editor of the *Asian Journal of Social Psychology*.

Jean L. Pettifor, Ph.D.

Jean Linse (Dixon) Pettifor identifies herself as a professional psychologist with over 40 years employment with the Government of Alberta, Canada, in Mental Health and Social Service Departments. Today, she teaches ethics in the Division of Applied Psychology at the University of Calgary. She has served in many capacities in psychology organizations for nearly 50 years, including positions of President of the Psychologists Association of Alberta, the College of Alberta Psychologists, and the Canadian Psychological Association. Her primary interest in professional ethics and value-based decision making is demonstrated in her publications, teaching, and international presentations. She has received many awards for her contributions to the profession. Dr. Pettifor has earned the following degrees: from the University of Saskatchewan a B.A. in English and in History, from the University of Alberta a B.Ed. and M.A. in English and a M.Ed. in Psychology, and from Wayne State University in the U.S. a Ph.D. in Clinical Psychology.

Angélica Riveros, Lic.

Angélica Riveros is a licensed psychologist, having graduated with honors from the National Autonomous University of México. Her main research interests include assessment of and change in factors that contribute to essential hypertension. She has completed continuing education courses from Mexico's National Autonomous University, the Mexican Psychological Society, the Ibero-American Society for Clinical and Health Psychology, and the joint program of the Department of Continuing Education at Harvard Medical School and Massachusetts General Hospital. Ms. Riveros has published articles in the *Journal of Clinical Child and Adolescent Psychology*, *Journal of Family Psychology*, and *International Journal of Clinical and Health Psychology*; she has presented over 20 peer-reviewed papers at congresses in Mexico and abroad. Ms. Riveros has coordinated the Mexican component of a joint transcultural studies program with research teams from Tulane University in the U.S. She currently oversees student-exchange activities in a joint program between the National Autonomous University of México and the Mexican Academy of Sciences.

Juan José Sánchez-Sosa, Ph.D., DHC

Juan José Sánchez-Sosa obtained his licentiate in psychology from the National Autonomous University of México (UNAM) and his M.A. and Ph.D. from the University of Kansas in the U.S. He is author/editor of nine books and some 70 articles and book chapters on educational, health, and professional psychology, and was editor of the *Mexican Journal of Behavior Analysis*. Dr. Sánchez-Sosa is a professor at UNAM and has been invited to serve on doctoral dissertation committees by universities in Spain, Switzerland, and the U.S. He was the founding president of the Mexican Academy of Applied Psychophysiology and Biofeedback. He has served as president of the Mexican Psychological Society, the Mexican College of Psychologists, Mexican Academy of Doctors in Social and Human Sciences, and International Society of Clinical Psychology. Dr. Sánchez-Sosa was vice-president of the International Union of Psychological Science and currently presides over the Division of Clinical and Community Psychology within the International Association of Applied Psychology. Dr. Sánchez-Sosa received a "Wilhelm Wundt" Meissen effigy for his keynote address at the 1980 International Congress of Psychology, a Fulbright fellowship at the University of California at Riverside, and an honorary doctorate from the University of Ottawa in Canada.

Leyla Faw Stambaugh, Ph.D.

Leyla Faw Stambaugh completed her Ph.D. at Fordham University in 2003. She then worked for two years as a researcher for the National

Clinical Assessment Service, a division of the National Health Service (NHS) in the United Kingdom. She also lectured in Psychology at Birkbeck College in London. She presented her dissertation findings at the 16th World Congress of the International Association of Child and Adolescent Psychiatry and Allied Professions in Berlin in August, 2004. She is now a postdoctoral fellow in the Department of Psychiatry at Duke University Medical Center. Her interests include developmental epidemiology and dissemination of evidence-based mental health interventions to underserved children.

Graham B. Stead, Ph.D.

Graham B. Stead was previously a Professor of Psychology at two South African universities. He is currently an Assistant Professor and a research methodologist in the College of Education and Human Services at Cleveland State University. He is registered as a Counseling Psychologist and as a Research Psychologist in South Africa. He has also co-edited *Career Psychology in the South African Context* (1999) and co-authored *Planning, Designing and Reporting Research* (2001) and *Undergraduate Statistics for the Social Sciences* (2005). His professional interests are in the fields of vocational psychology and qualitative and quantitative research methods.

Michael J. Stevens, Ph.D., DHC

Michael J. Stevens is a professor of psychology at Illinois State University and a licensed clinical psychologist. He will become President of the Division of International Psychology of the APA in 2007, having previously chaired its International Liaisons and Information Clearinghouse Committees, and co-chaired its Curriculum/Training and Program Committees. He is a Fellow of the Division and received its Recognition Award and Outstanding Mentor Award. He is an honorary professor at The Lucian Blaga University in Romania, where he completed a Fulbright grant and received the Doctor Honoris Causa degree. He has been invited to lecture in Argentina, China, Cyprus, Finland, Tajikistan, and Uruguay. Dr. Stevens has published over 80 articles and book chapters and presented over 90 papers and symposia. Recent scholarship related to global psychology includes the *Handbook of International Psychology* (2004) and *Psychology: IUPsyS Global Resource* (2005, 2006). Dr. Stevens' professional interests include the globalizing of psychology and the psychology of terrorism.

Harold Takooshian, Ph.D.

Harold Takooshian of Fordham University, has been involved in international psychology since 1979, when he completed his doctorate at City University of New York. As a teacher, he taught at five U.S. and three Latin-America universities, and later in four cities in the Soviet Union as a U.S. Fulbright Scholar in 1987–1988. As a researcher, he has done cross-cultural work comparing attitudes and behaviors across nations. Since 1997, he has served the International Division of the APA as a charter fellow, program chair, officer, and President. Since 2003 he has been a member of the six-person team that represents the APA at the U.N.

Thomas P. Vaccaro, M.A.

Thomas P. Vaccaro is a doctoral candidate in psychology at St. John's University. He holds an M.A. degree in psychology from St. John's University and a Cand. Mag. degree from the University of Oslo. He has worked as a Volunteer Coordinator for the Department of Corrections in Alaska and as a Milieu Therapist in Oslo, Norway. He has written articles on the history of psychology and international psychology. He is currently a psychology intern at the Albert Ellis Institute in New York City.

Michael G. Wessells, Ph.D.

Michael G. Wessells is Senior Child Protection Specialist for Christian Children's Fund, Professor of Clinical Population and Family Health at Columbia University in the Program on Forced Migration and Health, and Professor of Psychology at Randolph-Macon College. He has served as President of the Division of Peace Psychology of the APA and of Psychologists for Social Responsibility and as Co-Chair of the InterAction Protection Working Group. Currently, he is Co-Chair of a U.N. Task Force on Mental Health and Psychosocial Support in Emergency Settings. His research on children and armed conflict examines child soldiers, psychosocial assistance in emergencies, and post-conflict reconstruction for peace. He regularly advises U.N. agencies, donors, and governments on the situation of children in armed conflict and issues regarding child protection and well being. In countries such as Afghanistan, Angola, East Timor, Kosova, Sierra Leone, Sri Lanka, South Africa, and Uganda, he helps to develop community-based, culturally grounded programs that assist children, families, and communities affected by armed conflict.

Richard A. Young, Ph.D.

Richard A. Young is a Professor of Counseling Psychology at the University of British Columbia. He is a registered psychologist in British Columbia and a Fellow of the Canadian Psychological Association. He is the co-editor of *The Future of Career* (2000) and the co-author of *Action Theory: A Primer for Applied Research in the Social Sciences* (2002). His professional interests are in the areas of vocational psychology, action theory, family, health, and qualitative research methods. He is currently leading a research team examining transition to adulthood as a family project.

Appendix B

Sample Course Syllabus

ILLINOIS STATE UNIVERSITY
DEPARTMENT OF PSYCHOLOGY
PSY 326 International Psychology (3 sem hr)

Catalog Description:

INTERNATIONAL PSYCHOLOGY   3 sem hr   F or S

PSY 110 or 111 req.
History, current status, and future directions of scientific and professional psychology applied to contemporary global issues.

Course Overview:

This course entails reading about, discussing, and writing on a variety of contemporary topics in the relatively new specialty of international psychology. Students will examine mainstream as well as alternative theoretical, methodological, and applied approaches that are relevant to the study and practice of international psychology. The topics selected will offer a broad and deep understanding of this field, specifically, an appreciation of psychology's relevance to the understanding and solution of global problems, as well as of how psychology itself is affected by events and cultures around the world.

Student Outcomes:

International Psychology will provide students with opportunities to develop and demonstrate competencies in the following areas:

1. Knowledge of the history, current foci, and future directions of a new and rapidly growing specialty in the discipline;
2. Ability to evaluate critically the appropriateness and consequences of mainstream psychological theory, research, and practices to global events and phenomena;
3. Familiarity with alternative models, methods, and interventions that have their roots in cultural, economic, historical, political, religious, and social contexts and their relevance to global events and phenomena;
4. Sensitivity to how global events and phenomena impact the psychosocial and sociocultural realities of diverse populations;
5. Understanding the education and training requirements for a career in international psychology; and
6. Use of the Internet to learn about the global activities of psychological and policy-making organizations (e.g., the application of psychology to unconventional settings) and how to communicate and collaborate globally.

Topical Outline, Including Required and Optional Readings:

The following text is required for this course:
Stevens, M. J., & Gielen, U. P. (Eds.). (2007). *Toward a global psychology: Theory, research, interventions, and pedagogy.* Mahwah, NJ: Lawrence Erlbaum Associates.

WEEK 1: THE HISTORY AND SCOPE OF INTERNATIONAL PSYCHOLOGY

Required:
Stevens, M. J. (2007). Orientation to a global psychology. In M. J. Stevens & U. P. Gielen (Eds.), *Toward a global psychology: Theory, research, intervention, and pedagogy* (pp. 3–33). Mahwah, NJ: Lawrence Erlbaum Associates.
Hogan, J. D., & Vaccaro, T. P. (2007). International perspectives on the history of psychology In M. J. Stevens & U. P. Gielen (Eds.), *Toward a global psychology: Theory research, interventions, and pedagogy* (pp. 39–67). Mahwah, NJ: Lawrence Erlbaum Associates.

WEEK 2: WESTERN PSYCHOLOGY AND ITS LIMITATIONS

Required:
Nair, E., Ardila, R., & Stevens, M. J. (2007). Current trends in global psychology. In M. J. Stevens & U. P. Gielen (Eds.), *Toward a global psychology: Theory, research, interventions, and pedagogy* (pp. 69–100). Mahwah, NJ: Lawrence Erlbaum Associates.

Optional:

Adair, J. G. (2002). How international is psychology? *International Journal of Psychology, 37,* 160–170.

Draguns, J. G. (2001). Toward a truly international psychology: Beyond English only. *American Psychologist, 56,* 1019–1030.

WEEK 3: CONCEPTUAL AND METHODOLOGICAL ALTERNATIVES

Required:

Moghaddam, F. M., & Erneling, C. E., Montero, M., & Lee, N (2007). Toward a conceptual foundation for a global psychology. In M. J. Stevens & U. P. Gielen (Eds.), *Toward a global psychology: Theory, research, interventions, and pedagogy* (pp. 179–206). Mahwah, NJ: Lawrence Erlbaum Associates.

Stead, G. B., & Young, R. A. (2007). Qualitative research methods for a global psychology. In M. J. Stevens & U. P. Gielen (Eds.), *Toward a global psychology: Theory, research interventions, and pedagogy* (pp. 207–232). Mahwah, NJ: Lawrence Erlbaum Associates.

Optional:

Gergen, K. J. (2001). Psychological science in a postmodern context. *American Psychologist, 56,* 803–813.

Prilleltensky, I., & Fox, D. (1997). Introducing critical psychology: Values, assumptions, and the status quo. In D. Fox & I. Prilleltensky (Eds.), *Critical psychology: An introduction* (pp. 3–20). London: Sage.

WEEK 4: THE INDIGENIZATION OF PSYCHOLOGY

Required:

Kim, U., & Park, Y.-S. (2007). Development of indigenous psychologies: Understanding people in a global context. In M. J. Stevens & U. P. Gielen (Eds.), *Toward a global psychology: Theory, research, interventions, and pedagogy* (pp. 147–172). Mahwah, NJ: Lawrence Erlbaum Associates.

Optional:

Adair, J. G. (1999). Indigenization of psychology: The concept and its practical implementation. *Applied Psychology: An International Review, 48,* 403–418.

Díaz-Loving, R. (1999). The indigenization of psychology: Birth of a new science or rekindling of an old one? *Applied Psychology: An International Review, 48,* 433–449.

WEEK 5: PSYCHOLOGY IN OTHER COUNTRIES

Required:

Stevens, M. J., & Wedding, D. (2004). International psychology: A synthesis. In M. J. Stevens & D. Wedding (Eds.), *Handbook of international psychology* (pp. 481–500). New York: Brunner-Routledge.

Sánchez Sosa, J. J., & Riveros, A. (2007). Theory, research, and practice in psychology in the developing (majority) world. In M. J. Stevens & U. P. Gielen (Eds.),

Toward a global psychology: Theory, research, interventions, and pedagogy (pp. 101–146). Mahwah, NJ: Lawrence Erlbaum Associates.

Optional:

Lundberg, I. (2001). Zeitgeist, Ortgeist, and personalities in the development of Scandinavian psychology. *International Journal of Psychology, 36*, 356–362.

Nsamenang, A. B. (1995). Factors influencing the development of psychology in sub-Saharan Africa. *International Journal of Psychology, 30*, 729–739.

Stevens, M. J., & Wedding, D. (Eds.). (2004). *Handbook of international psychology*. New York: Brunner-Routledge. [Chapters on psychology in 27 countries]

WEEK 6: INTERGROUP CONFLICT
AND PEACE BUILDING

Required:

Eidelson, R. J., & Eidelson, J. I. (2003). Dangerous ideas: Five beliefs that propel groups toward conflict. *American Psychologist, 58*, 182–192.

Optional:

Dovidio, J. F., Gaertner, S. L., & Kawakami, K. (2003). Intergroup contact: The past, present, and the future. *Group Processes and Intergroup Relations, 6*, 5–20.

Montiel, C. J., & Wessells, M. (2001). Democratization, psychology, and the construction of cultures of peace. *Peace and Conflict: Journal of Peace Psychology, 7*, 119–129.

WEEK 7: SOCIETAL TRANSFORMATION
AND NATIONAL DEVELOPMENT

Required:

Wessells, M. G., & Dawes, A. (2007). Macro-social interventions: Psychology, social policy, and societal influence processes. In M. J. Stevens & U. P. Gielen (Eds.), *Toward a global psychology: Theory, research, interventions, and pedagogy* (pp. 267–298). Mahwah, NJ: Lawrence Erlbaum Associates.

Optional:

Maton, K. I. (2000). Making a difference, The social ecology of social transformation. *American Journal of Community Psychology, 28*, 25–57.

Stevens, M. J. (2002). The interplay of psychology and societal transformation. *International Journal of Group Tensions, 31*, 5–30.

WEEK 8: THE NATURAL ENVIRONMENT

Required:

Vlek, C. (2000). Essential psychology for environmental policy making. *International Journal of Psychology, 35*, 153–167.

Optional:

Chapman, R. (1999). No room at the inn, or why population problems are not all economic. *Population and Environment: A Journal of Interdisciplinary Studies, 21,* 81–97.

Lidskog, R., & Sundqvist, G. (2004). From consensus to credibility. *Innovation: European Journal of Social Sciences, 17,* 205–226.

WEEK 9: PHYSICAL AND MENTAL HEALTH WORLDWIDE

Required:

Draguns, J. G. (2007). Psychotherapeutic and related interventions for a global psychology In M. J. Stevens & U. P. Gielen (Eds.), *Toward a global psychology: Theory, research, interventions, and pedagogy* (pp. 233–266). Mahwah, NJ: Lawrence Erlbaum Associates.

Optional:

Krippner, S. C. (2002). Conflicting perspective on shamans and shamanism: Points and counterpoints. *American Psychologist, 57,* 962–977.

Tangenberg, K. M. (2003). Gender, geography, culture, and health: Emerging interdisciplinary approaches to global HIV/AIDS services. *Journal of Social Work Research and Evaluation, 4,* 37–48.

WEEK 10: SPECIAL TOPICS—GLOBALIZATION

Required:

Nikelly, A. G. (2000). Globalization and community feelings: Are they compatible? *Journal of Individual Psychology, 56,* 435–447.

Optional:

Alexander, B. K. (2000). The globalization of addiction. *Addiction Research, 8,* 501–526.

Bhugra, D., & Mastrogianni, A. (2004). Globalization and mental disorders: Overview with relation to depression. *British Journal of Psychiatry, 184,* 10–20.

WEEK 11: SPECIAL TOPICS—TERRORISM

Required:

Stevens, M. J. (2002). The unanticipated consequences of globalization: Contextualizing terrorism. In C. E. Stout (Ed.), *The psychology of terrorism: Vol. 3. Theoretical understandings and perspectives* (pp. 29–54). Westport, CT: Greenwood.

Optional:

Bourne, L. E., Jr., Healy, A. F., & Beer, F. A. (2003). Military conflict and terrorism: General psychology informs international relations. *Review of General Psychology, 7,* 189–202.

Staub, E. (2002). Preventing terrorism: Raising "inclusively" caring children in the complex world of the twenty-first century. In C. E. Stout (Ed.), *The psychology of terrorism: Vol. 4. Programs and practices in response and prevention* (pp. 119–129). Westport, CT: Greenwood.

WEEK 12: SPECIAL POPULATIONS—WOMEN

Required:
Murphy, E. M. (2003). Being born female is dangerous for your health. *American Psychologist, 58,* 205–210.

Optional:
El-Gibaly, O., Ibrahim, B., Mensch, B. S., & Clark, W. H. (2002). The decline of female circumcision in Egypt: Evidence and interpretation. *Social Science and Medicine, 54,* 205–220.
Walker, L. E. (1999). Psychology and domestic violence around the world. *American Psychologist, 54,* 21–29.

WEEK 13: SPECIAL POPULATIONS—CHILDREN, ADOLESCENTS, AND THE ELDERLY

Required:
Gielen, U. P., & Chumachenko, O. (2004). All the world's children: The impact of global demographic trends and economic disparities. In U. P. Gielen & J. Roopnarine (Eds.), *Childhood and adolescence: Cross-cultural perspectives and applications* (pp. 81–109). Westport, CT: Praeger.

Optional:
Nair, E. (2000). Health and aging: A perspective from the Far East. *Journal of Adult Development, 7,* 121–126.
Sarasthwathi, T. S., & Larson, R. W. (2002). Adolescence in global perspective: An agenda for social policy. In B. B. Brown, R. W. Larson, & T. S. Saraswathi (Eds.), *The world's youth: Adolescence in eight regions of the globe* (pp. 344–362). New York: Cambridge University Press.

WEEK 14: SPECIAL POPULATIONS—REFUGEES, MIGRANTS, AND THE POOR

Required:
Richmond, A. H. (2002). Globalization: Implications for immigrants and refugees. *Ethnic and Racial Studies, 25,* 707–727.

Optional:
Bourhis, R. Y., Moiese, L. C., Perreault, S., & Senecal, S. (1997). Towards an interactive acculturation model: A social psychological approach. *International Journal of Psychology, 32,* 369–386.

Leisinger, K. M. (2004). Overcoming poverty and respecting human rights: Ten points for serious consideration. *International Social Science Journal, 56*, 313–320.

WEEK 15: EDUCATION/TRAINING
AND PROFESSIONAL PRACTICE

Required:

Marsella, A. J. (2007). Education and training for a global psychology: Foundations, issues, and actions. In M. J. Stevens & U. P. Gielen (Eds.), *Toward a global psychology: Theory, research, interventions, and pedagogy* (pp. 333–361). Mahwah, NJ: Lawrence Erlbaum Associates.
Pettifor, J. L. (2007). Toward a global professionalization of psychology In M. J. Stevens & U. P. Gielen (Eds.), *Toward a global psychology: Theory, research, interventions, and pedagogy* (pp. 299–331). Mahwah, NJ: Lawrence Erlbaum Associates.

Optional:

Francis, R. D. (2002). The need for a professional ethic: International perspectives. *Educational and Child Psychology, 19*, 7–15.
Lunt, I. (2002). A common framework for the training of psychologists in Europe. *European Psychologist, 7*, 180–191.

WEEK 16: THE FUTURE

Takooshian, H., & Stambaugh, L. F. (2007). Becoming involved in global psychology. In M. J. Stevens & U. P. Gielen (Eds.), *Toward a global psychology: Theory, research, interventions, and pedagogy* (pp. 365–389). Mahwah, NJ: Lawrence Erlbaum Associates.
Stevens, M. J., & Gielen, U. P. (2007). Epilogue: Some questions for the future. In M. J. Stevens & U. P. Gielen (Eds.), *Toward a global psychology: Theory, research, interventions, and pedagogy* (pp. 391–398). Mahwah, NJ: Lawrence Erlbaum Associates.

Required Tasks/Assignments, Including Performance Evaluation Methods:

There are four diverse tasks and assignments that will provide the basis for determining an overall grade for this course. There is also an opportunity to earn extra credit. These tasks and assignments include: five in-class reactions, three written summaries, a group project, and two examinations.

1. IN-CLASS REACTIONS

Five times during the semester, there will be an unannounced written reaction to an issue or topic that has been the focus of class. In-class reactions will involve the clarification, development, or defense of a particular point of view. Sample topics might include some of the following:

"How is American psychology limited in its capacity to explain global problems?" "What are the psychosocial and sociocultural benefits and costs of globalization?" "If most psychologists worldwide practice with a bachelor's or master's degree, why does the American Psychological Association insist that psychologists have a doctorate?" Each in-class reaction should be about one page long and turned in at the end of class. In-class reactions will receive a numerical grade from 0–10. A maximum of 50 points can be earned through in-class reactions.

2. WRITTEN SUMMARIES

Three times during the semester, turn in a five-page summary of one of the optional readings listed above. Summaries must be typed, double-spaced, and follow the fifth edition of the *Publication Manual* (APA, 2001). Approximately two-thirds of the summary should capture the central points of the reading in an impartial fashion; the remainder should include psychologically probing reactions (i.e., support and criticism) to theoretical, methodological, and practical material. In addition, it is important to link key elements of the optional reading to the material in the reading required for the week. Summaries must be turned in sometime during the same week that the optional reading is listed. A numerical grade from 0–50 will be assigned based on the accuracy, organization, style, thoroughness, and thoughtfulness of the summary. A maximum of 150 points can be earned through the summaries.

3. GROUP PROJECT

Small groups of randomly assigned students (3–5) will complete an Internet project. The project entails locating the web site of a scientific or professional psychological association that is global (e.g., International Association of Applied Psychology, International Union of Psychological Science), regional (e.g., European Federation of Psychologists' Associations, Interamerican Society of Psychology), or national (e.g., American Psychological Association, Romanian Psychologists' Association), or a global policy-making organization (e.g., U.N. World Health Organization). The goal of the project is to produce a 10–page report, which should have two parts: (1) a description of how the psychological association or policy-making organization is addressing global issues or problems that have a psychological dimension, and (2) recommendations for how that association or organization can improve the impact and scope of its global mission and activities. Each group member is to share equally in planning, implementing, and preparing the report. Reports must be typed, double-spaced, follow the fifth edition of the *Publication Manual* (APA, 2001), and turned in on the last day of class. A numerical grade of 0–100 will be assigned to the group based on the accuracy, organization, style, thoroughness, and thoughtfulness of the report.

4. EXAMINATIONS

Midterm

The midterm will be closed-book and worth 100 possible points. Questions will consist of true-false, multiple-choice, and short-answer items. The midterm will cover readings, lectures, media presentations, and classroom activities from the first through the eighth week of the course. Sample questions will be provided to familiarize students with the content and format of the exam. Accuracy, organization, style, thoroughness, and thoughtfulness are the dimensions on which short-answers will be evaluated.

Final

The final will be a non-cumulative, closed-book exam structured along the same lines as the midterm and worth 100 possible points. The final will cover readings, lectures, media presentations, and classroom activities from the ninth through the fifteenth week of the course. Sample questions will be provided. Accuracy, organization, style, thoroughness, and thoughtfulness are the dimensions on which short-answers will be evaluated.

5. EXTRA CREDIT

The maximum number of extra-credit points is 10, equaling 2% of the total possible points for the course. Extra credit may be earned by attending the International Studies Seminar Series, sponsored by the International Studies Program. The International Studies Seminar Series takes place on Wednesdays from 12–1 p.m. in Stevenson 401; it is open to the public and includes a free lunch. Turn in a one-page, typed, double-spaced summary of each seminar attended. Two-thirds of the summary should capture the main points of the seminar, whereas the remainder should include thoughtful reactions, including how the topic relates to material covered in the course. Summaries must be submitted on or before the last day of class. Each summary will receive a numerical grade of 0 (incoherent and carelessly prepared), 1 (adequate), or 2 (accurate, clear, organized, and thoughtful).

5. GRADING SCALE

Grades will be determined on a strict percentage system based on five in-class reactions, three written summaries, the group project, the midterm, the final, and extra credit:

450–500 points or 90–100%   = A
400–449 points or 80–89%   = B
350–399 points or 70–79%   = C
300–349 points or 60–69%   = D
Fewer than 299 points or less than 60%   = F

PSYCHOLOGISTS WHO HAVE DEVELOPED OR TAUGHT COURSES ON GLOBAL OR INTERNATIONAL PSYCHOLOGY

John M. Davis, Ph.D.
Department of Psychology
Texas State University
San Marcos , TX 78666, USA
Tel: +512–245–3162
Fax: +512–245–3153
E-mail: jd04@txstate.edu

Uwe P. Gielen, Ph.D.
Department of Psychology
St. Francis College
180 Remsen Street
Brooklyn, NY 11201, USA
Tel: +718-489-5386
Fax: +718-522-1274
E-mail: ugielen@hotmail.com

Gloria Grenwald, Ph.D.
Behavioral and Social Sciences Department
Webster University
470 E. Lockwood Avenue
St. Louis, MO 63119, USA
Tel: +314 968–7073
Fax: +314 963–6094
E-mail: grenwald@webster.edu

Sondra Leftoff, Ph.D.
Department of Thematic Studies
John Jay College of Criminal Justice
899 Tenth Ave., Room 432T
New York, NY 10019, USA
Tel: +212–237–8452
Fax: + 212–237–8955
E-mail: sleftoff@jjay.cuny.edu, sleftoff@hotmail.com

John E. Lewis, Ph.D.
Center for Psychological Studies
Nova Southeastern University
3301 College Avenue
Fort Lauderdale, FL 33314–7796, USA
Tel: +954–262–5729; 800–541–6682, extension 5729
E-mail: lewis@nsu.nova.edu

Anthony J. Marsella, Ph.D., DHC
Department of Psychology
University of Hawaii
Gartley Hall, Room 110
Honolulu, HI 96821, USA
Tel: +808–956–6701
Fax: +808–956–4700
E-mail: marsella@hawaii.edu

Kurt Pawlik, Ph.D.
University of Hamburg
Psychology Institute
Von-Melle Park 11
D-20146 Hamburg, Germany

Tel: +49–3641–945200
Fax: +49–3641–945202
E-mail: rainer.silbereisen@uni-jena.de

Michael J. Stevens, Ph.D., DHC
Department of Psychology
Illinois State University
Campus Box 4620
Normal, IL 61790–4620, USA
Tel: +309–438–5700
Fax: +309–438–5789
E-mail: mjsteven@ilstu.edu

Author Index

Note: Page numbers in *italic* refer to reference pages; those followed by "n" refer to footnotes.

Subject Index

Note: Page numbers in **boldface** refer to tables; those followed by "n" refer to footnotes.

A

Abuse of powers, in macro-level interventions, 274
Academic coursework, in global psychology, 355–356
Accreditation. *See* Training and accreditation of psychologists
Action theory, 213–217
Activism, **339**
ADL, 244
Adolescents. *See* Children and adolescents
ADS, 293
Advanced Research and Training Seminars (ARTS), 71
Advocacy, in global psychology, 7–8
Affect regulation research, 245
Africa. *See also* South Africa; *specific countries*
    growth of psychology in, 75–76
    history of psychology in, 57–58
    macro-level interventions in, 277–278, 287–290
    professional psychology in, 310–311
    psychotherapy in, 250–251
    research activity in, **128–137**
    traditional healers in, 246–247
Alternative psychologies. *See also* Indigenous psychologies
    core concepts of
        collective construction, 190–193
        meaning-making, 189–190
        normative explanations, 194–196
        overview of, 187–189

time-dependent processes, 193–194
    future of, 197–199
    in historical context, 181–183
    impact of, 196–197
    international movements in, 187
    liberation psychology, 183–187
    as trend, 180
Amae, 153–154, 251
American Association for the Advancement of Science, 375
American Council of Learned Societies, 375
American Philosophical Society, 375
American Psychological Association (APA)
    in global psychology training, 349–350, 378–379
    number of members in, 310
    origin and evolution of, 45–46, 61–62, 368
    as resource, 370, 372
    9th International Congress and, 43
    trends reflected in, 77–80, 303, 342–343
American Psychological Association of Graduate Students (APAGS), 371
American Psychologist, 368
American Society for the Advancement of Pharmacotherapy, 78
Analectics, 185
Analysis of Social Issues and Public Policy, 79
Angola, 277–278, 288–290
Annual per-capita income, 104

Collective control, 155, 161
Collectivism, 190–193, 252–253
Colombia
  indigenization in, 312
  trends in, 84–85, 93–94
Committee on International Relations in
      Psychology (CIRP), 368
Commons dilemma, 17
Communications technology, 83, 107, **335**
Community empowerment, 287–290
Comparative psychology, 89
Competencies, 352–353, **353**
Conceptual fragmentation, 180–181
Conscientization, 184, 186
Consciousness, **338,** 349–350
Control, direct versus indirect, 155
COPE program, 291–292
Corporations, global, **335**
Credentialing. See Mobility of psychologists;
      Training and accreditation of psy-
      chologists
Critical consciousness, 349–350
*Cross-Cultural Perspectives in Introductory
      Psychology* (Price, Crapo), 380
Cross-cultural psychology, described, 9
Cultural psychology, described, 9
Cultural sensitivity
  in macro-level interventions, 289–290
  in psychotherapy, 250–251
  as trend, 85–86
Culture
  in Asian economic attainment, 162–166
  in Asian educational attainment, 159–162
  changes in psychology and, 345
  defined, 156–157, 354
  in discourse analysis, 218–219
  in global psychology training, 350,
      353–355
  psychotherapy and
    cultural characteristics and, 250–253
    sociocultural context and, 246–250,
      256
  relocation and, 377
  as research variable, 212
  in value of global psychology, 369–370
Curriculum, for global psychology, 8,
      351–352, 378–381

D

David Liberman algorithm (ADL), 244
Declaration of Global Ethic, 323

Declaration of Madrid, 321
Defense mechanism measures, 244
De-ideologizing, 184, 186
Delinquency, in Asia, 161–162
Democratic Republic of Congo (DRC),
      287–290
Denmark, 91, 319
Depression, 23, 25
Desegregation, as policy change, 275–277
Developing countries
  defined, 103–105
  facilitating psychology progress in,
      141–142
  future of psychology in, 393–394
  in global psychology, 102–103
  psychologists' work in
    education and training for, 111–116
    equipment and facilities and, 108
    information access and, 106–107
    professional practice of, 116–118
    research funding and, 109–111
  research activity in, 118–141, **120–137**
Developmental psychology, 88–91
Dialectics, 185
Digital divide, 83, 107
Direct control, 155
Discourse analysis, 193–194, 217–221
Discursive acts, 188
Diseases, in developing countries,
      112–113
Distance learning, 8, 380
Distrust, intergroup conflict and, 12–13
Diversity, global psychology training and,
      350
Division of International Psychology (of
      APA)
  described, 372
  history of, 368
  as resource, 379
  trends reflected in, 78, 303, 343
Domestic violence, 25
DRC, 287–290

E

Earth Charter, 279
Economic attainment, in Asia, 162–166
Economic psychology, described, 10–11
Economics, growth of psychology and,
      49–50
Editorial Mentor Program, 78